Odyssey

For Lex,
 May you continue
to find excitement &
satisfaction on your
own odyssey with
Lexited.
            XO
            Tricia

Odyssey

Pepsi to Apple . . .
A Journey of Adventure, Ideas, and the Future

JOHN SCULLEY
with John A. Byrne

PERENNIAL LIBRARY

Harper & Row, Publishers, New York
Cambridge, Philadelphia, San Francisco
London, Mexico City, São Paulo, Singapore, Sydney

APPLE and the APPLE LOGO are registered trademarks of Apple Computer, Inc. and are used with the express permission of the owner.

The statements, opinions, positions, and views expressed herein are solely those of the author, John Sculley, in his individual capacity, and do not and are not intended to represent the statements, opinions, positions, or views of Apple Computer, Inc.

A hardcover edition of this book was published in 1987 by Harper & Row, Publishers.

First PERENNIAL LIBRARY edition published 1988.

Copy editor: Ann Adelman
Designer: C. Linda Dingler
Indexer: Elan D. Garonzik for Riofrancos & Co.
Photo insert researched, edited, and designed by Vincent Virga

Library of Congress Cataloging-in-Publication Data

Sculley, John.
     Odyssey: Pepsi to Apple...a journey of adventure, ideas, and the future.

     "Perennial Library."

     Includes index.
     1. Sculley, John.   2. Businessmen–United States–Biography.   3. Apple Computer, Inc.
4. Computer industry–United States.   I. Byrne, John A.   II. Title.
HD9696.C62S38   1988   331.7'61004165'0924   [B]   87-45142
ISBN 0-06-091527-7 (pbk.)

88   89   90   91   92   FG   10   9   8   7   6   5   4   3   2   1

To Leezy
for her love and support
through everything

Contents

CONTENTS

Illustrations follow page 178

Prologue

Through the glass wall of my office, anyone could see we were deeply engrossed in private conversation. Steve Jobs, the young, brilliant computer whiz kid, the co-founder of Apple Computer, and me. It would have been a familiar sight. He had become my closest friend, a soul mate and a constant companion.

But anyone catching a glimpse of us today would have known that something had gone wrong. There were no smiles, no animated gestures, no sense of fun, excitement, or adventure. We spoke quietly and sadly. A break in our partnership seemed inevitable. It would destroy our friendship, it might destroy our company, and it already had destroyed my confidence.

A month earlier, on April 11, 1985, the board of directors had endorsed my decision to remove Steve Jobs from his base of power in the company. Several times before I had resisted this decision, but I couldn't resist it any longer.

Only a year ago, I had raised a toast: "Apple has one leader, Steve and me." He had confided to me: "You're like one of the founders of the company. Woz and I founded its past, but you and I are founding the future." Now all we had were vastly different visions of how to give our failing company a future. I was beginning to feel like a pulp fiction character. But Steve had that effect on people—he evoked an overly emotional response.

For over an hour, Steve pleaded with me for a second chance. When he failed to gain that concession, he pleaded again—this time for more time. Over and over. Again and again. I refused to relent.

Then, overcome with emotion, he suddenly burst from the room. I was left, wanting only to hide. My head bent and heavy, I searched for a corner of the room to awkwardly disguise my pain. I turned my face to the wall. Echoing in my mind was Steve's indictment that I was the cause of Apple's trouble: "You're wrong for Apple . . . I'm the only one who can save the company." The only one . . . the only one . . . I wept there, wondering how it had come to this.

I began a journey, a true odyssey, into this near-fantasy world two years ago. Silicon Valley was then a corporate Camelot: Apple was its Round Table and Steve was its King Arthur. It was so different from what I knew. For sixteen years at PepsiCo, I competed with the best of them in corporate America—where power is measured by the size of one's office. I had led the creation of a "Pepsi Generation" that for the first time dethroned Coke as the number-one brand in the most important market in the U.S.A. I was on the verge of getting all that I had worked so hard for, a serious contender for the number-one job in what I thought was the number-one company of the "old world."

Then, Steve called. Like so many others, I bought into the dream of this precocious, mesmerizing kid.

Together—he as chairman and me as chief executive—we would become the unbeatable team to put a personal computer into almost every home and every classroom and, in so doing, change the world. I was to create an "Apple Generation" and find new markets for the company's "insanely great" products.

What I discovered at Apple was a community without boundaries. A free-form environment, an artists' workshop. At Pepsi, we were warriors. We fiercely competed on a tenth of a percent of market share. And we sold what Steve disdainfully called sugared water. At Apple, we are dreamers. We are driven by a passion to change the world, to make it a better, more productive place for every individual. And we sell, not refreshment for the body, but tools for the mind. "One person, one computer"; that was our dream.

It nearly worked. One day we were the "Dynamic Duo." The next, it seemed, the Marx Brothers—unable to get anything right. Our sales dropped with our hopes. A computer slump, the long shadow of IBM, a mixture of poor judgment and bad luck—and

Apple Computer had plunged into a severe crisis. All of it occurred with dramatic suddenness.

Nanette Buckhout, my executive assistant for more than a decade, eyed me pressed into the corner.

"John!" she called, entering my office. "What's wrong? What happened?"

I slowly turned toward her, revealing a flood of tears from a pair of weary, reddened eyes. She was stunned. At Pepsi, Nanette had known me as a hard-charging, dynamic, and unequivocal executive. She knew me nearly as well as I knew myself—not as the cool, distant professional portrayed by the press, but as reserved, private, and always under control. Now it was as if I couldn't hold back anything.

I closed the office door and slumped into a chair, my hands on my forehead.

"Steve wants more time to prove he can change. I told him it's all over.

"But, my God, I came here because of Steve, because I wanted to work with him. I picked up and left everything so we could work together. And now he's gone. I'm left here alone. What do I have? Maybe I'm not good enough or competent enough?"

"John, I've never seen you like this. I've seen you deal with problems at home, with tough situations here. But nothing like this. You're a broken man," she said, nearly sobbing herself.

Her words struck me like a bullet. She was right—I was broken. For the first time in my career, I was failing. My confidence was gone. Financially, I was ruined: my Apple stock options, worth less than nothing as the price did a free fall, would put me deep into debt if I walked out of the company. With all Apple's problems, I would probably never be offered another job in corporate America.

And in the midst of it all, I had to cut off the visionary founder from his own company. For months I had been either unwilling or unable to go through with it.

When I finally cut the cord, I felt lost in a world I only barely knew.

A Note to the Reader

I hope that as much as this book reveals about me and Apple, it also reveals something about the power of information and ideas. At Apple, we trade in both. Our products are only as good as our ideas. As Walter Wriston has said, ideas are the new currency in corporate America. Silicon Valley is not just at the vanguard of product development, but of new-age business principles, too.

That's why I wanted to tell not just a story, but the story of ideas that have changed my life. To do that, I had to wrestle with the constraints of a book's linear format. In books, the reader typically finds himself in a state of pure passivity, marching at the pace of the author if he is to get all the book offers, or skimming in a hit-or-miss fashion. Here, I hope to provide a more interactive reading experience; rather than a clear beginning, middle, end, I've put in all sorts of detours—chief among which is the tutorial.

So, in reading this book, you might concentrate on the tutorials —the short essays that follow each chapter and are meant as the fuller explanation of a management or marketing lesson the story raises. Or, you could simply follow the story and go back to the tutorials. There are, in short, multiple access points to the book's material.

My model for the experience of reading this book is personal computing, which enables the user to summon up any information he needs, in the dosage he requires. I hope that together the lessons and stories will allow you a variety of windows into the book. I have tried to think of ways to make this book more than a passive experience.

The ideal reader, I have come to believe, is Skeptical Man. The future belongs to the skeptic—not the cynic—and a culture in which computers become as essential and invisible as the telephone will give rise to him. Skeptical Man does not take ideas on faith; he uses a multiplicity of information to compare and contrast. The computer makes such information available easily and in great quantity.

Following this model, I have drawn on the clues and inspiration for business systems in the future from new disciplines and new paradigms—from biological cell theory, from Tao, from architecture, and from art. When I draw on metaphors from these disciplines, I am offering the reader different points of view that enlarge one's interpretive powers. The text will generate more questions than answers, questions which I hope will tease your curiosity and encourage a search for new points of view.

What excites me so much about what I have learned at Apple is that the computer is more than a tool, it's a medium. Just as the typeface standardized information—changing us from a society where information was at the mercy of monks busy with hand copying into a fact-loving society where non-fiction outsells fiction—so the computer will change the way we look at the world. A twenty-first century renaissance sparked by a new information class? I can only hope so. Thus I have also taken pains here to describe technology and to depict the romance of it. It, too, is an integral part of the story in structure and meaning.

We want technology to be the source for new tools for creating a new world. The new world we already have created inside Apple, where creativity permeates every facet of our work environment, is but one small example of what an exciting new company can be in the information age.

The story I tell here is about a personal journey toward the twenty-first century, the seeds of which already are planted and the ideas already incubating. It's an odyssey of adventure and romance, filled with risks and surprises.

Above all, it's the story of how a person who had the opportunity to experience both worlds—old and new, East Coast and West Coast, linear and multi-dimensional—has so dramatically changed in the process.

1

Boot Camp

At Pepsi, we lived for the smallest details.

The moment I entered the boardroom, I knew the meeting would be momentous. For years, these executive sessions had followed a carefully orchestrated ritual. Today, there was a subtle, though telling, difference.

Ordinarily, the conference table's 21-foot-long surface, polished to look more like glass than the rare burl of Carpathian elm, would be touched only by PepsiCo board members, and then no more than twelve times a year. Today, the fitted leather covering that hid the gleaming top was removed.

I had been in this room at least a hundred times. I had sat worried at this table and I had nearly soared at it. I had witnessed tense colleagues—friends—being publicly hung for questions of performance, and I had seen them applauded, just as I had been here, for marketing ideas and strategies.

But this meeting was different. The table's exposed top said so. It made the spacious, windowless room all the more imposing. Like nearly everything else at PepsiCo, Inc., the room's stately power and elegance made you stand a little straighter. A large abstract painting by Jackson Pollock's widow, Lee Krasner, dominated the far wall. Custom-designed carpeting in earth-tone colors cushioned the floor. The bronze-plated ceiling, perhaps more appropriate for a church, reflected burnished mahogany-paneled walls. High-backed beige leather chairs, so imposing they could have carried corporate titles of their own, surrounded the boardroom table.

Every two months the marketing gurus of Pepsi—the company's heart and soul—would gather here, on 4/3, the executive floor of PepsiCo's corporate headquarters in the New York City suburb of Purchase, for a private ritual in the public war of the colas between Pepsi and Coke. A. C. Nielsen Co., the country's most prestigious market-research firm, would formally present what became popularly known as the Nielsens—closely guarded market-share figures that showed how we were faring in our competitive battle with Coca-Cola Co. The Nielsens defined the ground rules of competition for everyone at Pepsi. They were at the epicenter of all we did. They were the non-public body counts of the Cola Wars.

Like the other meetings, this one was a ceremonial event. We marked it on our calendars many weeks in advance. Everyone wore the unofficial corporate uniform: a blue pin-striped suit, white shirt, and a sincere red tie. None of us would ever remove his jacket. We dressed and acted as if we were at a meeting of the board of directors.

The Nielsen executives were the first to arrive. They carried themselves like accountants—good presenters with bland personalities in blue and gray suits. They were followed by Pepsi's junior executives, the support staff of market researchers and brand managers who could provide a stray fact or figure for the division officers and vice presidents who filed into the room next.

Everyone in this room was on the fast track, which at Pepsi was more like a racecourse. The senior officers here were the best of the best. In a corporation populated with bright, ambitious achievers, they were peerless. They had proven they were intellectually and physically fit survivors in America's corporate Marine Corps.

As president of Pepsi-Cola, I entered the room next. Corporate formality dictated where all of us sat. The company's top officers gravitated to the front of the table, the junior execs toward the back. Staff people found chairs away from the table along the walls. When everyone was in place, I went across the hall to alert PepsiCo's president, Andrall E. Pearson, who then joined us.

Everyone chatted away until the heavy wooden doors opened once again. The room fell quiet as a big-boned man with a frizzy shock of white hair strode in. PepsiCo chairman and chief executive Donald M. Kendall, fifty-seven, was no taller than six feet one, but he was a man of enormous presence, respected and feared by colleagues. Today, Kendall was feeling great pleasure. He worked the room like a politician, gripping hands, slapping backs, and giving an occasional bear hug—a patented gesture of strength and affection that Kendall reserved for only a few.

The meeting began precisely after Kendall took his seat and a black butler in a white jacket arrived with his drink on a silver tray: a Pepsi in a Tiffany tumbler set on a napkin in front of him. The recessed lights dimmed as the electric doors on one wall pulled away to reveal a projection screen. A Nielsen official began flashing the latest figures on the screen under Kendall's watchful eyes, explaining the minutiae of data that the company was spending nearly $10 million annually to collect.

Today, there would be no stern warnings, no sharp commands, no snapped orders to the platoon of executives around the table. Kendall's unabashed ebullience proved infectious. He broke out a box of his favorite Cuban cigars early and passed them around the table. Clouds of smoke, even laughter, engulfed the room as the figures revealed an achievement it had taken nearly a decade to create: Pepsi had surpassed Coke in sales as the leading soft drink sold in the nation's supermarkets.

"This is what I've longed for during my entire career," Kendall exulted, "to beat Coke fair and square."

Finally, in the spring of 1978, Pepsi was number one, the leading revenue producer of the more than 20,000 items sold in a supermarket—the freedom-of-choice market. The Nielsens proved it. The numbers on the screen showed that we had captured a 30.8 percent share of the national market to Coke's 29.2 percent, a slice of business worth more than $3 billion. We had inched ahead of Coke in some bimonthly periods a year earlier, but now we could claim a clear, unshakable full-year victory.

It was one of those moments for which you worked your entire career. We always believed, since the early seventies, when Pepsi was widely viewed as the perennial also-ran, that we could do it. All of us started out with that objective, and we never took our eyes off it.

My fixation on this goal surfaced as soon as I joined the company as a trainee in 1967. My success, my reputation as a marketing wizard, all were dependent on the Nielsens and this race to gain the seven share points—some $700 million in additional sales—that would put us over the top. I became at the age of thirty Pepsi's youngest marketing vice president in 1970, when I began to speak publicly about how we were going to dethrone Coke. Most people, including our own bottlers, thought we were crazy. But Coke was a little like the Wizard of Oz—so powerful was its image that few foresaw that the company was vulnerable to attack by new ideas. Seven years later, partly on the basis of those ideas, I was named the youngest Pepsi-Cola president.

If I was brash or arrogant on my way to the top, it mattered little to me. I was an impatient perfectionist. I was willing to work relentlessly to get things exactly right. I was unsympathetic of those who couldn't deliver the results I demanded. I was driven, not by simple power or raw ambition, but by an insatiable curiosity and skepticism as to business's accepted notions. I considered myself a builder, someone whose success was dependent on building products and markets, on changing an industry's ground rules, not merely competing. I felt as if I were an architect of new ideas and concepts. Yet I was happy to meet the tests of competition, and at Pepsi they appeared frequently.

Every two months, we would meet in the same elegant boardroom with Kendall and Pearson to chart our progress. The meetings served as a constant reminder that Pepsi wasn't the typical, faceless corporation. Rather, there were two demanding taskmasters at the top in Kendall and Pearson, the latter once singled out as one of the toughest bosses in America by *Fortune* magazine. They held our soles to a fast-burning flame called competition.

These sessions weren't always euphoric. Often, the tension in the room was suffocating. Eyes would fix on Kendall to capture his response at every gain or drop in every tenth of a market share. The stakes were high: a single share point translated into $100 million in sales, a substantial portion of which directly hit the bottom line. No silent gesture or comment went unnoticed. Kendall and Pearson, always seated at the front of the table, occasionally exchanged whispered remarks about the numbers that everyone strained to hear.

If we had a bad Nielsen period, there would be no backslapping, no cigars. Kendall's steely blue eyes would pierce through the executive whose Nielsens were lagging. You could count on Kendall to be direct and bold.

At Pepsi-Cola, this was our day of reckoning, our day of accountability. The results of every decision made in the field or at corporate headquarters could be measured here in the fine print of the Nielsens. When you performed, you were rewarded by the approval of your peers, increased responsibility, significant raises, and future promotions. When you didn't, the pressure became intense. We knew our careers rode on swings of a fraction in share point.

An executive whose share was down had to stand and explain —fully—what he was going to do to fix it fast. Clearly in the dock, he knew that the next time he returned to that room, it had better be fixed. It was the kind of experience you wouldn't want to go through very often. Indeed, you couldn't. Those who had trouble quickly repairing the damage didn't get a chance to explain a third time. Either your numbers went up and continued to grow, or you began to comb the classifieds for a job elsewhere. Always, there was another executive in the room, ready to take your place.

We all knew and understood the rules. Because we played by the same ground rules, we didn't complain about the tension they provoked, like Olympic athletes who don't grouse about the competitive pressures because they enjoy them. We competed as if at war, and the public combat between Pepsi and Coke made the competition evident to everyone.

The Cola Wars pierced the popular culture, touching the lives of everyone from the corner grocer to the inhabitants of the White House. When President Nixon took up residence on Pennsylvania Avenue, Coke vending machines disappeared. When President Carter arrived, the Pepsi machines went out. Coca-Cola patriarch Robert Woodruff was a lifelong Democrat, while Kendall was a loyal Republican who delighted in mixing with the leaders of the party. The politics of the leaders permeated the cultures of the companies. Coke was a company whose roots were in the South. Its executives were true Southern gentlemen. Pepsi was a two-fisted, self-made Republican corporation in the East.

We would not have been able to surpass Coke if not for our tough corporate culture. It put us on a search-and-destroy mission against a Goliath. The driving environment was in tune with our bottlers, who were hungrier and leaner than Coke's. Unlike Coca-Cola's third-generation bottlers, our business partners hadn't yet made their fortunes, and while Coke executives may have been a lot nicer and friendlier, Pepsi's were more ruthless and driven. Pepsi executives are pitted against each other to grab more market share, to work harder, and to wring more profits out of their business. Winning is the key value. Consistent runners-up find their jobs disappear. You must win merely to stay in place. You must devastate the competition to get ahead.

The culture demanded that each of us be in top condition, physically fit as well as mentally alert. At lunchtime, the glass-walled corporate fitness center was packed with the rising stars of the corporation. Like me, they were the kind of people who would rather be in the Marines than in the Army. Even our exercise regimens became part of the competition. Placards on bulletin boards charted each executive's progress against his colleagues.

Characteristic of the cultural differences between Pepsi and Coke was the impact of the Nielsens on each organization. At Coke, the numbers seldom worked their way into top management. They were largely employed by Coca-Cola's marketing people. Pepsi's top managers, however, would carry in their wallets little charts with the latest key Nielsen figures. They became such an important part of my life that I could quote them on any product in any market. We would pore over the data, using it to search for Coke's vulnerable points where an assault could successfully be launched, or to explore why Pepsi slipped a fraction of a percentage point in the game.

We often knew the likely mood of these meetings three weeks in advance. That's when we would get our first glimpse at the numbers in the form of an early Nielsen flash. No matter where I was at any time of the day, when the Nielsen flash came out, I wanted to be the first to know it. I didn't mind a problem, but I hated surprises. The last thing I'd want was Kendall calling for an explanation behind a weak number without having had the chance to see it myself. I'd scribble the details down on the back of an envelope or whatever else was convenient. Within an hour, some sixty or seventy people at Pepsi also would get the results and begin to work on them. We knew then whether the next three weeks were going to be horrible or wonderful, whether you would face a reprimand or approval from Kendall.

A week after the flash, the Nielsen decks, 3-inch-thick computer printouts, would arrive. They provided a wealth of detail, a nationwide sampling of how Pepsi was faring in nearly 2,200 supermarkets in 68 areas by brand, product, and package size. The data not only compared performance to other competing soft drinks but to snack foods and detergents, too, so we could account for any marketplace anomalies from strikes to price wars.

Winning, to me, was an obsession. I was driven not only by the competition but by the force of powerful ideas. I demanded the best of myself. If I walked away from an assignment not totally consumed or absorbed to near exhaustion, I felt guilty about it. Dozens had failed at this regimen; but to me, Pepsi was a comfortable home.

Our celebratory meeting around the yacht-sized conference table acknowledged a milestone, not a goal, in our battle with Coke. Pearson maintained that our victory over Coke wasn't enough. It proved that Pepsi had become a "fine corporation," but we still strived to emerge a "great corporation" in the tradition of a much-admired IBM or Procter & Gamble.

"We can't rest on our laurels," I agreed. "We've got to use this not as a victory but as a strategic building block."

We discussed how to exploit our victory in the supermarkets as a major attack against Coke in international markets, in vending machines, and in fountain sales, all areas in which we still trailed our nemesis. We had to persuade others that consumers preferred Pepsi when they were given a choice.

Now, however, everyone could taste blood.

"We can never relax," warned Kendall. "We have to have it all. We have to beat Coke in every market. This just proves we can do it."

The company wasn't always this way. The man at the front of the table made it so. Don Kendall was the devoted master of it all. His personality came to dominate the company and its changing culture. For years, Pepsi had run a distant second-place finish in the cola sweepstakes. When Kendall became chief executive of Pepsi-Cola in 1963, it was a modestly profitable soft-drink company with $300 million in sales. Some twenty-three years later, in 1986, he retired as chairman from a highly profitable $9 billion corporation with dominant power in beverages, snacks, and fast foods. He achieved the growth through boldness and risk taking, forging one of the most successful mergers in American business history in 1965 with Frito-Lay, the Dallas-based snack-food maker, a move which resulted in the founding of PepsiCo.

An ex-Golden Gloves fighter, Kendall joined the company in 1947 as a fountain syrup salesman. A decade later, he had worked himself into president of Pepsi's international division. It was here that Kendall gained instant notoriety in 1959 when he agreed to take a trade exhibition to the Soviet Union after Coca-Cola declined the invite. He did so, however, to the chagrin of a disapproving boss, who thought it a waste of money.

In Moscow, Kendall cleverly arranged to meet Vice President Richard Nixon for the first time through publisher William Randolph Hearst, who had been married to his wife's cousin. Both Hearst and Kendall urged Nixon to drop by the Pepsi-Cola booth with Khrushchev.

Nixon complied with the request. By a stroke of luck, the political leaders engaged in their famous Kitchen Debate as a smiling Kendall maneuvered between them with a Pepsi bottle in hand. The world's photographers were there to snap the moment. The following day the picture appeared on the front pages of every newspaper in the world. The publicity not only saved his job, but helped to further launch his Pepsi career.

Kendall and Pearson lured to Pepsi a thriving corporate class of competitors. In 1970, Kendall moved the company's world headquarters from Manhattan to a 140-acre site in Purchase, New York, where he personally selected and supervised the installation of an elaborate sculpture garden. He brought to the campus the symbols of power that PepsiCo would come to represent. On its approach to Westchester Airport, the corporate jet would routinely circle over Pepsi headquarters, providing a glimpse of the P-shaped, man-made lake on the lavish corporate campus. A limousine would greet you, ready to sweep you back to headquarters. It made me feel that I belonged to an elite fraternity, that there was no better corporation for which to work.

The ultimate perk was a button beside Kendall's desk that controlled the Pepsi fountains which shot a powerful stream of water more than 40 feet into the air above the lake. It conveyed a natural strength that he brought to the corporation as an extension of his own personality.

Don etched an indelible mark on people, too. He became a close friend and a distant mentor to me. I married his stepdaughter in 1960, a year before graduating from Brown University. I had planned to study architecture to become an industrial designer, with the goal of someday opening my own design firm. While I was a graduate student at the University of Pennsylvania's School of Architecture, however, Kendall convinced me my career was not as an architect but as a marketer. I would visit him at his home and overhear his conversations with ever-present Pepsi colleagues. Then we would sit around until late in the evening discussing them. Kendall said he thought I had good instincts for marketing and that marketing experience would even be helpful to me as an industrial designer.

As a summer intern at a New York industrial design firm, I had discovered that marketers, not the designers on the drafting boards, were calling the shots. Kendall's advice put me over the top, prompting a switch to Wharton, the university's graduate school of business. Armed with my MBA, I joined a New York advertising agency as a trainee in 1963.

The job with McCann-Erickson unwittingly provided an initiation into Kendall's world. The agency's most prized account was the Coca-Cola Co. Pleased with my work, the agency assigned me to a secret project: the analysis of Coke's A. C. Nielsen market-research books.

Coca-Cola wanted the agency to forecast the potential for the then-emerging market in diet soft drinks. It only recently had introduced its first diet drink, Tab, while Pepsi had begun testing Diet Pepsi as a replacement for its Patio Diet Cola, which had flopped. Coke management was convinced Pepsi blundered by stamping its own brand name on the diet product. Coke then believed that selling a diet soda under the Coke label would cannibalize Coke's sales. The company was further dissuaded from such a decision due to an old, unique contractual agreement with the Tennessee-based Thomas Co. The pact required Coca-Cola to pay Thomas an override of 10 cents on every gallon of soft-drink syrup sold in a broad geographic area from Chattanooga to Buffalo, N.Y., under the Coke name.

Pepsi, on the other hand, wanted to harness the value of its brand name by calling its diet product Diet Pepsi. While my analysis confirmed Coca-Cola's suspicions that Diet Pepsi was siphoning sales from Pepsi, it also was far more profitable than regular Pepsi, in part because cyclamate was cheaper than sugar. The study also forecast an explosion in the diet soft-drink market, which then accounted for a mere 5 percent of industry sales. Today, it's nearly a third of the market.

Coke had only recently made a major commitment to Tab and wanted to be told there was a new, major market emerging for it. The advertising agency also wanted to convince Coke to support the new brand with heftier advertising dollars. So I pored over the books with great enthusiasm, often crunching the numbers until 1:00 a.m. with a noisy Friden calculator. The secrecy of the project made it all the more tantalizing. For weeks, I would begin each morning by signing the books out of a vault. The volumes tracked, down to a share-point fraction, the market share between Coke and "the imitator"—not "the competitor"—as Pepsi was referred to, but an imitator attempting to steal what Coke presumed to be a God-given right to a market. Every night I returned them so they could be locked away. When the shocking news arrived that President John F. Kennedy had been shot, I was leaning over a Nielsen book. We gathered around a radio, listening in sadness to the news of his death. New York shut down that day, and I wandered home.

I didn't realize, of course, that I was getting an introduction to something that would dominate my life for nearly twenty years. What the agency didn't know was that at the time I was doing this secret work on the Coke account I also was the son-in-law of the chairman of Pepsi. If anyone had known, I would never have been allowed to work on those documents. Kendall had no idea what I was working on; he would have been outraged if he knew. But since I never discussed anything confidential, I didn't feel bad about it.

When I joined McCann-Erickson, advertising agencies plotted the marketing strategies for most companies. By 1967, though, more companies were beginning to set up their own marketing departments in house. I felt the time had come in 1967 to make the switch from agency to client.

Kendall's stepdaughter and I had divorced in 1965, and Kendall severed his relationship with her mother in the same year. We no longer were related through marriage, although we remained good friends. I spoke to Kendall about my desire to work for a client.

"Why don't you interview with Pepsi?" he asked.

"Don," I told him, "I don't think it will work. People know that you and I were once related through marriage. Even though we're both now divorced, I'm sure that's going to carry over."

"I think you ought to at least talk to the Pepsi-Cola people," he suggested. "From there on you're on your own."

He agreed to arrange an initial introduction. After that, we both decided that if I joined Pepsi, I would indeed be on my own and would steer clear of him. I never wanted anyone to think I was getting a free ride or special treatment from the boss.

So I joined Pepsi-Cola, the soft-drink part of PepsiCo, in 1967 as a new oddity: their first MBA. Like every other new recruit, I was shipped off to a company-owned bottling plant in Pittsburgh for the first leg of a six-month training program. It put me through every phase of bottling work, from sorting and inspecting returnable bottles to duty at the soaker, the bottle washer. I put on a uniform and went out as a driver-salesman on a Pepsi truck. One of my first jobs: to repack 16-ounce returnable Pepsi bottles into eight packs from six at the Giant Eagle supermarket in Mount Lebanon, a Pittsburgh suburb. I never worked so hard in my life, sitting in the middle of the floor, repacking bottle after bottle of a 1,000-case display the size of a room, while shoppers moved and shoved around me. After a few days, my fingers were all gnarled and bloody because they would catch on the rough edges of the crimpled bottlecaps.

Moving the returnable bottles up and down the cellars of Pittsburgh taverns, I realized I wasn't strong enough to withstand the rigors of the work. Kendall, himself a model of fitness, demanded that his executives be physically fit. He once had gotten a visiting executive from Mexico roaring drunk one evening and then dragged him out of bed for an early-morning run. The executive, who wasn't much of a jogger, collapsed by the roadside, while Kendall sprinted off in his Army boots, pleased he had outraced someone several years younger than he.

I was a shadow of the large, strong Polish men of Pittsburgh. Their rugged looks contrasted with my scrawny frame and pale complexion. So at night, I lifted weights at the Bigelow Health Club to build the strength that would allow me effortlessly to haul a half-dozen cases of soda bottles on a two-wheel truck up and down the steps of cellar taverns.

This was my first exposure to merchandising. I felt I had to understand the basics of the business, how value was added in each step of the process, from when the concentrate was mixed with sugar, water, and CO_2 gas to create the product; how it was poured in the bottles, how the bottles were slipped into cartons and cases, how they moved to stores, and how they were priced to deliver different margins. How they were merchandised and how money was collected—all the ins and outs of the business.

I coaxed Chuck Mangold, the Pittsburgh plant manager and the man who became my mentor, into allowing me to collect and provide him with sales and promotion information at the plant level that top execs at Coke were getting with the Nielsens. We began to compare the effects of merchandising products different ways in different stores. We analyzed promotions. This was brand new, because Pepsi had always operated by gut instinct.

Outside of work, Chuck, who had a warm family of eight children, treated me as if I were one of his sons. He invited me to his home on evenings and weekends for dinner and a game of croquet with his family. Other times, we would go camping in Pennsylvania where driver-salesmen and their families would gather to grill kielbasi, guzzle beer, pitch horseshoes, and swim in a watering hole where the focal point was a rope swung from a tree. It wasn't only my submersion into a new job, but my submersion into a new people. It was so distant from the life to which I had been accustomed in New York.

Yet it was nothing like the life I was headed for. After four months, I was sent to Phoenix, Arizona, for the second leg of my training—becoming a member of the blitz teams that would descend on supermarkets at 2:00 a.m. to rebuild their soft-drink sections, giving Pepsi as much prominence as possible on the shelf. Some days I worked in the field with a crew of Mexicans, putting up large metal Pepsi signs on buildings. We had to do all kinds of favors to get people to allow us to erect signs on their property. So I ended up repairing doors and, in some cases, rebuilding tin roofs on shacks. At midday, the temperature would hit 120 degrees in the sun and we would be up on sheet-metal roofs putting up yellow Pepsi signs. I had to wrap water-soaked handkerchiefs around my pressure points to keep from passing out in the sun. Even the swimming pool at the Caravan Inn where I stayed for $5.21 a night was too hot to swim in.

I always believed that you make your own luck. I was trying to absorb everything I could. I watched how people worked and spent their time. I observed the guts of the business, and in the process learned the nomenclature of the industry. The knowledge would later prove invaluable in quickly establishing a rapport with Pepsi's bottlers: I could speak their language and identify with their problems because I had been there myself.

My training completed, I headed back to Pepsi's ten-story glass-and-concrete headquarters at 500 Park Avenue in New York. A surprise awaited me upon my return: the new products job I had been promised didn't open up. Instead, I was assigned to Pepsi-Cola's marketing-research department across the street from Pepsi's main headquarters. It was supposed to be a temporary way station until the company found a new spot for the current manager of product development.

It was an inauspicious start. My MBA proved a detriment. Many of my new colleagues hadn't acquired a college education, never mind a graduate degree. Then word got around that I had been married to Kendall's stepdaughter and everyone wondered if I would get favored treatment. If anything, it was harder for me because Kendall judged me against a higher standard. Still, I was given neither an assignment nor an office.

I was disillusioned but determined to take advantage of my time. So I would arrive each day, find a place to sit, and begin to sift through every research file I could find. I just sat there all day and read, voraciously read every piece of paper the research department had on file. Most of it related to consumer behavior. What became clear was that I was in an essentially meaningless department. Little of its work was utilized by the higher-ups. The researchers went off and researched, then the sales and marketing staff went off and made their own decisions, independent of each other.

It was a difficult time. Blocked from the job I had been promised and rebuffed by my new colleagues, I felt bitterly disappointed. If this experience was a harbinger of what life at Pepsi was like, it was hardly for me. One day, I left the office for a walk off Fifth Avenue. Just as I made the mental decision to quit, a large, shiny black limo pulled up to the curb and the window rolled down. Inside sat a smiling Kendall. At his invitation, I hopped into the car.

"How are things going?" he asked.

"Things have gone better," I replied. "I'm not sure I made the right decision."

Kendall's mood turned serious. He quickly began a stern lecture. "You're too impatient," he said. "Give it some time. Things will work out."

Divine intervention? Impeccable timing? Whatever, the advice helped. Still thwarted in the job, I persevered and eventually landed the new product development position nine months later. With the benefit of some good timing and luck, I compiled a series of accomplishments that brought me increased responsibilities and a major promotion.

My first success came in the new products post, a wide-ranging job that broadened my perspective of the corporation. Seeking to leverage our snack-food and soft-drink business, I tested a snack-food franchise concept with a Pepsi bottler in the Canary Islands. Just as Pepsi shipped its concentrate to bottlers to turn into Pepsi-Cola, my idea was for Frito-Lay to ship a concentrate in pellet form to bottlers who could fry them up, turn them into snack foods, bag them, and deliver them to the same customers on the regular soft-drink routes. It was an incredibly exciting idea, and it became very successful.

Pepsi-Cola, though, was in a slump. It had been losing market share steadily for nearly four years. Kendall began to wonder if the company's management could turn it around. He engaged consultants at McKinsey & Co. to study the company and report on its management. But by 1969, McKinsey was about to resign the Pepsi account because its consultants couldn't get the cooperation of the company's soft-drink division. McKinsey sorely needed market research and financial data to do its analysis; Pepsi-Cola management, fearful that the study would reflect poorly on their efforts, was none too happy to cooperate.

For months, I had spent hours upon hours as a nonentity in the research department, gathering a plethora of information on Pepsi-Cola. I didn't know if it would ever be useful. Now, it provided the catalyst for a crucial lucky break. I knew where all the critical research was on the soft-drink business and Pepsi, and I knew how to get it. I was pulled off my new products project to work with a team of McKinsey consultants. I didn't realize what the McKinsey experience would mean for me until months later.

In the meantime, I got another important break when the government banned cyclamates on October 19, 1969. CBS Evening News asked Kendall to appear on television as an industry spokesman when Coca-Cola chief executive Paul Austin couldn't do it because he was traveling abroad. Kendall, who had a previous commitment and little trust in the management of the soft-drink division, drafted me.

"John, you're going on television tonight," Don told me.

"I've never been on television in my life. What do I do?"

"You're smart. Just give them straight answers, look them straight in the eye, and never stop smiling."

On my ride to the television studio, Pepsi officials were generous with advice. The company's legal counsel sat to my right, feeding me answers to hypothetical questions as if I were a politician about to hold a press conference. I kept telling myself to ignore them, to remember only what Kendall had said.

My television debut with Walter Cronkite lasted all of thirty seconds. But I managed to act smart and smile so the following day all the bottlers were calling in and asking, "Who is John Sculley?" They had never heard of me before. Suddenly, I was elevated to spokesman for the soft-drink industry. The crisis led to other important exposure as well.

Tipped off to the ban three days earlier, Kendall called me and a few other executives into his office to put together a plan to deal with the crisis. He wanted to scoop Coke by getting to market a reformulated version of Diet Pepsi within hours of the ban's announcement on a Friday.

As the new corporate director of market development, I was tapped to make what was my first presentation before the board of directors with only forty-eight hours of preparation on a Monday morning. We removed the cyclamate, replacing it with a combination of saccharin and sugar. It didn't taste as good as our banned product, but it was better than nothing.

I worked through the weekend, long into each night, surveying consumers by telephone on their reaction to the ban and our new diet formula. My presentation on the ban's impact and our response to it helped raise my profile. The same day, October 22, a mere three days after the government announcement, we ran a full-page ad in *The New York Times* proclaiming that cyclamate-free Diet Pepsi already was on the supermarket shelf. Over the next ten days, we rolled the product out in all our major markets. It was quite a coup —in the market and in the boardroom.

Four months later, I went from a nonentity in the market-research department to the youngest vice president of marketing in Pepsi's history by racking up one accomplishment after another. My success in the Canary Islands, my performance during the company's cyclamate crisis, and the assistance I provided the McKinsey team made all the difference. And it would not have been possible if I had allowed my early experience in Pepsi's research group to discourage me.

The McKinsey study, as Pepsi-Cola managers had feared, soon spurred a shake-up. Victor Bonomo, United Vintners president and a former General Foods executive, was recruited to head the newly organized company, and he named me marketing V.P. A chain smoker and coffee fiend, Bonomo was a tall, methodical executive with the utmost integrity. He demanded complete thoroughness from all his reports. I initially wondered if I could please him in the job. I obviously had no experience running anything, but I did demonstrate a good knowledge of the industry and Pepsi's place in it. Still, I had done everything by myself. I had never had to manage people before; that's not something you're taught in a business school. Yet here I was, at the age of thirty, the youngest of the seventy-five people in the department, and I was in charge. I knew most of these people. Some of them had gone out of their way to keep me in limbo when I was in research. Now their worst fears had been realized.

I arrived with a mandate from Bonomo to cut expenses. So within one month, I showed little hesitation in slashing the payroll.

I collapsed the market-research operation from thirty-one people to only four, the public relations department from thirty-three to three, and the display advertising group from twelve to two.

Word traveled quickly that Sculley had a hatchet in his hand. I dismissed each person individually; then he would go back and let the others know what was to come. It was as if I had lined them up outside my door. A lot of people went away pretty mad. It didn't help that I belatedly discovered that you just didn't say goodbye and good luck; you had to work out severance arrangements, too. So I spent nights figuring out each case individually.

Not surprisingly, I developed a reputation for being insensitive. At the time, I failed to understand the importance of teamwork. Pepsi's new, emerging culture, under Kendall and Pearson, allowed me to be more insensitive.

When I told Mangold, who had come to New York only months before as Pepsi-Cola vice president of sales, he was appalled.

"You've got a lot to learn about handling people," he lectured.

I came to rely heavily on Chuck because I was young, somewhat arrogant, and inexperienced. He constantly tried to impress upon me that people were the real strategic advantage of the corporation. In Pittsburgh, I could remember him staying at the plant until 9:00 p.m. to talk to his employees about problems with their children or marriages.

Chuck didn't speak the analytical language of the MBAs and consultants who were being recruited to Pepsi in increasing numbers by Pearson, yet he instinctively knew how important people are to an organization. My instincts were to dive into the data and work on the marketing itself as if it were unrelated to people. I was infatuated with the idea that the organization counted above the individual. It's the fate of many MBAs who come out of graduate school with misplaced priorities. Too few of them ever get a chance to work with and through people. When they do, they often fail. Unfortunately, I didn't learn the lesson fast enough.

Chuck's ideas always were focused on mobilizing our bottlers, knowing them as people and motivating them, in the fight against Coke. He was right: our bottlers were one of the hidden strengths of the company. They enabled us to surpass Coke in the supermarket.

But I was often stubborn, too, and didn't always utilize Chuck's advice. We were in our new jobs less than a year. Although we had halted the decline in the Nielsens by coaxing Pepsi bottlers into becoming more aggressive promoters, I glimpsed behind the figures a much bigger problem still looming. Our share gains largely were occurring at independent stores which were becoming a smaller part of the industry. I discovered that our sales were declining far more severely in the more important chain stores. I showed Chuck my analysis and suggested we divulge this to Pearson in a private meeting the following day. Chuck disagreed.

"John," he said, "if you show Pearson the share problem we have with the big chains, all he's going to do is get upset because we don't have a solution yet."

"Chuck," I replied, "don't worry. I think he's going to be pleased that we identified the real problems. PepsiCo management really wants to know what they are. We've got to show them that we understand them."

"John, I don't think you should lay out all those problems," Chuck said. "I don't think he's aware of just how bad this thing is."

"They'll think we really have a handle on it," I argued.

The next morning, after the presentation, Pearson was none too pleased.

"Well," he barked, "this is a fine mess we have. And if you two jokers can't get it straightened out fast, we'll get two other guys that can."

Pearson turned his attention to a set of neatly stacked papers on his desk and we walked out of the meeting dejected. It was obvious to us that Pearson meant exactly what he said. Few bosses were more direct . . . or categorical. Pearson remembers that:

"What I inherited at Pepsi was a competitive organization that lacked focus. Almost every company does better if it has a single competitor to focus on. Once I focus on you, I'm going to make progress. I have a standard and a goal. It makes all the difference because competition is what the world is all about. It fosters innovation because you're trying to beat someone. It pushes the organization because you've got a goal to reach. It works in sports, like the Celtics against the Lakers. They do better because they know who to beat. In the classroom, kids compete against

*each other. So why wouldn't it work in business? We were fortu-
nate to have a deadly competitor to focus on.*

*"I didn't want to come here to preside over a slow-growing
Pepsi. I wanted our sales and profits to grow substantially faster
than the national averages.*

*"It has to be a demanding work environment. You have to
expect a lot of people, including yourself. Otherwise everyone is off
on their own thing. A lot of the pressure we put on individuals was
to make sure they had a strategy which gave us a competitive edge
versus a lot of dreaming. We were trying to inch our way into
leadership.*

*"I was tough. But there's a big difference between tough-
minded and a tough son of a bitch. Maybe I was that but that isn't
what I tried to be. I may not be everybody's idea of a choirboy but
I'm not a son of a bitch, either.*

*"Our code included openness. We told people where they stood.
We were fair."*

We had a big job ahead of us. I learned that you don't simply
identify problems at a company as competitive as Pepsi, you come
equipped with the solutions.

Pepsi, I realized, was sorely in need of some radical solutions.
Or miracles. The problem involved nothing less than dethroning
Coke where it was strongest. No one had been able to do that before,
and yet every solution—from pricing more cheaply to redesigning
the bottle to overhauling the advertising—had been tried.

For the first time in my career, I felt I could possibly face failure.

Changing the Ground Rules

Most marketers grossly underestimate their competitors. They're quick to poke fun at and to exaggerate their mistakes, and just as quick to disparage and minimize their successes. Scott Paper initially scoffed at Procter & Gamble when it acquired Charmin, the bathroom tissue maker; Pillsbury did the same when P&G bought Duncan Hines, the cake mix company. Neither took the great consumer marketer seriously when what was a soap company initially moved into paper and food products. Both paid a substantial price in lost market share.

My goal always has been to know more about my competitor than he knows about himself. It calls for an insatiable curiosity about everything your competitor does, about how he is perceived by others and how other competitors react to him. My vantage point always starts with the product and how the market perceives its strengths and weaknesses. Then, I ask myself questions, like "What's it worth to me if I can nullify that particular strength?"

Usually, you can only nullify a competitor's strength by changing the ground rules of competition, not simply meeting a competitor on the same field, with his rules. Too many marketers, however, attempt to play within the existing competitive framework. Competing head on requires you to compete like everyone else. Suddenly, a company is restricted to pitting its own resources against its competitor's resources. Against a larger, stronger rival such as Coca-Cola or IBM, it would likely be a losing strategy.

If you can change the rules, however, you often can take away a competitor's advantage by forcing him to move from his natural strengths. You can rob your competitor of his advantages, making him compete on a field in which he isn't familiar or comfortable. This is the true power of marketing creativity.

Coca-Cola, for example, owned one of the world's most distinctive trademarks in its 6.5-ounce, hourglass-shaped bottle. The bottle design nearly became the product itself. It made Coke easier to stack, more comfortable to grip, and more sturdy to withstand a vending machine's drop. As much a part of this country as Mom and apple pie, it was the only company logo a person could pick up in his hand.

Convinced that the bottle was Coke's most important competitive advantage, Pepsi spent millions of dollars and many years studying new designs to no avail. The company came up with the "swirl" bottle in 1958, but as an imitation it never achieved the recognition of Coke's hobble-skirted model. Instead of pulling back and asking what the consumer really wanted, Pepsi executives thought of competition strictly in terms of a bottle. The company had become so obsessed by its competitor that it lost its perspective on the market.

Seeking to shift the ground rules, I discovered our marketing opportunity not in the shape of the package, but in its size. When I was put in charge of marketing, I initiated one of the company's first massive consumer-research studies, an extended, in-home product test with 350 families. We gave them the opportunity to order Pepsi and other competitive brands weekly at discounted prices. To our astonishment, we discovered that no matter how much Pepsi they ordered, they would always consume it. It dawned on me that what we needed to do was design packages that made it easier for people to get more soft drinks into the home. When consumers entered a supermarket in the early 1970s, they could only buy a soft drink in a single can, in a six-pack of small bottles, or in a 28-ounce non-returnable bottle. The research told us that if you could get it in the door, there were few limits to its consumption.

Instead of redesigning the standard bottle, it became obvious that we should change the rules of the competition entirely. We should launch new, larger, and more varied packages. The research proved it. So did my earlier experience on the floor of a Pittsburgh supermarket. By rebuilding a huge display, repacking Pepsi in eight-packs instead of six, we had significantly increased our volume. Shoppers wanted more, but they wanted to be able to carry it home with ease.

The best business concepts are often surprisingly simple, yet elusive. Successful strategies build on advantages over the competition, while trying to minimize the disadvantages. The realization that we needed to compete differently met both those tests. We could minimize our disadvantage of not having a distinctive bottle and transform it into an advantage over Coke by moving into larger and more varied packaging.

It wasn't until we shifted the ground rules to larger-sized packages that the marketing advantages to Coke of having such a unique bottle began to erode. New packaging, in generic shapes with straight-sided walls that were inexpensive to manufacture, allowed us to shift logo designs from bottle shapes to four-color label graphics. We tapped into the desire of consumers to purchase soft drinks in larger packages. Coca-Cola couldn't successfully translate its valuable silhouette to the larger-sized plastic bottles. The result: a trademark familiar to more than three generations of Americans became virtually extinct!

Other consumer packaging brands have pursued similar strategies with great success. In the 1960s, for example, people complained about how long it took to pour Heinz ketchup from the bottle. Competitors' products were a lot easier to use. Pondering the dilemma, Heinz officials wondered if a different formula or a new bottle design was the answer. Either solution would have represented the more conventional approach to solving a marketing problem—meet your competitor on the same field, directly responding to his latest salvo.

H. J. Heinz, however, wisely discovered an eventual panacea not through conventional thinking but by changing the nature of the competition. The company's marketing management began using a new advertising approach to convince consumers that the reason Heinz ketchup was slower to pour was because it was a lot thicker (and therefore must taste a lot better). By employing the "slowest-pouring ketchup" theme in advertising, Heinz's ketchup has dramatically improved its market share over the years from 19 percent to about 50 percent today. The company managed to turn what had initially been a disadvantage into a competitive advantage by changing the ground rules.

Sometimes, of course, it takes clever positioning of a product to benefit from such a strategy. When Lever Brothers initially launched All detergent, its advantage in the marketplace was that it was twice as concentrated as Procter & Gamble's market-leading Tide. To emphasize the difference, Lever Brothers introduced All in small packages, suggesting that the homemaker didn't need as much. Consumers, however, either didn't fathom the significance of the difference or, if they did, they didn't care. They wanted the most powerful detergent, not the most concentrated. Lever Brothers had shifted the ground rules by competing with a different product, but failed to impress the consumer with the difference. If anything, consumers thought they were getting less for the same money because the packages were smaller.

Not until All was packaged in large containers did it become successful. Users then scooped out the same size cupful of detergent they had been accustomed to using with Tide and other products. The result was a more powerful solution which made clothes cleaner. All's share of market zoomed as word traveled about its effectiveness.

Traditional marketers are obsessed with the notion that marketing is a quantitative process where success is won upon awareness, reach, and frequency, three of the profession's sacraments. Successful marketing, however, cannot be merely reduced to a set of quantitative skills or measurements. While such skills may reduce the risks of making a big mistake, they are a poor substitute for true creative vision.

That comes from builders, fundamentally creative-driven people who attempt to get mentally inside their products. It takes a passionate belief in the power of your own ideas and the conviction to see them through to the end. It can sometimes be a lonesome and a long battle to win. Visionaries are constantly fighting conventional wisdom because they see the world ahead in terms of what it can be if someone is willing to look at things in very different ways. By definition, they are more dependent on their own instincts. They invest their lives in a product by becoming totally absorbed by every aspect of it. They are usually demanding, stubborn, uncompromising, and difficult to be around. But when their perseverance and instincts match up, they are really right.

This is a far cry from the more common systematized competitor, skilled at fighting it out in today's market with an arsenal of B-school marketing tools. Competitors believe every battle counts, especially their most recent one, so they are too focused on the outcome of the month or the quarter. Visionaries are constantly looking over the horizon to tomorrow. If their vision is on target, it will change the market and they will prosper—even if it means losing a few battles along the way.

2

The Cola Wars

Within Pepsi, we were a band of obsessive misfits, thrown together by luck and circumstance. There were six of us, six very different individuals who would shape the company's marketing in the early 1970s and take on our Atlanta nemesis.

Three of the six, Chuck and Jim Mangold and Larry Smith, had worked their way into management jobs through the bottling ranks. Three of us were outsiders: Harry Hersh, formerly a financial analyst at General Electric; John Corbani, an advertising manager; and me.

Out in the market, we faced a huge task in battling back for market share against Coca-Cola. Inside Pepsi, we faced pressure from top management, particularly PepsiCo president Andrall Pearson, who had little respect for our small group. PepsiCo executives traditionally came out of the bottling business, like Chuck, Jim, and Larry. But Pearson wanted less parochial executives with broader marketing experience, and he began to actively recruit them from General Foods, General Mills, Procter & Gamble, Ford Motor, and ITT. Our group didn't neatly fit the new corporate image.

I was constantly in the position of almost having to hide the excellent work of Smith and the two Mangold brothers because it wasn't in the typical lingo and style of classical marketing. Pearson and Pepsi-Cola president Vic Bonomo wouldn't accept it without my MBA translation.

I had been trained both at business school and in market research in the ways of classical marketing. I understood the methods developed by Procter & Gamble which made marketing a systematized process. Marketing, as defined by P&G, wasn't an art. It was a discipline, reduced to a predictable, highly quantitative, analytical system.

My ideas about marketing leaned toward the creative and intuitive—not the rigidly analytical. I approached marketing from the back door, entering not with an overwhelming desire to become a professional marketer but to gather enough experience to leave and eventually set up my own industrial design firm. So I focused on the creative side and worked well with people who also scorned traditional methods.

All of us shared a respect for ideas and a desire to change the soft-drink industry; and each of us brought a different set of skills to make it happen. Chuck, an incessant worrier and pipe smoker, had the people skills I lacked. Larry, a well-read cynic with a sarcastic sense of humor, boasted an eclectic and sharp mind. Chuck's younger brother, Jim, was an exceptional analyst who could do complex math in his head. Harry Hersh, the former GE analyst, brought a measure of financial insight to the team. John was our bridge to the ad agency.

In 1970, we were faced with a problem no conventional business logic could help us solve: how to dethrone not just a number-one brand, but an American icon. Coca-Cola represented part and parcel of the good life the American dream guaranteed. At home, during peacetime, Coke became a form of self-expression. Abroad, during war, homesick GIs found comfort in Coke's red-and-white logo tooling out of bottling plants General Eisenhower had set up near all battle fronts.

As Pepsi-Cola's new, thirty-year-old marketing vice president, my future hinged on breaking us out of the number-two position. Being second to a Goliath might not seem so bad, but in reality it's even worse than it sounds. In a two-horse race, it means being last. Ever since an Atlanta druggist mixed the first batch of Coke in his backyard in 1886, we became the also-ran. It wasn't until twelve years later that Caleb D. Bradham, a North Carolina pharmacist, concocted Pepsi-Cola.

All of us badly wanted to beat Coke. I was very young to be marketing V.P., and I was unproven in the eyes of my peers. I wanted to gain their trust. But this wasn't just a marketing war; it was a civil war, and the South kept winning. For years, it was an unwritten rule that the word "Pepsi" was never to be uttered in front of strangers visiting Coca-Cola's massive headquarters in Atlanta. Their Nielsen books referred to Pepsi only as "the imitator." The "Real Thing," however, had outspent us, outmaneuvered us, and outdid us in almost everything.

For Pepsi ever to become number one, we needed to get a series of building blocks into place that would eventually allow us to reach three important goals: the best image, taste, and bottlers. I saw that Coca-Cola's overwhelming advantage was based on image, not product superiority. Pepsi never would be able to gain market share unless we could improve its image. So it made sense to attack it from this vantage point.

I asked myself how we could take advantage of external events that were shaping the world. The 1960s and early 1970s were a time of change and turbulence. A president had been assassinated; another president was in trouble. Riots broke out in the cities and on student campuses. People were marching in the streets in protest of a war they didn't believe in, and I was among them. These events were creating incredible anxiety. I wondered if we could use them in a positive way to unseat this mythical giant in Atlanta. My point of view shifted. I began scanning the landscape, looking for ideas that ranged beyond the narrow product specifications that classical marketing made gospel.

One of the things that caught my attention was a speech by Margaret Mead, the famous anthropologist. She said the single most important fact for marketers since the end of World War II was the emergence of an affluent middle class. I began to think about how we could tap into the children of this generation, the baby boomers.

Demographically, we were in the midst of a baby boom, and many baby boomers had already reached their teens. They had a lot of discretionary money to spend, but neither they nor their parents had any experience on how to spend it. Articulating a lifestyle they could aspire to was potentially a very powerful idea.

After viewing reels of Pepsi's commercials over the previous ten years, I was struck by the brilliance of its 1963 "Pepsi Generation" campaign. Launched by advertising agency B.B.D.O., and then advertising vice president Alan Pottasch, it helped to create a new genre of advertising in which lifestyle took centerstage to the product. The commercials, under the theme "Come Alive, You're in the Pepsi Generation," captured the exuberance of youth splashing through ocean waves, flipping Frisbees through the air, and driving dune buggies on a sandy beach. The message was that Pepsi was an integral part of this enviable lifestyle. Pepsi-Cola president Jim Somerall, however, inexplicably abandoned the lifestyle approach in 1965 in favor of a product sell campaign that touted Pepsi as "The Taste That Beats the Others Cold."

The decision to drop the Pepsi Generation was puzzling to me because, among other things, it seemed to address what research had shown to be a major competitive disadvantage we suffered against Coke. When people served soft drinks to their friends, they would pour Pepsi in the kitchen and bring it out in glasses. These same people, on the other hand, wouldn't hesitate to serve Coke out of the bottle because it had a more positive image. We had to convince people to take Pepsi out of the kitchen and into the living room.

The timing seemed perfect for a new Pepsi Generation. I thought we could use the campaign to say the blasphemous—that Coke was outdated and old-fashioned. We could take Coke's greatest strength—its great history—and try to convince people this was its greatest weakness. This could only be accomplished by focusing on the lifestyles of the people who were going to consume the product. We were saying, Yes, we are the smaller product, but we are the ones that a new generation is latching onto.

That was a powerful idea. First, it suddenly threw Coke on the defensive. Secondly, the demographics worked in our favor. We were appealing to an expanding group of young people who had very high per capita soft-drink consumption habits. Persuading them to switch to Pepsi had greater value to us because they would drink three times as much soda as the average person. Their culture wasn't the three square meals a day that to their Depression parents meant safety and security. They were the generation that invented snacks. Soda became their beverage staple.

The positioning was believable, too. Coca-Cola would have a harder time convincing people that a drink which had universal appeal for generations suddenly was a youth product. In Pepsi's case, a lot of people knew very little if anything about the drink. Pepsi started with almost a clean slate with many people.

The early Pepsi Generation commercials may not have been produced with this idea in mind. But as I studied them, I realized how incredibly insightful they were. The decision to dump the campaign after only a two-year run didn't make sense. Yet many marketing types frequently stumble into two ubiquitous traps. First, they think advertising loses its effect far more quickly than it actually does. They see and notice a campaign all the time; consumers, though, get nowhere near the same exposure. So they're quicker to ax a campaign and move on to something else, even when it isn't necessary to do so. Second, when an executive comes into a new job, he wants to quickly make an impact. Oftentimes, he naively changes things, not because they don't click, but because of the pressure to make his mark in the organization.

If the commercials didn't work before, it might have been because they were too contrived—like those low-budget soap opera commercials showing Marge and Madge, who were actresses, not real people, arguing over whose wash is brighter or whiter. We didn't have to settle for the low-budget "Marge and Madge" spots that were the province of P&G brand managers; we didn't have to settle for slogans, either. As a single-brand company though, we had the advantage of being able to direct large sums of money behind the brand. We would move from the slogan era to the image era; the images would sell emotion more than product differences.

I knew that Pepsi could never dislodge Coke if it didn't look like number one. Our theme, "You've Got a Lot to Live and Pepsi's Got a Lot to Give," was the basis of big-budget, sixty-second ads featuring real people who appealed to genuine human emotions.

We treated our commercials as if they were miniature movies, and we recruited Hollywood's best filmmakers to shoot them in cinematic quality. Most companies then were spending between $15,000 and $75,000 to produce a commercial; Pepsi began spending between $200,000 and $300,000 for a single spot. It was unheard of in those days. But we had to make Pepsi a "necktie" product, one that people would be happy to wear, to take out of the kitchen and into the living room.

Marketing, after all, is really theater. It's like staging a performance. The way to motivate people is to get them interested in your product, to entertain them, and to turn your product into an incredibly important event. The Pepsi Generation campaign did all this in scaling Pepsi to epic proportions and making a brand bigger than life. It broke with the more scientific classical marketing.

Working late at night, almost every night, our six-man team developed and implemented these upstart plans. We not only took Coke by surprise, we shocked Pepsi. We had overturned their classical marketing icons and gentlemanly ways.

The resurrected Pepsi Generation immediately clicked, winning awards and becoming the longest-running campaign ever to run on television. Suddenly we had a revived product and a whole social group who identified with Pepsi as if it were a new religion. The commercials were successful because they articulated a lifestyle to which a new, more affluent, generation of Americans could aspire, a generation which, of course, drank Pepsi. It showed life as people want it to be, without complication or distraction—a young boy playing with puppies in a field or a cute little girl who dropped a piece of watermelon on her dress. The vignettes of life's "magic moments," as John Bergin and Phil Dusenberry who led the B.B.D.O. creative team put it, captured America's imagination. They evoked cherished middle-American values, of familial love and the innocence of children. The commercials subtly positioned Pepsi as the modern American soft drink, and by contrast, Coke as the old-fashioned cola.

The Pepsi Generation reached people's minds through their hearts. It captured people's imagination at a time when they were vulnerable to a reassuring message that there was still reason to be optimistic about America. The campaign came at a time when America needed such a jolt.

So did my team.

Within Pepsi, we were heroes but still outsiders, mavericks. Our success only gave us license to throw the switch higher on our steamroller ways.

Pepsi hadn't seen anything yet. Neither had Coke.

As critical as advertising is, most of marketing is not advertising, it's implementation. Without the infrastructure to support our new ideas in packaging and merchandising, they would have been doomed to failure.

My team moved through Pepsi, rigging it for major changes. We would break with the conventional marketing concepts of the time in other ways as well. P&G's classical brand management structure gave brand managers great power. Often viewed as the president of his own little company, the brand manager focused on a single product or a small family of products. He orchestrated everything from market research and manufacturing to sales, package design, and advertising by drawing upon specialists within his company.

Each brand manager had profit-and-loss responsibility over his product. In a huge, marketing behemoth, the system fostered small, entepreneurial enclaves. It gave managers "ownership" over a part of the corporation, allowing a P&G to be more nimble and innovative than most large corporate entities.

At Pepsi, we saw something radically different. The company and the brand were inseparable. As a single-brand company, Pepsi was twenty times larger in volume than some of P&G's products. Our product boasted wider distribution, and some 95 percent of the population would drink cola annually. When a brand is so large, it makes sense to take its pieces and put individual effort and focus against them.

After all, a new P&G product would be a rousing success if it could grab a mere 2 percent of its market. But a new soft-drink package could easily capture a 3–4 percent stake. Our insight was simple: If packages were as critical to the soft-drink business as new products were to the consumer-packaging business, the structure of the organization should emphasize it.

In much the same way that P&G appointed a brand manager for Head & Shoulders shampoo or Cheer detergent, Pepsi could have managers for each of its packages, merchandising equipment, and distribution channels. And our accounting methods should underscore their individual efforts by devising ways to measure the profit and sales figures for each sector, just as P&G did for its brand managers. I hired many P&G people with brand management experience, making them 16-ounce returnable bottle managers, merchandising display managers, or convenience store managers.

The new organization and our method of guerrilla warfare helped us blitz Coke. Each could feel "ownership" over his area of purview, and the Nielsens provided the numbers to measure their impact. Our focus on convenience stores, for example, led to an unprecedented $50 million gain in volume in a single year. Our concentration on merchandising resulted in a new stand-alone display that led to phenomenal sales increases of 800 percent to 1200 percent during promotional periods.

The new individual focus allowed us to take greater advantage of every market attribute. Drugstore chains, for example, had become a new retailing phenomenon in the 1970s. Their growth and the further decline of the Mom and Pop corner drugstore—whose fountain sales often were the province of Coca-Cola—provided Pepsi with a major marketing opportunity. By having an individual manager for drugstore chains, he could tailor marketing and promotional campaigns for them. He could prove that Pepsi could drive additional traffic into their stores and help them make more money. The way to make money in retailing always is to use someone else's money. We ran tests and analyses which showed we could turn over Pepsi inventory in a drugstore chain four to five times before it had to pay us. Suddenly we were talking the retailers' language and they heard what we were saying.

After all these many changes—the revived advertising, the standardized Pepsi logo on all packaging and merchandising, the introduction of new, larger groups of packages, and a supporting management structure beneath the changes—we saw results. The downward slide in the Nielsens stopped and a long, consistent climb in market share began. A close inspection of the numbers disclosed that Pepsi had even moved ahead of Coke in some regional areas. As the changes rolled out across the country, the national figures began to change. It was exhilarating to everyone on the team. Starting in 1970, the ratings were up for sixty-four consecutive audit periods, about three and one-half years, the longest consecutive series of gains A. C. Nielsen ever recorded on any brand.

Ironically, as we gained on Coca-Cola, we realized the Atlanta-based company was in reality a sleeping giant. Coca-Cola was still tracking market share on the basis of the number of bottles (units) sold, not ounces. A 48-ounce Pepsi bottle would count as much as a 6.5-ounce Coke bottle in the survey. Because so much of Coke's business was in its small 6.5-ounce hourglass bottle, their Nielsen data tended to disguise the real advances Pepsi was making. We converted our Nielsen numbers to 8-ounce equivalent cases because it more accurately showed the trend toward larger packages. This made sense, too, because Pepsi and Coca-Cola were in the business of selling beverage concentrate; the more cola ounces consumed, the more concentrate bottlers would buy from us.

Chuck Mangold remained my mentor and coach. He was the only person who could control me because I wanted to do everything myself. Chuck would lecture me, telling me to get a haircut or making fun of the brown suede desert boots I'd often wear with my suits. He realized how impatient I was—with myself and with others. I'd have fifteen balls up in the air at any one time. Two thirds of them may have been virtually worthless. Chuck would sit back, puff on his pipe, and say, "John, I don't know what I'm going to do with you. You just have to slow down and concentrate on a few things. We just can't do all the ideas you want to do." Mangold held the team together. As he recalls:

"I was like the father to the group. Occasionally I'd have to keep them in line . . . cool, calm, collected, and working together. They were all young—in their late twenties and early thirties. I was in my mid- to late forties and had been with the company so long that I was like the old shoe.

"We had great esprit de corps. If a job took thirty-six hours a day, we did it and loved it. Somebody would come up with a promotional or marketing idea and the gang would work on it until it was done. There was a lot of laughter and kibitzing.

"John was impatient with himself. He was always coming up with an idea and as soon as he had one it was, 'Katie, lock the door, baby, here we go.' He was all over it and didn't care how many hours he worked.

"It was not extraordinary for one of his department heads to be awoken by the telephone at two o'clock in the morning and hear John saying, 'Hey, I just happened to think of this. How about meeting me at five-thirty tomorrow morning and let's see what we can do with it?' It didn't make a damn bit of difference to John."

No one could do his work well enough to meet my standards. Other than the six-man team settled around me, I was just going through people, chewing them up. I went through four marketing-research vice presidents in two years. Eventually I ended up doing the job myself and firing them. I still hadn't developed my skills as an operating manager. I didn't understand how important it was to build an organization. Pepsi was much smaller then, so I could still succeed in it. Nonetheless, I was getting a reputation for being someone you'd want to steer clear of. I didn't care: I was convinced that what I was doing was right, that I had to get my marketing ideas out, and I wasn't going to let anything get in the way.

Chuck was a counterbalance to everything I did. When I had a "better idea," nothing was going to get in the way of making it into something. Chuck would sit me down, close the door, and say, "Wait a minute. How are we going to make it work with the people and how will we manage it through?"

And he put up with my impatience, as did all the members of our team, even from the very beginning. At our first big meeting before PepsiCo management, the six of us were reviewing our presentation when the slides I had asked for finally arrived. It was already after work hours, the evening before our presentation, and the slides came in wrong. Our analysis, so carefully compiled for management, had been constructed in tables and charts that didn't reveal what was really going on.

We had just changed our Nielsen data from units to ounces and the new data showed we were winning against Coke and suggested incredible growth opportunities for Pepsi. But the slides didn't reflect this.

In my frustration, I tossed them on the floor of the boardroom and vowed to do my own. One of my associates scurried out of the room to tell Chuck what had happened. Mangold dashed into the boardroom.

"What's going on?" he demanded. "Someone told me you threw out the only slides we have for the presentation. He thinks you're crazy!"

"We are going to do the whole analysis again," I told Chuck. "I can make the charts myself. All we have to do over is the analysis."

Our presentation was scheduled for 9:00 a.m., and we were already well into the evening.

"How in the world can you throw away the slides the night before the big presentation?" Chuck asked in disbelief. "You can't do that! Can't we just talk around what we have?"

"No," I insisted, "it's not right."

Hersh took out a calculator and began recompiling all the information by hand. Lunch had been sandwiches at the desk. So dinner would be another bag of Frito-Lays, which Larry and Jim, who began reviewing the management data, poured onto the table. At about 2:00 a.m. I sent them all home—at that point I just had to make the charts. I stayed up all night, finishing the charts ten minutes before our meeting with Kendall and Pearson. There wasn't time to shower or change clothes, but all that mattered were the ideas. The presentation was a great success—because it allowed PepsiCo management to see the huge opportunity for us in large-size packages.

I lived for work. I was possessed by it. Commuting to Purchase from a small apartment in New York City, I would leave early in the morning after a run through Central Park, only to return late at night. On my way back, I'd customarily stop at a neighborhood pizza parlor, bringing dinner home with me in a flat white box. The apartment reeked of pizza, evidence of a routine that became habit. Part of the ritual would have me propped up in bed, a slice of pizza at my side, as I read one book after another, things like Tom Wolfe's *The Kandy-Kolored Tangerine-Flake Streamline Baby.* It was a life much different from that led by many of my older Pepsi colleagues who lived with their families in the suburbs. As a bachelor again, I was also a loner who felt at home in New York. I enjoyed the pace of the city, the anonymity it conferred on its residents.

On the weekends, my youngest brother, David, who then worked as a product manager for Lever Brothers, would stroll with me through supermarkets, exchanging marketing and promotional ideas and searching for intelligence on our competitors. He would critique Pepsi's packaging and displays; I would do the same for Lever Brothers' detergents.

Certainly, there were no attachments that would prevent me from accepting what for me would become a new, very different adventure at Pepsi. Before readying for a European trip to attend a Pepsi meeting in Switzerland, Pearson asked that I stop off in Paris to tour a newly acquired potato-chip factory. He wanted my impressions of this new Pepsi unit.

When I arrived, I couldn't believe my eyes. The factory was completely out of control. A flood of water, oil, and potato waste effluent covered the floor, requiring that we don large black wading boots for our tour of the plant. Cooking oil leaked from what was the world's largest potato-chip fryer, mixing with the water on the smooth tile floor. You had to hold on to the plant's pillars to prevent yourself from slipping and possibly drowning in the mess.

The factory's management planned on more than $10 million of sales a year, but the sales department failed to bring in the orders. Unfortunately, however, no one told the production department to stop or slow down on ordering materials. Carload after carload of materials were backed up on a railroad siding. Hundreds of thousands of dollars of packaged goods were dumped in a warehouse where this oily water was seeping. I went around with a little Minox camera taking pictures like crazy.

"How in the world did we ever buy anything like this?" I asked the plant's manager.

He rolled his eyes and said, "I don't know how we're going to get out of it."

"Well, good luck. I'm sure glad I'm not involved with it."

I then went off to the Pepsi meeting in Switzerland. Within my first day, Pearson called me over and said: "We've got a wonderful opportunity for you."

"Oh, what's that?" I innocently asked.

"Well," he said, "I know how much you've always liked international. How would you like to run our International Foods operations?"

"You mean including that French thing I just saw?"

"Yes," Pearson replied, "including that."

The French potato-chip fiasco was only the start of it. The international business was a ragtag group of money-losing companies scattered around the world: a cookie maker in Sweden, a pasta company in Venezuela, potato-chip and pretzel companies in Brazil, snack-food outfits in Mexico, Japan, Canada, Spain, and Puerto Rico. All told, this unlikely bunch of businesses was losing $16 million a year on $83 million in revenues.

I asked Pearson for some time to think about it. Then I came back and posed three questions to which I needed favorable answers before I would commit myself. I asked if PepsiCo was serious about being in the international snack-food business; if Pepsi would continue to invest in new opportunities in which return on investment was good despite our past misadventures abroad; and if Pepsi would allow me to hire my own team of young managers, most in their middle twenties, from inside the company. Pearson agreed, and I took the job.

People thought I had lost my mind. Nearly every Pepsi executive shipped abroad in this job before had never again reappeared in the corporation. It was the corporate equivalent of going off to Siberia, the dead end for managers who couldn't cut it in PepsiCo's highly competitive environment. I was surrendering the number-two job at Pepsi-Cola, the corporation's largest single business, with $700 million in sales, to run the only Pepsi division that was in the red. Many surmised I was taking a humiliating step downward. It seemed a losing proposition, a disaster from which I wasn't likely to survive. People assumed I must have committed a corporate faux pas to get saddled with the job. They were sure that I was being sent into the wilderness to mend my maverick ways.

The truth was I embraced the opportunity. It didn't matter whether this low-prestige job would enhance my career. I had always loved the idea of having the adventure of traveling around the world. And then, there was the allure of the turnaround challenge: building a successful entity from a losing business.

My first decision was to shutter the French operation that had been acquired only ten months earlier. It was not a popular move. After proposing the $14 million writeoff on the plant to the board, I met with Don Kendall in his office. I remember his icy stare, his habit of backing you up against the wall. He had an intimidating way of taking over your space.

"I'm damn mad about this whole French thing," he said. "We never should have gotten into France in the first place. We got out because it was the right thing to do. I sure as hell want you to ensure we never get into another problem like this again. And I'm counting on you, John, to make absolutely sure of that."

I had to demonstrate that we could not only fix the problems but could build our motley collection of companies into a substantial business. I knew that if we couldn't bring it up to a $500 million business by the end of the decade, no one at the corporate level would be interested because it would represent too small a part of the corporation's overall sales.

What Don didn't know was that we had only recently acquired two companies in Brazil that could face a similar fate as France: a modestly profitable pretzel plant and a disastrous potato-chip factory.

Located in a series of apartments built on a steep hill in São Paulo, the potato-chip assembly line resembled a Rube Goldberg concoction. At the top, trucks dropped off 220-pound sacks of potatoes; at the bottom, trucks carted off boxes of bagged potato chips. In between, the product was dropped through each floor to the next apartment below.

The process began in the first apartment on the hill. There, workers in black rubber boots emptied the dirty cloth sacks into a trough where the potatoes were washed down with a hose. They'd scoop the potatoes up in old washpans and throw them in the hopper of an antiquated machine that would peel and grind them up into moist slices.

The slices were manually dumped out of pans into a huge, raised hearth filled with hot oil to fry the potato slices. Tired men, their clothes soaked in sweat, picked them out with colanders wired to the end of broomsticks and dropped them onto a plywood table. Teenage girls dressed in blue smocks and bandanas shook salt over the chips, tumbling them at the same time, while someone else pushed the chips through a hole in the table where yet another worker held a small cellophane bag underneath. The bag was weighed on a small kitchen scale, heat-sealed, and thrown onto a pile to be packed in cardboard boxes. They'd drop the boxes through a hole in the floor to another apartment which was the storage area.

The process—which would have flunked most U.S. health laws —created what tasted like the world's most unedible potato chip. The potatoes had too much sugar in them, so they were very brown. The machine sliced them too thick. The frying oil was rancid. The cellophane bags couldn't keep the greasy product fresh. By the time it hit the stores, it was often stale.

Both this business and the pretzel plant clearly suffered from a lack of sound business basics. Merchandising and promotion wasn't given a moment's thought. The result: both brands lacked an identity in the marketplace. There were virtually no financial controls, not even a management process, at the potato-chip plant.

The task of turning the business around was further complicated by Brazil's roller-coaster economy. If we couldn't grow the business at dramatic levels, it would quickly go bankrupt.

To clean up the mess, I brought in Frito-Lay managers to hire and train new staff. We found new sources of potatoes and bags to enhance the quality of the product and keep it fresh. We completely rebuilt the chart of accounts, established financial controls, and put in a new organizational structure, process, and people. We added route trucks, merchandising equipment, advertising campaigns, new package designs, and promotional concepts, all designed to accelerate the business's growth rate.

It was difficult to justify new automated equipment because the teenage girls worked for a mere $2.60 a day. So we scoured the States for old machinery, broke it down in small pieces, and carried it across the border in our suitcases—a necessary deception given the embargo on equipment shipments for non-essential industries which the oil crisis inspired.

We operated the business as if it were our own. The São Paulo plant, for example, was plagued by sewage problems which we solved with an old trick I learned in Bermuda as a kid. We bought some goldfish, put them in the septic tank, and they ate up the waste material. They cleaned our water lines and helped us meet the government's environmental requirements. All without the need for expensive pollution-control equipment.

From Frito-Lay, I surprisingly discovered that the potato-chip business was barely profitable. The chips paid the overhead of the company's infrastructure, while corn-based snacks like Cheetos racked up virtually all the profit. In both Brazil and Spain, then, we had to shift into these higher-margin snacks to ensure long-term profitability. Europeans, however, largely associated corn with animal feed, so we had to figure how to convince them to eat it. We eventually came up with corn-based snacks disguised by a covering of a mild, white cheese and simply didn't advertise the fact they were made from corn. Within eight months, the business was growing at a rate of 40 percent to 50 percent a month.

We would go off on trips for four to six weeks at a time, often traveling together as a close-knit team: Harry Deckard, Ron Bellamy, Norb Sobek, and Ted Bonds—four Frito-Lay renegades from Texas, and the son of an Argentine rancher, Mauricio Pagés, who delighted in entertaining the Spaniards by wearing cowboy boots with blue jeans and large belt buckles. It would not have been possible to turn around the business if not for our team of competent individuals. Deckard, the oldest member of the group, in his fifties, was our manufacturing sage—along with Bonds, who upgraded the facilities. Bellamy, Sobek, and Pagés were the financial wizards, who helped to establish internal discipline and controls. With colored pencils and paper, I designed new packaging, point-of-sale materials, and racks.

For three and a half years, I crossed either the Pacific or Atlantic oceans at least once a week. My friends were the people who traveled with me all over the world. I was completely in charge of my own life. I loved what I was doing. I was running and starting little companies, and I had a wonderful group of young, bright people with me. Within three and a half years, the $83 million business that has been losing $16 million a year was selling more than $300 million in snack foods and making $40 million pre-tax.

Back in the States, meanwhile, Bonomo was tiring of his job as Pepsi-Cola president. The position could easily burn you out. As president he was under constant pressure, having to spend hours in delicate negotiations with the Pepsi-Cola Bottlers Association. Any change in concentrate prices, funding, or marketing had to be negotiated. It could be a grueling experience. Because the bottlers knew and trusted me, Bonomo urged that I take his place.

I resisted the move, turning down Bonomo, Pearson, and Kendall several times over a six-month period. "Come on, John," they said, "you've had your fun for three and a half years. Now it's time to come back." I finally relented. But I returned kicking and screaming.

There was an informality and spirit of teamwork that seemed missing back in Purchase, New York. Kendall often asked me if there were barbers in Barcelona or São Paulo because my hair grew shaggy. The thought of having to be confined to the United States was terribly demoralizing. It just wasn't what I wanted to do with my life.

During my stint in International Foods I had, however, fallen in love with an attractive woman I thought I would someday marry. I first met her at a dinner party in 1971. I was then on my second marriage, while she was married to a Pepsi executive. She impressed me as an interesting, warm, and sensitive person, who enjoyed art and antiques. A year later, I saw her again at a Pepsi dinner I was hosting at New York's Sign of the Dove restaurant. By now I was again divorced and working closely with her husband, Harry Hersh, a key member of our marketing team. After fetching Leezy a glass of white wine, I chatted for a few minutes and then went off to speak with other guests.

When her husband transferred to Frito-Lay in Dallas, they separated and eventually divorced. It was during one of my return trips from abroad that I met her again and invited her out to dinner. I discovered her to be warm and creative, yet street-smart and feisty. We started dating, although it was difficult because I would be away for six weeks at a crack. I fell in love with her, and I realized that I never could have a real life with Leezy while trotting around the world. Our relationship made the final decision easier than I thought.

Yet I was hardly ready to marry again. I had little time to pursue a personal life. I was so stimulated by work that I openly worried whether I could be a good husband to anyone. I had failed twice before, once with Kendall's stepdaughter. What assurance had I that I wouldn't fail a third time?

Leezy, however, could put up with my obsession for work. She understood me better than most people. She had an appreciation for the eighteenth-century English landscapes and portraits I collected. She could have as enjoyable an evening as I just sipping wine in front of a roaring fire at night, listening to fine music. And her bubbly, extroverted personality balanced my reserved nature perfectly. On March 7, 1978, we exchanged vows at home before a local justice of the peace, a friend, and a blazing fireplace.

It was a controversial marriage. The corporate wives at Pepsi branded her an opportunist, accusing Leezy of trading in a vice president for a president, even though she had been divorced for three years before we began dating. But Leezy wasn't the typical quietly conforming corporate spouse. An independent-minded woman, she could be quite irreverent. I admired her independence and her spunk.

One day I was a bachelor, traveling around the world. The next, it seemed, I was riding in a station wagon with a new wife, a new ten-year-old stepdaughter, a cat, a golden retriever named Duffy, and a pair of hamsters. My professional life at Pepsi, of course, changed dramatically as well.

I found myself drawn back into the more formal, accountable world of Pepsi's headquarters in Purchase. This was an important promotion to one of the top jobs in the corporation. It presented a new set of demands as well. Under Bonomo, the Nielsens had continued their upward climb, contributing to some of the headiest growth in Pepsi's history. There was no turnaround job for John Sculley at Pepsi-Cola.

Our efforts to get Pepsi out of the kitchen and into the nation's living rooms had been successful. By the mid- to late seventies, the new challenge was to aggressively push ahead of Coke and to establish new competitive advantages over our nemesis. The strategic competitive advantages we had pioneered no longer provided the combative edge they gave us in the early seventies. They had, by now, become standard throughout the industry. Even regional soft-drink companies rushed to duplicate them.

The success of all businesses is based on a strategy of achieving sustainable competitive advantages, of gaining and holding the initiative over a competitor. Pepsi's advantages were eroding as the industry began to emulate many of our practices—from larger-sized packages to new distribution channels.

The figures my new team and I had were the soft-drink equivalent of pure plutonium: Pepsi tasted better than Coke, and if asked, most people agreed. This fact was just what we needed to overturn Coke. I didn't suspect we'd unhinge Pepsi in the process.

It was one of the surprising findings of the market research I'd initiated back in 1971. The study showed that on a blind basis, consumers overwhelmingly favored the taste of Pepsi over Coke. But Pepsi only won the taste test when both Pepsi and Coke remained unidentified. At the time, we didn't know how to exploit this competitive advantage, so we didn't act upon it. Pepsi hadn't done comparative advertising then, and Coke could beat Pepsi when consumers knew in advance which brands they were drinking. Therefore, it had seemed more important to establish strategic advantages in packaging and merchandising.

Now, we needed to do more powerful things, to build upon our megabrand marketing concepts. The natural evolution of this became our effort to combine public relations, advertising, and promotion into an all-out, frontal attack against Coke. Just as the one-sight, one-sell concept helped to imprint a single image of Pepsi in the minds of the consumer—who had been confused by dozens of different logos in all sizes and colors—this, too, would help us leverage our taste advantage against Coke. The all-encompassing marketing blitz we would launch would have an impact that would far exceed a simple, Madison Avenue commercial campaign. The irony is that we initially began to launch our power campaign from weakness, not strength.

The Cola Wars had effectively stopped at the Mason Dixon Line, due to Coke's dominance of the South as a true Southern company. No market proved more impenetrable, however, than Texas. The Lone Star State was Coke territory. Here, Pepsi wasn't only a distant number two to Coke, it was a far-removed third behind Dr. Pepper. In the crucial Houston and Dallas markets, where Pepsi had two company-owned bottling plants, we fought hard for a meager 7 percent market share against Coke's 37 percent. It was hardly a contest.

Out of sheer desperation, Larry Smith, who had become an executive V.P. for Pepsi's company-owned bottling plants, urged an advertising effort more powerful than Pepsi's lifestyle approach. Not wanting to tamper with our hugely successful Pepsi Generation campaign, Pepsi advertising executives and B.B.D.O. resisted. Undaunted, Smith hired his own advertising agency in Texas and dispatched his vice president of marketing, Harry Hersh, to help it put together something that would represent a radical departure from what we or any other company had ever done before. The result amounted to one of the most devastating advertising and promotional campaigns ever devised. The Texas agency called it the "Pepsi Challenge."

The first commercial showed an old Southerner sipping two colas, one labeled L, the other M. When he was all done, the masks were pulled off the bottles to reveal that his choice was Pepsi, even though he claimed to be a lifelong Coke drinker. "Pepsi-Cola!" he exclaimed. "Well, I'll be darned. Well, I've got to go. Millie's waiting for me." He went racing off to Millie, and we went showing that commercial over and over again in Texas. The Pepsi Challenge was born.

All advertising, of course, suffers from lack of believability. But this is particularly true of highly competitive advertising. Indeed, Brillo soap pads were then running a comparative advertising campaign against SOS. Each brand lobbed claims and counterclaims against the other with little effect. The problem with most comparative advertising is that it most frequently features a manufacturer making claims about its product's superiority. In instances where real consumers are shown giving product testimonials, the advertising often seems contrived. In either case, the lack of believability prevents the commercial from having a strong impact on consumers.

The Challenge took a dramatically different approach. Its inherent strength was that we could show ordinary folk proclaiming that Pepsi was best. When you showed real people saying, "I've tasted the two and I prefer this one," it had credibility. No less crucial, it was a local, not a national, advertising campaign. People who viewed the commercials in any given area might even have recognized the people on the screen. They certainly would recognize the outdoor settings for the taste tests in their own areas. Then, when they left their homes for the supermarket or the shopping mall or the county fair, they were challenged to take the taste test themselves. The Challenge recreated those advertising moments in public places; it made what initially appeared to be a mere advertising campaign real —and bigger than life.

Moving to comparative advertising changed the ground rules of competition as well. Just as our competitive advantages in packaging and design had eroded over the years, our impact from pure lifestyle advertising wasn't as great as it once was, either. Coca-Cola and other major television advertisers had picked up on lifestyle advertising. So the Challenge offered people something different, too: it was the complete antithesis of the Pepsi Generation campaign. Indeed, one of the early commercials used three generations of a family. A weathered Texas grandmother was shown taking the test with her daughter and granddaughter. When the covers were slipped off the bottles, the little girl shouted: "Grandma picked Pepsi!" "I can't believe it," the older woman said. "I've drank Coke all my life." Never before had comparative advertising had such spontaneity.

More important, though, the campaign had what most other comparative advertising efforts did not: believability. It appealed to Americans' natural instincts to root for the underdog. As a weak player in the Texas market, we gained more attention and market share than we ever could have, simply by leveraging off of Coke's popularity. It was a war between the colas in which all of America could play—and it was wildly successful.

While we hadn't knocked Coke from its leadership position in Texas, we scored major gains. Bottling territories that for decades had been habitual losers were transformed into stronger, profitable areas because the Challenge significantly boosted our market share. Hersh and Smith expanded the Challenge outside Texas and began to build a merchandising campaign around it.

I was senior vice president of all U.S. sales and marketing operations when the first Pepsi Challenge debuted. I then left to head up PepsiCo's international operations in 1973. When I returned to Pepsi-Cola as president four years later, I saw the Challenge as a far more powerful idea than just a program for distressed Pepsi markets. If it could gain attention in markets where Pepsi was weak, why shouldn't it be even more effective in markets where we were strong, where we could better leverage our strength and resources into spectacular public relations and marketing events?

The timing seemed perfect. In my absence abroad, the mood of the country had dramatically changed. The Vietnam War was over; a president had been forced to resign. A born-again Christian had been elected President. America was getting its social conscience back. People became interested in fairness, values, and ethics.

As a marketing campaign, the Challenge jibed perfectly with the changing social climate in America. It seemed fair and ethical. It was a grass-roots campaign and that's how the country's newest president won election.

Somehow the challenge seemed to symbolize the ideas of the

country's new mood. It seemed to mirror where America was going at that point, which is what marketing and architecture have in common. Architecture mirrors society. Just as the cathedral mirrored the medieval towns and life around them, so marketing at its best reflects modern society.

But the best marketing doesn't mirror society where it has been; it anticipates where society is taking a turn to a new direction. That is where really powerful marketing emerges. Ideally, the most powerful marketing leverages external events that reflect social change.

Marketing is theater. In theater, you think of the audience as having a role. They may laugh and applaud or they may get up and walk out. When you show a Pepsi Generation campaign, you're trying to reach their emotions and touch their hearts. In a Pepsi Challenge, we tried to lure them into our campaign, to pull them across the line between where a commercial ends and reality begins.

The Super Bowl is evidence of this. It has nothing to do with athletics, really. The athletes are mere actors on a stage. Most people don't really care who wins or loses the Super Bowl because it's not their hometown team, anyway. What they care about is the Super Bowl event and all the pageantry that goes with it. It is a stage production, marketing as theater at its best.

Marketing is an art form. When I go through the Museum of Modern Art, I see not only paintings but artists who were driven by powerful ideas and who went through the identical process to what we do in marketing as theater. The power of it was not trying to duplicate an image realistically, like a photograph, but trying to capture the feeling of a striking idea or moment and then presenting an image of that feeling in a powerful way. The canvas becomes a mini stage production alive in a different medium.

It took a lot of hard work to get the Pepsi Challenge campaign off the ground. It wasn't like the Pepsi Generation, which everyone loved. To run Generation ads was a popular decision. The same, however, could not be said for the Pepsi Challenge. Advertising gurus at Pepsi and B.B.D.O. warned that we would be trading away the youthful, heartwarming imagery we'd spent years developing in the Pepsi Generation for what might be short-term market-share gains. They correctly argued that each advertisement must be considered a contribution to brand image, with every step becoming a long-term investment in the total personality of a brand. Those concerns prompted us to conduct market research into the new campaign's impact on our image. We found, in fact, that the Challenge didn't harm it at all.

Still, the debate raged loudest in markets where Pepsi already was ahead of Coca-Cola. Why, some asked, do you want to challenge Coke when you're already the leader? Couldn't it possibly jeopardize Pepsi's position, backfire like many comparative advertising campaigns by giving a weaker competitor free publicity? We decided to find out for ourselves in one of our company-owned territories.

The first big success occurred in Los Angeles. Students at the University of Southern California, a Coke stronghold, were coaxed into holding an on-campus shootout. If Pepsi won, college officials agreed in advance that we would get their vending contract. We set up our booths, proved once again that Pepsi was better tasting than Coke, and the college threw Coca-Cola off campus. Our cameras were there to capture the event and the subsequent commercials generated tremendous publicity. The Challenge doubled our market share in Los Angeles within a year and a half. The L.A. campaign was devised and led by Jack Pingel, who would later go on to lead our national rollout of Pepsi Challenge.

The decision stirred a major controversy within our bottler ranks. Many thought we were becoming too obsessed with competition; they feared a direct attack on Coke would spark price wars in their markets. Was PepsiCo willing to underwrite their losses if Coca-Cola retaliated? Were we sure that Pepsi would win when bottlers used beet sugar instead of cane sugar? Coke was allowing their bottlers to use a blend of sugars that cut their costs by using less expensive corn-based sugar. If we weren't going to permit Pepsi bottlers to do the same because of its potential effect on the Challenge results, were we willing to lower the price of our concentrate so Pepsi bottlers wouldn't be at a cost disadvantage? Were we sure that Pepsi could beat Coke in plastic bottles or cans?

Our major chain bottlers, who represented much of our volume in major cities, often tried to hold out for special concessions. They were hard negotiators, each demanding favors from Pepsi-Cola in return for their commitment to the Challenge. Even after a bottler agreed to go into the Challenge, it was not unusual for him to call back a few days later saying he suffered many sleepless nights from nightmares that he had lost the Challenge in his franchise.

Our task was made even more difficult because we usually needed four or five neighboring bottlers, who made up a single television-signal area, to all agree they would mount a Challenge. In order to stave off a war with the bottlers' association, I had to agree that we would not force any bottler to go into the Pepsi Challenge against his will. A single holdout in any given market, therefore, could lock us out of the area.

Frantic telephone calls from bottlers would come into Pepsi-Cola day and night. Bottlers pleaded with us to "stop this madness." No one doubted that the Challenge was effective. Our research showed that it worked in all markets, whether Pepsi led or trailed Coca-Cola in market share. But bottlers didn't make money on market share. If price wars resulted, a bottler's unit sales could easily go up while his profits plunged.

Neither was the Challenge a simple campaign. It had to be planned and executed as if it were a warlike attack. At Pepsi we would boast a thirty-five-member team to mobilize local bottlers' personnel so that eventually hundreds of people would be intricately involved in any single Challenge. The team would attend to every detail—from recruiting attractive young women to locally administer the test to arranging local Pepsi-sponsored sports events under the Challenge flag. We customized high school basketball games, 10K foot races, soccer matches into Challenge events. Even our delivery trucks were repainted into Challenge trucks.

Pepsi bottlers would set up Challenge booths at shopping malls, county fairs, schools, and supermarkets to invite local consumers to taste tests. We would film the contests, turning them into commercials for each local market. Eventually, we made a pool of nearly 300 commercials so we could boast that "Houston Chooses Pepsi" or "San Diego Chooses Pepsi." The tag line of each commercial would be that "More Coke Drinkers Like Pepsi Than Coke." Not only would people view them on television, but when they went shopping they would be invited to try it themselves. We'd also invite the local television stations to cover the Challenge. Combining public relations, advertising, and merchandising efforts gave us far broader impact for our dollar.

We treated each Challenge as a major event, a battle to be fought in our long-term war against Coke. Weeks before a Challenge would debut, we would begin quality tests on the product. If it failed to measure up, we would improve its taste so that a subgoal of the contest was to upgrade the overall quality of our product. The evening before a Challenge was to debut, I would often fly into an area on the corporate jet to give a rousing speech at a kick-off meeting held for bottlers and their families. One time, Coca-Cola ringed a Pepsi building with Coke trucks in which a kick-off session was being held. Coke wanted to intimidate the local Pepsi bottler. Instead, it attracted more attention from the local media, allowing us to garner even more publicity.

The taste difference, of course, was subtle. Indeed, I made the mistake of publicly taking the Pepsi Challenge once at the Daytona 500 car race in Florida. We had timed a massive campaign in the state to coincide with our sponsorship of the race, which we had transformed into a Challenge event as well. I took the Challenge and chose Coke! Fortunately, the media weren't there to witness my embarrassing gaffe. Pepsi people were terrified that someone would find out that the company president preferred Coke over his own brand.

A few weeks later in Hawaii, a television reporter asked me to take the test. Thanks to my earlier experience, I explained that wouldn't be fair. "The whole point is to let people choose what they think is best, not the manufacturer," I said. "Why don't you take it and decide?" She did, as thousands of others did, and decided that Pepsi tasted better than Coke.

The campaign heightened the competitiveness between us. There was nothing subtle about it; it was an attack against a very strong competitor. And it was all the more effective against Coca-Cola because the line between the commercials and the public relations campaign disappeared. We were turning the commercials into real life, making them bigger than life. It was a monumental success, a national marketing phenomenon.

Coca-Cola began to take the Challenge seriously. For years, it was an unwritten rule that the word "Pepsi" was never to be uttered in front of strangers visiting Coca-Cola's headquarters in Atlanta. Now Coke was publicly attacking us by name, charging that the Challenge was unethical, that it would destroy the soft-drink industry by turning soda into a commodity. Coca-Cola became obsessed with the idea that someone else actually had a better-tasting product. They ran secret taste tests which found that Pepsi really did taste better—a revelation that eventually led to New Coke years later.

I was surprised at how violent a reaction the Challenge had provoked in a competitor. We were being attacked by Coke on every legal front possible. They tried to dissuade the networks and local stations from running it; they tried to discredit us with commercials that poked fun at it. They even developed taste test commercials that had chimpanzees sipping colas to see which one they preferred. They attempted to turn it into the absurd, running ads in which people tasted a glass of tennis balls. Coca-Cola resorted to staging counter-Challenge events, hiring football player Mean Joe Green to smash Pepsi vending machines with a sledgehammer to the cheers and screams of Coke drivers. But Coke never found anything that was ever able to stop the Pepsi Challenge.

When Coca-Cola's efforts to disparage the campaign failed, the company shifted its strategy to enlist outside support from our own bottlers. In an important speech, Donald Keough, then Coca-Cola U.S.A. president, maintained that comparative advertising had gotten out of hand. In the best interests of the industry, he said, Coca-Cola was going to unilaterally halt all comparative commercials. He hoped Pepsi would have the courage and decency to follow its example before these commercials eroded consumer confidence in the industry. It was a clever ploy that sent shock waves throughout our already jittery bottler network.

If Coke did its research, of course, it would have known that consumers overwhelmingly chose Coke over Pepsi when the brands were identified before the sip test. Coke had invested millions of dollars and many years to build a positive, quality image. That work was enough to make people choose Coke over Pepsi regardless of taste. It was the missing piece of research that could have unraveled our campaign. Indeed, a close look at the Nielsens showed that virtually all of our gains were coming not at the expense of Coke but of other weak and fragmented brands. Coke users were satisfied with the taste of the product. Nonetheless, the Challenge helped to flatten Coke sales, allowing Pepsi virtually all the gains.

Failing to erode the Challenge's effectiveness, Coca-Cola hit on another strategy. It became far more aggressive in the early 1980s under new Coca-Cola U.S.A. management. Ironically, the new man selected to head Coke's U.S. operations was not unlike myself. Brian Dyson, an Anglo-Argentine intellectual, was a driven, intense executive and an insightful strategic thinker. He began launching local assaults against Pepsi bottlers who dared to adopt the Challenge in their markets.

Dyson saw a strategic opportunity to leverage Coke's near-monopoly position in fountain syrup. Coke claimed more than 75 percent of this market; Pepsi had little more than 10 percent. By raising prices in this captive market, Dyson generated a war chest of funds that could be dumped into the Nielsen markets to escalate the price wars. The message to every Pepsi bottler was clear: If you're in the Challenge program, we're going to go out and kill you. Coke would blitz a market, running major promotions, slashing prices, in effect, terrorizing the local Pepsi bottler. This strategy did make it affordable for Pepsi bottlers to go after the fountain market more aggressively because Coke's higher prices improved Pepsi's margins too, but it also scared enough of our bottlers so that the Pepsi Challenge never reached more than 75 percent of the country. Dyson successfully stopped the Pepsi Challenge rollout dead in its tracks.

Still, the Challenge had pushed us over the top, allowing us to unseat Coke as the number-one soft drink in supermarkets. The victory was a great morale booster because it came in the freedom-of-choice market where consumers could buy either Pepsi or Coke on the same shelf. That was a major difference from competition in vending machines and fast-food outlets where the consumer didn't have a choice. Becoming number one altered the stakes of the Cola Wars. It was strategically important as well because it increased the value of the Pepsi territories and provided incentive for the weaker bottlers to sell out to the stronger ones, helping to strengthen the bottling system. We also could leverage our victory to make inroads into the food service market. Now we could point to the Nielsens and the Challenge campaign and ask fast-food chains, "Why aren't you giving your consumers the cola taste they prefer in the freedom-of-choice market?"

After years of relentless work, of learning and managing through crises and changes, my business and personal life had finally come together. In 1982, at the age of forty-four, I felt as if I was on my way to achieving everything in business in which I was interested. Some people began to speculate that I would someday succeed Don Kendall as chief executive of the corporation. Headhunters, who viewed Pepsi as a fertile hunting ground, considered me "untouchable." Many of my young managers from the early 1970s had now moved into positions of power throughout the corporation. My friendship with Kendall, however distant because of our previous relationship, continued to grow. My life with Leezy seemed more settled and happier than ever.

What I didn't yet know was how restless I had become. The Challenge remained a vital competitive force; we had launched a new division to get Pepsi into the fast-food chains, and we introduced a new product in Pepsi Free, beating Coke to market with a caffeine-free cola by more than a year. Pepsi Free was a big new hit. Yet most of my time as president of Pepsi-Cola was spent lobbying for corporate resources from PepsiCo president Pearson and in negotiations with our bottlers.

One day, just before I was getting ready to leave the office for the upcoming Thanksgiving Day holiday in 1982, I received a telephone call from an acquaintance. It was a brief, hurried call that would eventually change every dimension of my life.

Why There Are
So Few Good Marketing People

It's a question I'm often asked. So often, in fact, that I'm convinced it's true: there are few good people in marketing. Part of it is
opportunity. I credit luck for a lot of the success I've had, being in
the right place at the right time. At the same time, the business
schools tend to turn out thousands of financial people but very few
marketers. Half of the MBAs from Harvard, Stanford, and Wharton
head for financial positions, perhaps because the opportunities to
learn marketing are few. Most large companies traditionally do their
training in house.

The other reason there are so few good marketers is that the
discipline has been falsely chasing the god of science, when it is
really an art. Market analysis, to take one false god, has failed to
predict all of the interesting and high-impact technological innovations of the twentieth century because it tends to look at trends.
But there is no trend that led from the railroad to the airplane.
There is no trend that led from the horse and buggy to the car; no
trend that led from the desk calculator to the pocket calculator;
no trend that led from the ditto machine to the Xerox machine; no
trend that led from the mainframe computer to the personal computer.

As the great mathematician Leonhard Euler said, "Science is
what you do after you guess well." The same is true of marketing.

Marketing is therefore less a single-minded discipline or set of
skills than it is an attitude, a way of thinking. A good marketer has
to be conceptually intuitive, to look for different points of view to

53

solve old problems. One has to step out of rational habit and linear thinking to see the world differently.

One also has to be incredibly resourceful in searching for different perspectives. It is crucial to develop an extremely wide band width to explore possibilities for quality, functionality, and service in every area of the company—customization, design, manufacturing, and so on. This is as essential in a service company as it is in a manufacturing company.

To develop this band width, an astute marketer must have the ability to zoom in and zoom out. To zoom in on something down to its finest details where true beauty is often hidden. Yet, one must also be able to zoom out to look for fairly fundamental shifts in buying styles. These are never obvious when you're looking at an industry on a quarter-to-quarter or even a year-to-year basis.

But this is not enough: the marketer also has to have courage to make changes. Many marketing people tend to play it safe and cede decisions to others. People who have the courage to take the risks are the people you'll tend to lose against.

Some of the best marketing comes from people who lack a marketing background but are simply good thinkers. I listen to the ideas of people who have great insight into products and services. Rarely do I have a conversation with Apple Fellow Alan Kay when I don't come away intellectually challenged. He usually sparks questions in something I thought I already understood, causing me to rethink what I thought I already had figured out. You should be able to quickly reorient your perspective from one vantage point to another as you think through the possibilities of how your service or product will be viewed by the customer.

Recently, marketing has become much more difficult. In years past, a Procter & Gamble would have had the persistence to stay with a product for eight to ten years to get it right. It had a different timeline, oriented to systematic advertising, research, and promotion. Today, the timelines are shorter; they don't provide for the long periods of market research so typical in the past. Few people seek marginal changes. They are searching for dramatic upheavals in product categories in months instead of years. The discipline puts a premium today on greater intuitive powers—something that really only comes from knowledge and wisdom in a given industry.

Yet, today marketing is assuming even greater importance for the most successful companies because it is playing an increasing role in adding value to what you sell and in getting that value recognized by the customer. If the best companies are to save their products from becoming undistinguished, undifferentiated commodities, they must sell on some perception of quality, functionality, or service.

Today, we are moving from a mass-production orientation to mass customization, as Alvin Toffler points out. As we gain the ability to customize products for people, localities, and regions, markets are splitting. There are many varieties of autos—you can order one built to your own specs in terms of add-ons. There is no one car market anymore. Consumers are not middle class or upper class; they're hybrids.

These days someone might buy a cheap digital watch, yet drive a BMW. Or drive to a fast-food restaurant in a Mercedes. To reach these hybrid consumers, we try to attract a "share of mind" rather than traditional "share of market." To do that, we have to position not just the product, which has an ever-shrinking shelf life, but the company—who we are, and why we are important to consumers beyond the life of the product, today and tomorrow. That's what we were able to do at Pepsi with the Pepsi Generation, and that's what we try to do at Apple.

I look for the same ability in marketers that I would in a chief executive. (In fact, the best way to train a marketer is to have him be CEO for a few years, then promote him into a marketing position. If only this were possible.) It takes years to gain the broad perspective to be a CEO, yet we generally ask a marketing person to have as much wisdom. Then as soon as someone demonstrates any ability at marketing, he or she is promoted, moved up and out, and effectively lost.

3

A Telephone Call

The calls came frequently enough. As president of Pepsi-Cola, I got a lot of them from headhunters of all kinds. I had won an enviable and visible place for myself in the corporate world. I was on the cover of *Business Week* magazine in May 1973, at the age of thirty-four. I was frequently quoted in the business columns of newspapers and magazines. And I was having fun running what then was Pepsi-Co's largest single business. Oftentimes, I wouldn't even return the calls. I had absolutely no interest in leaving Pepsi.

Only one headhunter could attract my attention. He was Gerry Roche, chairman of Heidrick & Struggles, Inc., in New York. A charming, gregarious man, Roche is the ultimate CEO power broker, a headhunter extraordinaire. He has recruited more chief executives and presidents to major U.S. corporations, from CBS to RCA, than any other executive recruiter. Gerry had spent nearly two decades of his fifty years networking his way into the boardrooms of the country's top corporations.

When Gerry called, there was a big difference. I knew he dealt only with the top jobs, and that if he was spending his own time on something, it was important. You would not fail to return a call from Gerry Roche.

I had known him as a headhunter and friend for years. In early 1977, he tried to interest me in the presidency of Norton Simon, Inc., the cosmetics company. Roche later tried again with the chairmanship of NBC, and more recently earlier in 1982 as chief executive of Warner-Amex, the cable television venture of Warner Communications and American Express.

I had no interest in any of those jobs. Pepsi was my life. I threw so much intensity into my work that I seldom looked up to ask if this was what I really wanted out of a career. My allegiance to Kendall and his company ran deep; I made the company my extended family. The mere thought of entertaining another job would have provoked the angst of a personal separation or divorce.

Gerry, however, is an engaging personality, a corporate story-teller who can effortlessly entertain someone for hours, and we developed a good friendship over the years. Gerry occasionally would check to see how my career and life were progressing. So when he called me at Pepsi two days before the Thanksgiving Day recess in 1982, I assumed it was another friendly check-in call. After exchanging pleasantries, however, he quickly got down to business.

"John," he said, "you and I have known each other a long time. I know that you're untouchable and not interested in outside jobs. And you know I wouldn't call unless it was something that was very important. But there is something which I think you've got to let me tell you about and hear me out."

Roche told me he was searching for a chief executive for Apple Computer, Inc., in Silicon Valley. I didn't know very much about the company. I had purchased one of their computers, an Apple II Plus, for my office, and was experimenting with setting up an information network among bottlers so we could share sales and promotion information. I was hardly interested in the job, however, and told him so.

"I know you don't want to leave Pepsi, and I hate to ask a favor of you," he said. "But please trust me. Would you make a trip to California and at least meet these guys?"

"Gerry," I said, "let me think about it."

Shortly after our conversation, Gerry dispatched a package of information on Apple by messenger to my home. That evening, a manila envelope from Heidrick & Struggles lay atop my stack of mail. I didn't open it at first. I brought it into my library, where I often would go at night to build a fire, listen to classical music, and read. I shuffled it to the bottom of a pile of reading material—a new *Yankee* magazine, other correspondence, and memos from a day's work at Pepsi.

I didn't open it until after dinner. Inside was a copy of the company's latest annual report and a ten-month-old *Time* magazine.

On the cover was a boyish-looking Steve Jobs with an arrow-shaped laser beam splitting a red apple balanced atop his head. The story, on "America's Risk Takers," gushed at how the mustachioed Jobs had practically created the personal computer industry single-handedly. It told an amazing tale of a passionate folk hero whose enduring dream was to allow individuals the power that only large corporations and institutions were able to wield. He accomplished this by personalizing the computer, once a distant, nearly ominous abstraction in the form of large mainframes, and bringing it down to scale so it could rest on a person's desktop.

Six years earlier, Apple was a company located in the bedroom and garage of his parents' home in Los Altos, California. Now it was a Fortune 500 company. Yet Jobs hardly played the part of a Fortune executive. A slender figure with long sideburns, he wore frayed jeans and cowboy shirts to our pin-striped suits. He had the appearance of a college student.

A child of the Valley and its dreams, he became intrigued by technology as a student at Homestead High School in Los Altos. At night, he would attend lectures at Hewlett-Packard, the Valley's huge electronics company. To the amazement of his high school electronics teacher, Jobs boldly called William Hewlett one day to ask for parts and equipment for his projects.

A college dropout, Jobs landed a job designing video games at Atari in 1972. After work, he would visit the Homebrew Computer Club, a haven for electronic hobbyists and computer hackers. It was there that he met Steve Wozniak, a self-taught engineer at Hewlett-Packard. "Woz," as he was known, and Jobs became friends and pranksters. They built and sold blue boxes that allowed users to illegally make long-distance telephone calls for free.

Wozniak was the computer wizard. He was working hard to construct a small, easy-to-use computer that he would bring to the group's meetings to show fellow computer buffs. He had little interest in its commercial appeal. Jobs, however, immediately saw its potential and convinced Wozniak, who later quit his job at Hewlett-Packard, to make the hobby a business. Jobs sold his Volkswagen van, while Wozniak parted with his Hewlett-Packard scientific calculator. The pair raised $1,300 and opened a makeshift production line in a garage, producing the computers in kit form for electronic hobbyists.

It was A. C. "Mike" Markkula, a former marketing manager for Intel, who would provide the needed business expertise behind the unique partnership. Steve discovered him through a venture capitalist recommended by Atari founder Nolan Bushnell. Markkula had retired only a year earlier at the age of thirty-three after stints with Fairchild and Intel, two of the most successful computer chip makers in the country. A dedicated family man, he envisioned a leisurely life on his Intel stock options which brought him multimillionaire status.

That was until Jobs persuaded him to visit his garage. Fascinated by what he saw there, Markkula began to help the two formulate a business plan, arrange a Bank of America credit line, and talk a couple of venture-capital firms to invest in Apple. Within a few months, Markkula put in $91,000 of his own money, and joined the company as its de facto chief executive.

The formal company's first product, shipped in 1977, was a redesigned prototype in a light, attractive plastic case, dubbed the Apple II. The company went public in December 1980. The annual report, only Apple's second as a public company, charted its extraordinary performance since then. Apple already boasted the largest installed base of any computer company in the world. Net income: up 56 percent to $61.3 million in the year ended September 24, 1982. Sales: up 74 percent to $583.1 million.

Beyond the numbers, the document impressed me with its elegant simplicity. Its cover featured a twenty-year-old quotation from President John F. Kennedy, "Man is still the most extraordinary computer of all." Inside, the report explained that Apple's technologies and products are created by those most extraordinary computers: its employees. Some of them were captured in stark black-and-white pictures that suggested they were far from typical employees. Rather, they were intense individuals on a dramatic mission.

Jobs and Markkula were pictured together, striding down a corridor at a quick pace, their shadows on the floor behind them. A gesturing Jobs in a white shirt and tie seemed to be lecturing, while an attentive Markkula, in a tweed sports jacket and baggy trousers, walked along at his side, hands in his pockets. The caption, written in script beneath the photograph, aptly described the mission: "Bringing technology to individuals through personal computers is, we believe, the extraordinary business of this decade."

It piqued my interest, if only because I didn't know much about

Silicon Valley or computers. Yet, as a youngster, I had loved to tinker with electronics. Gerry called the next day, but I put off a decision to meet then. Over the Thanksgiving Day holiday, Gerry and I arranged to get together in New York.

We met for lunch at the Sky Club in New York's Pan Am Building, one of Gerry's favorite haunts. It wasn't an out-of-the-way restaurant, but I didn't think of myself as a potential candidate sneaking out of the office for a preliminary job interview, either.

Gerry wasted no time, quickly sketching out the details of his assignment. Apple Computer's board of directors had engaged him to find a successor to Markkula, who had become chief executive on an interim basis after the previous president left unexpectedly. But he had promised his family he would step down as soon as he got the company on track and found a successor. The board, Gerry said, believed that Steven Jobs, now Apple's twenty-seven-year-old chairman and co-founder, was too inexperienced to take over.

"How does Jobs feel about that?" I asked.

"He agrees. He wants to find someone who is really great who he can learn from. The new chief executive reports directly to the board. Steve is focused largely on product development.

"I've met these guys and have spent a lot of time with them," Gerry went on. "I think I really understand what Apple is like and what they're looking for. They're looking for someone who is smart, good at marketing, flexible to work in a very different culture, and has international experience. If he doesn't understand electronics, they want him to at least not be intimidated by computers and electronics.

"They've been searching for someone for quite a while," he said, "for many months, and they've looked at an awful lot of people. But let me tell you, you're the only guy I know who fits all of those criteria. I don't have anyone else.

"Even if you have no interest in the job," Gerry urged, "you ought to at least meet them. You're going to meet a couple of extraordinary entrepreneurs who have done something that nobody has ever been able to do—build a Fortune 500 company in less than five years. If nothing else, you'll really enjoy meeting them."

As a youngster, I had been hopelessly captivated by technology and inventions. It was an interest I somehow discarded through most of my years at Pepsi. I always welcomed the opportunity to meet exceptionally bright and successful people, and I had been planning a trip to the West Coast to visit with Meg and Jack, my children from my first marriage, who were living with their mother in Los Angeles. So I told Gerry I would visit Apple, but only on the understanding that I would pay my own expenses. I didn't want any obligation. I wasn't looking for a job, and I didn't want them to get the wrong impression.

"I totally understand," said Gerry. "It's just a friendly thing between you and me."

I flew out to Los Angeles on Saturday, December 18, and quickly convinced Meg, nineteen, and Jack, seventeen, to visit a computer store with me. We found one that was about to open on Santa Monica Boulevard. Although not officially open, the store was selling pocket calculators and had the Apple II on display. We hung around for an hour as an endless stream of young people came in and out of the shop. It was clear that no one had given much thought to how to merchandise a computer. Computer packaging was fairly mundane. The advertising was too technical. There were no elaborate in-store displays. Yet I was surprised at how enthusiastic the store's visitors were about the products. I bought a few computer magazines, and we left.

Driving back in the car, my kids asked me why I was so interested in computers. I told them I was going to meet Steve Jobs at Apple.

"Steve Jobs?" asked Meg excitedly. "You're going to meet Steve Jobs!"

I was astonished that Jobs could prompt such a reaction, particularly from my children. They had grown up in a Hollywood environment; they went to school with the sons and daughters of movie and television stars. Celebrities couldn't turn their heads. But the mere mention of Steve Jobs seemed something else.

When I arrived at San Francisco International Airport on Sunday night, I rented a small compact and drove into the city to stay at the Fairmont Hotel. I got up early the next morning to jog. I sprinted down Nob Hill, through Taylor Street to Fisherman's Wharf, and then back up the hill, about a mile-long run at a steep 40-degree incline. As I climbed the hill, I told myself: "If I can't make it all the way up without having to stop for a breath, then I shouldn't be out here." I made it.

With a map and a Hertz car, I navigated my way south on Route 280 to Silicon Valley in a downpour so heavy it caused mudslides in the landscape. The strong winds pushed my rented Datsun around the freeway. It was a thirty-mile drive through fog and rain to Apple Computer in Cupertino.

The city, I discovered, was one of a handful of the sprawling suburbs of Santa Clara County that had become known as Silicon Valley. A generation earlier, the Valley was little more than a prune patch, supplying half of the world's dried prunes. Now, it was a center of technological innovation. The transformation spawned hundreds of new companies.

Viewed from above, the area looks not unlike a massive integrated circuit, with row upon row of prefabricated buildings occupied by little start-up companies. I had expected the buildings to look hi-tech. Instead, they were monotonous, flat, rectangular structures with tilt-up walls. It somehow seemed inappropriate for what had emerged as the technological center of the world.

As I came off the freeway exit onto De Anza Boulevard in Cupertino, the first building I saw with an Apple logo in front was the three-story glass-and-concrete Mariani Building. I thought this must be Apple's headquarters building because it was the only large building around. It wasn't.

Instead, the company was headquartered in a much smaller, more modest building on Bandley Drive, which cut through the middle of Apple's hodgepodge campus. At one end of Bandley was the Any Mountain Ski Shop, at the other end a supermarket. In between were a spate of flat, one-story huts from the Taco Bell school of architecture. At each entrance was a redwood sign carved with the company's rainbow-striped Apple emblem.

I was taken aback when I found that Jobs and Markkula were ensconced in a two-story wood-frame building with a shingled roof. It seemed more appropriate as a branch office for an insurance company than the executive office of a fast-rising corporation. Outside the building hung a small employment sign. As I parked the car, I noticed a surprising number of Mercedeses and Porsches in the adjacent parking lot. One sported a license plate with the letters THX APPL.

The brown building was referred to as "Bandley Six," meaning it was the sixth building Apple occupied on Bandley Drive. After entering the building, I was asked to go outside again to climb an exterior stairwell to reach the second floor. Inside, there were no closed offices, only open cubicles, tightly packed together. The scene resembled a labyrinth. The corridors—no more than 3.5 feet wide —would have violated most fire codes. Each cubicle had a personal computer sitting on every desk. In the background, there was a constant grinding noise, the sound of dot matrix printers producing computer-generated documents.

Mike Markkula greeted me in shirtsleeves and a pair of casual trousers. I was the only one on the floor in a suit. I felt awkward and surprised that most people at Apple were less formally dressed than PepsiCo's maintenance staff. Mike had a small corner cubicle for an office, with a round table in its center. It was neat and orderly. Behind him were three Apple computers, one of which flashed stock quotes on a video screen.

Mike is a wiry man of small stature, the definitive laid-back Californian. A modest, informal person, he began to unfold the story of Apple, what it was like during the early days and what it had become. I spent most of the morning with him, rummaging through the experiences of my ascent at Pepsi. A chain smoker, Mike filled the room with smoke, finishing off nearly two packs by the time we broke to meet Steve for lunch.

Steve's office, in the other corner on the floor, was nothing like Mike's. It seemed the epicenter of activity. A line of people stood outside, waiting to get in. The telephones rang constantly. Curiously, Steve had no computers in his office; instead, electronic parts and cases of products were scattered about the room. It was cluttered and disorganized, with posters and pictures taped onto the walls. He had just returned from Japan with a new product that he had taken apart. Pieces of it were on his desk. Whenever Steve saw something new that he was curious about, I discovered, he would buy it, take it apart, and try to understand how it worked.

He was sitting in a small 9- by 9-foot conference room next to his office, gesturing and pointing in a meeting with four other people, all in their early twenties. Steve wore blue jeans and an open checked shirt, his sleeves folded back. We waited a few minutes outside his office while he finished up his meeting.

"Hi," he said, when he emerged, "I'm Steve Jobs. It's really great you came out here. I'm really happy to meet you."

We walked to Anthony's Pier One restaurant, a few blocks away on the edge of the Apple campus.

"Look," I told them, "I want you to know I'm not really here for a job interview."

"We understand," said Mike. "We're excited about the chance to meet you and understand your marketing ideas."

Steve ordered a vegetarian dish, a salad of some kind. Over my filet of sole, I began to run through many of the same things I had just covered with Mike. Steve barely said a handful of words during the first half hour. He sat and listened, his sharp, brown eyes intently fixed on me in a commanding stare.

It wasn't until I began speaking about how I hoped to use the Apple II Plus Computer to communicate with Pepsi bottlers that he perked up. "We're going to make it even better," he said. "We've got some incredible ideas that will revolutionize the way people use computers. Apple is going to be the most important computer company in the world, far more important than IBM."

It was characteristic of Steve to speak in both vivid and sweeping language. "What we want to do," he explained, "is to change the way people use computers in the world." Steve launched into an explanation about how personal computers were going to change the workplace forever, maintaining that Apple had secured the lead role in this transformation because it understood the future better than any other company. It was started by people who loved the products they were building. "I can't talk about it," he said, "but we're going to be doing something that is really going to blow everybody's mind with a neat new product."

The new computer, called the Lisa, would be introduced by Apple at its shareholders' meeting in one month. Unlike the Apple II, the Volkswagen of computers, it was expressly made for the Fortune 1000 market. The advent of a software program called VisiCalc brought the electronic spreadsheet to Apple II and allowed its use by business. But IBM had been making considerable inroads in the corporate market since the 1981 introduction of its personal computer, known simply as the IBM PC.

"I don't know much about computers," I confessed, "but I can tell you the kind of things that I think business people want to be able to do with them."

We talked about how computers had to become more functional, and I explained some of the things I could and couldn't do with the Apple II Plus. At Pepsi, I found the Apple to be more work to use than it was worth. We tried monitoring our mail and phone calls and discovered it wasn't worth the time. We tried typing letters on it, but couldn't get a letter-quality printer then. We also began to talk about marketing, which Steve said he knew little about.

"I'd be really interested to come back and visit you sometime and learn more about marketing," he said. "I really like New York and, in fact, I'm even thinking of getting an apartment there. Maybe we can get together sometime in New York."

"That would be great," I responded.

At the end of the luncheon, we walked back, I got in my car and headed for the airport that afternoon. It was a brief meeting, but it left an instant impression. I thought Apple was different from anything I had ever seen before. On the flight, I took out a piece of hotel stationery I had saved and began to write a letter, outlining my concepts of what a personal computer should be able to do.

I informed Mike I was canceling my plans to replace my Apple II Plus with an IBM PC, at least until Apple announced its newest computer on January 19. All this was a unique and foreign vocabulary for me. Yet I knew I could somehow make a contribution. So I jotted down a collection of thoughts and reflections about some of the things we had discussed. The result was an eight-page letter, filled with underlined phrases and words, diagrams, cubes, and boxes of conceptual models and decision-making tools. From my own experience at Pepsi, I had found that the hierarchy of an organization would work against the microcomputer's entry into corporate America. Steve told me Apple was about to introduce a personal computer expressly for the corporate world.

Corporate management information systems (MIS) managers then had little understanding of or experience with personal computers. When I asked Pepsi's MIS department for their evaluation of the Apple II Plus and IBM PC, they told me about the computers' hardware and software features, but could not articulate what I could do with a powerful personal computer.

"To reach upper management," I wrote, "you need to promise *decision power,* not features. Upper management needs to see the opportunity for micros to *coexist* with mainframes and minis. As big a breakthrough as VisiCalc is, upper management doesn't do much spreadsheet analysis . . . and is already pressed for time. So using a personal computer will be looked at as *adding* more work on a crowded schedule; the time/cost vs. benefit must be rewarding."

To get the personal computer into the executive suite, I felt it had to be useful in strategic planning, a primary task of upper management. Ideally, it should link a company's large database with the conceptual models top management employed in strategic planning. The personal computer, I thought, should produce documents that combined text and visual models.

"Spreadsheets, pie charts, and bar charts don't have much sex appeal for this group," I advised. "Build structural visual models that can be animated on screen . . . make it possible to rotate a cube, slice it, explode and rotate out a building block and reformat data into other matrix designs. If you could do this and give upper management a way to manipulate data and options within the models, I think you could really have something great!"

Given my paucity of knowledge about computers, I had no idea if any of this was possible. What I did know was how to market to consumers. So I told Mike and Steve not to stop with hardware and software innovation, but to also work hard to merchandise the company's technology.

Invest in in-store merchandising that *romances* the consumer with Apple's potential to *enrich their life!* Here's where I think both IBM's PC and Tandy's TRS-80 are vulnerable. It will be hard for IBM to ever forget they are in the data processing business offering a range of systems/services, or for Tandy to separate itself from the "do-it-yourselfers" who are looking for the latest affordable gadgets.

You have a unique opportunity to differentiate Apple from the others, so don't miss it. Use bold animated color graphics and VCR instruction modules which will give consumers an exciting experience when they try an Apple at your display. Make your merchandising as "turnkey" as possible, letting the computer and its associated technology *do its own selling.* This is an expensive and important project *deserving of as much creativity as any of your major new products.*

It was the same approach I had taken during my years at Pepsi, treating packaging and merchandising concepts as if they were new brands. "I really enjoyed meeting you both and want to thank you for an exciting day," I concluded. "What you have already done is impressive, but your vision for Apple's future is even bolder and really captures my imagination." I was careful, though, not to suggest I felt like a candidate. If I saw Steve again in New York, it wouldn't be as a candidate for a job but as a casual acquaintance. I had no interest in giving up my career at Pepsi, but I was taken with this young, impetuous genius and thought it would be fun to get to know him a little better.

Leezy and I had just driven up to our home in Camden, Maine, for the Christmas holiday. I had been there only a few minutes when I received a call from Gerry Roche. It was one of what soon would be many such calls.

"How did you like the trip to Apple?" he asked.

"It was really interesting," I said. "I enjoyed meeting those guys. It was totally different than what I expected. I really didn't get to see an awful lot, but I particularly enjoyed meeting Markkula and Jobs."

"Well," Gerry said, "they enjoyed meeting you. These guys are very excited about their meeting with you. John, I know you're not interested in this, but you really owe it to yourself to meet with them again."

"Gerry," I explained, "the understanding was that I would just go out and look at it, and I told you I'm not looking for a job. I don't think I want to get more involved with this. This is only going to cause me more problems later on, so I would just as soon end it now."

Gerry, whose persistence has been known to wear down the resistance of many executives, refused to take no for an answer. He asked me, instead, to think about it for another day. Within twenty-four hours, the phone again rang with Gerry on the other end. He apparently spoke with Steve during the interim.

"Steve Jobs told me that he's coming to town after Christmas," Gerry said, "and he would love to get together with you for just a few minutes. So you don't have to go anywhere. All you have to do is meet him, and he'll meet you anywhere you want."

"Well, that's okay. I guess if I don't have to go to California, I'll go and meet him. I did say I'd get together with him sometime when he came to New York."

We scheduled an after-work meeting for January 12. The plan was for me to meet Steve at the Carlyle Hotel in New York. It was a cold night, with snow on the ground. When I introduced myself to the concierge at the Carlyle, he told me I was expected. I took the elevator to the twenty-first floor and walked down the hall to Steve's room. The door was ajar and I could hear excited voices inside.

My knock brought a young woman to the door, part of Steve's Apple entourage. When the door opened, I could see a group of young people, all in their twenties, surrounding a computer with a lit display. Steve emerged from them in a loosened tie and rolled-up shirtsleeves. The group was at the end of a long and tiring day.

"We've had sneaks all day," Steve said.

"What are sneaks?" I asked, mystified.

Steve explained that a sneak is a preview of a new product on a confidential basis to a member of the press. Apple was showing off its newest product, the Lisa, to selected writers from *Time, Business Week, Fortune,* and other major magazines and newspapers. The Lisa was the product Steve wouldn't mention to me over lunch a few weeks earlier. It was Apple's first attempt to crack the all-important business market. At $10,000 a machine, Lisa was Apple's most expensive computer yet. But it also was a highly advanced and surprisingly easy-to-use machine.

"Boy, it has gone fantastic," said Steve. "Everyone loves the new product. It is really incredible. I want to show this to you."

He introduced me to his associates as the president of Pepsi-Cola. He told them he was giving me a "sneak" because Pepsi might be interested in being one of the first major corporations to get behind the Lisa.

John Couch, a medium-built man with a small mustache and slightly drooping eyes, demonstrated the computer. The Lisa division's general manager, Couch explained how a small hand-held device, called a mouse, controlled a pointer on the computer screen. When you rolled the mouse over a desktop, the pointer moved across the screen, allowing you to point to graphic symbols or instructions. Just a click of a button on the mouse controlled the computer's functions. The mouse vastly simplified the computer's operation, allowing people to learn how to use the Lisa in only one sixtieth the time it took to grasp other personal computers.

"Why don't you try it?" Couch said.

I sat down, created a few parallelograms on a program called LisaDraw, and made a cube of it. Then he showed me how to merge the graphic with text on the same screen. An Imagewriter printer spat out my creation within seconds.

Every time Couch explained something, Steve would interrupt. Couch spoke about what the computer did, while Steve always talked about how it would revolutionize life and work. Steve's comments were as irrepressible and impetuous as Couch's explanations seemed temperate.

"We're going to blow IBM away," Steve boasted. "There's nothing they can do when this computer comes out. This is so revolutionary, it's incredible."

I sensed a rivalry between the pair. Couch, a former Hewlett-Packard engineer and another of Apple's multimillionaires, had been given the job of running the Lisa division in 1980 when Steve wanted it himself. Markkula and then-president Michael Scott, however, thought Steve lacked the experience to hold an important operating position. A disappointed Steve Jobs went off to take charge of a much smaller technical project that was developing a computer under the code name Macintosh. Steve bet Couch $5,000 that his group would ship Macintosh before Lisa. Steve, of course, lost the bet and had to pay up later that spring.

At the same time, there was another fellow in the background named Paul Dali, one of the co-general managers of Apple's personal computer systems division which produced the Apple II products. Dali kept trying to explain how his group was introducing the Apple IIe, an enhanced version of the Apple II Plus in my office. But everyone seemed far more interested in the Lisa product.

Steve suggested that the four of us go to the Four Seasons restaurant for dinner. The maitre d' sat us at a corner table, arranged for a vegetarian meal for Steve, and took our orders. I talked about the origins of the Pepsi Generation campaign and its impact on marketing, how we articulated to a new generation of young people a new lifestyle, and how Pepsi became part of that. I explained how it became a phenomenon, almost a cultural dimension of American society, a campaign that was able to survive longer hairstyles, protests in the streets, riots on college campuses, all of the country's turbulent changes of the sixties and early seventies.

The campaign succeeded because it focused on the world's

more positive side, providing a message people yearned to hear at a time of great uncertainty. It gave a comforting glimpse of life at its best moments. And because the commercials used real people instead of actors, people could identify with them.

It was an important marketing lesson. News reporters like to report bad news in the belief that conflict and tension attract greater readership and viewership. Inherently, however, that's not what people always want to hear. They want optimistic, positive messages. When President Jimmy Carter began talking about the malaise in the country, people tuned him out. When Democratic Party nominee Walter Mondale campaigned against President Reagan, he too spoke about problems, not opportunities. It was no accident that the same advertising pros who put together the Pepsi Generation worked on the strategy that helped President Ronald Reagan gain reelection.

But how could high technology best be sold to the public? To persuade parents to buy computers for their children, one company showed a family with a child who lacked a computer. The message was that without one, the child could get left out. It was a negative message. Why not focus on the child who has the computer and enjoys using one? Our research always had shown that the positive message has greater impact in virtually every case.

"When we created the Pepsi Generation, we were selling to teenagers," I said. "The campaign continued to appeal to the same people as they hit their twenties. Now, the Pepsi Generation is old enough to buy computers and buy them for their kids in school. I think Apple's got a chance to create an Apple generation."

They were clearly taken with the notion. I said you needed to get a critical mass of attention behind it before people would become aware of it. I explained how the Pepsi Challenge brought together public relations, advertising, and marketing to create media events that brought us massive publicity. They related that back to their "sneak" program, laying the groundwork for a successful launch of a new product. By giving reporters and Wall Street analysts an advance peek of the Lisa, journalists could write about it more intelligently and interview knowledgeable third-party analysts when it was launched. This increased the potential for more favorable publicity.

As we continued to talk about marketing concepts, we discovered it was now eleven forty-five and we were the last people in the restaurant. The waiters were hovering, wanting to close up. So we walked back to the hotel. "This has been one of the most exciting evenings in my whole life," Steve said. "I just can't tell you how much fun I've had tonight."

As I drove home, I thought I hadn't had as much fun since I was in International Foods. It rekindled my dinner meetings at Las Caricolas in Barcelona with my small team of people, when we spoke about building a new worldwide business for PepsiCo in snack foods. It stimulated me, roused my long-held desire to be an architect of ideas. In some queer way, I felt more kinship with these young renegades from Apple than I did with many of the people I had been working with at Pepsi-Cola for years.

Beyond the Pepsi Challenge campaign, an increasing amount of my time was being consumed by administrative issues back at PepsiCo's headquarters in Purchase, New York. I found myself spending far more time than I wanted to in negotiations with bottlers over concentrate prices and contractual issues. No less crucial, I was having a more difficult time convincing PepsiCo to commit more resources to our soft-drink business.

Under Pearson's prodding, however, the company had become intent on developing a third business segment that would leverage our strengths in soft drinks and snack foods. Diversifying into fast-food restaurants, PepsiCo gobbled up Pizza Hut in 1977 and Taco Bell in 1978. But the corporation's newfound interest in this area prevented me from gaining more capital investment for soft drinks.

I was one of Kendall's most competitive soldiers, yet after sixteen years of being constantly tested, I was discovering that I didn't enjoy competing. I enjoyed building. At Pepsi, I was driven by creating new concepts in marketing that no one had ever thought of before. The Pepsi experiences I most enjoyed, in International Foods, were what Apple seemed to personify.

Still, I wasn't interested in leaving Pepsi. Once Pearson had our fast-food segment up and running, I knew I would have greater access to corporate funds. And although I disliked the direct competition in which I was placed, I was one of the few people deemed a serious contender to succeed Kendall.

When I returned home, it took me a long time to fall asleep. I had just spent an evening with people who were excited about all the ideas I spoke about. They were as turned on as I by the experience. I realized that I was having a lot of trouble trying to get people excited about building things at Pepsi. All of the things they wanted to build seemed confined to the restaurant business, which was where Pepsi's main interest lay at that time. I couldn't get them interested in buying bottling territories.

The next day, Gerry was on the phone again.

"John," he said, "I talked with Steve and he said he had the most wonderful night of his whole life. I don't know what you guys did last night, but let me tell you, Steve Jobs is ecstatic!"

I told Gerry I wasn't interested in the job, but that I too had had an enjoyable evening. It wasn't long after our conversation that a pattern began to emerge. Every three or four days I would get a call from either Steve, Mike, or Gerry. Sometimes, the calls wouldn't relate to anything. Typically, it would be Steve saying, "Hi! How are you doing?"

Initially, I didn't realize why they continued to call. I had never gone through this kind of thing before. It soon dawned on me that Gerry must have advised Mike that he and Steve would have to keep the contact up, under any possible excuse, if they had any hope to change my mind.

I was getting concerned that my initial curiosity had been misinterpreted. "Gerry," I said on the telephone, "this thing is going too far. I told you I wasn't interested in a job. And now, all of a sudden, I'm getting calls all the time.

"We've got to explain to these guys that I really like them and I'm excited about their company, but I don't have any interest in working for them. I just don't want to lead them on."

Mike called again to say he would be coming to New York on a business trip in early February. He wanted to arrange a meeting with me. I saw it as an opportunity to put an end to the process. He flew to New York in his own private jet and visited with me at PepsiCo. When he entered my office, he seemed surprised. At most traditional corporations, size equates to power. An executive's importance and authority often are measured by the size of his office. My suite, a 30-by 20-foot room, was comparable in size to the White House Oval Office. A Persian rug covered the hardwood floors, antiques and fine paintings decorated the space. Nine windows looked out over the sculpture gardens and a small private garden below it. I had a private bathroom, an entry foyer where my executive assistant, Nanette, and my secretary sat, and another private office where I kept my computers.

We sat down and chatted a little. I congratulated Mike on the phenomenal publicity the company was generating. Apple had just introduced its Lisa computer and recently held its annual shareholders' meeting. *Fortune* magazine featured Steve on its cover, while *Time* had named the personal computer the "Man of the Year," the first time it picked a machine in all its fifty-five years. It seemed that everywhere I turned, people were writing about Apple Computer. I couldn't pick up a newspaper without seeing yet another article on the company. Still, I was intent on trying to discourage him from thinking that I was the candidate for Apple.

"Mike," I said, "you really ought to go look for someone else. There is an outside chance that I would consider it, but I think you'd do much better to look for someone else. I'll even help you come up with some names. But I don't know about it. This doesn't make any sense to me. I've got a great job. I have a pretty good idea of what my future can be. Let me just be a friend and an adviser. I don't want to work for you guys."

A few days later, Steve called me. He said he had been thinking about getting an apartment in New York and wanted to know if I had some ideas for him. He'd like to stop by and visit me while in New York.

This time, Steve showed up at my home in Greenwich on a Sunday afternoon. He looked more like a kid than a chairman of a company when he stepped out of a stretch limo in blue jeans, a leather jacket, and a pair of gray running shoes with Velcro straps. I introduced him to Leezy and showed him around our home. It was a California-style house on four and one-half acres, secluded by evergreens and the Fairchild Gardens. We bought the house five years earlier, while it was still under construction, and I had personally redesigned it, installing custom floor-to-ceiling windows among other things. Steve seemed much interested in the custom-built 300-pound doors made of oak. Their massive weight required special brass hardware for support, yet they were so perfectly balanced on ball-bearing hinges that they would swing open or closed with the push of a finger. Steve was fascinated by that because he is, as I am, a perfectionist. The details interested him, just as they fascinated me. We realized we shared a love for products.

We settled into my library, a paneled room with a Palladian window and a black-slate hearth fireplace. Steve, always taking everything in, cruised my bookcases, noticing my eclectic collection of books—not only on business and management but Zen, philosophy, architecture, art, and astronomy. We sat down.

"Steve, why are you talking to me?" I asked. "Why don't you go talk to somebody at IBM or Hewlett-Packard? Why do you want somebody out of the soft-drink industry? I don't know anything about computers."

"What we're doing has never been done before," he said. "We're trying to build a totally different kind of company, and we need really great people.

"My dream is that every person in the world will have their own Apple computer. To do that, we've got to be a great marketing company. You really understand marketing. I got excited about the idea of an Apple generation after our dinner in New York. I really want us to get to know each other better because I just have a feeling that this could be very important for all of us."

Steve's visions went beyond the business of computers. He saw in Apple a model of what the modern corporation could be. At the time, he wanted to build the ultimate campus for Apple, a 1980s company town in California where bright people would congregate to build a new future. Steve envisioned a massive complex of automated factories, employee condominiums, recreational facilities, even a Disneyland-like monorail to transport people about the grounds. He wanted the buildings to make an architectural statement and thought of enlisting a great architect to help him do it.

Given his interest in developing a corporate campus for Apple, we decided to visit the PepsiCo grounds. We hopped into Leezy's 450 SL convertible and drove to Purchase. The Pepsi grounds are as lavish as Apple's makeshift campus is austere. A long, meandering driveway through manicured lawns, sculpture gardens, and fountains brings you to the Pepsi complex of buildings. When you come into the presence of Pepsi's headquarters, you feel as if you're at the most important company in the world. It's the elegance of the grounds and the power they convey.

The 144-acre site was the personification of Don Kendall, who envisioned a new corporate environment that would integrate three art forms—architecture, landscape, and modern sculpture. He attended to every detail, just as Steve had at Apple. If he spotted an unusual tree in another part of the country, Kendall would haul it back on the corporate plane and supervise its planting on the campus. One day, he noticed a Coca-Cola can in a bush on the courtyard. It became a cause célèbre as Kendall became intent on tracking down the miscreant who dared to toss such a thing in Pepsi land. Security guards were called to comb the gardens for any other trash.

Steve was wide-eyed as we walked up the main entrance. It leads to a formal central courtyard in the shape of a Greek cross where a David Wynne sculpture stands in a round pool. The piece, a soaring acrobatic woman with a dolphin, is one of nearly forty sculptures by some of the world's most recognized artists, each personally selected by Kendall, who also brought European stonecutters to Pepsi to cut by hand the Italian cobblestones in the courtyard.

Seven three-story buildings, all linked to one another at their corners, comprise the Pepsi complex designed by architect Edward Durrell Stone. They form a circle around the courtyard, open only on the north side, where Steve and I entered the building.

I showed him the corporate fitness center, the separate entrances and locker rooms for executives and employees. The locker rooms were identical with the exception of a whirlpool bath, a luxury reserved only for executives. "You mean," he said nearly astonished, "that the executives are in a separate area from the employees?"

"Yeah. I don't like it. As a matter of fact, I was against it and I go over and work out sometimes in the employees' area. It gets everybody mad because they think I'm just doing it to make an issue out of it."

"Boy," Steve said, "this is really great. That's weird having an executives' area. But it's a great facility."

I took him upstairs to the executive offices on 4/3. He looked at them in amazement, as if he were a child visiting his father's office for the first time. "Wow, people really work in these big fancy offices?

That's really different." I quickly learned that "different" to Steve meant he wasn't yet ready to openly criticize something but that it clearly wasn't his style.

In anticipation of his visit, I had prepared videotapes of television commercials from the Pepsi Generation and Pepsi Challenge campaigns. As we watched them on a small screen in my office, I explained how important it was for an underdog to convey a leadership image through quality advertising. If you're going to be number one, you have to think and act like number one. Our commercials had to be every bit as elegant, if not more so, I said, than our competitors'.

"That's just how we want it," Steve said. "That's really high-quality filming. That's what we want. We want to have the very best advertising, the highest quality possible."

After the tour, I suggested we drive to IBM's headquarters in Armonk, about five miles away, off Route 684. IBM's entry into the personal computer market was being hailed as a major success, and IBM had become Apple's primary competitor. While IBM was nearly always on his mind at this time, Steve had never seen the corporation's headquarters. He was eager to catch a glimpse of what his nemesis looked like. "You're going to be really surprised when you see this because it looks very different from what you just saw," I told him.

As I drove up to the single building, I announced, "Here it is." IBM's headquarters is a modest building of industrial gray concrete set into the side of a hill. The landscaping is minimal. The few apple trees that dot the grounds are sprayed with chemicals so that they blossom but don't bear fruit because IBM would rather not have fallen fruit spoiling the lawn. "Rotten apples are forbidden fruit at world headquarters," I had recently read about IBM. The antiseptic touch was echoed by the parking lots that circle the building. All this hardly enforces IBM's invincible image. Unlike PepsiCo's elegant grounds, there is no sense of arrival.

"This is it?" Steve asked. "This is their headquarters? I want to charter a 747 jet, and I'm going to fly the entire Macintosh division out to see this. I can't believe it."

All Steve could talk about for the remainder of the day was IBM's headquarters. In Silicon Valley, IBM was viewed as this huge, monolithic corporation in East Coast corporate America. Steve anticipated an imposing monument to that image. Instead, he found that IBM's headquarters looked like any other nondescript office building. Flying the Macintosh team to Armonk to witness the same, he thought, would boost their morale.

His visit ended about 4:30 p.m. when the chauffeur-driven limousine pulled up to the house to whisk him back to the Carlyle in New York.

"Steve," I said, "I think we're developing a good friendship, but please keep your search on and keep looking for someone else. I will think about Apple, but my sense is that this is a hugely important decision for you and Mike. You ought to look at as wide a range of people as you possibly can because I'm not convinced it even makes sense to bring someone in from the soft-drink industry to run your company."

"Okay," he said. "But I want you to keep thinking about it."

I went back into the house, anxious to ask Leezy her impression of Steve. She has always had good instincts about people, and she has never been shy about expressing them, a trait I much admire in her. But when I asked her this time, Leezy said she just didn't know.

"Well, do you like him?" I asked.

"No, I just don't know."

"Well, do you dislike him?"

"I don't know," she said again. "What did you think of Steve? Did you have a good time with him this afternoon?"

"I had a fabulous time with him," I replied. "I enjoy being with him because he's so smart and understands and appreciates the things I care about. My eyes are opening to things I didn't know were out there. It's really interesting."

"You're not really seriously considering this thing, are you?" she asked.

"No, of course not. But he's a neat guy."

By now, however, it was more than that. I couldn't yet admit it to myself or anyone else, but I was captivated and intrigued at the possibility of going to Silicon Valley to make a new life for myself, to share in Steve's dreams. My meetings and conversations with him had sparked a rediscovery of myself, a part of me I seemed to have lost at Pepsi.

My background was nothing like Steve's. Far from being a free child of Silicon Valley, I grew up in a formal, tradition-bound world on the Upper East Side of New York. My mother, a soft-spoken woman who left a trail of laughter wherever she went, usually wore gloves in the city. My father, a Wall Street lawyer, wouldn't be seen on a city street without a hat. As a young student at the Buckley School on East 74th Street, my uniform consisted of a little blue cap with an embroidered B on its top, a lapel-less jacket, white-collared shirt and tie, and shorts with knee socks. Coats and ties also were mandatory at St. Mark's, a strict Episcopal Church school in Southboro, Massachusetts, where I was dispatched to attend boarding school at the age of eleven.

It was as regimented a life as a teenager could possibly have: chapel twice a day, three times on Sunday. We awoke by bell, slept in iron beds with thin mattresses in large dormitories, and took our showers by schedule. It was a stark contrast to the freewheeling days I had known in my mother's native Bermuda as a young child.

My youth was restricting in another, very painful way: I suffered from a serious speech impediment up until my middle teens. As a child, I had such a severe stammer that I couldn't speak a single sentence without incredible difficulty. It drove me into a world of my own where I would fantasize about building my own car or conducting my own scientific experiments—inspired from early-morning sessions reading the Books of Knowledge. I'd express my thoughts on paper because I couldn't get them out of my mouth.

It was a painful and frustrating experience. There was so much I wanted to talk about, and yet I couldn't even walk into a candy store and ask for a pack of Lifesavers without stumbling over the words. Eventually I was able to overcome the problem with the help of a medical hypnotist. But, as usual, I became completely consumed by hypnosis—to the point that I not only learned auto-hypnosis but began to experiment on my fellow students at St. Mark's. I had planted in one of my friends the post-hypnotic suggestion to freeze at my command.

It was during an evening chapel service that I triggered the post-hypnotic suggestion, halting an entire procession of students into chapel. I had to step inside the chapel doors and give another command to get the student moving again—my stunt almost got me suspended from school.

When I returned home from boarding school, my father would march me over to Otto, the local barber. He insisted that my hair be cut so short that it was never more than a quarter of an inch long on the sides. My father would sit there patiently watching as Otto went to work with electric shears connected by a cord to a ceiling outlet.

A senior partner at Jackson, Nash, Brophy, Barringer & Brooks, my father was devoted to his three sons, Arthur, David, and myself. He was willing to sacrifice anything in his own life to ensure we had the opportunity to become successful. We were his pride and joy, and he badly wanted at least one of us to follow his footsteps into law. When I was a youngster, he would take me to lunch at the Broad Street Club, a gathering spot for Wall Street's lawyers and bankers. All I wanted to do was plot my getaway so I would have enough time to walk to Cortlandt Street where many of the surplus radio equipment stores made their home.

I loved tinkering with electrical things as a child. I hardly ever played with toys. When I was five, I remember getting a dry-cell battery, a buzzer, and hook-up wire for Christmas. I started blowing fuses in our apartment at that age, too. I'd wake up early in the morning, reading *The Radio Amateur's Handbook* and *Radio & TV News,* studying the schematics, until they were shopworn and dog-eared. By the time I was ten, my friends and I were taking radios apart to convert them into intercoms, and we were building remote controlled robots with used radio components, erector sets and other old, discarded parts.

I became a ham radio operator at the age of eleven. At fourteen, in 1954, my fascination with electronics led me to invent a color television cathode-ray tube using a single electron gun with three separate grids placed before the colored phosphor screen and appropriately charged to direct the emitting electrons to the right colors at the right time. My father helped me find a patent attorney, but a competing one from the inventor of the cyclotron particle accelerator, Dr. Lawrence of Lawrence-Livermore Laboratories, was applied for only a few weeks before mine. His patent, later acquired by Sony, eventually became the forerunner for the technology that led to Sony's fabulously successful "Trinitron" color television tube.

My father was a proud, precise, and competitive man—so competitive, in fact, that he often had cortisone injected into his arm muscle when he suffered from a "tennis elbow" so he could play in neighborhood tennis tournaments. But he was never interested in nor could he understand my fascination with technical things. I had no interest in law, no interest in golf or tennis or the social side of life—all things that mattered greatly to my father. He was far more satisfied in the fact that I had been president of my class, captain of the soccer team, and head monitor at boarding school. To him, these were tangible signs of achievement.

When I wanted to skip college and attend art school, he was greatly disappointed. "I sent you to one of the finest preparatory schools in the country," he lectured. "I sacrificed everything. You've had every advantage in life and you don't even want to go to college. You want to study design. I can't believe it."

We compromised. I would go to Brown University if I could attend the Rhode Island School of Design at night. When I decided to pursue advertising after graduating from Wharton, he thought it was the worst possible field I could enter.

None of us became lawyers, but he instilled in us high expectations for success of some kind, and we were blessed with common sense, creativity, and vision. My brother David also pursued marketing, becoming president of H. J. Heinz U.S.A., while my brother Arthur is a senior vice president at Morgan Guaranty, in charge of its international private banking practice.

My mother, Margaret, an eternal optimist whose guiding principle in life was "doing right," had a far greater influence on me in many ways. Born in Bermuda, she was an exceptional woman. A gentle, stoic person with British reserve, she was described by her friends as something of a saint. Her twinkling brown eyes always would bring a smile to someone's face. A renowned horticulturist and a prize-winning flower arranger, she loved art, flowers, and animals. In Bermuda, she kept a pet monkey, Tarzan the Ape, that my grandfather got from an incoming sea captain.

My mother's father, W. B. Smith, seemed always interested in what I was doing. An irresistible raconteur and inventor, he was a man of adventure. He looked the part, too, like a weathered seaman; his nose had been broken several times. Born in Bermuda in 1875, he became a naval architect and engineer in Liverpool, England. Energetic and creative, W.B. was the chief design engineer on the world's first submarine built at the turn of the century. He also built

boats out of cedar, ship pumps, bridges, and docks, and even designed the equipment to produce perfume in a factory he started.
During my summers in Bermuda, we would spend hours talking
about Eastern mysticism, space travel, Einstein's theory of relativity,
W.B.'s invention to turn salt water into fresh, and his sailing voyages
across the Atlantic in the nineteenth century. He delighted in telling
how he sneaked cargo from Barbados to Bermuda in his 140-foot
schooner during World War II.

As a teenager, I'd wake up at 4:00 a.m. to sit and chat with him
about the future. A tale about a flying saucer he spotted in Bermuda
so fully captivated me that the next day I stalked out on patrol, a pair
of binoculars in hand, searching the sky for aliens. Failing to find any,
I eventually invented a flying saucer myself on a new circular-wing
design based on Bernoulli's principle.

My single-minded concentration on success at Pepsi somehow
caused me to discard my early interest in inventions and technology.
I had put aside my love of electronics twenty years earlier to get on
with my life and never realized how sorely I missed it. Now conversations with the Apple people were reawakening those fond memo-
ries of my past. Despite that obvious latent interest in electronics,
my background was vastly different from Steve's. Even the analogue
electronics that enchanted me as a child had little relation to what
was occurring in the digital world of Silicon Valley today.

Years earlier, you could open up a box, look inside, and see
what was happening. If a vacuum tube wasn't lit, you knew it had to
be replaced. When I opened up my Apple II at Pepsi, I couldn't find
anything. Amazed, I wondered what they were selling. The silicon
chip inside lacked soldered wires, warm tubes, and the gadgetry to
which I had been accustomed. I knew virtually nothing about this
new microelectronics. This was Steve's world. He'd say that people
in my generation were B.C., meaning before computers. I just
couldn't imagine how we could ever possibly work together.

Still, I found myself irresistibly drawn to Steve's world. As Apple's allure continued to grow, I felt more tension. In a week's time,
I had to fly to Hawaii for the annual Pepsi Bottlers Convention. I
agreed to visit with Steve again while on the West Coast. I already
had decided that my speech would be on personal computers. It was
my own little test for myself. I wanted to discover whether I would

have as much fun giving a speech about personal computers as I did about marketing soft drinks.

The speech, called "The New Wave," before a couple of thousand Pepsi bottlers in the Hawaii Ballroom at the Sheraton Waikiki, centered on how bottlers could use personal computers in the future to better manage their businesses. I didn't know it at the time, but I had recently appeared before the board of directors for what would be my last presentation: a proposal to spend $15 million for a Hewlett-Packard computer system for our company-owned bottling plants. The system would have allowed us to closely monitor the 300,000 individual accounts served by the Pepsi-Cola bottling group. I believed our independent bottlers could use personal computers to accomplish some of the same things. I borrowed heavily from my Apple meetings in discussing some of the Lisa's features and how they would make it easier for bottlers to learn how to use computers as a strategic tool against Coca-Cola.

After the speech, Frank Rupp came up to me. For twelve years, he was the producer of these events, ever since I recruited him and his entire staff from our advertising agency in 1970. I worked with him closely throughout. Indeed, at the end of each day, I would wander back into his creative department to get a feel for what was going on. It was a way to partly escape what seemed to me to be endless meetings I had to attend as president of Pepsi-Cola. The bottlers were still cheering as I stood in the dark off centerstage, my eyes moist with tears.

"What's wrong?" asked Frank.

"I think that's maybe the last time we ever do this together, Frank."

He didn't know how to interpret my odd remark. But I was choked up because I knew in my heart that I was now comfortable talking computers and I felt real good about it. In my mind, I had crossed the line. I realized I had more fun talking about the information age than I did talking about soft drinks. It convinced me that I was emotionally and psychologically ready to make the change. The irony was that I discovered it not at Apple, but in front of 1,500 bottlers at a soft-drink convention. It was an emotional moment.

Before returning to New York, I stopped off in Cupertino for another visit with Steve, who wanted to give me a peek at the company's next new product, the Macintosh. Steve had been in charge of the project, originally conceived by an Apple programmer named Jeff Raskin, since 1981. There seemed little in life that Steve was more interested in at the time. The Macintosh group was his obsession, his attempt to recreate at Apple the garage which launched the company's first big success.

"This product means more to me than anything I've ever done in my whole life," Steve said. "I love this product, and I want to share it with you. I want you to be the first person outside of Apple to see it."

Steve guided me into a small conference room, closed the door, and put on a lopsided smile. He placed a vinyl bag on top of the table, unzipped it, and gently pulled out a small computer. He dipped his hand into the bag again to remove a keyboard and a mouse, and plugged them into the unit. Steve slipped a disk out of his pocket and clicked it into the computer. He seemed more a showman on a stage than a businessman. Every move seemed calculated, as if it was rehearsed, to create an occasion of the moment.

"This is Macintosh," he announced with a sense of theatrics.

The 9-inch, black-and-white screen lit up with some pre-release graphics and a few funny quips. It looked to me like a miniature version of a 1952 television set, a little, funny-looking box. I tried to seem enthusiastic, but it hardly overwhelmed me.

Steve then demonstrated a program called MacPaint. He showed me how he could draw an elaborate picture, erase it, and dump it into a trash basket on the screen. The computer boasted many of the Lisa's capabilities, but it was designed eventually to sell for only $1,000, one tenth the cost of the Lisa.

Once I saw it in operation, I thought the machine was really impressive. Steve explained that it would cost a lot less to build because it didn't have as much memory as the Lisa, nor as complex an architecture. It didn't have expandability, either. It had a smaller screen and only one disk drive instead of two. The computer's entire circuitry was on a single board, versus Lisa's five boards.

The computer meant a lot to Steve, and now he wanted to introduce to me the people behind the product. The group then numbered about thirty-five and Steve introduced them as "the pirates." He spoke of his team, recruited from other parts of Apple as well as the outside, with extraordinary pride. "I've assembled a team of the absolute best people I know in the world," he said. "There is no one who can do the things they do any better than they can."

Then, he brought me to their cramped, Herman Miller cubicles. The first person I met was Andy Hertzfeld, a short, stocky animated programmer in his twenties. Hertzfeld studied science and mathematics at my alma mater, Brown University, then moved to Berkeley to live in California. He acquired an Apple II within six months of its introduction in 1977 and began hanging out at a local computer club, writing programs and designing peripherals. For my visit, Hertzfeld had worked up a little demo so he could get Pepsi-Cola cans and bottlecaps on the Macintosh screen. As they popped up and swirled about the display, Andy waved his hands in the air out of sheer excitement. He grinned like the Cheshire Cat. Never before had I seen anyone so enraptured with a machine.

Next there was Bill Atkinson, another young, brilliant software expert who had written the MacPaint program that Steve demonstrated. He nearly completed a Ph.D. in neurochemistry until he decided his real love was computers. He wore frameless glasses and sported a mustache and overgrown curly hair. Steve had him "on loan" from the Lisa team. Another young, bright star was Burrell Smith, a short technological whiz, his long hair in ringlets at the sides, who had been discovered in Apple's service department where he was a technician. One of the first hires on the team, he was designing the digital circuitry of the machine. Smith referred to his designs as "poems." With a large smile and a lot of pride, he handed me his business card. It identified him as "Hardware Wizard." Another engineer gave me his card. His title: "Software Evangelist." Never before had I seen titles like these.

Steve then introduced me to Debi Coleman and Matt Carter, who were to give me a presentation on their plans for making the Macintosh. Steve personally recruited Coleman from Hewlett-Packard to the Mac team as the group's financial controller. A Stanford MBA, she did her senior thesis at Brown University on "The Nature of Art in Nabokov's Major Novels." Carter, a burly young man with black hair, was in charge of building a state-of-the-art manufacturing plant for the Macintosh.

Lisa was being built by hand and Steve thought the whole process was wrong. He insisted that the Macintosh needed to be built in automated factories. Coleman said they were going to use robotic equipment and the latest and most sophisticated manufacturing techniques to build a superior product. She explained that they would build Macs using the most automated equipment available.

Mike Murray, yet another young face with curly hair and a small mustache, was the Macintosh marketing manager. Steve wanted me to meet him to talk over the marketing ideas for the computer. Murray said he conceptualized the Mac as an appliance like the Cuisinart. It was something that you could live without, but it would help you process food with more variety. The Mac was the desktop appliance that could process information in different ways. You could live without it, but after you tried it, you wouldn't want to.

I could never figure out why someone would want a computer if he wasn't a hacker. I kept thinking to myself that appliances serve a useful function in the home, but what would the average consumer do with a computer? No one could give me a satisfactory answer about the benefits to the end user. Whenever I would ask, I would get strange looks. "There's a revolution going on out there," I was told, "people are lined up trying to buy them. The Macintosh is even better and easier to use, so more people will try it and buy it."

I felt as if I were in a different world. Everyone here worked in small, cramped cubicles, almost as if they were part of a medieval guild. There was no sense of boundaries or barriers. I was amazed at how creative and open an environment it was. It had the intellectual feel of a university, not a corporation. A picture on one wall showed the Mac team sitting lotus style on the floor, enraptured by a lecturing Steve Jobs, their charismatic leader.

Steve called them artists, not engineers. Some of them were teenagers. I was the only person here who wasn't in his twenties. Nearly everyone dressed in jeans, T-shirts, and scruffy running shoes. Yet there was so much passion in their eyes. They were mesmerized, possessed almost, by what they were doing; they were universally young, passionate, idealistic, and brilliant. They wanted to change the world. If they had been born a decade or so earlier, they would have been part of the sixties culture that lived in communes and protested the Vietnam War. They didn't have a cause in a war or a president, however. Instead, they focused their energies on changing the world through products. The group demonstrated a cultlike dedication to working, sometimes through the night, to solve a technical glitch.

Before I left, I met with Mike, who made me a formal offer: $300,000 annual salary with an equal bonus, and options on 500,000 shares of Apple stock. The options, priced at the stock's current market value of $36 a share, were the real lure, Mike suggested. He believed that eventually Apple's stock would climb to between $150 and $200 a share. If that happened, he pointed out, the options would be worth more than $50 million.

I didn't accept or reject the offer, but I was surprised at how low the actual salary was. I was making about $500,000 a year as president of Pepsi-Cola, and I had hundreds of thousands of dollars more tied up in deferred compensation and pensions.

Gerry called the following day, after I flew back to New York.

"Gerry," I said, "there isn't any way I would consider. I really like Apple, and I'm thinking about it, but I want you to know that there are some issues which I would never accept, and one is that there isn't enough compensation for me to give up what I have. I have long-term deferred compensation, pensions, and things which Apple doesn't have at all. To go and take a salary which is not much different than what I'm already making is no sale. I'm not going to do that.

"Second of all, what's really important to me is that I've always had to work hard. I've never had a lot of freedom, but I want to make sure Leezy is really happy if we go to California. I want a house comparable to our home in Greenwich. California living is much more expensive, so I don't want to have to worry about that."

"Those are both fair points," Gerry said. "Let me talk to Markkula about that."

Steve, hearing that I had turned down Mike's formal offer, later called to arrange yet another meeting. This time the plan was to rendezvous with him on Sunday afternoon, March 20, at the Carlyle. I drove in, parked my car in a garage on 79th Street, and walked down a few blocks to the Carlyle. There was a new intensity to this meeting. Before, our sessions began more out of curiosity. Now, it was becoming real and more stressful. A formal offer was on the table, and I knew I was going to have to make a decision quickly. If I chose to leave Pepsi, I knew I would have to face Kendall.

We met after lunch at around one-thirty. Steve and I decided to take a walk through Central Park. No sooner had we left the hotel than a passerby walked up to us and asked if the young man next to me was really Steve Jobs. We crossed Madison Avenue and another stranger introduced himself to Steve. "My God," I thought, "I'm trying to maintain a low profile and I'm walking through New York with a celebrity."

"How are you feeling about things?" he asked.

"I'm really excited about what you guys are doing," I said. "I think you *are* changing the world."

"Well, I really think you're the guy. I want you to come and work with me. I can learn so much from you."

I privately wondered, though, how this could be true. Steve was highly opinionated about almost everything. He did not have the patience of Job. Indeed, he showed little patience for anyone or anything that seemed to get in the way of his vision of the future. He had no tolerance for people who weren't bright because intellect was a requirement to accomplishment. He showed no patience for other computer companies because he thought they only confused people about the computer's true potential. Steve particularly sneered at the so-called MIS experts in corporate management information systems departments. He didn't think these professionals, who decide what kind of computer equipment big business would buy, knew much of anything about products. He thought IBM treated the individual as a mere node, a connection point, to its institutional mainframe computers. Apple, he felt, began with and stood for the individual, not Big Brother. He had extraordinary foresight and vision for his age.

As we walked through the Park, Steve used his hands and arms to make or stress a point, as if conducting an orchestra. His conversation veered between a disarming nonchalance and an emphatic, almost argumentative, style. Either way, he had the rare skill to win over even the most skeptical. I was smitten by him. Steve was one of the brightest persons I'd ever met. I shared with him a passion for ideas. Yet I was amazed at how much he had accomplished at the age of twenty-eight. He turned his ideas into products that created a new industry. I always had been the person who achieved things before else at my age. Now I met someone, nearly sixteen years younger, whose accomplishments had come at a much earlier age. I was intrigued by him, stirred by his intellect, his ability to conceptualize the future.

What I didn't know was whether we could work together. How do you work with someone who already has become a figure in his own right? Our backgrounds, our experiences were so different. I had to search for a common language, and it would have to be built around ideas. Lacking computer know-how, I decided to test the ground in art. Although Steve didn't have the benefit of a formal college education, he demonstrated an unquenchable thirst for knowledge. His mind was fertile. He was interested in poetry and writing, and he desired to know subjects in detail.

I steered us in the direction of the Metropolitan Museum of Art, up the stairs, through the glass doors. We took a left turn toward the Greek and Roman classical exhibits in sculpture and pottery. I explained the differences between the Archaic sculpture of the sixth century B.C. and the Periclean sculpture of the fourth and fifth centuries B.C. He was fascinated by it, often relating what we saw to Apple.

"Apple wants to stand for great design," he said. "Anything that Apple does, we want to be the best. It has to be the best." What Steve liked most was simplicity and elegance. As we left the museum, wandered past the Park's Lewis Carroll figures and around the model boat pond, I gained a sense that I could be a teacher to a brilliant student. I saw in him a mirror image of my younger self. I, too, was impatient, stubborn, arrogant, impetuous. My mind exploded with ideas, often to the exclusion of everything else. I, too, was intolerant of those who couldn't live up to my demands.

We jumped from one subject to another. We talked about Pepsi and Coke, about IBM and Apple, art and music, New York and Silicon Valley, about our romantic notions of life. I told him how I'd go to Paris on vacation with my sketchbooks to draw on the Left Bank, spending a few hours in the Louvre every day. I confessed that if I weren't in business, I'd probably be an artist. Steve revealed that if he weren't working with computers, he could envision himself as a poet in Paris. The passing joggers, bicyclists, and baby carriages, the people who sat on the park benches with their Sunday papers were oblivious to us.

We wandered out of the Park, down Broadway, to Colony Records at 49th Street. Steve wanted to show me the music he was interested in. In the store, he fingered through records by Bob Dylan, Joan Baez, Ella Fitzgerald, Windham Hill jazz. My tastes were much narrower than his. The classical music I listened to was East Side New York. It occurred to me that the cluttered record shop was something of a museum, too, that Steve was showing me the art he treasured just as I shared with him the sculpture and paintings that informed my life.

Steve wanted me to understand that at Apple he would work for me. Never before had he worked for someone he really respected, he said. Steve felt he could only work with someone who was as bright and intelligent as he was. The next few years were important to him, he said. He believed they would be the most productive years of his life. Steve had wonderful ideas to contribute to the world, yet he realized he had to grow and learn to become more successful to achieve them. I was the person, Steve said, who could teach him the most.

We walked up Broadway to the San Remo apartment building on Central Park West and 75th Street, only a couple of blocks from the exclusive Dakota building, where ex-Beatle John Lennon, one of Steve's heroes, had been killed. The San Remo was designed and built in the golden age of New York architecture, a building that recalled another era. We passed the concierge and the doorman and got into the elevator that would take us straight to a penthouse suite Steve was thinking of buying. It was a two-story apartment in one of the San Remo's twin towers, some thirty floors above the ground, that had been owned by Jacob Rothschild.

By way of an outdoor stairwell, we reached a terrace that wound around the tower. I don't like heights and I had this terrible vision that the fire door would slam and we would get stuck out here. So I stayed close to the inside of the balcony as Steve showed me the building's commanding views—across the Hudson River to the New Jersey side, down to the Statue of Liberty and up to the George Washington Bridge, all the way out to a distant LaGuardia Airport across the expanse of Central Park. It seemed as if the two of us were standing out there above the world, above the world of New York that I knew and that Steve was now trying to discover, and above the world he was going to change.

We were on the balcony's west side, facing the Hudson River, when he finally asked me directly: "Are you going to come to Apple?"

"Steve," I said, "I really love what you're doing. I'm excited by it, how could anyone not be captivated? But it just doesn't make sense."

I explained that even if I wanted to join him at Apple, the financial package wasn't right. I told him I needed $1 million in salary, $1 million for a sign-up bonus, and $1 million in severance pay if it didn't work out.

"How did you reach those numbers?" he asked.

"They're nice big round numbers," I replied, "and they make it a lot easier for me to talk to Kendall."

"Even if I have to pay for it out of my own pocket," Steve said, "I want you to come to Apple. We'll have to solve those problems because you're the best person I've ever met. I know you're perfect for Apple, and Apple deserves the best."

"Steve," I said, "I'd love to be an adviser to you, to help you in any way. Any time you're in New York, I'd love to spend time with you. But I don't think I can come to Apple."

Steve's head dropped as he stared at the pavement. After a weighty, uncomfortable pause, he issued a challenge that would haunt me for days: "Do you want to spend the rest of your life selling sugared water or do you want a chance to change the world?"

It was as if someone reached up and delivered a stiff blow to my stomach. I had been worried about giving up my future at Pepsi, losing pensions and deferred compensation, violating the code of loyalty to Kendall, my ability to adjust in California—the pragmatic stuff that preoccupies the middle-aged. I was overly concerned with what would happen next week and the week after next. Steve was telling me my entire life was at a critical crossroads. The question was a monstrous one; one for which I had no answer. It simply knocked the wind out of me.

Steve showed no sign of disappointment in my reply. He didn't know the word "no." It never meant anything to him. No is just a temporary hurdle that Steve always seems to surmount. He had an uncanny ability to always get what he wanted, to size up a situation and know exactly what to say to reach a person.

We left the apartment and walked back across the Park to the Carlyle. It was nearly four-thirty and the sun was beginning its descent. I had turned him down. Yet as I said goodbye, I realized for the first time in four months that I couldn't say no.

The Third Wave

Today's executives speak of "decentralization," of going "back to the basics," and of respect for "culture." All cures for the malaise that affects American industry? Hardly. It's not a question of a quick fix; it's realizing that the basic corporate model, the one we've followed for more than fifty years, may be outdated.

Alvin Toffler, peering into the future, foresaw the managerial third wave; John Naisbitt, clipping periodicals, tracked its occasional occurrence. But I've lived and worked in Pepsi, one of the best second-wave companies of the industrial age, and in Apple, one of the best third-wave companies in the age of information.

I've poured myself mentally and physically into the world of industrial competition. I've also discovered a new world where business has less to do with competition and more to do with building markets, where success is measured not by share points but by enlarging the playing field for everyone, thereby making the industry stronger—not just for us and at another player's expense.

Ironically, most of the successful leaders in the industrial age's early days were builders, not competitors. Institutionalization, in some respects, made them stronger competitors.

Third-wave companies are the emerging form, not only for high-tech companies, but for all institutions. Simply put, the source of their strength lies in *change*—in the ability to transform their products and organization in response to changes in the economy, in social habits, in customer interests. By contrast, the source of strength in industrial-age companies is *stability*. Everything about them is geared to establishing stability—including their emphasis on title and rank rather than on making a difference, on structure over flexibility, on putting the institution's needs before the individual's. No wonder the second-wave company is slow to respond to external changes.

This is the signal difference between second- and third-wave firms. The difference is growing even more crucial as the tempo of change increases due to the acceleration of the information age. The first-wave companies were built in the agricultural age. Second-wave companies, the model for the industrial age, are *built for growth,* with a more-of-the-same attitude, not an appreciation for change. Think of the corporation in the sixties and seventies. There were few things managers had to do but mind the store while growth simply happened. There were few dependencies on the outside world. Pepsi, for instance, is a totally self-sufficient community. It has its own restaurants, its own doctor, its own sculpture garden. Inside the second-wave company, the CEO presides over this closed system like an emperor.

That's why most second-wave companies, when they venture outside of themselves, enter the international marketplace from a domestic point of view, in the form of *multinational* outposts. A third-wave company takes a global point of view, with a *multilocal* focus.

Second-wavers tried to remake foreign markets in the image of their domestic markets. They rigidly tried to impose their identity abroad. If it worked in San Francisco, it would work in São Paulo. This is wrong. Abroad, Apple adjusts to foreign norms and conditions. As Mike Spindler, senior vice president of Apple International, puts it: "Apple beats with two hearts—our California heart and the heart of the local company." Our home office then adapts some foreign ways. Apple—under this multilocal scheme—became the number-one personal computer company in France. And we're experiencing explosive growth in Japan.

It is still possible to succeed under the old second-wave model: IBM and PepsiCo seem to prove it almost every day. They succeed because they are good at competitive analysis and strategy, at reducing tasks to quantifiable objectives and policing performance, at consistency in implementation throughout the corporation. These are the traditional strengths of second-wave companies. But the world of today is not the same as the world of the mid-twentieth century, when these companies' business styles were refined. Volatility and interdependency are concerns second-wave companies were not built to handle; success may prove more elusive for companies which fail to transform themselves.

What the second-wave model often lacks are the ingredients that will determine success in the information age: flexibility, creativity, and innovation. All are hampered because each level of the hierarchy in a second-wave company is a filter. Every level has the right to say no, but seldom does it also have the right to say yes. If good ideas percolate to the top of the organization, they do so slowly. That means new products and new emerging markets aren't quickly seen in a second-wave company. That was acceptable when time wasn't a factor. But few of us have the luxury of time anymore.

Lots of high-tech companies are in the third wave. That's because technology allows things to be done better and cheaper than before, and because high-tech companies are attractive to people who aren't burdened by the experience of traditional management. But not all third-wave companies are in this sector. Chapparral Steel is an example of a company in an archaic business that has nevertheless successfully made the leap and is doing quite well as a result.

Flexibility

At Chapparral, people hold flexible cross-functional jobs so that the vice president of administration has actually doubled as a switchboard operator. The organization is flat, lean, and flexible. Growth by vertical integration is viewed with disdain, and the factory is considered a true laboratory for experimentation. Employee productivity is almost four times that of the average U.S. steelworker and nearly twice as much as the Japanese.

There are also "flexible walls" at Apple. People like the idea of working in open spaces with cubicle partitions that can be assem-

Contrasting Management
Paradigms*

Characteristic	Second Wave	Third Wave
Organization	Hierarchy	Network
Output	Market share	Market creation
Focus	Institution	Individual
Style	Structured	Flexible
Source of strength	Stability	Change
Structure	Self-sufficiency	Interdependencies
Culture	Tradition	Genetic code +
Mission	Goals/strategic plans	Identity/directions/values
Leadership	Dogmatic	Inspirational
Quality	Affordable best	No compromise
Expectations	Security	Personal growth
Status	Title and rank	Making a difference
Resource	Cash	Information
Advantage	Better sameness	Meaningful differences
Motivation	To complete	To build

* Inspired by James E. Cook, technologist, entrepreneur and former technology vice president of Computervision Corporation.

+ See tutorial on "Living Out the Genetic Code" on page 318.

bled and reassembled over a weekend. In most cases, we lease facilities. The culture doesn't put a premium on what one's office looks like. It gives us immense flexibility to reorganize.

Reorganizations, in fact, are looked at positively. In many corporations, they're viewed with anxiety. People wonder, "Where do I go, what will I do?" That's especially true in companies that have had no layoff or have cradle-to-grave employment policies. In Apple, it's constant change. People expect buildings, structures, offices, and people to change. Organizations shouldn't have permanence.

The Network Organization

For the first time, alumni of the sixties generation and the Vietnam experience are moving into the ranks of business leadership. They are loosening the bonds of leadership from a hierarchical to a network model.

The beauty of a network is that it has no center. It is a process more than a structure, composed of modular groups that establish themselves to take on specific tasks—not to build fiefdoms as traditional "departments" do. Depending on the situation, the leader can thus also be a follower and a peer, offering inspiration, not his own dogmatic views. Often I am a leader in one network but a follower in another, as I take a back seat to players who are stronger in product development or manufacturing. The corporate leader is not necessarily a paragon of wisdom: in most second-wave companies he is the end product of a process of elimination, not a process of cultivation where talent and ideas shine.

How then can the third-wave leader add value? He still sets the agenda—he says, Here's what's going to be important for us, and thus decides where the resources will go. His job is to empower the network. In a second-wave company, by contrast, the network is an informal one and is simply tolerated.

Why is the network so important? Because that is the natural course of how ideas flow. Third-wave companies are designed for management by dissent. Second-wave companies are built to foster consent, which is considered healthy. Apple would never develop the products or principles it has if not for the love for colliding ideas.

Structure has no permanence. Third-wave companies are not necessarily centralized or decentralized. There are times when you want to change structures; the network shifts to accommodate the change. Our network is made up of temporary teams that are formed and then disbanded as events necessitate.

The network also calls for fewer employees. Consider Digital Equipment Corp. (DEC), one of the real computer success stories in recent years. It had $6.5 billion in revenues and 89,000 employees in 1985. Apple, on the other hand, racks up more than $2 billion in annual revenues with little more than 5,000 employees. If we were to grow three and one-half times DEC's size and increase our workforce by the same rate, Apple would have all of 17,000 employees versus 89,000 at DEC.

We're able to keep so lean because we rely on an independent network of third-party business partners—independent software developers, makers of peripheral equipment, dealers, and retailers. We provide a conduit for creativity and innovation. The true entrepreneurs, then, are those who take advantage of the network.

Some critics wrongly assert that such arrangements have led to the emergence of the "hollow corporation," a vulnerable shell whose survival is dependent on outside companies. When you look behind these seemingly large entities, they contend, you discover a facade—no manufacturing, no sales channels, very little other than services.

The critics have misjudged the vast advantages that accrue to such organizations. When Apple fell into its crisis in 1985, our dependence on this network of outside companies significantly heightened the pressure on us. If they abandoned Apple, our future would have been less than secure. But the flexibility we gained from it far outweighed the disadvantage. If we had greater numbers of people, as DEC does, if we owned our buildings, if we were more vertically integrated, we would have faced an even greater and more painful crisis. There is a great source of strength in having a corporation with few people.

For every dollar of revenue in the catalyst company, the external infrastructure may generate three to four additional dollars of sales. Vertical integration, therefore, assumes less importance, and corporate size becomes less significant. Of far greater import is the enhanced flexibility to turn change and chaos into opportunity. Our network helped us turn desktop publishing into a marketing phenomenon by providing the software and peripherals.

Motivation

Second-wave companies are in the business of getting bigger. Size is their religion. Third-wave companies are more interested in finding a better way.

This leads to a primary third-wave goal: to make yourself and your own products obsolete. No one should be more competent at that than you. Our Macintosh replaced the Lisa, Apple IIgs was designed to replace the earlier Apple IIs. What we do is find ways to give people a growth path—upgrade—to the next product, to the future, not abandon customers who have bought the now-obsolete product. The way we renew ourselves is to supply our customers with meaningful differences. In second-wave companies, the product objective is generally meant to give customers better sameness —an improved version of their same old product.

This is a very contrarian idea. Second-wave companies do everything they can to defend what is already theirs. They will spend more and more money to do so or acquire a company to control the competition.

Individual vs. Institution

At Apple, we take this conflict for granted while most second-wave companies ignore its existence. We exist for our people, who are our lifeblood, not the other way around.

Second-wave people are motivated by promotion, salary, and bonuses. Third-wave people are motivated by commitment to an ideology, by the chance to personally change the world, the chance to grow as a person. The second-wave company does not offer this as a possibility, not in the promise of lifetime employment and the lure of a pension. As a result, third-wave people are more likely to take risks, to court failure. They are playing according to a different standard—their own, not the company's. Their attitudes are based on the possible rather than the actual. They must, as a result, be given high rewards for their high risk, especially in stock options.

Quality

In this new wave, quality takes on a broader definition. It doesn't apply only to the product; instead, quality is pervasive throughout every part of the organization. Quality, without compromise, is expected in every function and every department, from finance to sales. It's everyone's job. And it's defined by anyone who wants to compete—not just who is bigger and has more clout.

That's one of the reasons why so many American companies fell into trouble. They measured quality in terms of what was affordable, meaning what level of predictable error was acceptable, rather than insisting upon perfection at the start. The proof of this is in some of the gains traditional corporations have registered in quality since the early 1980s; the increases are shocking not for their improvement but because they reveal how bad things actually had gotten.

So what does all this mean? The differences between second- and third-wave companies require vast revolutions in attitude and behavior. These differences are worth noting during the time of transition we are in currently. The third wave is a model we would do well to begin implementing.

4
Fish on a Hook

"Sugared water . . . or a chance to change the world." I couldn't stop thinking about the challenge Steve put to me. For hours and days, the remark lingered in my mind.

For the first time in sixteen years, I had peeked outside the Pepsi world and discovered that as great as PepsiCo was, there were great things occurring at other places, too. For most of my career, I naively thought I was doing the only exciting things in the world, that I worked with the only bright people in the world. I knew now that wasn't true. To someone who had rarely looked up from his work, it was no small revelation. Apple's interest in me forced me to think about the things I most enjoyed in life.

It wasn't running large administrative organizations. The things I enjoyed most were working with small teams, creating ideas and turning them into products or market opportunities, solving problems in small companies as I did in International Foods, or personally devising marketing strategies as I did in the early seventies when Pepsi-Cola was still a small corporation.

As exciting and successful as Pepsi was, I probably would never have the chance to do those small team, hands-on projects in the future. Yet I was being offered an opportunity to head a new company in a new industry, to participate in the very things I most enjoyed. Whenever I returned from a meeting with Apple people, I always felt reinvigorated and excited that I had learned something new. I found myself having more fun than I had had in years.

Contrary to popular conception, I never was a standardized,

sanitized professional manager. Throughout my Pepsi years, I had broken with convention. I was a maverick in a highly standardized world. I had given up a good job in the advertising world to lug soda cases up and down dirty cellars. After landing the job as vice president of marketing, I succeeded by changing the ground rules of competition—the way packaging, merchandising, and promotional concepts were employed—not by playing it safe and competing on traditional grounds. I was captured by the intellectual power of an idea and how it could change things, less interested in beating a competitor in a market-share race.

I then abandoned all this for a job that most people considered a demotion. Yet I still wasn't interested in the power: I was driven by the experience, the adventure of life abroad. When offered the job as president of Pepsi-Cola, I turned it down twice and finally came back kicking and screaming. As many speculated that I was the leading contender to head the corporation, here I was seriously considering abandoning it all for a smaller company 3,000 miles away that was populated by people half my age.

My experience in International Foods built my self-confidence, convinced me that I could handle as challenging a job as Apple was offering. I knew from firsthand knowledge that running an entrepreneurial business in a roller-coaster environment was difficult but not impossible. I had done it in Brazil, with both a company and an economy raging out of control. It provided the confidence that I could succeed in a dynamic, exploding industry like personal computers.

I wanted to build businesses, products, and markets. Increasingly, however, I found myself an administrator. One month, I was going through the tedious experience of concentrate price negotiations with the bottlers. PepsiCo felt the bottlers weren't investing enough in marketing; the bottlers argued that Pepsi wasn't doing its share. The next, I was faced with constant negotiations to get the bottlers to agree to a fundamental change in their exclusive territorial agreements over fountain syrup. In between, I would fly to Washington, trying to prevent saccharin from being banned or attempting to persuade the Federal Trade Commission that the exclusive territories of our bottlers were not anticompetitive.

Many of the bottling territories had little logic to them. Set up at the turn of the century, they were based upon how far a horse and buggy could travel to collect empty bottles to be washed and refilled at the plant for delivery the following day. In the 1980s you had to have 10 million cases to compete in a different industry and there were huge economies of scale. Equipment needs were different. It became extremely inefficient for the small bottler to compete.

Bottlers' territories were increasing in value after the passage of a law, the Interbrand Competition Act, which secured their value. I felt PepsiCo needed to take an active leadership role in reshaping them. Coca-Cola's new management, under the aristocratic Cuban Roberto C. Goizueta, who succeeded Paul Austin as chairman in 1981, was far more aggressive. It began buying its bottlers out, combining them, and refranchising them in some cases as leveraged buyouts. They were perfect leveraged buyout candidates. They were asset-intensive; the assets were understated in the books, and they boasted a predictable stream of earnings. We began to face stronger, more aggressive bottling competitors in every market refranchised by Coca-Cola.

It was a brilliant move, and it was driving me nuts, particularly because we already had a competitive advantage over Coke that would have allowed us to better take advantage of that strategy.

About 25 percent of Pepsi's U.S. sales came from company-owned plants, while only 8 percent of Coca-Cola's domestic revenues were attributable to company-owned facilities. So there was a big opportunity for Pepsi to exploit its larger position. I wanted to buy out additional territories and spin them out into regional groups which could go public or could be refranchised to existing bottlers. But I couldn't get PepsiCo to spring for it. Most of the corporation's resources were now being siphoned off by its fast-food businesses, Pizza Hut and Taco Bell.

By this time, Kendall had set up a spirited three-way competition between myself, Frito-Lay president Wayne Calloway, and PepsiCo Food Services president Donald Smith. The winner would succeed Kendall as chief executive and chairman of the corporation. Kendall strongly believed it was his job to nurture a choice of top candidates as successors from which the board could choose. At Pepsi, we were not only in competition with our competitors, we were put into competition with each other. For the first time, however, I felt directly in competition with Calloway, a good friend, and I disliked it.

It became a distraction, too. People openly speculated over who would win. The subject became the total preoccupation of the managers. The tension was apparent, and you could overhear the conversations about it in the halls. "I saw Pearson with Smith today," one would whisper to another. "I wonder what that means."

Kendall began sending out signals that the competition had started a year earlier when he asked the three of us to get more involved in corporate decisions. We became board members of the PepsiCo Foundation, charged with recommending how the corporation should spend its foundation grants; we were encouraged to get involved with outside activities, and we were tested, too, on our performance inside the corporation. One of those tests had involved a white paper recommendation on what Pepsi should do with its transportation business, which included North American Van Lines and Leeway Transportation, two motor carriers. While Leeway was losing money, North American was fairly profitable.

Smith, recruited from Pillsbury's Burger King division, urged that Pepsi continue to invest in the transportation business. Calloway suggested that if someone came along and offered us a high enough price, we should be willing to get out. My recommendation was more controversial. I suggested that we not only dump the two companies, but that we also should ditch Wilson Sporting Goods and any other business not involved in soft drinks, snack foods, or food service—our three major business segments.

I felt the stock market would look favorably upon the restructuring and that it would, more importantly, give us an opportunity to redeploy our resources into the refranchising of our U.S. soft-drink territories. I posed a common-sensical question: When opportunities were greater in its three-core businesses, why was PepsiCo in businesses that never would amount to a large part of its total revenue?

The deregulation of the trucking industry was driving prices down dramatically and making it hard for any but the strongest companies to survive. The sporting goods industry was inventory-intensive, with a huge number of products that prevented a company from achieving the higher gross margins available in soft drinks and snack foods.

Kendall disagreed. "We worked too hard to build this corporation and we're not going to go selling off businesses that can be fixed with better management," he said.

"Don," I unsuccessfully argued, "it has nothing to do with management. It has to do with what kind of a corporation are we trying to build strategically."

Still, I could not convince him. Since then, however, PepsiCo has sold off all of those businesses and has become an aggressive acquirer of bottler territories. In the last two years, Pepsi has spent nearly $1 billion buying soft-drink territories. But at the time, food service operations were soaking up most of the company's capital investment. The best we could manage was some consolidation in the Southwest.

I was getting a little frustrated that I couldn't get the backing for all the things I wanted to do at PepsiCo. In 1982 I even entertained the notion of starting my own entrepreneurial business on the side. The concept was a center where people could rent a personal computer by the hour. At that time, a fully configured Apple II cost about $3,600, and few people thought they needed to own a personal computer. Small business owners could put their mailing lists or accounting systems on the computers during the day, while businessmen or students could use spreadsheets or word-processing programs at night. Next to each computer, I would have television screens so a user could slip a videocassette into a recorder and receive step-by-step instructions for each task.

I sketched the layout of a prototype store, worked up a business plan, and was going to place one in Greenwich, Connecticut, near a high school where students were already using Apple computers. Nothing ever came of it, partly because of my obligations to Pepsi, but it was an indication of my growing restlessness at the time.

I had been president for five and a half years, and I was getting tired, physically tired, of doing what I was doing year after year. No one at PepsiCo had been measured by Nielsen share points for so long. No longer did I wake up in the morning excited about the job as I used to years ago.

It seemed to me I was building a cathedral. I looked at my role as creating new concepts in marketing that no one had ever done before. I derived my satisfaction from the thought that these new ideas would help change an industry. Size and power didn't mean that much to me. Other people at Pepsi were on a search-and-destroy mission.

If I stayed at PepsiCo and succeeded Kendall, the most that I could hope for was to live in his shadow. No one would ever know whether the reason I got the job was because of my friendship with him or whether I earned it on my own. That, too, was important to me because I never sought anything on any other basis than merit.

Gerry now knew he had a fish on the hook. But he also realized he could lose the whole thing. It was becoming apparent that if this deal came together, it would be the biggest headhunt ever to occur. Wherever I turned, it seemed, there was another telephone message from him. He told me he would be making another personal appearance at the annual black-tie dinner of the New York Wharton Club in the ballroom of the Waldorf-Astoria Hotel on March 22. William S. Paley, the soon-to-retire founder and chairman of CBS Corp., was named Wharton's "Man of the Year," an honor Kendall had received several years earlier.

I was on the dais sitting next to Procter & Gamble president John Smale in my capacity as chairman of Wharton's business advisory board; Gerry was present as a member of the board and a friend of Bill Paley's. For Gerry, it was like wandering through a candy store. The Wharton dinner was a unique gathering of some of the most influential executives in corporate America. He was not inconspicuous in a crowd like this—if anyone was seen speaking to him at length, it would give many cause to wonder. Of course, the last thing I wanted was to be seen next to Gerry Roche at this event.

In Paley's speech before 1,000 guests, I was amazed when Paley, a symbol of America's corporate establishment, said that the future was being made today by a group of young people in Silicon Valley. "I wish I were young again," he said. "I wish I could do it all over again with them."

His remarks sunk in. I was now looking for signals that either told me, "This is crazy, put a stop to it . . . " or, "Should I really take the chance?" I sometimes thought Apple's courtship of me was an eventful interlude that would soon end so I could again concentrate my energies back on Pepsi. It wasn't.

After the event was over and the crowds cleared, Gerry pulled me off to the side. We went into the hotel's lounge and found a quiet table in a corner for a drink.

"How am I going to get myself out of this thing?" I said. "I feel like I've dragged everyone along and I don't want to misrepresent things. Up front, I told you I'm not interested in this job, and yet everyone keeps coming back. I have to admit I'm having a good time getting to know Steve and Mike, but it doesn't mean I want to work for Apple."

"I know this would be a huge decision for you," Gerry said, "and you probably will decide that you don't want to leave. I can understand that, John, because you're the hottest property in corporate America right now and you've got a wonderful future ahead of you at PepsiCo. Or you can write your ticket anywhere you want to in corporate America.

"But, John, you ought to know that something is happening out in this Valley. I've been thinking about it a lot. Silicon Valley is different from anything else I've ever experienced. It's like Florence must have been in the Renaissance. It's where all the bright minds are coming together and it's a place in time where wonderful things are going to happen."

I stared at him, half startled by the comparison. But Gerry knew I was a romantic at heart, and he knew it would capture my attention.

"What do you mean?" I asked.

"Look what's happening out there. We're moving into an age where technology is becoming extremely important in people's lives. Steve Jobs and Mike Markkula are two of the pioneers in the Valley. They're coming up with a whole new culture of what corporations can be and they have visions of how the personal computer is going to change the world. The geniuses of today aren't working on ceilings or marble, they're working on gallium arsenide chips and software. If Michelangelo were alive today, don't you think he would have been using some of these tools?"

"He probably would have, you know," I said. He was starting to get to me a bit. I cut him off before he could say much more and asked, "Gerry, can't you come up with any other candidates for these guys?"

"I've looked at other people, but nobody excites them as much as you do," he said. "I've got to tell you, these guys are not going to give up. They are determined to convince you that this is the right thing for you.

"It's your decision," he continued. "I'm not going to put any pressure on you, but I want you to know that I'm here to advise you as a friend."

"Well, let's just suppose I did go to Apple," I said. "How in the world would I ever tell Don Kendall? I can't even picture in my own mind how I would approach him."

"That would obviously be a difficult thing for you to do," Gerry agreed. "But, John, you've got to think about your own life and your own future and where you can make the best contribution."

Markkula had by now come back with a revised offer that was acceptable to me. The deal included $1 million in annual pay, 50 percent salary, 50 percent bonus, $1 million up front to come to Apple, and $1 million in severance should things not work out. In addition, Apple agreed to make up the difference in cost to buy an equivalent home in California, a feature that would later cost the company another million dollars. Mike said, however, that the board decided to lower the number of options in the package by a fifth, to 350,000 shares.

If successful, the package guaranteed my financial independence. I mulled over the pros and cons, again and again. The Apple job would put me on the cutting edge of technology, almost completing the loop of my childhood fascination with electronics. It was a small company in a high-growth industry where I could again feel that I was a builder. The move would bring me closer to Meg and Jack in California. The job also would be an escape from my increasing frustrations at Pepsi.

There aren't many people during your lifetime that you feel you can really learn from. I thought Steve could be one of them. I was fascinated by his mind and his vision and my place in it. I could help Steve become the Henry Ford of the computer age. Steve would frequently speak of Ford, how he understood what the automobile was about, just as Steve understood what the computer was all about.

Ford was the builder who transformed the automobile from an expensive curiosity for the wealthy into a commodity for the masses. He hadn't invented the car, just as Steve hadn't invented the com puter. But by using mass-production techniques and producing every car the same way in one color, he brought the power of transportation within reach of the common man.

Steve wanted the computer to be like Henry Ford's famous Model T, a product available to everyone. He would define what the new personal computer would be in the Macintosh, and each one would be produced under a highly automated manufacturing process. The design of the computer would allow it to be priced as a consumer product. As a marketer, I could ensure that as they came off that assembly line they would get into the hands of the common man. I could apply the consumer packaging and marketing lessons I had learned at Pepsi to complete Steve's vision.

The positives far outweighed the negatives, but they didn't seem to make the decision any easier. The risk of going to a new business and not succeeding was high. Gerry had told me the success ratio for an outside CEO moving into a like industry could be as high as 50 percent, but he conceded the odds were strongly against someone transferring into a different industry, particularly one as volatile as computers. The conventional wisdom was that fewer than one out of five succeeded.

"What if this doesn't work out?" I asked. "What are my chances of getting back into corporate America?"

"I have to be honest with you, John," he said. "It will be very hard because you will come back as a failure. I can get you almost any job in corporate America today. But if you fail out there, I can't promise you anything."

"Well, what if I'm unhappy, and Apple is unhappy, and I leave? What can you do?"

"I can't do anything," he replied. "My contractual agreement with Apple says that you would have to get someone else to help you."

Apple's decision to agree to a severance contract at least provided a short-term insurance policy if something went wrong. It would allow me some time to figure out how to get myself on my feet again. While the risk of failing was real, my self-confidence prevented it from being a significant drawback. Far more troublesome for me was having to sever my ties with Kendall and the Pepsi family. The inevitable confrontation with him, I sometimes thought, might have been enough to forgo the Apple opportunity.

How in the world could I tell him? My relationship with Kendall ran deep. It had little to do with a company organization chart. He was more than a professional mentor, even more than a friend. Loyalty was extremely important to Kendall, and it was important to me. Loyalty had been important to my father as well. Maybe too important.

My brother David was quick to remind me of the consequences of our father's loyalty to his law firm. The Depression had forced my father to drop out of Columbia Law School, but he was given the opportunity to work for a law firm. He completed his degree during nights at Fordham University, eventually becoming a senior partner of the firm. He stayed there his entire career, rejecting other opportunities that would have guaranteed him greater financial security and success.

As other partners retired and drew off the firm's earnings, the company fell on hard times; my father refused to leave out of loyalty. His income dropped to $15,000 a year. The lifestyle he achieved in the fifties became much harder to maintain in the sixties. He borrowed heavily to send his three sons to the best schools and lived well beyond his means. The strain took a severe toll. Under heavy stress, he began drinking, gaining weight, and aging rapidly until his death at the age of fifty-five.

Kendall knew and liked my father. I remember the support he lent at my father's graveside. He walked away from the grave with me and, in his characteristic way, put his arms around me and gave me a bear hug. It was a side of Kendall few got to see. Most people glimpsed him as this powerful, pugnacious executive. I knew him as a warm, gentle romantic who loved the arts and was far more sensitive than his outward image suggested.

When Kendall's own father was killed in an automobile crash in Washington State, I visited with him at his home. It was one of the few times I would ever see him alone because I had no interest in exploiting our personal relationship. His eyes welled with tears because he said I was the only Pepsi executive who personally visited with him after the death of his father. Another time, I accidentally discovered that Kendall had been reaching into his own pocket to help pay health-care expenses for the child of a Pepsi vice president.

Few saw that side of him because, on the job, he demanded the best of people and refused to tolerate anything less. He had the instinctive capacity to sniff out anyone who tried to snow him. I remember when Kendall and I once visited Pepsi's research labs and one scientist talked about cyclamates and how they should be tested. Sensing he didn't know what he was talking about, Kendall began to stare him down. He let him talk and talk, and when he was through, he said, "You don't know a goddamn thing about what you're talking about. I was in Washington last week and this is what's going to happen . . ." Kendall moved within six inches of his face, taking over his space, and suddenly this man burst into tears. He couldn't handle it. His hands were shaking.

You probably could not have found two people more different than Don Kendall and myself, yet our relationship continued to grow. He was physically large; I was slight of build. He was gregarious; I was a private person, almost shy. He loved competitive sports and the outdoors; I enjoyed reading and drawing. I would go hunting with him, but I would rarely shoot a gun. I'd go along for the conversation. I'd fish with him, yet I could hardly catch anything. It nearly exasperated him.

Don, however, understood, even more than my own father, how important it was for me to feel that I had contributed to the success of growing and building something. While competitive sports didn't mean much to me, I understood what made a champion out of an ordinary person. It was the ability to reach inside yourself and find that inner strength at the right moment. Throughout my career, I was able to draw upon that strength even when I was tired to the state of exhaustion. Kendall always could reach down to find a reservoir of endurance and energy, too.

It was a curious coincidence that Kendall came to Pepsi much as I had many years later. It was Kendall's father-in-law, Admiral Edward McDonnell, then a Pepsi-Cola board member, who arranged for his hire as a soda fountain syrup salesman in 1947. Just as Kendall, by then my former father-in-law, had arranged for an initial introduction at Pepsi for me.

We were, in other ways, similar. I shared Kendall's work ethic, his obsession with getting things done right, without compromise. I was driven by the vision of wanting to build something. Kendall was basically a builder, too. He built PepsiCo into the great corporation it is today. He says:

"In the early days, I was looking around for the legs of the stool to put it together. Part of it was opportunistic and you have to have luck. If you look back in the fifties who would have thought that Pepsi and Frito-Lay would have gotten together? But when an opportunity comes along you have to have sense enough to recognize it.

"We could promote the products together, but the critical thing was the management. We didn't have any problems when we put the managements of those two companies together. People could walk into my office or Herman Lay's and they would get the same answer to any question from the both of us.

"I've always talked about the company as a family. That's one of the reasons I moved it out of New York City. At 500 Park Avenue, our people were scattered around and we began to lose that family atmosphere and spirit which made the company special. The best compliment I ever got was when someone said we were the smallest big company he had ever seen. We kept the values of a small company even when we got big."

Kendall thrived on the idea of having gigantic obstacles to overcome. So did I. I could tough it out when the chips were down.

As Kendall watched my development at Pepsi, I had glimpsed his. When I first met him twenty-five years ago in 1958, for example, he was far from an effective speaker. I remember going to hear him give his first political speech at the launching of a new cruise ship being named in honor of his father-in-law, the late Admiral Mc-Donnell, in New Orleans. He didn't perform very strongly at all. Kendall overcame it. By dint of hard work, he would become an accomplished orator.

I, too, had to work many hours to improve my skills as a speaker. Not only to overcome my severe stammer as a boy, but to gain the confidence to speak before large groups of people—without a prepared text or notes. When I was named marketing vice president, I was determined to build a strength out of what was originally a weakness. I went to the theater to watch how performers positioned themselves on stage. I'd practice for hours. I became obsessed with the idea that I was going to become better than anyone else as a business communicator.

Three months before my first speech in front of Pepsi's bottlers,

I began work on a forty-minute presentation so I could do it without notes, centerstage in front of several thousand people. I memorized every one of over 200 slides which appeared in a complex animated format on five screens behind me, and indicated when each one should be changed. But I recall my anxiety as I was standing in the wings. I remember thinking that maybe I would go out there and my mind would blank out. There was nothing to fall back on, no notes, nothing. I had to keep my composure and just go out and do it. It was only after a few seconds on the stage that I got the strength to continue, and the speech was a great success.

Like Kendall, I turned my ability to speak in public into an important management tool. I began booking a rehearsal room with banks of slide projectors in advance of every bottler meeting. I had been working on my delivery with a speech coach, Lilyan Wilder. I'm a terrible singer, but she would have me croon "My Way" because of Frank Sinatra's perfect timing and phrasing, elements crucial to effective public speaking. It didn't come easy to Kendall, and it didn't come easy to me.

How could I tell him I was ready to leave? The big numbers somehow made it a lot easier. One of the reasons I insisted on such a large compensation package was so that it would be very clear to Kendall that I was not leaving out of disloyalty to him or to Pepsi, but that it was an opportunity that no one could turn down. It had to be an incredible sum of money that nobody could have possibly turned down.

I sought advice from only a few close friends and associates, including recently retired General Electric chairman Reginald Jones. I had known and respected Jones from my work as an alumnus of Wharton. Like Kendall, he was a true corporate statesman, a person whose opinion I desired. When I told him of Apple's offer in his Stamford, Connecticut office, he expressed shock and surprise.

"John," he said, "I just had dinner with Don recently and he told me how much he thought of you, and how you were one of the leading candidates to succeed him. I just can't imagine that you would want to go all the way to California to a hi-tech company. There's a lot of risk there."

My old friend and mentor, Chuck Mangold, was just as skeptical. Ironically, several of his children now worked for IBM.

"Do you know what you're letting yourself in for?" he asked. "You and I have done a lot against Coca-Cola over the years, but you're going to go up against IBM. And Apple is a little, tiny new company. I hope you know what you're getting yourself into, John."

He talked about the pros and the cons, and he quickly realized I was seriously considering the offer.

"You really have your mind set on this, don't you?" he asked.

"Yes, I really do."

"Well," he said, "I guess you've got to do it. Go talk to Don."

I couldn't completely accept the idea of leaving Pepsi to go to Apple; but I was so close to reaching that final decision that I simply had to tell Kendall about the offer. Anything less would not have been fair to him or to Pepsi.

Although I reported directly to Pearson, I knew I had to tell Kendall first. Kendall despised cowards, and it would be cowardly to do anything but sit right in front of him, look him straight in the eye, and tell him I was seriously considering Apple's offer. He couldn't hear it from anyone else. He never would have forgiven me.

Yet I knew it would be one of the hardest things I would ever have to do. So fearful was I of telling Kendall that I spent days rehearsing in my mind the likely dialogue of our talk. More than anyone else at Pepsi, Kendall understood my early fascination with electronics. Somehow I had to relate my interest in Apple to that. While Kendall would be shocked, I felt he could at least rationalize it, saying, "Yes, it's true, John always did like and understand electronics." I knew that would track in his thinking.

Most important, though, was the money. I wanted Kendall never to face any embarrassment over my departure. I wondered what he would say to the other chief executives and politicians he traveled with when they asked how he lost the person who was supposed to be the most loyal to him. The very best explanation was the money.

I arranged through his executive assistant to see him after work on a Monday evening at his home. It was a cold, blustery night. Kendall didn't know why I was going to visit him privately. I simply told him I wanted to talk. But he knew that I had never asked for a meeting like this in the sixteen years I'd worked for PepsiCo.

I dressed early and tried to sit down with a book to mark some time. I couldn't concentrate. I began playing with the dog, looking out the window, anything to occupy my time. It occurred to me that I could speak before 2,000 people without a butterfly in my stomach, yet I feared a private meeting with someone I had known for nearly half my lifetime.

I lived only a mile from Kendall's house in Greenwich so my drive there was brief, if apprehensive. Down a winding road, past a small, frozen pond and fields blanketed with snow, I came to a dense wooded area. It led to a clearing and an expansive driveway with an oversized mailbox emblazoned with Pepsi's logo colors, a wavy red, white, and blue. Kendall and his wife, Bim, a German baroness, lived in a huge Tudor-style mansion about 400 yards from the front of the driveway.

I parked the car in the snow off the circular driveway and walked to a large entrance portico. As I stood outside the door of his house, I could hear my heart pound loudly. Then the door opened and out stepped a formally suited Kendall. He greeted me warmly, with his customary bear hug. To reach his living room, we walked through a long expanse, a 120-foot-long hallway that looked like a European cloister. At one end was a massive altarpiece, crafted with inlaid wood, from the chapel of Bim's family castle in Germany.

We entered a square, sunken room, dominated by a pair of large, overstuffed sofas. A glossy black Steinway sat in one corner. A fire roared from the room's stone fireplace. Paintings and sculpture, mostly contemporary or from Russia, decorated the spacious room. A pair of maquettes, miniature models of sculpture Kendall had commissioned for the PepsiCo gardens, provided an elegant finishing touch.

Kendall moved behind a bar to methodically fix our drinks. It was agonizing to watch ... I only wanted to get on with it. He prepared them with characteristic care, washing the ice—an old Pepsi trick found to enhance a drink's flavor—carefully slicing a fresh lime, pulling out a frosted bottle of a limited edition of Stolichnaya vodka. It was his normal drink, ever since 1972 when in a historic trade pact with the Soviet Union he had secured the right to import and distribute Stolichnaya in exchange for Pepsi-Cola syrup.

With a Perrier in hand, I stood in front of the fireplace with him, talking about things in general. Kendall, always fond of traveling and politics, spoke about his recent trip to Washington for a luncheon with the President. Now and then I nodded, contributing a word or two. I really wasn't paying much attention, to tell the truth. My mind was riveted on the conversation that would likely follow this preliminary chitchat.

We went into Kendall's large, formal dining room, and sat down at one end of the long table. Kendall sat at the head of the table; I sat toward his right side, so I'd have access to his better ear. Five years ago, under very different circumstances, I had sat at this table with Leezy, the Kendalls, and Gustavos and Patti Cisneros, who owned Pepsi's bottling operations in Venezuela, one of the largest in the world. It was shortly after our marriage and Kendall rose to toast us. "I'm certainly glad John Sculley has gotten married," he joked, "because I'm not going to have a potential chairman of PepsiCo single."

Now, however, it was just the two of us, and we began to talk as the butler poured both of us a glass of white wine and served dinner. I started, with much difficulty, to tell him about a fabulous opportunity that was not in PepsiCo. He looked at me intently, not uttering a word.

"You know, Don, when you and I first met," I said, "you gave me two old television sets from the late forties you had down in the basement. I took them apart and rebuilt one of them into a color television set."

He sipped his drink, staring intensely at me.

"I've always loved electronics. There is something incredible that's going on in the world now, and it's in computers and it's all digital electronics. It's a whole new kind of electronics that I've never been a part of before. I've had a chance to get exposed to it and nothing has excited me as much since I was a kid."

His silence was deafening as I struggled through my monologue.

"I've got an opportunity to be part of all this. There is something, a revolution going on in Silicon Valley, and I have a chance to be a part of it. In fact, I have a chance to run a company that is maybe the most exciting company in all of Silicon Valley."

Kendall, his face impassive, still didn't say anything. He continued to eat his veal, eating and staring, sipping his wine in total silence.

"I haven't made my final decision yet, but I'm really thinking about this and it's something that I really want to do. I know what

I'd be giving up and I know that you and I have always believed loyalty is the most important thing. I'm just trying to find a way to discuss this with you without feeling disloyal. I can't do it. I feel awful about this."

Kendall finally broke his silence. "Well," he said in a stern voice, "I'm shocked! I never thought that you and I would be having a conversation like this, John. How serious is this?"

"It's real serious," I replied.

"Well, what company is it?"

"Apple Computer." It was obvious Kendall had no idea what Apple was.

"Well, can you tell me more about it and what they're offering you?" he asked.

"Don, they're giving me an offer that Pepsi couldn't even begin to match, if we can build the company into what we think we can. But there is a lot of risk. It may not happen exactly that way. The Apple people think it will."

"Well!" Kendall boomed. "What are they offering?"

"A million dollars salary and a bonus of a million to join and an equal house in the Northern California peninsula area to what I have here in Greenwich, plus three hundred fifty thousand shares of options in Apple stock."

"And what's Apple stock at today?" he asked, his bushy eyebrows curling higher on his brow.

"About thirty-six dollars, but the Apple people think it's going to be worth, you know, between one hundred fifty and two hundred dollars a share."

"John," he said, "that's something like fifty million dollars!"

"Yes, I know it."

"Well, that's a hell of a lot of money, John. Why do you think you're good enough to be worth all that money? I always thought that someday you would have a chance to lead this corporation. I haven't made my final decision, but we both know that you're a lead contender for it.

"Do you realize what you're giving up?" he asked, not waiting for an answer. "If you were to do something like this, you're giving up everything you've worked for in the last sixteen years. And you're going out to a place you don't know anything about, in an industry that's just starting. I think you've got to think long and hard and not let this money distort your perspective. Because hell, a million dollars, you're going to make that kind of money at PepsiCo with the kind of deferred compensation program we have. I don't think that's any big deal."

Now Kendall was dominating the conversation.

"The only thing that's a big deal is the stock options. What guarantees do you have that the stock's going to go up that much? I just don't think the money should be taken that seriously because it's all bet on the come.

"You're a marketing executive; you're not a high-technology executive. I know you love and you've always loved electronics and I remember that, but I know John Young at Hewlett-Packard and he's got an engineering background. It's a technology business and that's a very rough industry. How much do you know about these guys? Are they for real?"

"I've spent a lot of time with them," I said. "I've been out there many times, and they've been back here. I've had a lot of meetings with them, Don. We've been in constant contact now since before Christmas."

Kendall seemed taken aback. He hadn't realized the courtship had been going on as long as it had.

"You really are serious about this, aren't you?" he asked, nearly incredulous.

"I am," I said softly. "I knew this would be the hardest meeting I'd ever have, and it really is."

"Well, John, I'm in shock. I just don't know what to say."

We finished dinner, adjourned to his drawing room, and stood around the glowing fireplace. The discussion made him reflective. He talked about his goals for PepsiCo and how he wanted to leave it as a great corporation. As Kendall approached his retirement only a few years away, he began spending an increasing amount of time on activities in Washington, Moscow, and other world capitals. But he had recently jumped back into operations because of a scandal in an overseas bottling branch that forced a huge writeoff in 1982. Executives in the Philippines and Mexico had inflated their unit's profits for several years by falsifying financial records. It was a severe blow to Kendall's pride.

"I've put my whole business life into this company," he said. "I don't intend to leave it unless it's in excellent shape. We've got some real problems today. I need to have the top people in this company pull together and get this to work.

"This is absolutely the worst possible timing that you could come up with something like this. And then you, the person I thought was my most loyal and trusted executive at Pepsi, to come and tell me that you're going to leave. I don't know what to say. But it's your decision. You've got to decide what to do.

"I'm not ready to say who the next chairman will be, but it's either going to be you or Wayne Calloway or Don Smith. One of the three of you is going to be the next chairman of this corporation. I want to begin working closer with all three of you over the coming months.

"This is a tremendous disappointment to me. But if you're going, if you're really serious, make sure they pay you a hell of a lot of money."

There was little else to say. I told Kendall I would make my final decision within the next few days. We walked out of the drawing room and he helped me with my coat. There was no bear hug at the end. The heavy wooden door closed with a thump. Outside, it was unearthly quiet and chillingly cold. A clear sky exposed a brilliant moon and stars. The ground was covered with a fresh frost. As I walked to my car, I could hear the frost crackle beneath my footsteps. It was an eerie sound.

My breath appeared as mist in the air. Everything was cold. My hands were cold. My car was cold. And I felt just awful. I had broken the code of loyalty. From the beginning, Kendall taught me that nothing was more important, little was more coveted, than integrity and loyalty. Yet I had just committed the unthinkable violation of one of our canons. It wasn't just loyalty to the corporation; it was loyalty to my friend and mentor.

Events seemed to take control of me. My car drove me home. I felt as if I were watching a movie, except I was the person in it. The drive seemed to take forever. When I arrived, dejected and forlorn, Leezy was waiting to hear about the evening she knew I had faced with such trepidation. "John!" she said. "What happened?"

"I don't want to talk about it."

"You have to talk about it. I'm not going to let you go to sleep until you talk about it."

I recounted the entire evening, down to the last detail. It was early in the morning by now, but I couldn't sleep. I felt nearly ill. "This is the most awful evening I can ever remember," I told Leezy.

The following day, Gerry was on the phone again. He, too, wanted to know about my evening with Kendall. With that issue nearly resolved, there was only one other hurdle to overcome. The final decision rested upon whether Leezy wanted to move to California. I knew I would be working very hard and that it was important that she felt she could build a life and a home for us in California. And whether our fifteen-year-old daughter, Laura, could find a school that she could be happy at. "The most important thing to me, more important than my job, is my family," I told Gerry. "If Leezy doesn't like California and can't find a house she would be happy with, then we're not coming."

I met with Mike and Steve while Leezy went shopping with a real estate agent. Leezy had already found a house she loved. It was the first one we saw in Woodside, about fifteen minutes from Apple's headquarters in Cupertino. The eleven-room house was an unpretentious English Tudor nestled on a hillside overlooking the Menlo Country Club and affording views of the Diablo Range in the distance. With a kidney-shaped swimming pool and wandering gardens, it was more like something you'd expect to see in Greenwich than California. We returned that evening to the Huntington Hotel in San Francisco and had dinner at L'Etoile next door.

"This is it," I said. "You know we've got to make our decision one way or the other. Are you happy with the house?"

"I'm ready to come."

We decided to sleep on it. The next morning I called Steve at his home in Los Gatos.

"Hi," I said. "How are you doing?"

"How are you?" he asked.

"Well, guess what? I'm coming to Apple."

"You're coming?" he said excitedly. "That's fantastic! That's incredible! This is the best day of my whole life. I can't wait to tell Markkula."

"No, let me tell him. Mike is the one who's hiring me."

I called him next and he was equally ecstatic. Then I called Gerry. Normally, he is very calm and cool; he had even counseled me against accepting the offer if it didn't feel right. That's why he's number one and can close a sale. When I told him, he simply screamed.

"I am so excited," he gushed. "This is the most wonderful thing. This is the best thing you've ever done. I am so happy for you, I'm so happy for Leezy. Marie, my wife, is happy for you!"

On April 4, two days from my forty-fourth birthday, I went up to Kendall's corner office on 4/3 to tell him of my final decision.

"What is it?" he asked, knowing the answer already.

"I'm leaving."

"I thought that's what it would be," he said sadly. "You know, I knew I'd lost you when we talked the other night."

There were now only the details to which I needed to attend. Kendall told Pearson that I had resigned. As a formality, I walked into his office and said goodbye. Andy Pearson had been a fine boss for me. I had learned a lot from him. He was smart and demanding; he had insisted on clear thinking and had little patience for fuzzy ideas. More even than Kendall, Andy had raised the standards of management excellence for which PepsiCo was becoming famous.

To my surprise, the meeting with Pearson turned out to be cold, perfunctory. He remained seated behind his desk as he said, "I understand that you're going to leave." Apparently annoyed he had to hear the news from Kendall, he didn't stand or shake my hand.

"Yes," I replied.

"Well, I wish you luck. I hope it works out for you."

News of my resignation swiftly traveled throughout the corporation. People were in shock. I was surprised at the reaction. Nanette, my executive assistant, told me people were crying. I was the last person they expected to leave.

"What are you hearing, Nanette?"

"People are just dumbstruck, John. They can't believe it. They just never thought you would be the one who would leave the company. They can't believe you're abandoning everything you've ever worked for and going off to a start-up company."

Apple already had leaped into the Fortune 500, yet most of the executives at Pepsi still considered it a mere start-up in an odd place called Silicon Valley. Strong-willed and sensitive, Nanette had worked with me for eleven years and was an important confidant and partner. I wanted her to come to Apple, too.

"John," she said, "of all the years I've worked with you, the time you were happiest was when you were doing something on your own, running the International Foods business and working with small teams. I think you're going to love it."

"Well, Nan," I said, "I'm only going to love it if you're coming with me."

"Don't count on that," she replied. "I'm not going to California."

"You have to promise me you'll come out and look at it before you say no."

Nanette made the trip, rolled her eyes, and reluctantly decided to come with me. "I've put up with you this long, I guess it's too late to back out now," she said.

When news of my departure was announced to the press, a blizzard of media inquiries came in to Pepsi. The overwhelming attention on my recruitment stunned me and my Pepsi colleagues. Apple, however, was the archetypical success story of what was emerging as the entrepreneurial age. Its recruitment of a person the media considered the consummate corporate professional was therefore deemed a major news event.

Kendall issued a statement, wishing me well. "John is an extremely capable executive who has helped Pepsi achieve leadership positions in several key growth segments of the soft-drink business," he said. "John has earned the respect and admiration of everyone in the PepsiCo family and we all wish him continued success in this new and exciting opportunity."

It was finally over. Pepsi decided to hold a going-away party for me. But when I saw the guest list, I was astounded. Only executives were to be invited. I wanted to ask all the people who had been my friends through the years—the secretaries, the guards, the chauffeurs, the attendants in the fitness center. I was told I couldn't do it. I said I wouldn't attend the party. They were allowed to come. But it was obvious to everyone that neither Kendall, who was traveling in Europe at the time, nor Pearson showed up. Pepsi presented me with a large maritime painting by James Carrow that hung in my office.

It was one thing to talk about leaving; it was another to physically walk out the door. I left with a feeling of emptiness. When I reached the downstairs Pepsi-Cola lobby, I noticed that my portrait, which hung next to Kendall's and Pearson's, had already been taken down.

My ties had been severed.

The New Loyalty

I left a world where loyalty meant a lot for a world in which loyalty doesn't mean nearly as much. I can still remember my surprise when I first heard someone remark, "I'm thinking of stepping outside of Apple." He meant he was leaving for a few years to start his own company. I've since learned that this kind of attitude—a commitment to one's own development above the organization's—has a great deal more meaning for the corporation. It's not blind allegiance, a social contract; it's commitment based upon a new ethic that drives the survival of the third-wave company.

I had viewed up close the effects of blind loyalty to know it less as a virtue than a disadvantage. I knew how important loyalty was to my father, and yet I saw the living evidence of how it had taken his life away from him. It was his personal loyalty that gave him a job in the depths of the Depression, that made him stay with the firm even when it fell on hard times and could no longer offer competitive pay.

That bond, between man and institution, represented a social contract in which the Organization Man traded his loyalty for security and lifetime employment. It was a Faustian bargain, which seemed to offer the job holder limitless wishes while robbing him of his freedom, his motivation, his creativity.

That social contract is no longer valid. Nor, perhaps, should it be.

Many people in third-wave companies aren't, after all, looking for security. They're looking for personal growth, for a chance to make an important contribution. They want to clearly understand the vision and direction of the corporation, why it's in business, and what that means to our society and view of the world.

The trappings of loyalty—pension, cradle-to-grave employment—have been replaced by attention to such things as creating opportunity, rewards, and challenges for people. In return, people pledge their commitment to do their absolute best. For themselves and for the company.

When I arrived at Apple, I felt that I had graduated from one school and entered another. In this sense, the corporation's best model is the academy. Learning doesn't end at the boundaries of the institution; it is a lifelong experience.

People tend to look at joining a company like Apple as getting a graduate degree at a university. You select Apple because you think it can offer you an incredible, life-growing experience. Indeed, we seem to have become one of the country's most elite "higher education" institutions, because there tend to be more than fifty applications for virtually every unadvertised job. People gravitate to us with the idea of staying three to five years and then going off to start their own companies. And there can be no better preparation for it.

For the corporation, it is looked upon as a process of rejuvenation, not unlike that which occurs in the academic world. The never-ending flow of young students through a university keeps the more experienced professors forever challenged. These professors bring a fresh perspective to the institution. They think young, even though they are much older than the students whom they teach and who teach them.

And those who leave the company don't deplete it. On the contrary, they expand our boundaries. The days when Silicon Valley and other companies were plagued with what Tom Wolfe called "defection capital" may be over. Not because it doesn't happen; but because of a change of attitude. At Apple, we think of our "ex's" as our "alumni": they tend to remain good ambassadors for Apple wherever they go. The new loyalty hinges on how a company defines its identity. Should we limit ourselves to the pool of the "currently salaried"? Or should the company's boundary extend to include its wider network of independent dealers and other interested third parties? I think a company is enriched, not threatened, by the broadest possible definition.

At most companies, it would be heresy for a senior executive to publicly state that his or her goal in life is to join another corporation. Yet when Debi Coleman, our thirty-four-year-old chief financial officer, says her goal is to succeed chairman and chief executive Jack Welch of General Electric, we applaud her determination and ambition. And her choice of Apple as her training ground for this goal.

These radically different expectations call for greater commitment. Second-wave companies don't demand as much from their people. You are asked to pour a part of yourself into the success of the company, particularly in a creative company. Indeed, in many ways the individual is asked for a greater commitment than in the days when he or she was simply a cog in the wheel of a systematized corporation.

In return, you should get an experience that sharpens your instincts, teaches you the newest lessons, shows you how to become self-engaged in your work, gives you new ways of looking at the world.

What hasn't changed or hasn't been compromised in this new model is integrity and trust, the foundations of true loyalty. Trust, of course, imposes a heavy burden on people. Trust is almost a way of testing a person's integrity. When I trust others, I build a relationship with them. In return, I expect them to be trustworthy back. I place an inordinate belief in this because trust is crucial in a third-wave company to allow the free and unguarded exchange of ideas and opinions.

Management by objectives is the method of setting goals in second-wave companies; trust is the method in third-wave companies. When I trust someone to do a job brilliantly, I have paid him or her the highest compliment possible. It empowers both of us with a sense of confidence.

In many traditional corporations, too many people are fearful of saying what they really think because they don't trust each other. People believe their opinions can get them in trouble. I lack the skills of a good negotiator who can hold things back. Instead, I tend to be open and say what's on my mind, and I expect the same from others. If someone violates trust, I don't want to work with them.

While I'm not asking for open-ended loyalty, I am asking people who are at Apple to buy in to the vision of the company while they are here.

When Apple was faced with a crisis in 1985, I made one of the most difficult and painful decisions of my career. It was to lay off 1,200 employees, the largest single cutback in the company's brief history. A remaining employee asked a simple, though tough question: "What loyalty does Apple have to its employees; what loyalty do you think it should have?"

We are not immune from the instability that has made many of our second-wave brothers volatile and vulnerable. What must remain stable, however, is the vision and direction of a third-wave company. Management has a responsibility to employees to protect that vision and not allow quarterly earnings to get in the way of its survival or growth. That's the kind of stability top people look for today. So, the first level of commitment accrues not to the company but to its sense of purpose.

At a company like Apple, therefore, you are expected to get financial rewards by being a risk taker. You participate in the rewards through the stock options and profit-sharing programs. You also are expected to grow; if we fail to provide that part of the pledge, the experience doesn't measure up.

A company today owes its employees one of the most rewarding experiences in their lifetimes, a chance to realize their quest to grow, to achieve, and to make a difference in the world. Nothing more, nothing less.

5

"The Guy from Corporate America"

The meeting was like nothing I had ever experienced. Ever.

I had been in my new job only a few days when we left Cupertino for a three-day off-site session at Pajaro Dunes, a popular enclave for Silicon Valley companies about an hour and a half's drive from Cupertino off Highway 1, which hugs the jagged California coast. A retreat of condominium beach houses, Pajaro Dunes is nestled along a stretch of sand dunes on Monterey Bay.

The setting was in direct contrast to the formal, tension-filled meetings in PepsiCo's ornate boardroom. We huddled in a large, functionally appointed apartment, with a kitchen, several soft sofas, and a big flip chart. The living and meeting room looked out over the Pacific Ocean. You could hear the surf crash against the beachfront and shorebirds screech as they glided over the coastal landscape.

All of us dressed casually, sans ties and jackets. Steve sat on the floor lotus style, in blue jeans, absent-mindedly playing with the toes of his bare feet. Some propped themselves up against the furniture; others slouched into the soft sofas. "The guy from corporate America," as I was sometimes referred to, settled into an armchair.

At the outset, I had decided that a sensible plan was to pursue a product-line strategy for the company, so I put that topic high on the agenda of this meeting. It was a logical place for a newcomer to start. First, it gave me a chance to understand the executive staff's opinions on our differing products and technologies. It also was clear to me that Apple might have too many incompatible yet overlapping product technologies. I couldn't see how we could effectively coax outside developers to support four different operating environments when the IBM world was beginning to focus on only one.

Apple was essentially four companies under one roof: the Apple II group, the Apple III unit, the Lisa group, and Steve's Macintosh development team. We needed to develop a strategy to strongly position Apple in each of its key markets—the classroom, the home, and the office. Should we continue to position the Apple II for both the education and business markets? Why were we trying to sell three solutions in the Apple III, Lisa, and Macintosh units for the business market?

I tried to direct the discussion around these and other issues placed on the agenda, but it was to no avail. The meeting became a free-for-all. Whoever could attract the group's attention controlled the floor. It was difficult to distinguish between facts and opinions. People would have side conversations during executive presentations; some would get up from their places to get something. It was virtually impossible to keep order.

I had requested that everyone write one-page memos for a strict agenda. Instead, it became a finger-pointing, no-holds-barred session over which disk drive should be used for which computer. It became clear that this wasn't a team at all; that we had a group of individuals, all running their own functions. People felt free to say anything they wanted to say about anyone or anything, and they often vented issues and attacked each other.

Many of them traded insults as often as kids used to trade baseball cards.

"You were wrong about this last time," one executive would shout to another.

"Well, I think you're the most incompetent manager that's ever come to Apple," he would retort.

"What makes you the expert on competence?"

Every once in a while, the conversation would become littered with technical talk I could barely follow. It was almost as if some of them spoke a foreign language: Winchester disks, seek times, GCR vs. MFM, the IWM chip. I feverishly scribbled the words and acronyms down in a little notebook—just as I did in Europe or Latin America when I heard words in Spanish or German and tried to do business in the native language at Pepsi's International Foods division. Later, I'd look up the words in a small pocket dictionary.

The discussion centered on disk drives, which spin the 5¼-inch circles of flexible plastic that store information. "Seek time" was the amount of time it takes for a processor to reach out to the disk, locate a file, and bring it up on the computer screen. GCR (group code recording) was the variable-speed formating of data on a floppy disk adopted by Apple in the early days, while MFM (modified frequency modulation) was the fixed-speed data formating of a floppy disk used on the IBM PC. The two approaches were incompatible with one another. None of this meant much to me then. I laughed when I discovered that the IWM chip really meant the "Incredible Woz Machine," the disk-drive controller chip designed by Apple co-founder Steve Wozniak. It was a whole new vocabulary for me.

Steve urged on us an alternative technology, a 3½-inch disk drive made by Sony Corp. of Japan, instead of one that would accommodate the 5¼-inch industry standard floppy disk. For one thing, the Sony disk would allow us to make the personal computer smaller, which also meant cheaper. For another, it permitted the user to safely carry disks, notebook style, in his shirt pocket. It was a great leap toward the truly portable "dynamic book" the pc's founders had originally envisioned. Apple hadn't had much experience in making disk drives before, preferring to buy them from outside vendors. So there were questions over whether we could get what was to be our own disk-drive operation up and running with the quality and volume that would make it successful.

Although our internal deadline to ship Lisa was June—a mere two months away—there was still considerable debate over the disk drive and future upgrades that the computer would use.

"Well," one of the group shot back at Steve, "you haven't delivered Macintosh! Why don't you wait to get a product out before you start being critical about this."

Others began to attack Steve as well. They were unsparingly critical of him. At Pepsi, no one would dare address Kendall in such terms. The chairman of the company had certain privileges; he was addressed in a tone of sober deference. Yet here nearly everyone began pig-piling on Steve. I had to pull them off of him.

"Come on," I shouted. "We've got to cut this out. Let's focus on the issues and not on personalities."

It was a revealing little episode, a fitting prologue to life at Apple. To a person accustomed to corporate discipline and protocol, it was hard to believe. At Pepsi, you kept your emotions and your personal thoughts private. Meetings were precise and disciplined, the discussion orderly and controlled. Indeed, even before a meeting, you had a pretty good idea of where everyone stood and what the probable outcome of a gathering would be. Even our off-site meetings at Pepsi were well-rehearsed shows at the Lyford Cay Club in the Bahamas. There were no surprises.

This wasn't a meeting, it was a rap session. The comments it provoked were unvarnished and natural, even stinging. It verged on anarchy. Now I knew what one wag at Apple's advertising agency meant when he joked, "What's the difference between Apple and the Boy Scouts of America? The Boy Scouts have adult supervision."

We hadn't been in the meeting more than an hour and a half when the lights flickered and the building began to tremble. We were in the middle of an earthquake.

"Head for the beach," someone shouted. We ran out the door, got fifty paces toward the beach, and someone else said, "Wait a minute. The last earthquake, we got a tidal wave. Head for the land."

The indecision, the contradictory advice, the specter of a natural disaster, only foreshadowed what was to come.

When I left PepsiCo, I knew I was discarding corporate orthodoxy for a different life. I left my old identity in a closet in Greenwich when I packed a bag of casual clothes, without a single suit. I flew across the country, not in a corporate plane bearing a Pepsi logo but in a commercial airliner. I left Leezy and our daughter, Laura, back east for the first five months after a brief vacation in Bermuda because I knew I had to immerse myself in the new job.

Apple arranged for me to stay at Rickey's Hyatt House, a high-tech meeting ground where venture capitalists gravitate to forge the deals that create new companies in Silicon Valley. It was an unassuming gateway into the Valley, a drab, dark, motel-like spot that looked as if it were imported from one of the exits on the New Jersey

Turnpike. I would get up at four-thirty every morning, run along El Camino Real, and work at Apple from 7:00 a.m. until 10:00 or 11:00 p.m.

As I walked to a building to have my photo taken for a security badge, it was as if I were walking across a college campus. Young, friendly people were everywhere. Many of them stopped, introduced themselves, and welcomed me to the company. When I asked people how long they had worked for Apple, they more often than not answered in weeks and months, not years. Those with the lowest numbers on their ID badges spoke with pride about them because it meant they were among the earliest to share the company's dream: a low number conferred a revered standing on an individual. Affixed to my security badge photo was the number 4,450, indicating I was the 4,450th person to be hired by the company. At the age of forty-four, I was one of the oldest Apple employees as well. The average age of an Apple worker was all of twenty-seven. In many companies, that would be years of service. As a result, Apple didn't have a pension plan.

Apple was a company populated by young people bent on making a difference, or at the very least an impression, upon the world. It was not a nine-to-five job for anyone. People were willing to work incredible hours to bring out products. They wore T-shirts that proudly proclaimed their dedication: *Working fifty hours a week and loving it"* would be crossed out and replaced with, *"Working seventy hours a week and loving it."* That would be supplanted by yet another phrase: *"Working ninety hours a week and loving it."* Every time a new product or project was started, a new series of T-shirts would be created to celebrate it.

I couldn't explain what was going on when I arrived. It was almost as if there were magnetic fields, some spiritual force, mesmerizing people. Their eyes were just dazed. Excitement showed on everyone's face. It was nearly a cult environment.

As I walked with Steve down Bandley Drive, he would talk nonstop about everyone's mission to change the world. "We're doing something that's never been done before," he'd tell me over and over. "We have a chance to really make a difference in the world and that's what makes people excited. We are a community that brings together the brightest minds in the world and the most creative people. Personal computers are changing the world, and we're doing things that are going against all odds of success."

It would have been scary if not for the fact that it was true. Stories were legend of people driving across the country in the proverbial Volkswagen bus which was sold upon arrival for food money until jobs could be had at Apple. Some people actually parked outside of the buildings, just waiting to get in to play a role at the company.

Typical among them was Joe Hutsko, a freshly scrubbed, bright, lanky kid from New Jersey who later joined me as my personal technical adviser. He bought his first computer at the age of fourteen, picked strawberries on a farm to buy his first Apple, and was tossed out of his data-processing class after crashing the high school's IBM computer system by pulling an emergency stop switch.

Joe was working as a computer operator and trainer for an Atlantic City gambling casino when he read about the Lisa computer. It hooked him. His role model became Steve Jobs; his dream company Apple. He phoned Apple every day for a month, lobbying for a job—any job—at the company. Turned down, he decided to fly out to Cupertino, selling an IBM clone to pay for the ticket, to make an in-person appeal. It worked, and he joined Apple at the age of twenty.

Steve sometimes described Apple as the Ellis Island of American business because it intentionally attracted the dissidents who wouldn't fit into corporate America. The Friday-afternoon beer busts, a ritual in the Apple environment, resembled the bar scene out of *Star Wars:* you would meet people from every nationality and race, varying from Indians in turbans to scruffy, bearded kids from New Jersey. Gender was a non-issue. It wasn't that Apple was just a good place for women to work, it was that no one gave a thought to whether you were male or female. Apple, in fact, boasted as many women managers as men.

Compulsive work mingled with outright fun. Deals were cut with local movie theaters so that in exchange for an Apple computer, they would close to the public for a day so Apple employees could see for free the latest movies, from *Stars Wars* to *Raiders of the Lost Ark.*

It was a heady time. The summer of 1983 was the height of the high-tech boom in Silicon Valley. Young people lived high, on their pay and stock options and especially their mounting debt. They speeded around in fancy sports cars, pampered themselves with lavish gifts, and often built funny-looking homes in the Valley's hills. I'd always driven a Cadillac at Pepsi, but now I too was headed into a Mercedes dealership, thinking about the possibilities. You couldn't walk into a restaurant, a bar, a hotel lobby, or a department store without hearing people talk about high technology. Whenever I asked the question "Do you think this is real and going to continue to grow the way it has?" I was confronted with incredulous stares. People looked at me as if I weren't a believer. Didn't I know that this was Silicon Valley? People were starry-eyed with excitement about changing the world with computers.

Apple's stock zoomed higher and higher, from $36 when I joined to a peak of over $63 per share in June. Because Apple has the most broad-based stock option program of any major corporation, the company's employees saw their wealth increasing dramatically. The most recent stock price was posted hourly on bulletin boards in every building. Within five months of my arrival, my options were worth more than $9 million on paper.

Someone figured that about 100 employees had become millionaires because of Apple. There wasn't a corporation in the world that wouldn't have done almost anything to get the kind of spirit and morale that people had at Apple because they were genuinely energetic about everything that was going on.

Within days, though, my Pepsi experience seemed out of another lifetime. I had come from a world in which top executives were relatively anonymous, dull creatures to one in which high-tech leaders were treated as if they were superstars. Requests for interviews from the local, national, and international press tumbled in. Outside Apple, people would recognize me, introduce themselves, and ask for autographs. I had never heard of a business executive giving an autograph before, and I couldn't imagine why anyone would want mine.

I had heard Apple described as a dream company and once thought it little more than hyperbole. But my first few months at the company exceeded all of my expectations. I was physically tired every evening to the point of exhaustion—but it was the kind of exhaustion that makes you eager for the next day's effort.

I felt younger physically and mentally than I had in years. I felt as though I were in a graduate school instead of a Fortune 500 corporation. What made it so unique was that not only were we in a relatively new, uncharted industry, but Apple was a corporation made up of a new generation, unencumbered by the traditions of corporate America. They hadn't been schooled to understand failure, and so they believed anything was possible. Despite my initial reserve, I felt myself taking on their coloration.

Their heads pointed upward toward the future. They rushed to embrace the information society and all its ramifications, for individuals in schools, the workplace, and the home. This was really a place where people had come to change the world. For me, Apple was more than changing jobs from one company to another. I was literally starting my entire life over.

Beyond the unbridled enthusiasm, however, was an undisciplined and fiercely independent company. Within days of my arrival, my first rule was that I wouldn't accept a memo longer than one page. The one-page memo forces you to become articulate and know your subject matter, but at Apple it was a rarity. Because every employee had a computer on his desk, business memos, proposals, status reports, and technical documents all took on a stream-of-consciousness style. Inundated with paper, I would nightly bring home suitcases full of documents to study. Finally, I simply refused to read any memo over one page long.

It did not take much time to discover, though, that little is accomplished on the basis of an executive order at Apple. The chief executive could issue a directive here, yet no one would pay much attention to it. Independence was encouraged to the point where people felt they could make their own choices.

Apple had developed a reputation with Silicon Valley as a company you could never get through to on the telephone. A basic problem was that Apple didn't have secretaries; it had area associates who were encouraged to do more creative tasks on their own. Unfortunately, this often meant that secretarial duties like answering the telephone went unattended.

Flustered, I went to our human resources vice president, Ann Bowers, and asked, "How do we get people to answer the telephones around here?"

She rolled her eyes and laughed. "That's one of the things that Apple has got to learn how to do," she said. "But you're going to discover that it doesn't happen by sending memos out."

After I first visited Apple, I remember advising Steve to stay in touch with the East and its management concepts. I felt that was important if Apple was to successfully develop computers for the business market. Just as Northern California is the "technology center" for innovation in computers, I had naively thought the Northeast corridor was the "management center" for innovation in business. "There are a lot of exciting concepts and tools being developed by business, business schools, and consulting firms in the East," I told Steve. "Make sure you are exposed to these leaders and their ideas."

What I didn't realize at the time was that Silicon Valley was a fountain of managerial innovation as well. If PepsiCo was a model of the successful second-wave corporation, Apple reflected what the third-wave corporation should become. Central to the difference was the concept of "buy-in management."

At Apple, we promote "buy-in management," a group decision-making process that recognizes individuals regardless of where they reside in the company. This was quite a difference from the "top-down management" style of so many American corporations, in which the boss simply issues an order from the top and the troops below meekly follow the command. It also was different from Japanese-styled "consensus management," which allows for a consensus of support to build in favor of a decision in an orderly fashion within the organization. Consensus often means a company is willing to adopt the "average" if everyone accepts it.

Buy-in, however, doesn't allow for compromise. If someone has an idea, he or she is obligated to sell and persuade others that it's important. Ideas and decisions in a buy-in company can originate anywhere—not from the top down as they do in many second-wave U.S. corporations, nor bubbling up through a rigid hierarchical structure as in Japanese companies.

Buy-in encourages unfettered group discussion of attitudes, policies, and ideas. Decisions are the product of long thrashing-out sessions. Just as I had marveled at the disarray at the Pajaro Dunes meeting weeks earlier, I began to understand that such exchanges were healthy. People didn't hold back their opinions on anything, which made it possible to get ideas across a lot faster than having to go through the formal filtering and posturing you tended to find in a more traditional, structured world. It was fair game for any employee to take on any senior executive about any issue.

People have the opportunity for virtually a free-form interchange of opinions, so ideas aren't easily squelched. In a more typical corporate setting, managers often have the authority to say no, but they seldom have the same authority to say yes. So they'll modify an idea or project, in effect saying no just enough so their imprint gets stamped on it, and then filter it up to the next level. By the time it reaches the top of the company it looks very different from what initially was intended.

The "buy-in" group weeds out the bad ideas from the good. The process may, in fact, take longer to reach a decision. But once a team achieves buy-in, its members will literally do anything, make any sacrifice, to ensure the success of a project. Once a decision was made at Apple, everyone somehow got together and everything happened. I never saw decisions implemented more quickly in an organization. It's because everyone has a stake in all decisions and a vital role in them.

The big difference in a buy-in organization where group dynamics are important is that people are looking to see if their peers and superiors add value to the way they work. It's not enough to emulate a traditional chain of command, to look at someone else's work, make some notations on it, and pass it up to the next level. At Apple, they've got to make some contribution. Along with the privilege to make a difference goes the responsibility to make a difference.

The management philosophy was symptomatic of all the other differences in the company's architecture. At Apple, you would rarely hear the word "win." At Pepsi, you would rarely hear anything else. At Apple, people would speak about changing people's perspectives and building things. At Pepsi, the locker-room war stories were about competition. How a manager seized a quarter of a share point in a state or region. How a company hero worked day and night over a weekend to get the syrup dispensers to work in vending machines in time for some special event. But the truth is that there isn't a soft drink that's ever been invented that has the potential to change young people as much as computers will in schools.

At Apple, the competition was for a long time considered just a fellow pilgrim on the way to building markets. I was far more captured by the intellectual power of an idea and how it could change things than I was by beating someone in a market-share race. Many of PepsiCo's managers were as competitive out of the office on a golf course or a tennis court as they were in the office. I'd rather spend my time going to a museum or a symphony concert, or reading a book.

When Markkula and Jobs hired the president of Pepsi-Cola, they thought they were employing a professional manager from a second-wave corporation. Having visited with me at my old office at Pepsi, Markkula had prepared a 20- by 20-foot executive suite for me in the new Sobrato Building—named after the developer who owned it—that the executive staff was going to move into in July. The plans called for custom rosewood furniture, marble tables, elegant paintings, and plush carpeting. Markkula apparently didn't want me to feel out of place.

We were two months away from moving into the building when someone showed me the plans. I didn't want a big office; it was totally out of character with Apple. When Steve saw the plans for his office in the same building, he refused to move in.

"This isn't Apple," he said. "We're far more informal than this."

Instead, he maintained his office in the Macintosh Building. I had the office walls moved and the space reduced to a more normal size. One wall was made of glass to make me visibly accessible. In place of the custom furniture Apple intended to order, I insisted on the standard Herman Miller-issue furniture that everyone at the company used.

If Kendall was the epitome of a second-wave manager, Steve surely represented the new wave. He didn't understand or respect corporate America. Kendall, on the other hand, badly wanted to belong to corporate America. The art and sculpture he brought to PepsiCo was in part an effort to gain that acceptance. At Apple our art is in T-shirts and posters. Outward symbols of power at Apple turned people off.

Not long after I joined Apple, Kendall came out to California and had an opportunity to meet Steve. It was like two animals circling each other. Kendall, his thick eyebrows arched, looked Steve over. Steve did the same. There was tension in the air when the two exchanged pleasantries.

"You took one of my best people," Kendall intoned. "I hope you're getting your money's worth."

"Apple deserves the best," responded Steve, as if suggesting that Pepsi didn't.

When the brief meeting was over, Kendall told me he didn't think Steve was all that impressive. Steve, unsurprisingly, said the same about Kendall. They were both self-made men without college degrees. Yet they represented two vastly different worlds of American business. Indeed, they were almost caricatures of the worlds from which they came.

For years I had been a wanderer searching for entrepreneurial ideas, experiences. The freedom and excitement of building a business had made my life at Pepsi's International Foods the happiest of times. In the back of my mind, I wanted to learn from Steve just how he had done it, so that after I helped groom him to become Apple's president, I might move on to a start-up of my own.

There was no better place to learn. Apple's roots were deeply embedded in the counterculture and the academic climate of the university. The revolution the company authored was almost incendiary. It challenged convention and the corporate establishment. Until 1977, when Apple was born, computers were institutional abstractions. Their use was confined to the support of the establishment, major corporations, and the government. Apple brought that power within reach of the average individual.

The dream began when two Steves met on Edmonton Avenue in Sunnyvale. Bill Fernandez, then a thin teenager and now an Apple employee with badge number 4, engineered the introduction. His family knew the Wozniaks, who were neighbors for twenty-three years. He had met Steve in junior high school. Next door to Woz on Edmonton Avenue lived Alfred Taylor, a technical troubleshooter for Lockheed Corp., whose neighborhood fame rested upon the fact that he owned a surplus electronics parts store. In exchange for cleaning up Mr. Taylor's unkempt yard, Fernandez and other neighborhood kids would barter for electronic parts. They kept track of their work for him in a spiral notebook inside the garage door.

On his way to see Mr. Taylor one day with Steve, Fernandez introduced Jobs and Wozniak to each other in front of Alfred Taylor's house. Years later, Woz, who had attended the first Menlo Park garage meeting of the Homebrew Computer Club in 1975, brought Bill and Steve along to other meetings. The club was a gathering place for computer buffs to trade ideas, swap hardware, and exchange copies of computer programs.

It was a dreamlike, Ken Kesey experience. The two Steves, both college dropouts, were Merry Pranksters who shared a common interest in electronics and telephone pranks. Woz dropped out of the University of Colorado after a year of playing bridge and designing computer games. Jobs quit Reed College after a semester of experimenting with Eastern religion and vegetarianism. Woz worked at Hewlett-Packard. Jobs worked at Atari and journeyed to India, where he shaved his shoulder-length hair and sought to follow the path of Buddha. This was something Kendall or few others at Pepsi could hardly fathom.

Instead, Jobs, becoming disillusioned with Eastern mysticism, returned to Silicon Valley and renewed his friendship with Woz. Woz invented a computer, dubbed the Apple I by Jobs. Wozniak saw his invention as a neat toy, something to play with himself and share with friends. It had an enthusiastic following at the Homebrew Club, even if rejected as a real product idea by Woz's bosses at Hewlett-Packard and Jobs's superiors at Atari.

Woz would tell me parts of the story from time to time.

"I never started out trying to pursue money. I just wanted to design a computer. I just knew I was going to be happy telling jokes all my life. We had great fun doing that, pulling pranks and selling blue boxes. One of our best pranks never really came off, but the idea was to turn the sprinklers on the parents at high school graduation on the football field. We came so close... a friend of mine from Berkeley who was a lockpick tried to pick his

*way into the school, I climbed up on top of the building and got
into half of it but couldn't get into the other half where the
switches were.*

*"We had read an article in a magazine labeled fiction and it
turned out not to be. I designed a blue box from this article and
we went to research libraries and figured out stuff. Steve started
selling them. I would go down and order parts under a fake name,
Pete Rose. I didn't know he was a baseball player. I got nailed once
because the World Series came to Oakland and Cincinnati was in
it with Pete Rose, and I was too embarrassed to pick up my parts.
Then we used handles instead of real names. I was Berkeley Blue;
Steve was something like Oak Toebark. Eventually, I had a couple
of guys who would buy ten at a time. We sold a couple hundred,
and I split the money with Steve all the time.*

*"If I'd had enough money, I would have bought a computer. I
could not afford to buy one so I built my own. I had to hear
everything going down about this revolution at Homebrew. I
would tell Steve what they were doing with microprocessors and
floppy disks and, boy, was he interested. I could see in his eyes:
there might be products at the end of this.*

*"I got turned down for personal computers at Hewlett-Packard
three times. But I was so into it that that was going to be the next
part of my life.*

*"I was sitting at H-P and I had gone through their legal de-
partment to get a release on the product they weren't interested in.
We went ahead and laid out a PC board. I brought it in and showed
it off to all my friends, the engineers, and they said it was the most
beautiful PC board in the world. I got a call the same day from
Steve saying, guess what? I just went down to the local store, the
Byte Shop, and I got a $50,000 order. We were expecting to sell
these things for $40 each at the club, holding them up over our
heads and selling them ourselves; we thought we could break even
and get our $2,000 back someday if we could sell 50 of them. So
here I get this call and it's the most shocking thing in the world.*

*"We were driving along the freeway once and started talking
about maybe starting a company and he said, how about this.
Apple Computer. We started tossing names back and forth. I threw
out a couple. He tried out a couple. It was clear nothing would*

beat Apple Computer for sounding so good. He'd taken a few months off to go up to his friends on a farm in Oregon and then he came back to work at Atari. I knew they had orchards at the farm. I just assumed there were apples there. I never asked. With Steve you never know exactly where an idea comes from. It might have been apple orchards or it might even be that there was a person in this orchard one day who joked about starting a computer company called apple."

It was under Jobs's prodding that the pair began selling the Apple I, assembled in Jobs's garage, for $666 to whoever would buy it, mainly electronics buffs, enthusiasts, and the *Popular Electronics* crowd. The computer led in 1977 to the Apple II, the first fully assembled, programmable microcomputer that required no knowledge of soldering, wiring, or programming. A new company and industry was born. Original Homebrew members would form more than twenty companies, but none achieved greater success than Apple.

Everything came together. The environment, the technology, and the people. Silicon Valley, as Woz quips, is "where computer technicians and computer nerds finally came out of the closet." And when they did, they found an army of other people who if younger would have been marching against the Vietnam War or hanging out in Haight-Ashbury. The early videotapes on "Apple Values" show an enthusiastic employee explaining that "we build a device that gives people the same power over information that large corporations and the government has had over people."

For Apple, it was as rich and vivid a birth and childhood as it had been for many of the pathbreaking companies. Yet unlike the tales of the Sloans, the Rockefellers, and the Carnegies, it grew from a desire not to make money but to make a difference in the world. The personal computer industry was an industry created by and for a new generation. I was thrilled to become part of it.

I divided my time between learning about Apple and how it worked, trying to think through the product strategy, and getting to know Steve. I carried notebooks everywhere, jotting down relevant pieces of information about the company and its technology. In my first year, I filled twenty of them. It was like being a student again. Each week I was preparing for exams—except my tests were public. In effect, I had to prove myself worthy to be chief executive of Apple.

I was quickly shedding my Pepsi education. At Apple, the conversation was sprinkled with words like "vision" and "values," words that were nonexistent back in Purchase, New York. They replaced other words in the vocabulary of the traditional manager, words like "discipline," "accountability," "competition," and "market wants."

Until now, I had lived my entire professional life being measured on market share and had great respect for it. But at Apple there were no Nielsens to lean back on. In an industry changing and growing as rapidly as ours, careful and considered positions of our products had to be the highest priority. Market positioning was more important than market share. We needed to develop a product line that would strongly position Apple in the office, education, and serious home-user markets.

The more the Valley glittered like an El Dorado, the greater the rush of competitors after the prize.

By 1983, everywhere we looked we faced increasing competition. Hewlett-Packard launched a personal computer; AT&T entered the market with a personal computer as well; Atari, primarily a video-game company, was reported to be gearing up to make a low-priced personal computer; and Commodore was planning a personal computer more advanced than its game machine in the marketplace. Software developers, such as VisiCalc and Lotus, now had to make programs for two standards, the Apple II and the IBM PC; dealers had to decide which of a limited number of machines they could stock; and consumers had to puzzle over which one was better.

The sudden problems in the industry started to reveal the problems within Apple and the reason why I was hired. Chief among these was that everyone had great ideas. But some structure was needed if people were to feel a greater sense of accountability.

As I met each member of the executive staff, I came away with a clear impression that there wasn't a common understanding of the company we were trying to build. In fact, there were many, competitive fiefdoms. A group called PCSD (Personal Computer Systems

Division) was responsible for the development and marketing of the Apple II. Within that division was a smaller splinter group in charge of the Apple III. There was the Lisa computer division, and Steve's Macintosh team, which hadn't yet introduced a product.

The Macintosh group, though, believed its product would be better than Lisa or anything else that Apple had ever done. The Apple II people highly resented the fact that they had been pushed into a building that was two and a half miles from the Apple campus on Highway 280. Macintosh people routinely referred to the Apple II people as "bozos." They maintained that all the best people were working on Macintosh; those who weren't were automatically bozos.

The elitism was blatant. Apple kept the refrigerator for the Macintosh team stocked with free fruit juice; and it paid a masseuse to work the tense backs of the Mac engineers. No other part of the company benefited from such perks.

The Macintosh would be incompatible with any other Apple computer, creating potential software and retail headaches. Steve correctly thought that the Macintosh represented a new generation in personal computers and that another standard was worth developing. Efforts to achieve some compatibility among Lisa and Macintosh were underway, but required greater resources for any chance of success. Our research efforts had to be consistent with our corporate mission to bring high-technology products within the reach of the consumer.

My first test as CEO was to establish both the parameters and the priorities for future product development, product introduction, and marketing support. The discipline I introduced was the gentlest of Pepsi transplants, but very necessary. I convinced Steve to at least make Macintosh compatible with the new Lisa 2 computer series, a modified version of the original Lisa. I reorganized Apple's product line-up into two distinct families, an Apple II family and a Lisa/Macintosh family, organizing the marketing team around both. The Apple II, because of its color display, the huge volume of software, and its dominant position, is being primarily focused in the home and K–12 education market. Lisa and Macintosh, our 32-bit computers, would be directed toward business and universities.

We put the lid on several new product ideas, esoteric software packages, and some peripherals to focus the company's efforts behind several key products. And we made the commitment to support the Apple II with significant marketing and product spending to ensure it as a mainstream product family throughout most of the decade.

When I arrived, I found people all over the organization doing the same thing. Three of four home-marketing groups, for example, existed. The product-line strategy we developed led to a new organization that eliminated a lot of the overlap, without causing massive layoffs. We centralized our marketing services; we began to consolidate our manufacturing.

I didn't want to insulate myself from the organization, either. I wanted to flatten the organization out so there would be lots of people reporting to me, both line and staff people, so I could assess all the pieces. I reorganized some thirteen autonomous divisions down to seven, asked three vice presidents to step aside, and moved in to become the head of the Apple II group myself. I felt this was a good way for me to learn how a product division worked. Two co-general managers reported to me: one ran the technical side while the other did the marketing.

I also became immersed in the company's financial details. In some cases, I went back to the chart of accounts to determine how Apple's financials were set up. We doubled our internal audit staff to get our arms around key financial expenses and to install tighter control policies. We increased the level of discipline and market focus among Apple's managers.

I thought I had done my housecleaning not a moment too soon. Then, like the family living in the dunes in the Kobo Abe novel, the sand began trickling in. And nothing could stop it.

I had been at Apple less than six months when I realized we had the makings of a class A problem. What began as a fantastic year for the industry ended in an industry-wide shakeout. Until the summer of 1983, no one could build enough computers to meet the demands of the market. The imbalance attracted hundreds of competing start-ups. Now, we were in an outright slump. By year's end, companies in the home computer business would lose $1.2 billion, five times more than IBM and Apple made combined in personal computers. Ever-dwindling prices at the low end of the market pushed Mattel,

Timex-Sinclair, and Texas Instruments out of the home computer market. Meantime, Osborne Computer, Computer Devices, and Victor Technologies all filed for bankruptcy. Apple, which began the year as the personal computer leader in market share, fell slightly below IBM.

Apple had started the year in a whirlwind of activity. The Macintosh group was not only building a new computer, it was putting up one of the most highly automated factories in the computer industry to build them. The $20 million plant in Fremont was designed to produce a Mac every twenty-seven seconds. Through automation, we hoped to cut direct labor costs to a mere 1 percent of production.

The Apple II group was feverishly working on a new portable product, code-named "E.T.," after the extra-terrestrial alien of the movie. The new product would exploit advances in customization of integrated circuits and lowered production costs. We gained an important new employee in Steve Wozniak, who rejoined the company after a two-year absence to design the "mouse" interface for the Apple IIe. His homecoming was hailed by Apple veterans.

Most pressing, though, was the recently launched Lisa computer. Lisa was our great hope to capture the business market.

I had little influence over Lisa because Apple had launched the product before I even arrived, and most of the marketing and operational decisions to support it already were in place. Among them was a multi-million-dollar advertising campaign to convince corporate America that Apple was serious about selling to corporations.

I was skeptical of the Lisa commercials, even though they used the signature Pepsi lifestyle approach.

One of the commercials featured a young woman playing basketball, another showing a man playing a flute carried the advertising theme of "Alone Again" to promote both the advanced technology of Lisa and Apple's overall image. Here we had this incredible product and we were doing the kind of advertising more appropriate for a soft drink. I thought we could do much better.

The advertising agency defended them on the grounds that they had to stand out from the clutter of commercials by dozens of other personal computer makers. The idea was that people who use Apple computers are individuals and they do fun things.

Lifestyle advertising worked well, particularly with undifferentiated products, because you lacked the meaningful product differences to show consumers why they should buy them. If you change the color of a package for an undifferentiated product, it's a major decision. With the Lisa, however, we had real product differences which I thought we should highlight. The packaged-goods market spent huge amounts of energy and resources making small differences appear very big. In high technology, you're constantly confronted with big differences that are changing all the time. It seemed to me we ought to take advantage of those big differences instead of selling with lifestyle advertising.

This was especially true in the computer business because personal computers at the time had only a 3 to 4 percent penetration rate of U.S. households. In a package-goods company, however, a marketer is trying to reach huge penetration. Some 95 percent of the U.S. population drinks cola in any given year. So you didn't have to convince them to buy the product, only to buy your brand. In personal computers, you still had to persuade them that a computer was worthwhile. The consumer's decision, to buy a computer system costing $10,000 versus a can of Pepsi for 35 cents, was a big one—and it's not easily reversible.

The Lisa, too, was a product for the more sophisticated business market. It was unlikely that the lifestyle approach could tap into the business world, which didn't buy products on emotion. Many consumers, in fact, don't purchase products; they buy ideas and lifestyles. But the same cannot be said for the business market, even though that's the approach Apple took.

Lisa didn't begin shipping until the end of June, missing our internal target date of April. But we had a large back order of sales even before it shipped. The media and the analysts were enthusiastic about it.

We believed that Lisa's 32-bit technology would usher in a second generation of personal computers and establish Apple as a strong competitor in the important business market. The soul of both the Lisa and the forthcoming Macintosh was the Motorola 68000 microprocessor. After it started shipping, however, its weaknesses were slowly revealed. It wasn't as fast as the IBM PC because the superior graphics capability of the Lisa consumed so much of the machine's higher processing power. But we believed that users would be willing to sacrifice speed for better graphics and ease of use.

Projecting that Lisa could be built into a $1 billion business, Apple had assembled a direct sales force of about a hundred people to sell the Lisa into the corporate world. The sales reps were becoming discouraged because they found that it was a lot harder to sell corporate America on a $10,000 computer made by Apple than they ever imagined. The commission-based sales team found they weren't getting any commissions to speak of.

They were told the product was too expensive and too slow; they were told it should be compatible with IBM and it should have the ability to work in a network with other Lisa computers. Initially, the criticism didn't alarm us because our back orders far exceeded our ability to make the computer. By early August, another internal forecast showed production and demand were coming closer together. Our orders at that time fell to 12,000 computers. It was a disheartening sign, but hardly a crisis.

The forecasts, however, continued to plummet. As business moved toward the IBM PC and the computer business slowed down, dealers began canceling their orders.

The ground rules of the marketplace were swiftly changing as the computer industry shuffled behind the IBM PC. Until 1983, businessmen universally used the VisiCalc spreadsheet program which was largely responsible for putting the Apple II on many business desks. But the debut of a new faster and more powerful spreadsheet program called Lotus 1-2-3 and the introduction in the summer of 1983 of the more powerful IBM XT forever altered the business market in IBM's favor. Their acceptance by business allowed them to capture nearly 28 percent of the market, compared with Apple's 24 percent.

By early September, we discovered that we would likely sell only 6,400 Lisas rather than the near 11,000 we knew we could build. We publicly disclosed that our backlogs were shrinking and our fourth quarter outlook was discouraging. These disclosures, coupled with the industry shakeout, caused Apple stock to drop eight points in a single day. For the Lisa, we had assembled the infrastructure, a factory, and people to support a $750 million business, and yet there were no sales. Even more troublesome and threatening was the situation over the Apple II. In early June, we had a month and a half of back orders on the computer; we couldn't build them fast enough. By the end of that month, the backlog also had disappeared, and by October, sales were extremely weak.

The new market realities imposed greater discipline on the organization. For years, Apple's heady growth masked many mistakes. When sales began to slow, expenses became more obvious and open to greater scrutiny. Head count, for instance, now outpaced our sales growth. Over the past year, we averaged 250 new people per month, as many as we could process through the door. Our plans called for 5,500 employees by the end of September, and 6,900 people within a year after that. We froze our head count growth, didn't replace those who left due to attrition, and selectively pruned the workforce based on performance appraisals. And in one of the most unpopular decisions, I lifted Apple's generous profit-sharing program.

By October, a *Business Week* cover story declared IBM the "winner" in the microcomputer race. I was furious, but no one at Apple seemed to notice. If it had appeared in *Computer Currents,* a freebie street paper in the Valley, the story probably would have had more impact. Apple people didn't really read business magazines. So absorbed in what they were doing at the company, many had no touch with the outside business world.

Still, a number of outsiders urged us to fall in line with IBM, to develop clones that would run on the same operating system. If Apple could find some safe harbor or niche unwanted by IBM, then Apple could survive, was the thinking.

I never got much satisfaction from being a survivor. I get my satisfaction by being a dreamer and a builder. We resisted the advice as our net profits tumbled 80 percent to $5 million in the final quarter of our fiscal year, ending September 30. Our stock fell from a high of over $63 in June to about $23 by early October.

Back at PepsiCo, Kendall called me up and asked me if I wanted to return to the company. He quipped that at a recent board meeting someone calculated that I had made $9 million and lost it in the first six months I'd been with the company. Kendall thought that was hilarious.

I could always play to any set of ground rules as long as I understood them. What was hard for me now was that I didn't always understand the rules because they shifted so rapidly. My perspective when I arrived was how we could make more products to fill what seemed an insatiable demand for them. Within months, I had the opposite job. I was still new in this business. I didn't know how everything worked; I didn't know where to go to get everything fixed. And yet, I felt I was making enough progress to know I made the right choice.

IBM's decision to launch the PCjr. in mid-October didn't help. Many analysts initially thought the product would smother us. We were very concerned that the Apple IIe would be overpriced against a real powerhouse of a product from IBM. Yet we could not successfully launch the Macintosh in January from a failing company. Somehow, we had to gain momentum through the seasonal period to help us introduce Macintosh.

To stimulate Lisa sales, we dropped the price, unbundled the software, and expanded the dealers who carried the product from 150 to 350. I believed this strategy would increase sales, but I knew it wasn't enough to get us out of the woods. We had to depend upon Apple II for a successful Christmas.

If we were wrong, we were going to have a disastrous Christmas selling season. But we had little choice. How could we introduce a revolutionary new product like Macintosh from a failing company? Momentum and timing are everything in marketing. Few people would want to buy a computer from a company that isn't doing well. We had to get the momentum back.

The Rise of Skeptical Man

When I saw a film of how computers could help the handicapped, I was moved. And then I realized . . . we are all handicapped.

We all have mental and muscular disabilities. Inside us is someone who strives for more than we can achieve. There is the sense of the computer returning to me something which is mine. This is why the Apple logo is so powerful, this sense of lost paradise.

The computer expands one's neuromuscular coordination. I have this fantasy of the computer making me fly over a sea of data, helping me see patterns. The key of real intelligence is to see isomorphisms where others don't. The computer is wings for the mind . . .

As Jean-Louis Gassée says, human beings are grossly handicapped by the limitations of our minds, limitations we seldom even recognize. In the next few years, technology will plunk the Library of Congress, catalogues of the great museums, and files of world-class institutions right into our laps, giving us access to a staggering amount of information. Until now, we've been limited not just in collecting data but in assimilating it and learning from it. Now to get information, you typically have to get into your car, drive to the local library, find a librarian, explain your question, walk to the stacks, and search. Soon the computer will do all that for you—instantly, wherever you are. The computer will thus reduce the barriers to information, lower the "emotional overhead" of tapping into these riches.

Assuming we can use the power of information to overcome our human handicaps, what will that do to us? How will we change?

"You don't understand anything until you learn it more than one way," says Marvin Minsky, one of the pioneers of artificial intelligence. I imagine that the greatest impact computers will make is not in guiding rockets to Mars, nor in eliminating payroll errors, nor in monitoring heart transplants so thoroughly they become infallible. No, the computer's greatest power lies in its capacity to breed a new race—a race of questioners.

The purest power computer technology affords is the ability to think in questions. Most of us worship answers, the result of religion and business's relentless Mr. Fix-It syndrome that interferes seriously with deep thinking about almost everything. Answers, as Socrates said, are often ignorance mistaking itself for knowledge. Realistically, there is never one right answer; there are only partial answers. It's the ability to ask questions that deepens our knowledge. Much more interesting than answers are different points of view, new attitudes, opinions, that eventually lead to a general truth.

Technology gives you a good reason not to take anything on faith. Suddenly there is so much information you can almost effortlessly find the facts for yourself. You can test your ideas and explore alternatives. Computing offers you every incentive to become skeptical.

The race of Skeptics that may well arise will be bred on such rich information and easy access. We will perhaps see the end of that cold Cartesian, Rational Man, for whom all knowledge was narrowly logical, based solely on reason. Skepticism also takes us beyond the self-imposed limits of Empirical Man, for whom knowledge was the sum total of experience and nothing else. Skeptical Man is kin to Socrates, the great questioner; but he is not a cynic, like those whose votes against Socrates caused his imprisonment.

Compare the book, which had such a great impact on society for its form as much as for its content. Marshall McLuhan claimed that books made knowledge portable and personal. Gutenberg, he said, thus triggered the age of individualized man, freed him from the tribal way of doing things.

The book triggered the age of individualized man, but the rise and dominance of institutions—from the Church to the Corporation—has in modern times obscured the individual's power. Only now have personal computers begun the work of rescuing the individual from the shadow of the institution.

Technology restores to us our sense of creativity, because unlike television and most of the other media with which we surround ourselves, it is not passive. It's a hot medium. It requires interaction. Ask a question, get an answer, ask another question, and so on. Socrates complained that writing forces you to follow an argument rather than participate in it. Computers aren't the extension of the book; they constitute a new medium, hence a new kind of literacy.

The culture of Skeptical Man will be different. Now, our culture is based on amplitude. In business, in social affairs, whenever we want somebody to listen to us, we talk louder. We mount bigger special effects on television, use more garish colors, engage in more gyrating and twisting. We surround ourselves with what Asians would call a very obvious culture. We only understand the dimension of amplitude. Asians find this offensive.

By contrast, Skeptical Man will communicate by details, which information offers in all its plenitude. *The computer will turn off amplitude and turn up the contrast.* What we really want to do with the computer is to compare, not just figures on a spreadsheet but points of view. (What is amplitude but a single point of view shouted the loudest?) Windowing technology is the first evidence that that is possible.

Steve Jobs had a great ability to shift points of view constantly, to compare, contrast. When he first glimpsed Woz's makeshift pc board, he realized the technology would be valuable in allowing individuals the computing power that IBM had up until then confined to corporations and governments—a brilliant comparative leap. He didn't stop there; he then brought Taoist notions to management. "The journey is the reward" became one of Apple's "laws." Steve could see the potential for high technology in a "low-tech" Cuisinart, and prophecy for the computer industry in a Bob Dylan lyric about war. His ability to draw rich contrasts helped make him a genius.

Would it be disastrous if we took nothing on faith? If we continually question the known world, would a race of Skeptical Men spark new existential worries over meaninglessness and absurdity? I believe just the opposite. According to psychiatrist Victor Frankel, the people who survived internment in the concentration camps with not just their lives but their sanity intact were those who had the ability to decide exactly how they were going to react to anything that happened.

They didn't sacrifice this order of control. With questions and information at his command, Skeptical Man is free to decide his own direction.

6

The Awesome Mac

I remember the first time Steve brought me to his home.

It was in a comfortable, upper-class neighborhood in the hills of Los Gatos, a neighborhood with manicured lawns, well-tended gardens, and gravel driveways. Except for Steve's. It was as if his house had been abandoned. His lawn looked as if it hadn't been mowed in a year. The grass was 12 inches high and blowing in the wind. Just like in the old sci-fi films, the shrubbery and weeds seemed ready to devour the property.

Parked in the garage was his BMW motorcyle which he would sometimes ride alone on the weekends along Skyline Boulevard, the same road, affording breathtaking views of the Valley, that he had traversed by bicycle as a child.

Steve had asked Leezy and me to come over for a Saturday-morning breakfast. Leezy brought along an omelette pan and the ingredients to cook up vegetarian omelettes for the three of us. He greeted us warmly. As we walked into his Tudor-style home, he prepared us for what we were about to see.

"I'm sorry I don't have much furniture," Steve said. "I just haven't gotten around to it."

Inside, his home barely contained a hint of human existence. The house seemed empty and still, virtually bare. Scattered here or there were a few scraggly plants. Yet there were a few items that obviously had been carefully selected. What he owned was either elegant and the very best of its kind, or it was just utilitarian. In his living room, there was a beautiful Tiffany lamp and some old wicker porch furniture with flowery Styrofoam cushions.

Upstairs on his small bedroom bureau stood framed pictures of Albert Einstein and Neem Karolie Baba, the guru Steve had followed when he was in India. A laser disk video machine was linked to a Sony Trinitron television. Otherwise the comforts were few for someone who lived alone in a large house.

The visit triggered a vivid recall of my frantic and Spartan life in a cluttered New York City apartment that stank of stale pizza and had only the most basic furnishings. I smiled at the association, and I understood it all too well. Above all, Steve's house reflected how little time he had for a personal life. All his effort was consumed by Apple.

"We all have a short period of time on this earth," Steve told us around an antique table in his dining room. "We probably only have the opportunity to do a few things really great and do them really well. None of us has any idea how long we're going to be here, nor do I, but my feeling is I've got to accomplish a lot of these things while I'm young."

I would come to learn that Steve believed he would die young; maybe he'd always felt the wind against his back. Out of a concern for how history would remember him, he felt pushed to accomplish more and greater things.

Steve was as different from Don Kendall as Apple was from Pepsi. At Pepsi, the protocols would not tolerate a demonstrably close relationship between Kendall and me. At Apple, there were no protocols. So while I made my way through a world so vastly different from what I had known, I also forged a friendship with a person I would come to think of as a friend, a younger brother, and even a teacher.

Steve and I became soul mates, near-constant companions. We spoke with each other for hours throughout every day. Initially, a well-worn path developed between our offices, which were no more than twenty steps away from each other. When Steve later moved into the Macintosh Building, we spoke on the telephone frequently. He would wander over and see me once or twice during the day, and I would do the same. We had an unwritten understanding that either one of us could interrupt the other in whatever he was doing. At the end of each work day, we often would meet for a brain dump —meaning, in computer argot, that you dump everything in your head into the other person's.

We tended to speak in half sentences and phrases, jumping from subject to subject: our pasts and our futures, marketing and technology, Trotsky and Marx, Coke and IBM. Most of it was pure business: details about new technologies and products. Our lives were wrapped up in business details. They would consume us. We were now putting all our faith and hope in Steve and his Macintosh group to reestablish Apple's momentum.

He'd stop anything if I wanted to talk to him. He would call me five or six times during the day. He'd think nothing of coming in and saying, "Sorry to interrupt you, but I've just got to tell you what's on my mind. You're the only one who will understand."

He'd come into my office in his jeans and a T-shirt and a blue sweater on his tall, slim frame and sit down, tucking one leg underneath him. When he explained an idea, his voice was quiet. He spoke slowly, in a rich vocabulary. You could almost hear his brain thinking out an idea. Then he'd leap from his seat, pick up a marker, and begin sketching diagrams and arrows on a whiteboard to explain a notion visually. His whole body would speak. His hands would come together as if he were holding a product in them. He would make you see what didn't yet exist.

While I wasn't as technically knowledgeable as Steve, I could at least test his ideas for logic.

"Yeah," I'd say. "That's interesting. But explain to me why that's better than the alternative. Tell me how it fits into a broader context."

On Sunday mornings, we sometimes met for breakfast in Palo Alto; other times, we'd grab a bite at a Japanese restaurant or get a pizza together. Oftentimes, we'd have lunch at the Good Earth Restaurant, a pseudo-health-food hangout within walking distance from the Apple campus. We discovered incredible similarities in the way we thought and in the respect we had for ideas. We held common interests in architecture, design, and great consumer products: Braun appliances, Sony television monitors, Mercedes-Benz sedans. We not only used these, we'd study them for design and function ideas. I once found Steve running through the Apple parking lot, analyzing what made his favorite cars so beautiful in order to adapt these ideas to the design of the Mac.

"Look at the Mercedes' styling, the proportion of sharp detail to flowing lines. Over the years, they've made the lines softer but the details starker. That's what we have to do with the Macintosh." He was as elated as a kid in a department store.

Steve also was intensely curious about the world I came from. He was very interested in corporate America, in marketing, in New York City, in East Coast dress, conversation, and way of life. For a while, he started dressing in oxford button-down shirts and khaki trousers which I ordered for him from Maine. We drove the same cars, a Mercedes 380 SEC, and Steve eventually would buy a home in Woodside where Leezy and I had settled.

Steve was nothing short of exciting. He was arrogant, outrageous, intense, demanding—a perfectionist. He was also immature, fragile, sensitive, vulnerable. He was dynamic, visionary, charismatic, yet often stubborn, uncompromising, and downright impossible. He was always interested in learning whatever I could teach him from my own experiences. Our most important bond, though, was the dream we shared for Apple Computer and its ability to change the way people work and live.

Nothing consumed Steve's interest more and nothing seemed more central to that dream than the doings of a team of young, dedicated fanatics who toiled under a pirates' flag in the Macintosh Building. Steve's "pirates" were a handpicked band of the most brilliant mavericks inside and outside Apple. Their mission, as one would boldly describe it, was to blow people's minds and overturn standards. United by the Zen slogan "The journey is the reward," the pirates ransacked the company for ideas, parts, and design plans.

Steve dreamed up the pirate metaphor, first springing it on his small Mac team at a retreat in September of 1982. "It's more fun to be a pirate than to join the Navy," Steve would say. It was Steve Capps, a software ace drafted from Lisa, and Susan Kare, the Mac's graphics designer, who had sewn together the black skull-and-crossbones flag that would become the group's symbol. It was a funny way to convey the fact that this was no traditional development team. This group shunned corporate orthodoxy and the conventions of society.

At the end of each day, Steve and I would wander into the building—known in AppleTalk as Bandley 3—sometimes after a quick dinner. We'd knock around the engineers' cubicles, looking over the progress of the previous day or week. A new piece of software; a change on the logic board. It was a stimulating respite from some of my other administrative tasks. I marveled at how at Apple, the company CEO was almost as invisible as a janitor. The real excitement and heroics rested in the product developers. They were the artists.

Even at midnight, it was a place that burst alive with activity. Young people gathered in the building's gracious central lobby, an area with a soft Mexican-tiled floor and white walls decorated with Ansel Adams prints. Everyone dressed informally, in shorts, faded jeans, baggy sweatshirts, T-shirts, sneakers or sandals. The low-slung cubicles were designed so that by standing in the center, Steve could see each member of his team, and they could see him—just like the captain of a pirate galleon.

A couple of pirates were hunched over the video arcade games, frantically working the joysticks to "Defender" or "Joust." Another pair played a vigorous game of Ping-Pong on a nearby table. An expensive, high-tech stereo system blasted the Pointer Sisters' "I'm So Excited" through 6-foot-tall, slim electrostatic speakers. Steve had ordered every single compact digital disc available on the market in early 1983 for the Mac team, and the music was as constant as the air conditioning. At the same time, someone else would play the concert-level Bosendorfer piano in the corner. Parked against one wall was Steve's motorcycle. A little Heathkit robot would scamper out in the hall from the software room. The scene looked more like a college rec room than a corporate product development center.

This was the post-Beatles generation making their contribution. The maverick stance, coupled with the peace and love sentiments these kids had absorbed, was now something they carried with them, sewn into the lining of their coat, in a phrase Tom Wolfe once used to describe how people who settled in this mesmerizing Valley were nevertheless not completely remade by its prosperity. The sixties ethic was something these kids had come to later than the Wood-stock and Haight-Ashbury crowd and so they had absorbed the de-cade's ideals without being scarred by its tragedies. Their abiding faith was in the power of tools made available to everybody. One person, one computer was the route by which they planned to change the world.

For this team, work became, as Picasso once said, the ultimate seduction. The Mac team thought of the product every minute they were awake. And they often worked through the night, forgoing sleep in a creative frenzy to resolve a technical enigma. When I would visit them, their hair was often mussed, their faces often creased with sleepiness, but their eyes always seemed to glisten with excitement. It was because Steve made the Macintosh *their* product. "Macintosh is the product I want for myself," Andy Hertzfeld, twenty-eight, employee number 8 and one of the Valley's best software wizards, would say. "It's the product I want my best friends to have even if they aren't rich enough to afford today's personal computers."

Steve and I would often venture back into the "fishbowl"—the nickname for the software room where some ten young engineers could be found leaning over their computers in small, open cubicles.

"Hi, Andy," I greeted Hertzfeld one night, "what are you working on?"

"This is really neat, you gotta see this," he said, pulling me over.

Andy was the architect for the Mac's systems software. He was a short, heavyset fellow with tousled hair who often wore a rumpled sweatshirt and faded jeans, and paraded around the building barefoot. He had just come up with a new refinement of the computer's scroll bars. Andy painted an explanation of how they worked in the air, swirling his hands and waving his arms in excitement.

Most documents, of course, are too large to fit in their entirety on a computer screen. The scroll bars, along the right and bottom of the Macintosh computer screen, allow a user to effortlessly move around a file. By dragging along the bars a white box—called a "thumb" for thumbing through the documents—you could see different parts of the document. The feature users now take for granted took Andy months of 100-watt effort and a trunkload of failed attempts at writing code until he got the program working.

"Hey, what's that?" Steve asked, coming over after a chat with another engineer.

"Steve, we got this really neat thing," Andy replied. "I want you to look at the way we're doing scroll bars."

"That's really neat! Look everybody, come on over," shouted Steve. "Look what Andy's done! It's the greatest thing I've ever seen."

A cadre of the engineers crowded around Andy's cubicle for a personal demonstration. They would get just as excited as Andy and Steve. Andy had scroll bars running on the Mac back in 1981, yet he still was refining more than a dozen subtle details to get to Steve's "insanely great" stage.

"Boy," another chimed in, "we're really going to make it!"

I left the building just before midnight to drive home in the darkness. In the background, I could hear the music blasting and I could see that the only fully lit building on the campus was Mac. Every other building was closed down for the night.

Steve was their inspirational leader, and they idolized him. In a story on Silicon Valley, Tom Wolfe once wrote about what psychologists call "the halo effect." "People with the halo effect seem to know exactly what they're doing and, moreover, make you want to admire them for it. They make you see the halos over their heads." That was Steve's power—to make people believe in him.

Some of the Mac team were his best friends—like Bill Atkinson and Burrell Smith and Andy. Steve longed for the good old days, reminiscing about what it was like when he and Woz started in the garage. And the Macintosh team was the good old days resurrected for what had become a large, successful company.

Steve made every decision, from whether the computer should have a fan in it to cool it down (he opposed them because they were too noisy) to what final shape it should take: he wanted it to have a forehead and be human-looking. He once admitted to hating the Lisa because the top of the screen and the top of the machine were almost even, giving Lisa's face "a Cro-Magnon look," he said.

He didn't create anything really, but he created everything. And when his decisions didn't make sense, members of the team would make others behind his back. "The Macintosh," Steve would say, "is inside of me, and I've got to get it out and turn it into a product."

In the midst of Apple's problems toward the end of 1983, Mac gave us great excitement and great hope. No matter how problematic the competition or our internal troubles, my spirit rebounded when I strolled into the Macintosh Building. We knew we would soon bear witness to an event of historical proportions. It would be the birth of Steve's great dream. It was a product that was the collective personification of a small group of pioneers who were about to open a new frontier for individuals. The product changed their lives, and we believed it would start to change the lives of others as soon as it debuted at our shareholders' meeting on January 23.

Much of the Macintosh's technology wasn't invented in the building. Indeed, the Macintosh, like the Lisa before it, was largely a conduit for technology developed at Xerox PARC (Palo Alto Research Center). PARC was a haven for Ph.D. scientists and computer science intellectuals who probed the frontiers of personal computers and artificial intelligence.

Back in the early 1970s, Xerox lured as many as a hundred computer scientists to its laid-back West Coast laboratory by generously lavishing research grants on them with few restrictions. At PARC, some of the world's top-class technology experts slouched in bean bags on the floor surrounded by circular blackboards dreaming up the future of computing. The group constructed the Alto, one of the first personal computers, as early as 1972, five years before Woz created a preassembled computer circuit board dubbed the Apple I in Steve's garage and six years before Apple Computer was incorporated as a company.

Prodded by others who knew firsthand about the center's work, Steve was invited to visit Xerox PARC in 1979. What he saw amazed him. He recognized almost instantly what Xerox itself apparently hadn't: that PARC's ideas and concepts might completely change the entire computer industry if they could be channeled into real products. Xerox scientists were working on a visual, intuitive way for users to interact with computers. While the personal computer had become a guilt-free slave which could follow rigid commands, the user-friendly approach reduced to near zero the frustrations of working a computer.

In some ways, Steve was not unlike the great inventor and conceptual thinker Thomas Edison, who only accepted praise with great reluctance. "Actually," retorted Edison, "I'm a good sponge. I absorb ideas and put them to use. Most of my ideas first belonged to people who didn't bother to develop them."

California was still a prospector's dream. Inventors could be heroes, but the real fame and rewards went to those who had the ability to sniff out the right people, the best ideas, and the sharpest products, and to nourish them along. No one was better at this than Steve. I remember once going with him to visit Dr. Edwin Land, the inventor and founder of Polaroid Corp., at his laboratory in Cambridge, Massachusetts. "The world is like this fertile field that's waiting to be harvested," Land told us. "The seeds have been planted, and what I do is go out and help plant more seeds and harvest them."

Riding back to our hotel in a taxi, Steve turned to me and said, "Yeah, that's just how I feel. It's like when I walk in a room and I want to talk about a product that hasn't been invented yet. I can see the product as if it's sitting there right in the center of the table. It's like what I've got to do is materialize it and bring it to life, harvest it just as Dr. Land said."

Steve lacked the engineering ability to create a product, but he instinctively knew what needed to be created to succeed. He insisted that Apple build the Lisa and incorporate into it many of the innovative ideas he glimpsed at PARC. Initially, Steve tried to negotiate with Xerox to gain a license on their innovative ideas. Discussions were held on the possibility of our acquiring certain technology from Xerox. Nothing came of these discussions. Steve later hired a few people from Xerox PARC, including Lawrence Tesler, who had demonstrated the concepts to Steve and others. Tesler left Xerox in May of 1980 and became a key member of the Lisa design team, which Steve wanted to head. But Mike Scott, then Apple's chief executive, considered Steve too young, too inexperienced, and too difficult to work with to be entrusted with such a massive project.

Steve always resented the decision, but could do nothing about it. Instead, he latched on to the Macintosh project, and had become critical of many of the things the Lisa group was doing. He thought of the group as a bunch of former minicomputer engineers whose large computer experience only biased them to make things far more complicated than needed. Lisa, Steve thought, might be a fine product for big corporations, but it wouldn't change the world the way he wanted. It was the Model A of the personal computer business. In the "one person, one computer" religion at Apple, "big minis" were pure heresy. The lines had been drawn from the start.

Steve sorely desired to create the Model T. His goal was to make Lisa technology available to the masses, to provide 70 percent of

Lisa's capability for 20 percent of the price. Not only would it be affordable, personal, small in size so you could lug it around with you. It would be simple, too.

All personal computers, including the Apple II, demanded that users spend hours learning how to use them. You couldn't take one out of the box, set it up, and put it to work paying bills, writing reports, crunching numbers. The Macintosh, however, was to be the first crankless computer—like the crankless automobile, a product that could be set up and used almost immediately.

Like Henry Ford, who offered the Model T in any color you wanted as long as it was black, Steve insisted on selling the Macintosh in only one configuration. That was essential to bring mass production to personal computers, to enable millions of people to afford to enter a new era of personal computing. Variety only complicated things. Steve would decide what people needed. He would make the computer a closed box—so closed that no one would be able to open it without a special tool. If they did, Apple would void the product's warranty. Steve insisted on the restriction because he believed that software, not hardware, would become more important in the computer industry. Therefore, he reasoned, it wasn't necessary to have access to the computer's innards to plug cards and other devices into it. He insisted that no cursor keys be placed on the keyboard so that people would be forced to use the mouse instead. Reliance on the mouse was so important because it replaced complex command key sequences with a more intuitive gesture of the hand. Steve remained the final arbiter, sifting through the technology and giving the Macintosh, in the end, his own signature.

The Macintosh leaned heavily on the Lisa's technology yet without the Lisa's heavy price tag.

Tradeoffs were inevitable, and we would speak of them often during our long chats together. The Macintosh had to have a smaller monitor, only one disk drive, and less memory because of its expense. The cost of a 128k chip, the largest then commercially available in large quantities, was $25.50. The only way to put more memory into the machine was to plug in more expensive 128k chips. Within a year, the cost of the same chip dropped to about $11. Today, it costs $1.50.

But the high cost of memory meant that the Mac pirates had to write elegantly tight computer code—not unlike poetry, which tolerates only the perfect word or sparest image. Andy Hertzfeld had to write some eighty pages of computer code—a task that took months —simply to explore all the scroll-bar alternatives before getting them down to twenty tight pages. "Elegantly simple" was Steve's standard for everything the pirates created.

Steve insisted that his engineers rewrite their computer code to get it tighter and tighter so more capabilities could be fitted into the Macintosh's 128k of ROM (read only memory). ROM is akin to a phonograph record. You can retrieve information from it but you can't add new information on it. RAM (the random access memory) is more like a cassette tape. You can add, change, or simply retrieve information from it.

Few thought it possible to compress as much capability in a graphics-based system with such economy of space. It required the Macintosh team to write code in either assembly or machine-level languages, a tortuous and time-consuming task. "You have to essentially throw out nine tenths of your work to get the one tenth that was really good," said Burrell Smith, the Macintosh's hardware wizard.

Steve provided phenomenal inspiration and demanding standards to get his team to do such things. He pushed them to their limits, until even they were amazed at how much they were able to accomplish. He possessed an innate sense of knowing exactly how to extract the best from people. He cajoled them by admitting his own vulnerabilities; he rebuked them until they, too, shared his uncompromising ethic; he stroked them with pride and praise, like an approving father.

He could celebrate their accomplishments with unusual flair. When the first prototype was finished, Steve uncorked bottles of champagne to toast the achievement. When Christmas of 1983 arrived, he rented the main ballroom of the classically ornate St. Francis Hotel in San Francisco for a black-tie party that featured Strauss waltzes by the San Francisco Symphony. And when the product finally shipped, Steve laid plans for a huge trailer truck to pull behind the Macintosh Building with one hundred computers bearing engraved nameplates for each member of the team. A lasting tribute was his order that the signatures of forty-seven Macintosh creators be embossed on the inside of the computer's back panel.

Yet, Steve also wouldn't hesitate to call their work "a piece of shit" and throw it back at them in an angry rage. Their faces would grow numb, until they could gather just enough energy to move to a chair, sit down, and start again. I was amazed at his behavior even when his criticism was correct. A few hours later they'd be back at the computer keyboard, starting to rewrite all the code over—knowing that they had probably two hundred or more hours of work ahead of them before they could show it to Steve again.

Steve would routinely walk up to someone, disarm him by saying, "Hi! What are you doing?" The person, who might have been up all night working on it for five nights in a row, would explain, only to get a sharp reprimand from a piqued Steve.

"Well, you're doing it all wrong," Steve would say. "Here's what we want to do. . . ." He would then launch into a long, technical harangue. "Why can't you do it right?" he'd demand to know. "It's just not good enough. You know you can do better."

Little details obsessed Steve. Time and time again, the engineers would come back to him, saying they couldn't design a piece of plastic to conform to the odd shape of the Macintosh computer case, which Steve insisted had to be all one piece. Its construction represented a manufacturing breakthrough.

"Steve, we can't do it. It's too complex," one of the industrial design engineers told him.

"I don't buy that," he snapped. "If you can't do it, I'll find someone else who can."

Eventually, it was done—but it took something like fifteen separate forming tools to make one piece of injection molding for the case.

When the Apple II engineers insisted they couldn't inexpensively design a mouse that could be used for both the Apple II and the Macintosh computer, he got Woz to do it, and it was done. When the Apple IIc was being built, Steve was adamant that they build into the machine AppleTalk—which allows users to connect their computers together into networks so they can send documents electronically to each other. The engineers groused that they couldn't get the product out on time, that it would cost too much, and that there wasn't enough real estate on the computer's board to install it.

In his quest for perfection, Steve put many people on the defensive. He'd fix his intense, dark eyes on you in an intimidating stare, focusing his eyes in and out. It was a stare that bore down on you, froze you like a 100-ampere headlight, a what-makes-you-think-you're-so-smart look. He could inspire people, and he could make them sweat. He could tell you things that only you knew about yourself. At one moment, he could drain all your self-esteem. At the very next, he could praise you, offering just a few complimentary crumbs that somehow made all the angst worthwhile.

At Pepsi, such behavior would not have been tolerated or understood. But it worked at Apple because Steve was Steve. He was a world figure, with incredible accomplishments to his name. One immediately thought of the impresario of an opera company, some-one whose changing moods and manners were hard to deal with. Yet everyone respected him and would nearly kill to receive only a few approving words from the master.

He instinctively knew how to reach people. One time, his fourth-grade teacher, Teddy Hill, came to visit Steve at Apple. She brought with her a photograph of the class on Hawaiian Day. Steve apparently showed up without his Hawaiian T-shirt, yet there he was in the middle of the picture proudly dressed in one. Teddy lovingly recalled that he had conned the shirt off the back of one of the other children. It was typical of Steve.

Outsiders had just as difficult a time with him. Steve would keep people who traveled from the East Coast for a meeting with him waiting for literally hours. It would drive some of the public relations people from Regis McKenna, our outside media relations consultant, into fits.

"I don't want to talk to them," he'd tell Jane Anderson, who personally handled all of Steve's and my press interviews and speech engagements.

"But they've been here for three hours waiting to see you," Jane would say.

"Well, I just don't feel like talking to them. Tell them to go back, and I'll talk to them another time."

They would go away, some enraged and others incredulous. But somehow, Apple went on and the people almost always came back.

Like everyone else at Apple, I accepted his behavior because Steve was unique. People made exceptions for him. They held him to the standard of a young, smart kid; they didn't really view him as an adult. Yet the few people who stood up to him earned his respect. If people caved in and became intimidated by him, he would lose all interest in them.

None of Steve's behavior alarmed me, maybe because I so clearly saw my younger self in him. People had often found me difficult to deal with during my early days at Pepsi, too. I never verbally attacked anyone, but I insisted on only the best from them, just as Steve did. So I tried to coach Steve the way Chuck Mangold coached me at Pepsi.

"You've got to learn to hold back some things," I told him. "All you're going to do is cause a lot of unnecessary frustration which isn't constructive."

"You're right," he said. "I know it. Keep talking to me, you're absolutely right. I know I shouldn't do that."

He'd promise to be better. But then he'd fall back into his old ways. Yet when he looked at me, it was a look of admiration, a what-can-I-learn look that was terribly gripping. In Steve's eyes, I couldn't do anything wrong.

I felt I could give him something he couldn't get anywhere else. He lacked real experience, and from experience you gain wisdom. No matter how smart or brilliant he was, he didn't have the advantage of wisdom. I became a teacher to him.

He was a teacher to me as well, instructing me about technology and computers. I'd hear him out on a lot of his ideas. Some of them were harebrained, and some of them were superb. We were walking down Bandley Drive one day when he told me he had the ideal solution to the nuclear imbalance between the United States and the Soviet Union.

"We should let the Soviets come over and put an atomic bomb of the highest capacity right in the center of Washington, D.C.," he said. "And they'd be in control of that one. Then we would go and build one in Moscow and we would be in control of that. We wouldn't need missiles anymore because if one of us blew up their bomb, the other would blow up theirs. That would solve the whole problem."

"Steve," I said, "that's ridiculous."

Yet, for every zany idea of his, he'd come up with a gem. It was Steve who foresaw the need to build one of the world's most automated manufacturing plants for personal computers, using state-of-the-art manufacturing techniques. It was Steve who immediately realized the potential for computers in schools, and it was he who thought of the idea to give Apple II computers free to 9,000 California schools.

He was the only person I ever met whom I could speak with on multiple levels. We felt we were living life on several different planes at all times. We spoke, thought, and worked in synchronization.

Every once in a while, Steve would pause, press his fingertips together, and muse in his boylike voice, "I'm having the 'funnest' time in my whole life. I am so happy that you decided to come to Apple. You're the best person that Apple ever could have chosen."

"This is the happiest I've ever been in my whole life," I said. "I never dreamed that Apple could be as much fun as it is, and I just love working with you, Steve." We had an incredible friendship.

Unlike the Ph.D. computer scientists at Xerox PARC, the Macintosh creators were very young, passionate artists. It may seem ironic that people largely without the discipline and training of computer scientists were able to seize a technology and make it commercial. But imagination can often triumph over hard fact. Futurist Arthur C. Clarke once said that it is not the one who knows most about a topic, and is the acknowledged master of his field, who can give the most reliable pointers to its future. Too great a burden of knowledge, he explained, can clog the wheels of imagination.

No such burden existed in the Macintosh Building. The Mac team acted as much on faith as it did on logic. Some of them looked so young that they wouldn't be allowed a drink at a bar. That's one of the reasons for its success. The Macintosh wouldn't be made by hundreds of engineers; it was started by a core group of about fifteen people who began in a cramped office more like a four-bedroom apartment a half-mile from the main Apple campus. By the time we launched the computer, there were not many more than one hundred people in the entire group, including all the marketing, finance, and manufacturing engineers who developed Macintosh.

Steve wanted Macintosh to have the most phenomenal introduction of any product ever launched in the world. "Mac deserves it," he said. "This is the best product that I've ever seen in my whole life and it's got to have the best introduction that any product has ever had."

We wanted to make a major event out of it—and the advertising would be a key part of the plan. I had been flabbergasted at the amount of public attention Apple was able to generate even when it didn't have an event. When Lisa was launched before I joined the company, Apple had received incredible publicity. For Macintosh, we wanted something on a much grander scale.

The decision to introduce Mac with a promotional splash, however, tied in to our discussions on how to price the product. I urged a higher price to support a dramatic marketing effort; Steve, on the other hand, was under pressure from the Macintosh engineers to come out with a lower list price, a price closer to what the masses could afford.

Originally, Macintosh was supposed to be a $1,000 computer. When it came close to production, everyone realized that a price of $1,995 was more realistic.

I thought we should charge an additional $500, however, to offset the cost of a huge promotional effort. For the first 120 days, product would be in short supply until we ramped up to full production in the Macintosh factory. We could get the product well positioned in the first quarter when demand outstripped supply, and we could have the option of lowering the price later on. I felt we should treat advertising as just another part of the product's development cost.

Steve and I debated the issue for weeks and weeks. I don't think a day went by when we didn't talk about it. Even when we disagreed, it was as if we were a single debater working through the thesis and antithesis to reach the best conclusion. Steve feared that at $2,495 the Macintosh would draw criticism from Apple's loyal followers, the computer enthusiasts, the hackers, and others who would think it too expensive.

"Well, then, you can't have any advertising campaign," I said. "You can't have it both ways. Without the money, there is no advertising and no event."

"We've got to have an event," Steve insisted.

"Then, it's going to cost $2,495."

He edged back and forth. One day, he would insist that it be priced at $2,000; another, he would agree with me on the higher figure. Sometimes we reversed roles, with me making a case for the lower price. Never would I have felt comfortable switching positions at Pepsi; when I reached a conclusion, I argued strenuously for it to Pearson and Kendall. Yet Steve and I enjoyed taking one position, arguing it as persuasively as possible, and then turning around and adopting another argument. We would constantly joust over what each of us thought about new ideas, projects, and colleagues.

Ultimately, we agreed to put a $2,495 price tag on the Macintosh. We couldn't ramp up to full production for a full six months, so there was little risk of selling fewer computers at the higher price, anyway. It was more important to deliver Macintosh with an ever-rippling splash. If Macintosh failed, there might never be another chance to prove that great individual achievement can outmaneuver the American corporate establishment.

For months, Chiat/Day had been working on an advertising strategy for the Macintosh that transformed the computer's creators into folk heroes. The campaign was to be focused around conversations with Mac team members who explained how important the product was to them. Our agency came back with touching footage of impassioned young people talking about the Macintosh.

I knew it would play well in Silicon Valley, but I doubted a campaign of that kind would sell a lot of computers in the real world. I didn't think it could reach East Coast America or Midwest America. Steve and I thought that if the product was great enough to change the world, then it ought to have an introductory commercial that was great enough to change people's minds. So we asked Chiat/Day to see if there was a way to take advantage of the fact that 1984 was the year that George Orwell chose for his famous prophecy of a totalitarian regime in which Big Brother controls all of man's actions and thoughts.

A few weeks later, Steve Hayden, a Chiat/Day copywriter, came back to the conference room in the Sobrato Building. Mike Murray, the Macintosh's marketing manager, was there. So was the rest of the Chiat/Day creative team.

"We've listened to your directive, and we think we have really come up with something great," said Lee Clow, a lean and lanky bearded man who was Chiat/Day's executive creative director. "You may think it's a little far out, but you have to hear it through because we think this may be the greatest commercial that we've ever done."

I'd heard this claim many times before and learned to greet it with great skepticism. He then turned it over to Steve Hayden, a bright man with a gentle personality who is always puffing away at a cigarette. Steve pulled out the commercial's storyboard, a series of drawings that allow the advertising world to convey a visual impression of the finished commercial. I had seen hundreds of these in my career. But never before had I seen one like this. Steve pulled out the first one and it showed zombie-looking fellows in pajama suits, chained together and walking down a corridor.

Then, he said, displaying another storyboard frame, it goes through a scene where you come into a large room and find a dramatic contrast between Big Brother on a screen, lecturing these seated zombies, and Apple, represented in the form of a heroine who is going to rush into the room with a baseball bat to smash the screen and save the day.

"That's going to announce Macintosh as this big event that's going to save the world from having to become inundated with all this boring sort of stuff that IBM represents," he said.

When the presentation was over, Steve and I just looked at each other. Someone in the room had shivers.

"That's weird," Steve said.

"I've never seen anything like this in my whole life," I added. "Can you really shoot this? Can you make this look like a commercial? It looks pretty hard to implement or execute."

"Look," Lee said, "we know we can do it. We've got exactly the right person to do it."

Chiat/Day had picked British director Ridley Scott, whose movie credits included *Alien* and *Bladerunner,* films that featured unusual and dramatic lighting effects. It would be one of the most expensive commercials ever made—the Chiat/Day team estimated it would cost between $400,000 and $600,000. The bigger issue was the cost of time to run it and how it would be perceived by the public. Chiat/Day proposed running the sixty-second commercial during the Super Bowl—at a likely cost of $1 million. What we were looking for was a blockbuster that would shake the world. What we didn't want was a flop that would backfire on us and distract from the introduction of the Macintosh.

"Well, John, what are we going to do?" asked Murray.

"I think we ought to build the commercial," I said, "but we're going to reserve the decision to run it until later on. The big decision in my mind is if Apple comes out of this quarter with a real sales disaster, then I don't know how we can possibly come out with a commercial that is this outrageous. People will think we've lost our minds. If we can get some real momentum in Apple II sales during Christmas, then that puts a whole different light on things."

We still, of course, had only one commercial.

"Once '1984' gets everyone's attention that there is a phenomenal new product, I think we've got to tell them why the product is phenomenal. The first big commercial doesn't show the product. We've got to follow with product-oriented commercials and we've got to do neat things with the product."

"Product commercials are boring," said one. "Yeah," chimed in another, "we don't want boring commercials. This is a great product. We're not going to have boring commercials."

"Well, who said anything about boring commercials?" I asked. "If the product's so phenomenal, why can't the product be the hero of the commercial, and we can show off its graphics? It must be able to do something that would look exciting on television.

"Is it worth exploring doing something like a Pepsi Challenge? There we had a better product than Coke, and we got credibility for it because we let people see the difference, and it wasn't just the manufacturer shouting it."

The media portray the news in black-and-white terms, so we needed a campaign that would focus on a two-horse race to leverage off of Apple's underdog status. Dozens of other computer companies were coming out with products and I was afraid we were going to get lost in the crowd. If we could create a two-horse race between us and IBM, we might be able to convince people that there are really only two computer companies competing in the marketplace. In any large consumer industry, few people remember the third- or fourth-largest competitor.

More often than not, there's only room for two big brands, whether it's Coke and Pepsi, Hertz and Avis, Budweiser and Miller, or hopefully IBM and Apple. We had to become the number-two player on the basis of innovation because IBM, as the industry leader, could leverage its traditional strengths of size and customer satisfaction. The advertising had to stake out our role as industry innovator in this two-horse race. Perhaps we could even stimulate a public computer war, not unlike the Cola Wars, because of the huge consumer interest in personal computers.

No less crucial, though, Apple hadn't yet realized that as a billion-dollar corporation it had immense advantages we hadn't exploited. It's almost impossible for a company with sales of $50 million or even $200 million to invest in the kinds of effective television advertising campaigns you need if you're going to leave any impression at all. Yet, much of the clutter in advertising came from computer companies which lacked the advantage of our size. So leveraging our larger resources was critical to raising the stakes to play in the game.

We got our first glimpse of what would eventually help us make Macintosh a milestone product in early November when Chiat/Day's team of copywriters and account executives returned to Apple to show us the result of their effort.

An enthusiastic Lee Clow stood up and said, "We have the most fabulous commercial that Chiat/Day has ever done."

During the intervening weeks, Chiat/Day had shot the commercial at Shepperton Studios in London with a cast of 200 people, including members of a British skinhead sect. Additional amateurs with full heads of hair were paid $125 a day to shave their heads and stand by for the week-long filming. A professional female discus thrower was recruited as the star.

We watched, our eyes glued to the video monitor at the end of the room, as the commercial began. With a thundering noise in the background, bald, emaciated figures marched along in baggy, colorless clothing. You could hear their cadence as they marched single file through long glass tubes, not unlike those in the Charles de Gaulle Airport in Paris.

The group trudged into a dimly lit, cavernous hall, showered in cinéma vérité sepia colors. The scene then showed all of them sitting down on hard wooden benches, surrounded by armed guards with Darth Vader helmets and clubs. You could clearly see this was a controlled society where people no longer had their own thoughts. Then, it cut to the black-and-white screen all of them were impassively watching, with a narrator talking in Newspeak.

My friends, the voice announced in an authoritative tone, *each of you is a single cell in the great body of the State. And today, that great body has purged itself of parasites. We have triumphed over the unprincipled dissemination of facts. The thugs and wreckers have been cast out. And the poisonous weeds of disinformation have been consigned to the dustbin of history. Let each and every cell rejoice! For today we celebrate the first, glorious anniversary of the Information Purification Directive. We have created, for the first time in all history, a garden of pure ideology, where each worker may bloom secure from the pests of contradictory and confusing truths. Our Unification of Thought is a more powerful weapon than any fleet or army on earth. We are one people. With one will. One resolve. One cause. Our enemies shall talk themselves to death. And we will bury them with their own confusion.*

The words appeared at the bottom of the screen, beneath an all-powerful and all-knowing image of Big Brother. Then, all of a sudden, the commercial cut to a youthful, athletic figure running toward the screen from the end of the hall in full, living color. She was dressed in bright red shorts and running shoes, with a white Macintosh T-shirt. The commercial built drama during her entry by cutting back and forth between the screen, the zombie-like audience, and this young blond, tanned woman who carried a sledgehammer with her. Finally, she stops in front of the screen, swirls the sledgehammer over her head, and hurls it into the screen.

The screen explodes in a blinding flash of light. Then, as the camera pans the crowd, their mouths open wide as they sit mesmerized by the explosion, a voice-over says: "On January 24th, Apple Computer will introduce Macintosh. (Pause) 1984 won't be like *1984.*"

When it ended, Steve broke a few seconds of dead silence in the room.

"Wow!" he shouted. "That is incredible."

He was beside himself with joy. It had all the arrogance, flamboyance, and outrageousness that appealed to him.

"That is just an incredible commercial," I nodded, smiling with satisfaction.

"It is just awesome," Steve said. "It's so radically different from what everyone else is doing."

"Are people going to think that we've lost our minds?" I wondered. "Are we going to blow the opportunity by getting so caught up in the theatrics of the commercial that people will forget the product?"

Everyone in the room was enthusiastic about it, yet we were scared of it, too. It was a stunning commercial, but it was a minute of advertising that broke all sorts of rules. It never showed the product. It mentioned Apple Computer only once. It was possible for viewers to leave this commercial without even knowing that Apple made computers.

Yet it captured the spirit of the product and how revolutionary it was. And it cleverly played off of the public's fear of computers. By and large, most people *were* intimidated by the personal computer. They were machines, many thought, that could control our lives, take over our jobs, invade our privacy. The commercial poked fun at these fears, making it okay for someone who didn't fit into the existing computer world to at least try it.

"But you know," I said, "we haven't made the decision whether we're going to run it yet. That depends on how we do for this Christmas selling season, and it depends on getting the Macintosh all together."

"Steve," I asked, "how do things look on Mac?"

"It's going to be real hard," he said, "but I think we're going to do it. We're having trouble on the finder, but I think we're going to be able to do it."

The finder was a novel piece of software that made the Macintosh as convenient as a desktop, but infinitely more useful. It transformed the computer's screen into a simulated desktop over which were sprawled documents and folders. By clicking on the folder icons, the user could electronically open up on a whole library of folders as if they existed in paper form on top of a desk.

"Well, sales are picking up on the IIe," I said. "It's looking a lot better, so we'll just have to see."

By this time, Chiat/Day had locked us in as commercial number six during the second half of the Super Bowl.

Steve also suggested we show the commercial to Apple's board of directors, who traditionally have played a major role at the company, far more than the perfunctory boards of many companies. It was a small board with only seven members, compared to the dozen or more people on other boards. Each of them was a power broker in his own right, with enormous experience that contrasted beautifully with Apple's youth. Dr. Henry E. Singleton was a legend in corporate America, having built from scratch Teledyne, Inc., one of the most successful diversified corporations in the country. Arthur Rock was similarly a legend in venture-capital circles. He was one of the first to invest in Silicon Valley, and his investments in Fairchild Semiconductor, Intel, and Apple made him millions. Peter O. Crisp, managing partner in Rockefeller's Venrock Associates, was an extremely bright and insightful executive from the East Coast. And Philip S. Schlein, then chief executive of Macy's California, brought excellent retail marketing expertise to the group. The others were Jobs, Markkula, and I.

Our regularly scheduled board meeting was only a few days away, so we arranged for Mike Murray to present the commercial as marketing manager of the Macintosh. Murray explained to the board how we were trying to position the Macintosh as an appliance to appeal to vast numbers of consumers—not only computer and gadget enthusiasts. That approach in itself was a bold step. No other company had thought to bring high tech down to the user. People, he said, were becoming intimidated by computers, and we needed something to stand out from the clutter of competing advertising messages.

"We needed to convey that a real revolution was about to take place in the industry. So we looked for the most revolutionary thing we could possibly think of, and here it is," he said, as the video clip filled a screen.

Sixty seconds later, a chill silence blanketed the room. One director leaned his head on his hands and just looked down at the table. Another stared in disbelief. The others just looked at each other, dazed expressions on their faces.

"Steve," one asked, "you're not really going to run that thing, are you?"

Most of them felt it was the worst commercial they had ever

seen. Not a single outside board member liked it. Murray was visibly crushed, absolutely devastated. He looked as if his whole life was going down before his eyes.

"We haven't made a final decision on it yet," Steve said, nonplussed, "but we had planned to run it on the Super Bowl."

"How much does that cost?" one director asked.

"About a million dollars," Murray replied.

"Oh, my God!" screeched another.

"John," a third said, "you're the advertising expert. What do you think of it?"

"Well, it's the most outrageous commercial I've ever seen. But we need advertising that is as revolutionary and awesome as the Macintosh itself. I think that you have got to delegate the final decision to management, and we have to decide whether the commercial runs or not."

"What do you think we ought to do?" Steve asked me after the meeting.

"I think we're going to look real silly if we don't get a good quarter together, and we don't know the answer to that yet."

"Maybe," Steve said, "we're going too far on this thing."

We both decided to tell the agency to try to sell our one minute of time on the Super Bowl. If they couldn't sell it, we would run the commercial but only if we had a good Christmas selling season. Chiat/Day, however, could get little more than half the $1 million we paid for the network time, so we held on to the Super Bowl time slot.

In early January, things looked bright. Our pricing and advertising strategy for the IIe worked handsomely. We shipped a record 110,000 computers in December alone, some $160 million in revenues. Lisa, although not strong, had picked up a little bit. IBM's PCjr. was getting devastating reviews from critics who among other things attacked its awkward Chiclet keyboard.

Macintosh, no less, was coming together on schedule. The entire company pitched in to help. Apple II people, usually in competition with Mac and Lisa staffers, volunteered to work over the Christmas holidays to pack Mac in boxes and help ship them out to dealers so they could be in the stores on the day we planned to introduce the computer. Only part of our new automated factory in Fremont was ready, so Apple II staffers began stuffing software and instruction manuals into Macintosh boxes, too.

Buoyed by the confluence of good news, we had little doubt that we would run the commercial. "1984" was going to go on the air. The agency actually had put the commercial on the air in late 1983, probably at 3:00 a.m. in some little town, just to get it into the advertising competitions for the year.

We had an incredible product to offer the world and we wanted the world to know it. Mac used a 68000 microprocessor, the same 32-bit microprocessor used in Lisa. And as Steve said, "It eats 8088s for breakfast." He believed that just as the 5¼-inch drive was an innovation in the seventies, the 3½-inch drive would become the disk of the 1980s. It was safer, sturdier, and could store over 400k bytes of information on one side of a disk that can be put into your pocket. It had over twice the number of dots on its screen of any current generation personal computer, meaning that its resolution and clarity were better than any other computer. And all of the power fitted into a box one third the size and weight of an IBM PC.

The ad ran during the third quarter of the Super Bowl as the Los Angeles Raiders pulled in front of the Washington Redskins. Even the sports announcers lost their composure. One said, "Wow, what was that?" Newspapers began writing up things that asked what were you doing when the "1984" commercial ran?

It became a phenomenon overnight. The commercial sparked widespread controversy. When word got out that we had spent nearly $1.6 million on a single sixty-second commercial, irate shareholders began firing off letters. They asked what right I had to take the company's money and plow it into something that no one at Apple had any experience with. Other so-called advertising gurus contended the commercial was utterly alien to the product. But the commercial also was the basis of news stories on all three networks, on nearly fifty local news shows, and in countless newspapers and magazines. Some 43 million people saw the film, even though we only paid for it to run once. It would go on to win the Grand Prix at Cannes—the first American commercial to do so in years—as well as thirty-four other international and national advertising awards.

I was Pepsi's new oddity: their first MBA. I spent time in Phoenix as a driver/salesman on a Pepsi truck. (*Inset*) Chuck Mangold, my mentor.

Inspecting the Frito-Lay line in Mexico. Ron Bellamy (*foreground*), the financial wizard; (*inset*) Harry Deckard, our manufacturing sage. People assumed I must have been sent into this wilderness to mend my maverick ways.

5

(*Above*) Relaxing in St. James, Long Island, with
my children, Meg and Jack, in 1964.   (*Right*) The
PepsiCo conference table's 21-foot-long surface was
polished to look more like glass than the rare burl of
Carpathian elm.

6

7

After a Nielsen meeting over market share
figures, at which careers were made or
destroyed, Don Kendall (*foreground*)
worked the room like a politician.
(*At left*) As senior vice president of Pepsi,
I was on the cover of *Business Week* at the
age of thirty-four.

8

Marketing is theater.

9

10

11

I fell in love with Leezy and realized we could never have a real life together while I trotted the globe for Pepsi's International Foods. (*Left*) In Kendall's library. Kendall convinced me my career was not as an architect but as a marketer.

13

Gerry Roche, the only headhunter in the world whose calls I would take.

12

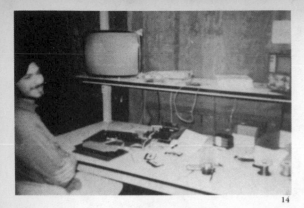

15

(*Left*) Steve Jobs, 1976. In six years, Apple moved from his parents' garage to the ranks of the Fortune 500. (*Above*) Woz, a self-taught engineer then at Hewlett-Packard, tries out a blue box.

14

16

The original Apple logo in 1977. (*Right*) Building the world's first Apple, which Steve Jobs named Apple I.

17

18

19

Mike Scott, the new startup's first president, with Mike Markkula, Apple's unsung hero, its stabilizing force, and "fifth Beatle." (*Right*) Viewed from above, Apple's Bandley Drive campus looks not unlike a massive integrated circuit.

The Macintosh building. It had the intellectual feel of a
university, not a corporation.

Steve Jobs issued a challenge
that would haunt me for days:
"Do you want to spend the
rest of your life selling
sugared water or do you want
a chance to change the
world?"

My father was a proud, precise, and competitive man.

W. B. Smith, my grandfather, an inventor and irresistible raconteur, was a man of adventure.

My mother, an artist and eternal optimist, had a great influence on me.

Me, age five, in 1944.

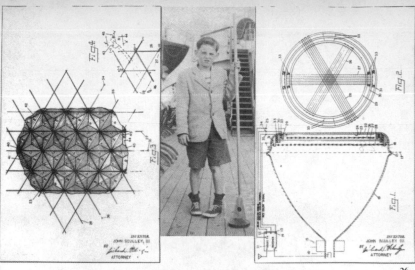

At age fourteen, in 1954, my fascination with electronics led me to invent a color television tube. A competing patent, filed only a few weeks before mine, was the forerunner of the technology that led to Sony's successful Trinitron tube.

(*Left to right*) Sean Sculley, my cousin, and my brothers Arthur and David with me in 1967. My single-minded concentration on success at Pepsi somehow caused me to discard my early interest in inventions and technologies.

1983. My first Apple badge. I left my old identity in a closet in Connecticut when I packed a bag of casual clothes without a single suit and flew west.

28

Do Not Disturb, Please!

29

Steve, me, and the Mac team gathered around the Bosendorfer piano. They called themselves the "Pirates" and proudly flew the skull-and-crossbones flag. (*Above, right*) Apple brings together a company of artists: Steve insisted that each of the Mac's creators autograph the inside of the original Macintosh case.

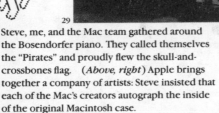

30

The original "1984" commercial television storyboard. The commercial had all the arrogance, flamboyance, and outrageousness that appealed to Steve. It captured the revolutionary spirit of Macintosh, "the computer for the rest of us."

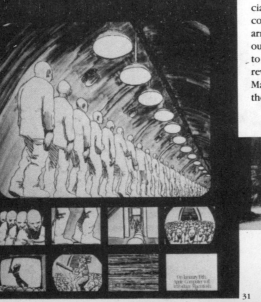

31

32   33

(*Left*) Introducing the Apple IIc right after the Mac introduction. Like
telephones and cars, computers would change the world, we thought.
(*Right*) Del Yocam, our general manager, me, and Steve Jobs at an Apple IIc
event. Our marketing events were described as religious revivals.

34   38

35   36   37   39

(*Above*) Sunrise in Hawaii, at the 1984 sales meeting. Steve and I had developed a
partnership and a friendship. It was a unique way to run a corporation. In November
Business Week called us the Dynamic Duo. Three months later we were a company
in trouble. Apple's outside directors: Dr. Henry E. Singleton (*top left*), a legend in
corporate America, who built Teledyne from scratch; Peter O. Crisp (*bottom left*),
managing partner in Rockefeller's Venrock Associates; Phil Schlein (*top right*), then
chief executive of Macy's California; and Arthur Rock (*bottom right*), one of the first
venture capitalists to invest in Silicon Valley.

40

41

(*Left*) I felt I could give Steve something he couldn't get
anywhere else: he lacked real experience, so I became a
teacher to him. He became a teacher to me as well, initiating
me in the magic of computers.   (*Right*) The automated
factory was almost a scene out of science fiction: machines
replicating machines: Macintoshes building Macintoshes.

Press conference (*left*) with Steve, winter 1985. Our troubles were just starting. (*Center*) Named "Adman of the Year" for 1984.   President Mitterrand (*right*) wanted to bring France to the forefront of the computer industry—by buying millions of Macs, we hoped.

(*Left*) We suffered a real credibility gap after our failure to deliver the promise of a Macintosh office in January 1985.

(*Left*) Our bid for Super Bowl fame: we made sure that every seat in the stadium had an Apple cushion that flashed over national television.   (*Above*) Apple Fellow Alan C. Kay. His job required him to be both a computer visionary and critic.

California JUN OPEN MAC CA 87

MS DOS Just say no.

I showed up in long woolen underwear and a painted face at our Halloween sales meeting in 1985. It was the first sign that the spirit of Apple hadn't died.

Bill Campbell

Jean-Louis Gassée and Al Eisenstat

Mike Spindler

Speaking in Sweden, 1987.

Debi Coleman

Dave Barram

What a group to lead Apple out of its quagmire! A soda pop executive from the East. An Ivy League football coach. A French intellectual. A seasoned attorney. A German conceptual thinker. A manufacturing whiz with an English literature background. And a Baptist philosopher.

55

56

57

58

Esther Dyson's February 1986 conference was something of a Trilateral Commission of personal computing. The industry heavies whose confidence I had to win were: (*top left*) Ed Esber of Ashton-Tate, (*bottom left*) Philippe Kahn of Borland, (*center*) Bill Gates of Microsoft and Esther Dyson, and (*right*) Mitch Kapor of Lotus.

59

60

(*Left*) Getting ready for the *Today Show* to spread the word that Apple's problems would not be fatal. Jane Anderson, my publicist, in the foreground.   (*Right*) In 1985 the news media widely portrayed me as the victor in a boardroom coup. Nothing could have been further from the truth.

61

62

63

(*Left*) Making my peanut butter and jelly sandwich for lunch.   (*Center*) My assistants Joe Hutsko and Nancy Kelly with me.   (*Right*) The turnaround taking hold: a chance to sign autographs at AppleWorld in 1987.

The power to be your best.™

64   65

(*Left*) At Apple's tenth anniversary party in January 1987, Del and I
present Mike Markkula and Woz with their ten-year pins.   (*Right*)
Apple Fellow Bill Atkinson, one of our most astute technologists,
receiving his hero's award medal. Bill is Apple's cosmic thinker.

66   67

(*Left*) Larry Tesler, now our vice president of advanced technology.
(*Right*) Nanette Buckhout, my executive assistant for more than a decade,
knew me nearly as well as I knew myself.

Inside Apple's creative services department.   68

We're back!

69

71

70

Leezy and me with Laura, and (*inset*)
Meg and Jack.

72

73

74

(*Left*) Woz had returned to Berkeley to complete his degree in electrical
engineering. Wanting to go incognito and being the practical joker that he
is, Steve enrolled as Rocky Raccoon Clark.   (*Right*) President Reagan gives
it a try.

It was about time a capitalist started a revolution.

Macintosh, 1984.   75

Lisa, 1983.   76

Macintosh II, 1987.   77

78

Twenty-first-century computer users may
have the "Knowledge Navigator," which
may become the tenth-generation
Macintosh. Grab the handles and drive into
the future. Document scanning, speech and
handwriting recognition replace keyboards
for data input.

79

(*Left*) A gift from students at Wharton.

The M.B.A. Students of
The Wharton School of the University of Pennsylvania
hereby declare
John Sculley III
Official Wharton Folk Hero
for his
Boggling Achievement
MBA
in Business Administration
April 1, 1985

80

81

The journey is the reward.

82

"I should like to rise and go / Where the golden apples grow." That line of poetry appeared next to my photograph in a book published back in 1944 when I was a child. I guess I finally understand what the line means!

Nothing could stop us. Not ourselves, not IBM. Not even gravity, it seemed. Not only did we understand each other, Steve and I rejoiced in our similar reactions to the world. We could complete each other's sentences because we were on the same wavelength. Steve would rouse me from sleep at 2:00 a.m. with a phone call to chat about an idea that suddenly crossed his mind. "Hi! It's me," he'd harmlessly say to the dazed listener, totally unaware of the time. I curiously had done the same in my Pepsi days. Steve would rip apart a presentation he had to give the next morning, throwing out slides and text. So had I as I struggled to turn public speaking into an important management tool during my early days at Pepsi. As a young executive, I was always impatient to get things done and often felt I could do them better myself. So did Steve.

Sometimes, I felt as if I was watching Steve playing me in a movie. The similarities were uncanny, and they were behind the amazing symbiosis we developed.

The evening before the Macintosh launch, Steve and I worked frenetically to ensure that everything would go smoothly. As exhausted as everyone on the Macintosh team was, there also was incredible excitement in the air. Up until tonight, the thirty to forty key members of the growing Mac team had worked for days without sleep to meet final deadlines. Even now, hours before its official debut, Mac's software team was putting the finishing touches on the demo programs that would be used to introduce the Macintosh to thousands of people.

In an empty and hollow Flint Auditorium a few blocks from Apple headquarters, Steve and I rehearsed our speeches, but Steve wasn't satisfied. He fumbled his lines, not knowing what he was going to say. He threw out slides. He was driving people insane, getting mad at the stagehands for every glitch in his presentation. I sat there and wondered how we were going to get through this the next day. Steve kept changing his remarks, altering his presentation up until the last moment. But I also could understand and relate to the nervousness he was feeling.

"I think of you just like Woz and Markkula," Steve had told me earlier. "You're like one of the founders of the company. They founded the company, but you and I are founding the future."

Backstage, before we went on, Steve turned to me and said, "This is the most important moment in my entire life. I can't tell you how I feel. It's the most incredible thing I've ever had to go through and I'm really nervous. You're probably the only person who knows really how I feel about this."

I grasped his hand, pressed it warmly, and whispered good luck. Steve strolled off onto the stage in a double-breasted charcoal gray blazer and a red bow tie and welcomed the crowd.

He opened the meeting by quoting lyrics from Bob Dylan's "The Times They Are A-Changin'."

Come writers and critics who propheticize with your pens
And keep your eyes wide the chance won't come again.
And don't speak too soon for the wheel's still in spin
And there's no telling who that it's naming.
For the loser now will be later to win for the times they are a-changin'.

Having revved up the crowd, he left the stage.

I strode to the podium to talk about the company's financial health. It was the typical businessman's speech about the state of his company and what the future held for it.

But before I stopped, I had to deviate from the script.

"The most important thing that has happened to me in these nine months," I said, "has been the chance to develop a friendship with Steve Jobs. The two of us have had tremendous challenges together in leading this company, and the rapport and friendship that have developed between us mean an awful lot."

Then I introduced Steve, who walked onto a darkened stage. The real show was about to start.

"It is 1958," he pronounced. "IBM passes up the chance to buy a young, fledgling company that has just invented a new technology called xerography. Two years later, Xerox is born, and IBM has been kicking itself ever since.

"It is ten years later, the late sixties. Digital Equipment Corporation and others invent the minicomputer. IBM dismisses the minicomputer as too small to do serious computing and, therefore, unimportant to its business. DEC grows to become a multi-hundred-million-dollar corporation before IBM finally enters the minicomputer market.

"It is now ten years later, the late seventies. In 1977, Apple, a young fledgling company on the West Coast, invents the Apple II, the first personal computer as we know it today. IBM dismisses the personal computer as too small to do serious computing and therefore unimportant to its business.

"The early 1980s—1981. Apple II has become the world's most popular computer, and Apple has grown to a $300 million corporation, becoming the fastest-growing company in American business history. With over fifty companies vying for a share, IBM enters the personal computer market in November of 1981 with the IBM PC.

"1983. Apple and IBM emerge as the industry's strongest competitors, each selling approximately $1 billion worth of personal computers in 1983.

" . . . The shakeout is in full swing. The first major firm goes bankrupt, with others teetering on the brink. Total industry losses for 1983 overshadow even the combined profits of Apple and IBM for personal computers.

"It is now 1984. It appears IBM wants it all. Apple is perceived to be the only hope to offer IBM a run for its money. Dealers, initially welcoming IBM with open arms, now fear an IBM-dominated and -controlled future. They are increasingly turning back to Apple as the only force that can ensure their future freedom."

Cheers erupt as Steve's voice grows deeper and faster.

"IBM wants it all and is aiming its guns on its last obstacle to industry control, Apple. Will Big Blue dominate the entire computer industry, the entire information age? Was George Orwell right?"

As the crowd hysterically shouted a chorus of "No's," the "1984" commercial hit the huge screen behind Steve. It was a brilliant bit of theatrics, a prelude to his official introduction of the Macintosh. Until then, there had only been two milestone products in personal computers—the Apple II and the IBM PC. Macintosh was meant to be the third milestone.

Steve walked over to a bag, unzipped it, and took the computer out, just as theatrically as he had done many months earlier when he was trying to lure a Pepsi-Cola president to the company.

As he turned on the Mac, the theme of the movie *Chariots of Fire* blasted from the auditorium's speakers.

"Today, for the first time ever, I'd like to let Macintosh speak for itself."

In a shaky voice not nearly as threatening as the machine-like diction of the authoritarian narrator in the "1984" commercial, Mac said: "Hello, I am Macintosh. It sure is great to get out of that bag. Unaccustomed as I am to public speaking, I'd like to share with you a thought that occurred to me the first time I met an IBM mainframe. Never trust a computer you can't lift. But right now I'd like to sit back and listen. So it is with considerable pride that I introduce a man who has been like a father to me, Steve Jobs."

The audience roared its approval. The first five rows of the auditorium were filled with members of the Macintosh team—all dressed in Mac T-shirts—who led the explosion. No one could help getting carried away by the hysteria. Not the shareholders nor the media. Steve, a knowing smile on his face, nodded his head back and forth. He knew he had them in the palm of his hand. For a moment, he had created more than "an insanely great" product. He had created a church.

The night before he had lurched through his rehearsal. Now he was spellbinding, his timing perfect. Everyone was captivated by his performance. It was a spectacular presentation. Backstage, Apple people hugged and kissed each other in pure delirious joy.

As the auditorium boomed with applause, Steve walked off the stage. In the wings, I grabbed him and we hugged each other. Both of us had tears in our eyes. I knew how hard Steve had worked for this moment, and I knew how important it was to him. I was thrilled to be a part of it.

Never before in my life had I felt such emotional exhilaration. Never before had I known a friend as well as I knew Steve.

"Steve, I am so proud of you," I said. "You've really done it!"

"It's really happened," he replied with a lopsided grin. "Mac is a real product now!"

Managing Creativity

Wanted: Impresario to orchestrate a workshop of wizards.

You're not likely to see an advertisement like that in *The Wall Street Journal.* Yet, when I walked through the Macintosh Building with Steve it became clear that he wasn't just another general manager bringing a visitor along to meet another group of employees. He and many of Apple's leaders weren't managers at all; they were impresarios.

It is an important metaphor for inspiring creativity. Not unlike the director of an opera company, the impresario must cleverly deal with the creative temperaments of artists. At times, he may coach because he knows that creativity is a learning process, not a management process. Other times, he may scold because he knows that creativity requires a demanding commitment of self. The impresario must, in fact, be alternately tough and admiring toward his people.

In art, he ensures that the setting and stage are conducive to the production of a masterpiece. His gift is to merge powerful ideas with the performances of his artists. At Apple, we bring together a company of artists; we build the infrastructure of set designers, stagehands, and a supporting cast; and we applaud the performances of our cast members who oftentimes emerge as stars on their own.

This is the difference between inspiring the growing numbers of "knowledge workers" in our economy and simply motivating people. Virtually all our models of motivation derive from industrial and postindustrial labor. Getting people to reach beyond their best abilities is knowing how to manage creativity itself.

Business literature reveals almost nothing about how to manage creativity. Nor does any other literature. For example, stories about Harold Ross, founding editor of *The New Yorker* and one of the greatest managers of creativity, go into detail about how much he drank, who he fought with, why he cursed writers—but nothing about how he got even the ordinary people under him to do extraordinary things. The same is true of one of the greatest impresarios of all time, Sir Rudolf Bing, the long-time general manager of the Metropolitan Opera in New York. Relentless in his demand for excellence from his artists, he believed in delegating authority, but he retained final authority and assumed all responsibility. "What goes right is the result of teamwork, and what goes wrong is my fault," he said.

The traditional management gospel only thwarts us in trying to understand creativity. Management and creativity might even be considered antithetical states. While management demands consensus, control, certainty, and the status quo, creativity thrives on the opposite: instinct, uncertainty, freedom, and iconoclasm.

The traditional corporation has largely been left-brained, systematized and quantified. The entrepreneurial model often errs on the other side. It's too loose and iconoclastic, so that when the company meets success, its managers find it difficult to control the accompanying growth without abandoning the very characteristics that led to its success. Yet, to nurture the creative impulse of any organization, there needs to be some reconciliation of the two states.

Apple Computer, obviously, starts with an advantage. It has none of the baggage of a second-wave corporation: no aging plants, no older workforce, and no unions. Many came to Apple precisely because they wanted to work in a different kind of company. So I largely work with people who already are motivated by the company's mission to bring the power of computing to individuals. The task is to get them to work at the highest levels of creativity, not just productivity. The difference is you want people to think, not necessarily work faster. The "Think" signs that Tom Watson scattered all over IBM offices in the 1940s are hardly enough today to get people to do extraordinary work.

The Macintosh team, for example, was a young group of disparate individuals going all-out to accomplish the creation of a product that they believed would change the world. To get each artist to exceed his or her abilities, Steve would go to any length. He wouldn't hesitate to ridicule poor performance publicly within the group, yet he was a master at celebrating milestone accomplishments with his team. A little recognition went a long way toward keeping a worn-out engineer not only working but passionate about his work.

He cared, too, about the environment. The Mac building's theme was great art and great artists. Its rooms were named after Picasso, Matisse, Rembrandt, and other creative luminaries. It transformed a building into a creative incubator because all these differences became symbols that Apple was dramatically different from the second-wave company.

At Apple, management didn't get in the way. In fact, Steve Jobs was less a manager and more an impresario. He knew that the role of management wasn't to stifle creativity through structure and process, but to foster it through unusually innovative means and thinking.

There are no six easy steps to anything in management or art. But there are general principles through which the impresario works to create a higher state of creativity within an organization. These help define the corporation's identity and architecture as well. Consider:

The safer you can make a situation, the higher you can raise the challenge. So says Tim Gallwey, author of *The Inner Game of Tennis,* and he's right. Apple impresarios try to remove all hierarchical obstacles, but they ensure that the resources are there when needed and help to build support for the work being done. The impresario makes things safe, which allows artists to do their work without having to deal with the structure of production. And we don't want people to worry about hitting a wrong note in trying to play an extremely difficult piece of music. But the piece has to be difficult. If you reduce the risk without raising the level of effort, you get high arrogance and complacency.

Don't give people goals; give them directions. We want to lead people to ideas they haven't dreamed of yet. Unlike most corporations, we don't so much try to define our identity; we try to make it recognizable—not too concrete. So we talk endlessly—and aphoristically—about what we do: "We build people, not computers"; or, "The best way to predict the future is to invent it." I know most culture gurus would have companies memorize their corporate vision. We define our identity as the company that "builds great personal computers," yet we resist hardening our vision to specifically defined goals, believing with Eden Phillpotts that "The universe is full of magical things patiently waiting for our wits to grow sharper." Creative people want to have a strong understanding of the standards of the company, even more than they need to know exactly what it's there to do.

We would rather remind ourselves that our products make a difference in customers' lives; whenever that happens, we can be truly proud. So we would rather say, "We help people grow," which refers to ourselves and our customers. The impresario must ensure that such goals and their nuances are thoroughly understood.

Encourage contrarian thinking. While an impresario must provide a sense of discipline, you always need some low level of dissent. There should be a level of tension between discipline and anarchy. I would worry if there wasn't always a little bit of anarchy in the organization. It's like arsenic: a little is medicinal but a lot can kill you. You want to impart medicinal levels of anarchy within an organization so that people feel they are free enough to express opinions without worrying about the implications.

As an impresario, I encourage and elicit contrarian views and contrasts. We want people to be able to see more than they ordinarily might. As psychologist Jerome Bruner has said, contrasting viewpoints are far better than absolute judgments, although many corporate leaders today overly venerate decision making and reward judgments. I find the process of reaching a decision more valuable than the results. It's important to place tension between points of view to extract the best from people. Dissent stimulates discussion, prompting others to make more perceptive observations. And it ultimately influences decision making for the better.

Build a textured environment to extend not just people's aspirations but their sensibilities. You can't buy creativity. You have to inspire it. Creative people require the tools and environment which foster their success. Above all, they require an atmosphere conducive to fun and to thinking in non-standard ways. The work environment needs to be informal and relaxed; it needs to remove the symbols of management, which in the traditional company means the uniform of the business suit, the closed-in offices, the overabundance of titles, the executive perks. We try to remove all those symbols, creating an egalitarian environment, because we don't believe there is a difference between the contribution of a single artist or an orchestrator.

But we go beyond this.

Managing creativity has nothing to do with people sitting around a square table "brainstorming." The atmosphere is too rigid. We almost never do anything important in any of our offices—that's where we're constrained into rational, rigid thinking. Apple Fellow Alan Kay talks about stimulating the "body mentality" by creating a tactile environment that jump-starts memory, feeling, emotion. At Xerox PARC, the researchers added showers to their office building as ideal "think tanks." When your consciousness is occupied in relaxation, your unconscious mind—the seat of creativity—is freed to act.

In some Apple buildings, each floor is outfitted with a red-topped popcorn cart, so everyone at Apple can even sniff how different we are. It's another symbol to remind us that Apple is not a traditional corporation, so doesn't think in traditional ways. And at the end of each work week on Friday, the company sponsors beer busts in every building. It's not that employees are into drinking beer; it's a weekly gathering point where people can informally exchange discoveries with each other, a way for a large company to become smaller.

Almost every building has its own theme, so meeting and conference rooms aren't identified by cold, impersonal numbers. Instead, they are named by employees who decide on the theme of their building. In our "Land of Oz" building, the conference rooms are named Dorothy and Toto. Our Management Information Systems Group has meeting rooms with names such as "Greed," "Envy," "Sloth," "Lust," and the remaining deadly sins. It's not accidental that many of these are the symbols of childhood (popcorn included). William Blake believed that in growing up, people move from states of innocence to experience, and then if they're fortunate to "higher innocence"—the most creative state of all.

If a traditional corporation did the same, would it work? Probably not. Because these elements of the new architecture only affirm the vision of the company and how it differs from second-wave corporate models.

Build emotion into the system. Defensiveness is the bane of all passion-filled creative work. We keep defenses down in several ways. One way is by thinking about problems differently—not as negatives, for example. We are considering giving people medals for problem finding, not just problem solving. Our world is moving so fast that new problems are being created all the time. The people who find them have tremendous powers of creative observation.

We also deflect defensiveness by our large and public system of rewards, which includes cash and stock option bonuses, individual research budgets, extra time off, even all-expense-paid skiing trips, as part of the reward system. There are special bonuses, separate from merit raises and base salary plans, that put thousands of dollars in individuals' hands within two to three weeks of authorization by their manager/impresarios. As crucial as these incentives are to inspire people to exceed their creative limits, however, they often play less of a role than the public celebration of a person's contributions within Apple. It can start with the simple acknowledgment of all contributors under the heading "Kudos" at the beginning of a company report. It ends, perhaps, with the company's Hero Award, the Apple equivalent of the country's Medal of Honor. It's a large and heavy solid brass medallion with a wide ribbon in Apple's rainbow logo colors.

Encourage accountability over responsibility. We don't give creative people traditional responsibilities, like being at the office every day from eight to five, or check on them for efficiency and punctuality. Instead, they are made accountable for the results of their work. People are given the flexibility to perform a lot of work at home. Indeed, some spend only a day or two a week at the office. Just as academia offers its people the freedom to structure their own time, we do the same, and yet people work incredibly hard. It goes back to our roots in academia.

The impresario must have a clear grasp of what it is we are all here to do. His artists need both the freedom and the discipline to let their creative ideas take us on incredible unexplored journeys. Someday, maybe we'll see more companies searching not for managers and employees, but for impresarios and wizards.

7

The "Dynamic Duo"

More than an advertising slogan for the Macintosh introduction, "1984 won't be like '1984'" emerged as the theme for Steve and me in what was shaping up as a dreamlike year. Everything seemed to go perfectly, as if according to a well-crafted, razzle-dazzle Hollywood script. It was a year of elation.

In the first hours of the launch, we sold $7.5 million worth of Macs in addition to the $53 million order we had on hand from universities over the next two years. Long queues of consumers formed outside the computer stores, so anxious were people to put their hands on the Macintosh keyboard. Apple people rushed down to computer stores themselves for the thrill of watching retailers set up displays for the product they had worked on for years.

Enthusiasm abounded. Dealers, analysts, software developers, and the media agreed with us that Macintosh was a technological breakthrough. Outsiders hailed the computer for its graphics capabilities which they said were unequaled in the industry. Some called it the best price/performance machine ever made. Others said it was the first truly easy-to-use computer. Few, if any, industry observers expected the Macintosh to be anything but an outstanding success.

I watched elatedly as we sold the 50,000th Macintosh not in the first 100 days as expected, but on Day 74. It was an unprecedented start. When virtually no one knew what a personal computer was, it had taken two and a half years to sell 50,000 Apple IIs. When one of the strongest corporations in the world got into the market, it took seven and a half months to sell 50,000 IBM PCs.

Steve and I were convinced we had the secret formula, a combination of revolutionary technology and marketing, to fulfill his vision for the personal computer. The "bicycle for the mind," the computer would be an intellectual tool to enhance the individual's work, mind, life. It was a rebellious, even subversive idea: back in the mid- to late 1970s—just ten years ago—few people could own a computer, even if they wanted one.

The personal computer revolutionized the idea of what a computer was. In the early 1950s, the Ice Age of the computer, the UNIVAC offered institutions less memory (roughly 1,500 bytes vs. 1 million bytes) than a Macintosh Plus. Yet it was 15 feet long, 7.5 feet wide, 9 feet tall, weighed about 5 tons, and was known as the "Giant Brain." The Macintosh weighs less than 17 pounds.

With the growth of the American economy in the 1950s and 1960s, American industry needed ways of consolidating information, especially financial data. The explosion in the use of such mainframe computers as the UNIVAC made "dedicated processing" such as payroll processing a milestone in productivity. The computer assumed a forbidding, godlike image: it was locked up—a completely segregated tool, set off in a large, air-conditioned room with department store–style windows, serviced by men in white coats who wheeled computer tapes around on trolleys. IBM's huge blue machines came to shape the industry and eventually dominate it. They became the world's greatest company based on service to institutions.

As the technology grew more powerful and cheaper, smaller companies got access to computers. It wasn't until 1964 that IBM introduced its System/360, the first family of compatible computers, which revolutionized computing. It was based on a new architecture that could take advantage of more memory, storage, and processing speed to come in the late sixties and seventies. Suddenly, computing had come of age and large blue boxes with whirling magnetic-tape drives in high-security rooms became status symbols as important for corporate America as the fleet of corporate jets. But the System/360 also altered the competitive game. In launching it, IBM made obsolete its own computers as well as many of its competitors', allowing the company to break away from Sperry Univac, Control Data Corp., Burroughs, and other card sorter and early mainframe makers. General Electric and RCA eventually ditched their computer operations.

IBM was caught napping in the early 1970s, however, when

Digital Equipment Corp. (DEC), a small company of engineers who made laboratory instruments, launched the first minicomputers. They were smaller, less expensive versions of mainframes that made the cost of processing so inexpensive that they could be placed next to users. In 1972, DEC had $100 million in sales; today, it's over $10 billion. The epicenter had begun to shift from stand-alone mainframes to "distributed processing," which meant computers had to be networked together.

The shift occurred because processing had become far less expensive and it didn't have to be confined to centrally air-conditioned computer rooms. Companies were also discovering all kinds of new and different users for computers. But this specialization had led to a need to link computers together in networks.

The last presentation I made before PepsiCo's board of directors was to recommend the $15 million purchase of Hewlett-Packard minicomputers for Pepsi-Cola's company-owned bottling plants. Computer networking became important because users needed a way to link all of their computers together so they should share data. None of IBM's computers would talk to one another. DEC's could.

For more than two decades, computers focused on institutions, not people. It was Steve's vision to give the power of a computer—until then available only to corporations and governments—to the people that allowed Apple Computer to spark a revolution. This individualistic approach made Apple unique.

The timing proved right. A slowdown in productivity growth during the late seventies and the recession of the early eighties prompted corporate America to look critically at its big, bloated, white-collar staffs who did little but push paper around. Personal computers helped companies manage to strip their staffs by taking over lots of white-collar work.

Up until only recently, IBM's vision of the personal computer was shaped by its mainframe history. The IBM PC was a complete anomaly compared to what the company had done in the past. IBM didn't seem to care if its machines lacked graphics or ease of use. It rushed a personal computer onto the market in 1981 because it didn't want to miss a new important market as it had with minicomputers. In its haste, IBM missed the importance of how the personal computer would change the world. So have many of the other corporations, such as AT&T, which also rushed to market personal computers.

"IBM has it all wrong," Steve said repeatedly. "They don't care about people. They sell personal computers as data-processing machines, not as tools for the mind."

But IBM was already entrenched in companies, which meant Apple could never have gotten started in a niche in the corporate market dominated by them. Apple had to move into rough waters and create its own business.

It was the Apple II, of course, that stirred the change back in 1977. By now, in early 1984, Apple had sold over 1.5 million units of the computer. Its success was critical to the company. Some analysts had warned that the seven-year-old computer was becoming obsolete.

Seven years is two lifetimes in the microcomputer industry. Though the Apple II had more than endured the times—our price-slashing strategy over the Christmas season created shortages of the machine when it had to compete with the IBM PCjr. for the first time—it was now time to launch a new version.

We took over the cavernous Moscone Center in San Francisco on April 24 and unveiled the Apple IIc, a portable, briefcase-sized version of our most successful computer. It was sleek and slick—the stylish result of a collaboration between our designers and award-winning German designer Hartmut Estlinger—and would sell for only $1,295, half the cost of the Macintosh.

Because we wanted to emphasize the smallness of the computer, we had hidden about 1,000 Apple IIcs under the auditorium's seats. At the moment I unveiled the product on stage, members of the Apple II division who were positioned throughout the auditorium brought them out and held them up in the air. The auditorium was a sea of sleek, shiny Apple IIcs. Then, they turned and handed the new, 7-pound computer to the dealers to the left and right of them. By the time Herbie Hancock delivered his last jazzy notes in the evening, we had taken more than 50,000 orders for the Apple IIc.

The day sealed a double pact Steve and I had made with one

another. It was a hyper-ambitious deal, not meant for the slow or unsure. "Apple II Forever," the theme of our Moscone Center event, proclaimed our desire to become first and foremost a consumer product marketing company. This was the first agreement.

Consumer marketing requires bold, major investments—not just throwing money into the market but investing capital to create capital. We spent $15 million to introduce the Macintosh, a sum that added up to the largest marketing effort in the company's history. It included 10 million copy inserts in business and computer magazines and twice-nightly advertisements during the Olympics. We had no television for almost a year; now we were back on national television in a major way. We made Apple one of the largest advertisers in the United States.

The Apple IIc event was a $2 million party that upped the ante in the computer race. We signaled our intention to introduce the largest advertising campaign in the company's history. If we could simply add just a 1 percent penetration of households a year, it would produce almost a million more sales for the Apple II family of products. We put more advertising support behind the IIc in May, June, and July than either Pepsi or Coke in both national magazine advertising and network television. We ran eight-page inserts for the IIc in *Time, Newsweek, People, Sports Illustrated, Money,* and *Omni* magazines. There was a major radio campaign in forty-two cities backed by local newspaper advertising, too. Within ten weeks of the introduction, some 34 million people would have been reached twenty times by our television commercials alone.

Behind the strategy was our effort to raise the level of competitive investment for anyone who wanted to be a serious player in the industry. There are things that a multi-billion-dollar company can do in terms of the affordability of television advertising, as an example, versus what a much smaller company can do. It's almost impossible for a company with $100 or $200 million in revenues to invest in the kinds of effective television advertising you need if you're going to leave any impression at all. So it was crucial to leverage our size against the hundreds of competitors in the marketplace. I wanted Apple to become not just a great product company but also a great marketing company.

One of the major differences between computers and soft drinks is that the soft-drink business is a large industry where the major competitors are fighting over fractions of market share. In personal computers, the growth was so phenomenal that market-share gains early on aren't nearly as important as making sure Apple is properly positioned in areas that are going to be significant to it in the longer term. Product positioning and company positioning were crucial. People needed to know that Apple stood for innovation, for being at the leading edge of technology. That is the basis for our differentiation from IBM, known for its industry stature and service.

We weren't too shy to do our own version of the Pepsi Challenge on the air—to continually drive home the notion that this was a two-horse race. Among our new Apple IIc commercials was a spot that playfully featured an IBM PCjr. being moved off-camera by a Charlie Chaplin cane, only to make the point that the new Apple IIc was the better computer. Observers agreed; many were already comparing IBM's offering to Ford's disastrous Edsel in the 1950s, a product which had become synonymous with failure.

The most ingenious of the commercials was a comparative ad that showed an IBM PC. The copy read: "This is a highly sophisticated office computer and to use it all you have to learn is this," at which point several huge manuals tumbled out of the air to a thump on the table that rocked the computer. "This is Macintosh from Apple, also a highly sophisticated office computer, and to use it all you have to do is learn this," at which point a single, slim manual floated down, landing gently on the tabletop. "Now, you decide which one is more sophisticated."

Common wisdom in consumer marketing tells you it's better to have market share and then figure out how to make money. That strategy hasn't always worked, however. Companies that rushed to develop market share in CB radios, digital watches, and hand calculators found out the hard way. So, it has the potential of being not a very good strategy in the personal computer business at the low end. We want to focus at the end of the business where there is a genuine difference, where personal computers are not merely toys but tools conferring power on users. So we positioned the IIc as a computer for the "serious home user."

The soft-drink industry already had saturated the marketplace.

Only 7 percent of the U.S. population used a computer then, and personal computers were in only 3 percent of American homes. And that figure included low-end systems made by the Ataris, the Commodores, and the Colecos. To crack the broader consumer market, it was necessary to demystify the computer, to make it as easy to use as a telephone or a television. Conquering the broader marketplace depended less on product wars and price cutting to gain market share than convincing Americans that the computer is a useful appliance.

For Pepsi to succeed, it wasn't necessary for Coke to fail. For Apple to succeed, it isn't necessary for IBM to fail. Indeed, IBM's entrance into the personal computer was good for Apple because it brought the legitimacy of the world's largest computer company, signifying that the market was for real. That's why, when IBM entered the market in 1981, Apple ran full-page national ads proclaiming: "Welcome IBM, seriously." At Pepsi and at Apple, the approach involved developing emerging markets rather than heading on a collision course with your chief rival.

Great marketing cannot sell a pedestrian product very well. If the product isn't great, no one is going to want to develop software for it. On the other hand, Apple had regarded marketing as a cost rather than an investment: it was important to establish a brand name that could command a premium price. There were more similarities, though. Apple sold its computers through independent dealers, just as Pepsi sold its soft drinks via independent entrepreneurs with their own bottling territories. The great leverage in soft drinks is coming up with innovative marketing programs and putting resources behind them. I wanted to make consumer marketing one of the important dynamics for success in personal computers.

The second part of the pact between Steve and me was one we would seal later. It could either free us from the competition or tie Steve and me together in a free fall from the heights. I wanted us to race to a critical mass to get Apple large enough so that it could afford to pursue its own technologies. Critical mass meant having sufficient resources for research and development of new products. It meant being able to afford far-reaching marketing programs. It meant automating manufacturing to drive down costs and increase quality. I was convinced that if we played it active, there wasn't going to be any room for a personal computer company with less than $1 billion in revenue.

I would talk to Steve about it the first chance I got. The plan was to race us all twice as hard as the Mac team had done only months ago. I was sure we could win. We'd already won by every other measure.

On May 3, there was a private event—to which few insiders and no outsiders were invited—that became in many ways as much a turning point in my adventure as either the Macintosh or Apple IIc launches. Nanette advised me that Steve wanted me to meet him for dinner at Le Mouton Noir in Saratoga, four or five miles from Cupertino. I was surprised. It was somewhat out of the way and I had no idea what he wanted to discuss.

When I arrived, the restaurant was filled with familiar, smiling faces, all the members of the executive staff, the board of directors and their wives. Leezy was there. Even Peter Crisp from Venrock Associates had traveled across the country to attend the event. Everyone swarmed around me, shaking my hand and congratulating me on my first anniversary at Apple. A beaming Steve stood in the background, nodding his head up and down and wearing a Cheshire Cat smile on his face.

After drinks, we sat down to an elaborate dinner. Then Steve got up and made a presentation.

"Everyone here knows that I love Apple more than anything that I've ever been involved with my whole life," he said. "And the happiest two days for me were when Macintosh shipped and when John Sculley agreed to join Apple. This has been the greatest year I've ever had in my whole life because I've learned so much from John."

Then he uncovered a large acrylic box, a montage of memorabilia constructed in a time line from the day PepsiCo announced I was leaving, including a miniature replica of Kendall's internal memo reporting my departure, to the present flurry of press reports on Macintosh and the Apple IIc. He said he had arranged for the montage as a reminder of the things we had accomplished together in the last year.

I was deeply moved by his generosity. I was even bemused by how the montage represented the up-to-the-last-minute effort by Apple people. Even through dinner, they were gluing in the final pieces.

"I've made a lot of decisions in my life," I said, "but never one that changed my life more, never one that I felt better about, than coming to Apple. It isn't working for a company; it's a chance to work with people who were part of shaping history."

I explained how Steve and I had developed a partnership and a friendship. Hopefully, Apple was benefiting from both of us. It was a unique way to run a corporation. Neither of us was caught up with titles. We shared a passion to make Apple a phenomenally great company.

"Apple has one leader, Steve and me."

I looked across the room and spotted Steve, a broad smile on his face, and it was as if we were in communication with each other. The board was thrilled, too, because somehow it was able to bring in an outsider who could work with this precocious, mercurial founder against all odds. I didn't stop to think about the quizzical look that crossed the face of Arthur Rock, and of a few others. I was basking in the conviviality, and our plans.

I didn't yet know it, but my statement proved to be a turning point. I was increasingly sharing with Steve the power to run the company. Although Steve had founded Apple, the operational power to run the company always had eluded him. It meant the difference between actually running the Lisa division, for example, and exerting some influence on the product in the laboratory. Markkula had it from the beginning; Markkula had it again after Mike Scott left; and then I arrived.

My paucity of experience in the computer industry caused me to defer to Steve on many technical questions from the start. Indeed, Steve and I began talking over most issues and making the decisions. We were running a top-down company and people were beginning to resent it. They wanted more participation in the decision process. The two of us were deciding all of the important things and weren't delegating enough to the people in the organization.

What all this did was elevate Steve into a position of power he never had before. As the Macintosh group grew in size, from a small product development team to a full-fledged division, his power increased. I raised his title from vice president to executive vice president when we merged the Lisa division into Macintosh shortly after the Mac launch.

It wouldn't occur to me until October of 1984 that maybe I had made a mistake. Our success not only gave us great confidence as a team and company, it made Steve more forceful as a manager. With my approval, he started to become far more vocal on everything that went on at Apple—not just the Macintosh division or new technologies. He began to dominate many of the conversations and discussions within the executive staff. The most visible evidence of his new role in the company occurred at our annual business plan meetings in October.

These were standard sessions at which middle managers and executive staff members made presentations for next year's budget. Steve proposed an "accounting transfer price" between Apple's different divisions. The central sales organization, for example, would have to effectively bid for the business of the Apple II or Macintosh groups. Steve believed it would provide each group with the incentive to manage its own profits. Instead of being just another department in a big company, a division could take on the feel of a small business.

Steve argued forcefully in favor of the approach, trying to ram it through the executive staff. But no one was really buying it. People were looking to me to take control, to get him to sit down and shut up, but I didn't.

As I was leaving the room later, I heard someone whisper, "Why doesn't Sculley shut him up?"

I was beginning to wonder the same thing, in a mood of cold self-doubt. I had put Steve in an operating job when he didn't want it, and now he suddenly decided that he wanted to be Steve Jobs the manager, not just Steve Jobs the product visionary. For the first time, I thought to myself that Steve was trying to lead the management decisions and that I wasn't being as forceful as I should. I felt as if I was losing control. But things were going so well that it didn't seem to matter that much. And after all, I had come to Apple to help make Steve a manager.

Increasingly, though, he became interested in demonstrating he was a manager as well as a brilliant product innovator. I had created someone who was becoming more of a peer from an operating standpoint, yet someone who was still symbolically over me as chairman.

Yet, just as Apple's tremendous growth hid many of its problems, our overwhelming success made it difficult to argue that the partnership approach Steve and I adopted wasn't good for the company. In hindsight, it would prove a mistake. It left the other vice presidents relatively powerless when it came to making decisions about resources, and it only aggravated the tensions between the Apple II and the Macintosh groups. But for the first year, it seemed the best way to run the company.

When the board reviewed my performance after my remarks in early 1985, it was pleased with what I had done. But the board members surprisingly raised concern that I wasn't running the corporation myself, that I was sharing too much of the power with Steve. Initially, I was startled. I had always thought that part of my role was to help Steve grow so that someday the board would have the option of allowing him to run his own company. Always in the back of my mind was that part of my job was to be Steve's mentor.

Indeed, when I agonized over my decision to leave PepsiCo, I had asked myself an important question. If someone had told me that I could have been the mentor to Alexander Graham Bell or Henry Ford, how could I have turned it down? I couldn't. So from the very start, I felt that part of my role was to nurture Steve from a prince to a king so he would someday be able to run the company he cofounded.

One of the first signs to emerge that something was amiss came across my desk as a short memo in early May from Alan C. Kay. A brilliant computer scientist, Kay had been put on the company's payroll as an Apple Fellow, a job that required him to be both a computer visionary and a critic. Steve first met him at Xerox PARC, where as a systems designer Kay invented Smalltalk, a high-level, object-oriented programming language used by non-programmers. Alan also pioneered the use of icons instead of typed codelike words for telling computers what to do. "If your dog and your kid can learn a simple English command, your computer should be able to do that," he once told me. He'd coined the phrase "personal computer" before the pc ever existed. And he conceived of the first truly portable computer, which he called the Dynabook, in 1968, an idea that sparked the imagination of future computer scientists.

An intense man of forty-four, with a mind as broad and playful as Buckminster Fuller's, the mustachioed Kay often talked about the computing pioneers he'd met as a graduate student at the University of Utah in the early 1960s, including Ivan Sutherland, who created the first computer graphics program, called Sketchpad, in 1962. It took more than twenty years before Apple brought to the mass market the idea in the Lisa, with LisaDraw. Another computer scientist hero of his, Doug Englebart, created with his team the mouse that had become an integral part of the Lisa and the Macintosh almost two decades after its invention by Englebart.

Steve got to know Kay after he left PARC to take on the job as chief scientist for Atari in late 1981. Kay remained there until Steve offered him a job as an Apple Fellow. The idea was for Kay to float through Apple's labs, planting seeds of ideas, and to counsel us on the future direction of personal computing.

Alan described his job to me as that of a lone wolf, a wild card in the game of advancing Apple's destiny. "The reason Apple has Fellows is not to reward them for past wonderfulness," he said, but because Apple was betting that a mix of divergent thinking "will be one of the special spices that turns a workaday technological kitchen into three-star dishes."

In his very first memo as a Fellow, however, Kay triggered Steve's anger by calling the Macintosh "a Honda with a one-quart gas tank." Macintosh is one of the world's best-designed transportation systems, he said, but claimed that "it can only take you to the corner store for celery and back. Impressive in your driveway, but you can't take it on a medium or long haul. Surely the Japanese would never let anything so unbalanced out of their factories."

Despite his misgivings, Kay also believed the Macintosh was the first personal computer worth criticizing. With a single disk drive and only 128k of memory, however, he didn't think it was powerful enough. He called the new Sony disk drive Mac's "Achilles heel." "The need for the second drive is all too apparent even before the first week is out," he said. After reading the memo, Steve forbade

Jane Anderson, our public relations representative, to let the media speak with Kay.

The lack of memory, however, grew into a significant disadvantage because it made it difficult for programmers to write software for the Mac. The easier it is for the user, the more complex it is for the programmer to write for. It didn't help that Apple hadn't yet published software tools to make it easier for them to write programs. Henry Singleton, the only board director who did a lot of programming himself, began to complain about the difficulty in programming the Macintosh.

"It's crazy that we have a computer out that nobody can program," he told Steve at several board meetings. "How do people program a Macintosh?"

"They program on Lisas," Steve would explain. "But we're going to fix that. It's not going to be a big problem."

Nonetheless, some developers who intended to create Macintosh software simply gave up; others found the complexity slowed the pace of their development, causing long delays in getting to market.

While we heard grumbles about the lack of Macintosh software, good news far outweighed anything else. Computerland, one of the most important computer retail chains in the country, decided to carry the Macintosh. That decision alone made the computer available in an additional 350 new dealer outlets. They came on the bandwagon after three other important computer retail groups agreed to become Apple dealers: Businessland, Sears Business Systems Centers, and the Genra Group. We installed a new sales organization which would call on our dealers directly instead of through independent manufacturers' reps. When we ran two ads in *The Wall Street Journal* to recruit 350 people for these jobs, we were inundated with more than 12,000 applications—so many people wanted to work for us. The deluge swamped the Cupertino post office for a week.

I put Alan Kay's memo in my desk drawer. No emergency here, I thought. I planned to study his remarks later.

The industry was booming and so was Apple. We were selling Apple IIcs and Macintosh computers nearly as fast as we could manufacture and ship them. In July of 1984, Steve and I found ourselves in his office, sketching out on a whiteboard how many computers and peripheral products we could possibly sell in our Christmas quarter, typically the biggest three-month selling period of Apple's year.

"You know, we could hit a billion dollars in a quarter," I said.

"Boy, that sends shivers up my spine," Steve said, nearly giggling with excitement.

If we could pull this off, it would be a near-miraculous coup. In a single quarter, we could rack up more revenues than Apple did in the previous year. We were bullish, and both us were having a lot of fun just thinking about the possibility. We examined the cash-flow implications of it and quickly discovered it would take an incredible amount of cash to build up the inventory to support a $1 billion quarter. It could consume over $100 million of the $155 million in cash we then had on hand. But we thought that if we could do it, it would give us an important lead over our competition in future years.

"We've taken risks before," I said, "and we bet the ranch. We bet the whole company on the Macintosh and we did it again on the IIc."

Steve and I looked at each other, wondering whether we should go for it again.

"Yeah, let's do it," Steve said. "Let's bet the company again."

Steve thought we could sell 80,000 Macintoshes a month by Christmas time. So we put in the capacity to handle about 110,000 units a month, to build inventory of Macs and Apple IIs so we could hit the $1 billion mark during the Christmas quarter. We got the board's approval to take our cash way down and convert it into inventory. They were very reluctant to see us do that, but we went ahead and everyone agreed.

The future looked amazingly bright. The home computer market was still growing by leaps and bounds, and we were well on our way toward developing the key products that would allow Macintosh to succeed in the business world. Steve's Macintosh group—at first a 25-person design group, then a 100-person team, and now a 700-person division—was readying some important products to help establish Macintosh as the "second standard in business." IBM's share of the personal computer business market in 1984 was estimated at 36.1 percent, while Apple's share was 12.7 percent. The "Macintosh Office," as we called it, was our key strategy for penetrating the business market. At the beginning of 1985, we expected more than seventy-five business software packages on the market, including a program by Lotus Development Corp. called Jazz.

Among them was a LaserWriter, a printer that produced near-typeset-caliber text and art-department-quality graphics. It is a replacement for the noisy impact printers like daisy wheel printers which could only handle text, not graphics, and are commonly found in offices. Next, we had a file server, which in effect created an electronic central filing cabinet where documents could be stored and shared among many people using various Macintosh computers in an office network. The key to all this was AppleTalk network, which permitted groups of up to thirty-two users to communicate with each other and share peripheral devices such as printers and file servers. It was easier to install AppleTalk than to connect a television to a videocassette recorder. And its cost was only $50, much less than the $300 to $1,000 that corporate buyers currently paid to connect machines to a network. Also under development was software that would allow an IBM PC to be put on an Apple network, a bridge between the first standard in business and the second.

We felt the Macintosh Office wasn't just good. It was great. Insanely great. Then why shouldn't we be really ambitious? I asked Steve to come over to my office.

"Steve," I said, "we really aren't thinking big enough on this thing. You've convinced me that we've come up with the technology that can basically change the way people use paper in business. But it's hard to see how Apple is going to capitalize on the commercial value of what you've created without strong distribution channels into large corporations."

Already, we had cut a deal with General Electric Information Services Co. to add the Macintosh to a line of office-systems products it sells to large corporate customers. We began talks with Roger Smith and Ross Perot of General Motors, with executives from AT&T, and with others as well, seeking corporate alliances for the business market. Steve and I agreed we needed to forge other strategic alliances to sway greater numbers of companies.

"Why don't we look at people who already have businesses

where this would be an evolutionary step as opposed to having to create the infrastructure as well as the entire technology and product lines? Maybe we ought to be looking at acquisitions with other companies that have a strong presence in the business market," I suggested.

"I guess we could probably get some small companies and put them together to make Apple bigger," Steve said.

"We don't want small companies," I stressed. "We're not thinking big enough. Maybe we should look at a big company. There is no limit today as to what size company can be acquired. Maybe we should expand our band width and think if there's a big company out there that could really help us take advantage of this technology. The obvious one to me is Xerox."

Steve, however, was no fan of the company. Only three months earlier, we had privately met with Xerox vice chairman Bill Glavin and Bob Adams, head of its computer systems group, to explore whether we could work together in some ways. Apple already had a sales relationship with Xerox in Latin America and Canada, and Glavin had called me to see if we could forge other alliances to our mutual benefit.

In advance of the breakfast meeting at Rickey's Hyatt House, I had coached Steve to be on his best behavior. Steve wouldn't hesitate to say exactly what he thought at the moment he thought it. And he had little good to say about any large, traditional corporation, Xerox included.

"I know you don't admire Xerox as a company because it hasn't been able to commercialize its computer products very well," I said to Steve. "But let's just go in and listen and keep our minds as open as possible. Let's demonstrate to them that we're really mature people, and we're able to handle ourselves with business meetings of this sort."

"Okay," said Steve, "I promise to behave and do my best. I'll behave."

We began the meeting in Glavin's hotel room, but we hadn't gotten more than a few minutes into the conversation when Steve began to attack Xerox.

"You guys are doing it all wrong, just doing it completely wrong," exclaimed Steve.

He believed Xerox, with resources far greater than Apple, was sitting on top of some of the best laser-printing technology in the industry, and yet it couldn't get a printer out that was as good as Apple's product. It frustrated him because he already believed Xerox "blew it" with the personal computer by not being able to successfully commercialize the inventions at PARC. Now he believed the same thing was occurring with laser technology.

Adams bristled, and things went downhill from there. Glavin glanced across the table at me and rolled his eyes.

"Now, let's step back and talk about this," I hopelessly interjected.

But Steve couldn't hold himself back. A pained look appeared on his face as the words came tumbling out of his mouth.

"I really shouldn't say this," he said, "but I'm going to say it. You guys don't have any idea of what you're doing."

Within fifteen minutes or so, it was clear we would accomplish nothing. So I pulled Bill Glavin aside and suggested that we call off the session and perhaps regroup at a later date. The meeting quickly ended and Steve and I left the room. I was incredulous.

"Steve," I asked, "why did you do that? I thought we had an agreement that you were going to control yourself."

"I'm sorry, but I couldn't help myself," he said contritely in a little boy's voice. "I went to Xerox PARC and saw that they had all the great people and they were doing all the great things and they just didn't see it. And they still don't see it. I believe in great products, and they haven't built great computer products with their technology. I just couldn't control myself. I'm sorry."

Steve and I never rescheduled the meeting with Xerox. After that set-to, it didn't seem possible that we could ever work with the company. I still felt that a Xerox-Apple alliance would be terrific. So why not buy it, acquire a $10 billion corporation that was more than five times the size of Apple? We felt we could spin off Xerox's Crumm & Foster insurance subsidiary and keep the rest. Xerox's major appeal was its massive sales and service organization which, I thought, could provide us a major jump on the market to sell our soon-to-be-announced "Macintosh Office" products into large corporations. Apple's entire workforce was a mere fifth of Xerox's sales and service staff of more than 30,000 people, an operation many recognized to be the company's most important asset.

Xerox was an intriguing target because few had seemingly grasped the fact that electronic publishing was going to become the market of the future. Increasingly, people needed better ways to communicate with each other, to more effectively persuade others of their ideas on paper. Alan Kay had taught me that the computer was "a communications amplifier" more than a numbers cruncher. "I consider the airplane a communications device," he said. "I consider the photocopier a communications device. The railroads thought they were in the railroad business and IBM thought they were in the computer business, but both were really in the communications business."

Steve believed that Xerox's electrostatic copier machines eventually would be replaced by laser copiers, and he envisioned a time when the two technologies would converge into one machine that would revolutionize the industry and deal a killing blow to the huge copier business. Why would anyone want to buy a traditional copier when they could use laser-printing technology to fulfill all their in-house printing and copying needs? Because the LaserWriter strengthened—amplified—the written medium, just as typewriting had amplified handwritten messages.

"Once they see the LaserWriter and what you can do with it, everybody's going to want it," Steve said. "No one's going to want to go back to anything else. I don't think those guys at Xerox really see what's going to happen."

"Do you think we could run a company that big? Because the Japanese are really coming after them with copier technology," I said.

"Yeah," said Steve, "you've run a big corporation before. You could go back and run it, and I could run the Apple part, and we could really make this whole thing work."

We even brought others into the conversation. We asked Bob Bellevue, an ex–Xerox PARC computer scientist who was the director of engineering of the Macintosh division, what he thought. Bellevue was an extremely bright engineer. It was he who had become instrumental in convincing Steve to go with the Sony 3½-inch floppy disk drive, and he now was the technological angel behind Laser-Writer and AppleTalk network. Based on his knowledge of Xerox technology, Bob believed we had the better technology, but cautioned that we should look at buying a number of smaller Silicon Valley technology companies rather than a giant like Xerox.

We mentioned the idea to Al Eisenstat, our general counsel. Al was the most experienced and seasoned of all Apple's top executives. An entrepreneur himself, he founded United Data Centers in the late 1960s, sold it to the computer services company Tymshare Inc., and became executive vice president and general counsel of Tymshare before joining Apple in 1980.

Al often brought us down to earth. Some jokingly called him the "Abominable No Man" because of his penchant for bringing measured reason and caution into Apple's business decisions. Al facetiously described himself as "the Last Angry Man." He didn't always win the arguments, but he often was right. Knowing we would face trademark challenges over Steve's decision to launch Macintosh under its original codename, Al had argued at full volume that Steve should pick another name for the computer. "Another name would sell the machine just as well," he said. "Find something!" Steve prevailed, but it ultimately cost us nearly $2 million in out-of-court settlements.

When we told him of our idea to acquire Xerox, he put his hands up to his head.

"Holy Jesus!" he said. "What are you two up to now? You've got to be kidding!"

"Al, what do you suppose the board would think of it?" I asked.

Not much, Eisenstat thought. Besides the huge difference in size, it was far from clear that Xerox would be able to fend off the Japanese in the copier market in the future. Although he helped convince us that maybe Xerox wasn't a good move, Steve said the discussion was one of the most exciting we had ever had. After a few days, however, we thought that acquiring Xerox was a little bit too outrageous, even for us.

At the time, in late 1984, we thought we held the future in our hands. We developed an intoxicating overconfidence. In October, Steve and I were on the cover of *Business Week* magazine, dubbed the "Dynamic Duo." Things had gone so well we literally didn't know how high was up. As Steve put it, it was like being in a room that was completely dark, moving forward even though you didn't know where the walls were. Our revenues had jumped 54 percent in the year ended September 28, to more than $1.5 billion. While our net income declined, it was because we felt it was more important to race toward critical mass than it was to increase profit at long-term expense. Even so, in our final quarter of the year we reported record profits. Already we were beginning to talk about hitting $5 billion in revenues in the near future and $2 billion in sales for the next year alone.

No company our size in the Fortune 500 had ever grown that much in a single year. But I felt that no company ever had the opportunities and the products and the people that we had, either.

We had established Macintosh as the personal computer industry's third milestone product, after the Apple II and the IBM PC. We were well on our way to selling 275,000 Macintoshes in 1984, and some 150 software packages were available for it. To the relief of many of our dealers, we also introduced an upgraded model of the Macintosh with 512k bytes of memory four months earlier than anticipated.

We changed forever the marketing ground rules of the industry by moving from a minor advertiser to one of the largest, most-talked-about, innovative marketing and advertising concerns in the country. Our bold advertising led to the highest brand awareness in the industry—even higher than IBM, which spent more money than us to make a Charlie Chaplin look-alike its computer spokesman. In fact, one independent survey found that we gained double the recognition of IBM in personal computers despite our smaller budget. It wasn't only because we believed we had better products and advertising. It was because Apple represented something very different about business.

Apple emerged as a symbol of hope and prosperity for America at a time when more people than ever were questioning our nation's ability to compete with Japan. Corporate leaders and politicians gravitated to our campus as if on a pilgrimage. Even Chrysler Corp. chairman Lee Iacocca visited Apple to praise our remarkable success. Presidential and vice presidential hopefuls asked us if they could come on the Apple campus to promote their candidacies.

Fan mail poured into the company by the thousands from customers, dealers, third-party developers, and the general public who shared our alternative vision. But one of the most touching and moving letters came from a six-and-a-half-year-old boy who wrote to Steve.

> Dear Mr. Jobs:
> I was doing a crossword puzzle and a clue was, "As American as Apple _____." I thought the answer was computer, but my mom said "pie."

By year's end, the Apple generation had even reached the White House. "When I was a boy," said President Reagan, "an apple was something you brought the teacher. Today, you learn on an Apple or a Macintosh."

The press seemed to reflect that we were infallible. We paid a price for the fame and popularity, however. We became targets for anyone who was envious of our success. At one point, I had received bomb threats at my home in Woodside. At another, there was an attempted kidnapping. One morning, on my usual jog, I noticed a car hidden behind brush not far from the entrance to my home; inside were two men who jumped from the car and began to run toward me. I sprinted back to the gate and got inside before they could reach me. Another day the police abruptly arrived at the school our daughter Laura attended to bring her home because of the threats on our lives. We ended up erecting a huge fence around the property. For a while I jogged with a gun-toting bodyguard, and ex-FBI agents slept on our living-room sofas with sawed-off shotguns for two months. No one was ever caught.

We had no reason to suspect that our success would not carry us in our race into the new year. If anything, 1985 seemed to promise as much or even more for us than any other year in the company's history.

Just then we were given another reason to strut: an invitation to a secret meeting between me and French government officials who were interested in making hundreds of millions of dollars worth of computer purchases. President Mitterrand wanted to bring France to the forefront of computer literacy, to leapfrog the United States and Japan, by setting up 40,000 computer centers throughout the country for both students and adults. France envisioned that upward of 70 percent of its population would change jobs in the next decade and saw these centers as a means to retrain workers and educate a new generation for the information age. Because French education already placed heavy emphasis on mathematics and conceptual skills, which are critical in software development, the government also believed the project could help it make software a huge new industry for France. Mitterrand had already gotten the recommendation that the Macintosh was the ideal personal computer for what the government proposed.

We were beside ourselves. Our business in France was very successful; we already were the number-one personal computer company based on sales of the Apple II, and Macintosh also was selling well there. Indeed, more Macintosh software originated out of France at this point than out of the United States. We figured it could represent the largest contract that had ever been put together for personal computers. At the very minimum, the French government indicated it would need 100,000 Macintoshes. This, however, was likely only the beginning. If Apple could export everything from the United States, the order could eventually be worth upward of half a billion dollars.

Steve had met Mitterrand earlier in the year when the French president came to Stanford for a symposium. He was especially interested in Steve because Jobs was a folk hero in France with the young people. As usual, Steve had been outspoken during his meeting with Mitterrand and had even contradicted him at one point by telling him he didn't understand how things really were out here in the Valley. The meeting apparently didn't put the president off Steve or Apple. Instead, Mitterrand, characteristically of the French, was impressed by the young, contrarian intellectual and co-founder of Apple.

So it was agreed that Steve and I would be invited to Paris to meet with various members of the government cabinet and possibly President Mitterrand after the Christmas holidays. We scheduled a lot of time to prepare ourselves for that meeting.

High over our success with last year's campaign, we asked the agency to come up with another blockbuster to run at next year's Super Bowl that would bring attention to the Macintosh Office.

I had begun to play a lesser role in Macintosh advertising, preferring to delegate it to Murray, the Macintosh marketing manager. But over the last few months, our advertising had taken a strong anti-IBM tone. One ad showed a businessman working on an IBM computer as the words "Syntax Error" came on the screen. The person would get so frustrated that he'd grab his IBM unit and smash it against the wall. Another one showed people using chain saws to cut their IBM computers apart.

Now, the agency was presenting the storyboard for a commercial that seemed to follow the same theme. It showed blue-suited, white-shirted, and blindfolded male executives marching single file —each one's hand on the next's shoulder—until they blindly and monotonously went off a cliff like lemmings into the sea. Ominous black clouds swirled overhead. The musical background for the commercial was the *Snow White and the Seven Dwarfs* tune "Heigh-ho, Heigh-ho" slowed to a funeral march by the agency.

The purpose of the commercial was to convey that most executives don't think about where they're going, they simply follow what everyone else does. At the end of it, one person peeks out from under his blindfold, looks around, and says, "Why am I doing this?"

When Chiat/Day showed us the storyboard, Steve and I both disliked it. It didn't have the panache of "1984," which left viewers with a positive image of Apple. "Lemmings" lacked the optimism of that commercial as well as its playfulness. More troublesome, though, was the fact that many might find the commercial offensive and could wrongly interpret it. Viewers might think we were ridiculing the very customers we were trying to gain with the Macintosh Office. I feared that it would convince people that we really had gone too far. Maybe we were the ones who had fallen off the cliff.

Chiat/Day argued that it was symbolic of people tumbling into the unknown, not death. We asked if they had any other ideas. They didn't.

"Look," someone at the agency said, "you guys didn't want to run '1984' last year, and then we finally ran it and it was a great success. Now we've got another one and we're going through the same thing again."

Although not nearly as enthusiastic as he was about "1984," Murray too favored "Lemmings." "I think this can be a good commercial," he said.

But it didn't register as well in our gut. Steve and I talked about it for days, yet we never really felt comfortable about it.

"I've been in advertising a long time and this is really a good commercial," said Jay Chiat, the chairman and founder of the agency. "You're going to make a terrible mistake if you don't let us make this commercial."

"I will put my whole reputation, everything on this commercial," argued Lee Clow, now the agency's president.

Finally, we relented and allowed them to make the ad. This time, the agency couldn't get Ridley Scott, the British film director who did such a magnificent job with "1984." Instead they settled for his brother, Tony Scott, who they believed had a similar style.

Five weeks later, they came back with the commercial. After I saw it, I felt worse than when the agency presented it on storyboards. It had taken a deadly serious tone that paled by comparison to "1984." The commercial lacked the hope and spirit as well as the good-versus-evil subliminal messages conveyed in the "1984" spot.

"This is not a great commercial," I said. "It just is not. You guys didn't come through with it."

The agency defended the piece, arguing it could fix some of the problems by better editing. "You're looking at a very rough print, slop prints," they said.

"Come on," I said. "I've been looking at slop prints for twenty years. This commercial is not as well filmed in my opinion as '1984.' And it has only exaggerated the concerns I had because it looks even more depressing than I thought it would. I don't like it."

Despite protestations by the agency, we instructed Chiat/Day to sell back the time. The agency was able to sell it back to ABC-TV, but in the following weeks mounted a strong lobbying effort to get us to run the ad. Chiat/Day continued to press Murray and called Steve on several occasions, hoping to reverse our decision. They suggested a plan to run the commercial in a group of cities instead of the Super Bowl game. We vetoed this suggestion, too.

Meantime, however, word had leaked out in the advertising community that we had this great commercial and had decided not to run it. Unexpectedly, we started getting a lot of publicity over a commercial we wouldn't run. There seemed more interest in the commercial that wasn't going to run than in "1984," which ran only once.

"This commercial deserves to run," argued Clow.

"I have never felt so strongly that a commercial should run as this one," added Chiat.

Steve eventually suggested we allow Murray to decide. "Mike has really done some great things for us in advertising for Macintosh," said Steve. "He's close to it and this will give him a real sense of responsibility that the agency feels that he'll be the decision maker on this."

I agreed, so we went back and reported our decision.

"We're going to give Mike Murray the final decision as to whether this commercial does or doesn't run," I said.

Under a lot of pressure from Chiat/Day, Murray decided to run the ad. The agency was able to buy back the time for $900,000, about $100,000 less than we had originally paid for it. We even ran teaser ads in newspapers just before the Super Bowl: "If you go to the bathroom during the fourth quarter, you'll be sorry."

Steve and I would get a quick reading on the public's reaction to the commercial because we planned to attend the Super Bowl game at Stanford Stadium in January 1985. We arranged for the commercial to be piped in and shown on a huge screen that had temporarily been erected in the stadium for the game.

As part of our efforts to gain publicity for the Macintosh Office launch, we had agreed to supply 85,000 seat cushions with the Apple logo on them for the uncomfortable wooden seats in the Stanford stadium. When we arrived ahead of time, it was an awesome sight. Every seat boasted a white cushion with the Apple logo face up. It turned out to be a public relations coup because whenever a television camera panned the stadium during the pre-game shows, it picked up the Apple seat cushions. They became instant collectors' items.

We were still getting threats, so Steve and his girlfriend, Tina, and Leezy and I were accompanied to the game by six security guards. Although we had bulletproof vests made for the occasion, neither of us wore them to the game; they were too bulky and awkward to be comfortable. Before we took our seats, the security guards checked them.

"Lemmings" didn't air until the closing seconds of the game, long after everyone knew that the Miami Dolphins would lose it. When the commercial went up on the stadium screen, everyone in the place stopped what they were doing, their eyes turning toward the screen. Some 90,000 people were dead silent. All of a sudden, I got this terrible lump in my stomach. "This doesn't feel good," I thought, wondering what the 43 million people across the country were thinking.

When it ended there were no cheers, only an instant of dreadful silence before attention returned to the field and the game. It must have been the only completely silent moment in Super Bowl history.

"Well," I said, turning to Steve, "there it is. I wonder how the other forty-three million people felt about it?"

He didn't have to answer. We simultaneously realized the commercial was a flop. What we didn't yet realize was that our $1 million, sixty-second advertisement would later emerge as a symbol that Apple Computer was out of control.

●

Laying Claim to "Share of Mind"

IBM: three of the most formidable initials in the history of American business. When I waved farewell to my colleagues at Pepsi, they stared in wonderment at the prospect of competing with yet another giant. They were wrong. IBM isn't just another giant; it is one of the most successful business organizations ever assembled in the world.

As the chief executive of an upstart computer company in Silicon Valley, I sometimes feel like I'm peering down the barrel of a nuclear-missile silo. The numbers tell an awesome story. IBM boasted 394,930 employees to Apple's 5,000; IBM's $40 billion in sales cast a long shadow over our $1.5 billion; IBM's $6.6 billion in net income, more than any other corporation in the world, compared with Apple's $64 million.

Those figures tell you that an assault on so mammoth an industry leader as IBM isn't likely to succeed. As I discovered at Pepsi, the leader by virtue of its preeminent position can often afford to cut prices, unleash a torrent of new products, or swamp you with an advertising blitz.

The trick is to nullify the leader's advantages, while summoning your own to your advantage. We had to leverage public interest in the company with a new product that could form the basis of a sustainable advantage over IBM.

Most marketing strategies hype the product. Event marketing goes well beyond the product. Apple had to sell personal computing more than the personal computer.

Every new, highly innovative product creates a new problem for society which only it can solve: The airplane made transportation by any other mode seem disadvantageously longer than in the era of the train and horse and buggy. The telephone made anything less than instantaneous communication a fearsome obstacle. So the Macintosh—the computer for everyone—was designed to make standard communication forms a severe limitation to personal productivity. Computers make us recognize our handicaps; without them we would realize how clumsy we are at drawing, how we often fail to express ourselves well, how there is, inside of us, someone who strives for much more than we can achieve. With the Mac, who would want to go back to using ditto machines and typewriters?

If Mac introduced a problem, we would have to sell the solution only it could provide. And we had to do this at the very moment the home computer market went bust. That was first. Then we had to sell what almost can't be sold because it didn't really exist: We had to sell the future, our vision for a world enhanced by personal computing. To sell our product, we had to alter the culture, reshape the public consciousness. We had, in other words, to lay claim to "share of mind."

To do any of this modestly or in traditional terms would have been to fail before we started. We viewed the Mac launch as if we were introducing the automobile. We needed a vehicle as ambitious and unique as our aims. Our intent was to create the impression that the problem and the product were everyplace, which in and of itself establishes credibility and staying power. So in 1984 we built up a crescendo of attention for Apple and for Macintosh with event marketing, which was one of the most thoroughly planned and comprehensive consumer marketing programs ever assembled.

The event became key. Every release of information about the product centered on a celebration of Apple and its vision. Through a convergence of advertising, promotion, and public relations, the experience of the event would have to match the experience of the product.

When you unite these strategies—solution selling and selling the future—with the intention of making your message unforgettable, you have event marketing.

By portraying our product as fascinating and exciting, what could the competition do for an encore? Unlike "share of market," "share of mind" is much more lasting. By this measure we were already way ahead of IBM and AT&T, the competitor everyone thought was gaining.

SHARE OF MIND

Apple:	**IBM:**	**AT&T:**
Innovation	*Customer service*	*My phones don't work*

In the space of forty-eight hours, Apple had communicated to almost the entire Western world that in creating the Macintosh, we had done something revolutionary. By definition, revolutionary acts have to be outrageous; they can't simply be evolutionary.

Selling the Solution

What we had in mind was dramatically different from the special-event sponsorship programs that many consumer marketing companies have employed to great advantage. Those campaigns, like Kentucky Fried Chicken's sponsorship of a bluegrass festival or Mercedes-Benz's backing of the New York City Marathon, link a product or service to a leisure pursuit. We wanted to go well beyond that concept to create a long-standing blizzard of attention.

Instead, we would sell personal computing as the solution to problems of personal effectiveness. "A bicycle for the mind" is what Steve called it. Jean-Louis Gassée went one better when he used the phrase "wings for the mind." We cast the broadest possible net, one that exceeded product lines.

Before the Pepsi Generation and the Challenge, many people perceived Pepsi as a Coca-Cola clone or compatible. Even though

Apple was the pioneer in personal computing, it began to suffer a similar fate: too many consumers failed to recognize the distinctions between a serious personal computer like the Macintosh and $300 toylike game machines. To boldly position Apple as competitor to IBM and lift us out of the fray, we decided to ignore product specifications and focus on images of individuality and achievement.

Up until the Mac, all high-powered computers were developed for institutions, not the individual. "Think of Mac as an appliance," Mike Murray wrote in his marketing plan. "The increased personal productivity combined with the opportunity for personal creative expression will hit hard our customers' psychic drives."

The Mac was a significant invention. On plugging in their machines, Mac users could do in minutes what had required a technological sophisticate twenty to forty hours to learn to do. These existing machines could not be called appliances. They failed to deliver great utility, didn't always increase productivity, took up lots of space, and weren't often priced for personal (as opposed to shared) use. The Macintosh was different, very different.

In Macintosh, Apple had an advantage over IBM's existing product. The product was a radical departure from all existing computer systems on the market with the exception of Apple's own more costly Lisa or Xerox's very pricey Star. The difference in our product was so great that if we could establish it as the third industry milestone, it would take years before an IBM could offer its own version of a graphics-based, easy-to-use computer.

Emphasizing product features might have made sense in the mid-1970s, when most buyers were hobbyists and were fascinated with the technology. But in today's market, most users aren't interested only in the technical features of a product. They want complete solutions to problems, and they want to enhance their abilities.

Positioning the Future

An event is a positioning vehicle. Marketing in a postindustrial society is not a marketing of function; it's a marketing of experience. What the excitement of the event had to embody is the experience—the "pure sex" of personal computing. Selling the feeling is more important than selling the feel, as Harvard's Theodore Levitt has explained. GM traditionally markets the adventure of owning a Cadillac—the feeling—rather than the comfort of the seats against your back. We knew we could sell the feeling.

But we decided to go further—to sell the future—to sell Apple's vision and its stake in an exciting industry. This is unusual in marketing. Buyers of cars, for instance, may have loyalties to Ford or GM, but these tend to be inseparable from product loyalties, to the Mustang or the Cadillac, for example.

How do you sell what doesn't yet exist? You have to make your event marketing a statement of where you are trying to take your company in terms of its position in the marketplace. What we tried to do was pull out in front of everyone in a very cluttered computer market to make it a two-horse race between IBM and Apple. It's a total waste of money if you're just out there to publicize what you're trying to sell that year.

An event must go beyond a simple product introduction; it has to tell you something about the company's direction. A new product by us is usually a major statement about the direction not only of Apple but where we think information technology needs to go.

"One person, one computer" carried a double resonance. It spoke to the individual and to society. It articulated our new vision of society—an egalitarian vision of an affordable, highly powered information tool. We repeated this message in different forms at each event.

We were trying to introduce and sell fairly expensive consumer items, so it was necessary for the public to know more about us. How much does the public know about PepsiCo or Procter & Gamble? Very little compared with their many brands of products. But the public knows a great deal about Apple as a company. And there's a good reason for the difference. Consumers want to know that the company will be there in the future to provide solutions and enhancements for them. They want to minimize the risk up front before making a large purchase.

It was important to sell Apple Computer with the Mac. We would sell "ownership" in Apple with each and every product. Every Mac owner could feel he had a vote in Apple's future, its direction, and its vision for the workplace of the future. The event, which became part revival, part information blitz, captured these themes. The publicity made even our executives well known and closely watched—more like a baseball team than a management team.

In soft drinks and other packaged goods, advertising is intensely focused on the product line. That makes sense because the industry is mature and products don't change that dramatically. But in personal computers, products can change overnight. So can distribution and advertising strategy. That's why it's so important that you anchor public interest and attention in your company's technological vision, the enthusiasm of your workforce, your values, rather than just in a product's technical specifications.

Company identification is growing as a strategic opportunity for firms in the computer business as well as in other industries, as consumers become better educated than ever before. This goes beyond a corporation's "good citizen" status. We had to reveal ourselves completely, sell ourselves and our capability. The result of all this is that when most people think of Apple, they think in terms of a crusade rather than a company.

We knew that Apple was viewed as the counterculture company in the industry, and also that there was a lot of public interest in the personal computer industry. But there's always the risk that a company will lose public visibility. I knew that nobody was going to forget IBM. But I couldn't be as certain that people wouldn't forget about us.

Here's how we made sure they wouldn't:

The Method

Some people have looked enviously at the amount of attention lavished on Apple and found it hard to understand how a so-called event can possibly garner so much press. What they haven't seen is the scene behind the stage door, the many hours, days, weeks, and months of preparation. Event marketing hardly materializes by itself.

Start by leveraging change. The trauma that comes with change opens up opportunities and often forces more traditional companies which cannot always move as fast to miss some of the emerging opportunities. Just as the Cola Wars took advantage of social change that affected consumers, the computer wars became important in the new growth industry about which people were curious. The fears surrounding the approach of 1984 and the public perceptions of a behemoth like IBM gave us a way of positioning ourselves.

We figured everyone would have a cliché on "1984." But we came very early in the year and we snooped around to see if there were any other major campaigns to be launched around George Orwell. There weren't any.

The result: sixty seconds of commercial film that set the stage for our event, that underscored why our approach to the business was dramatically different from IBM's. In an industry with hundreds of competitors, it thrust Apple into a two-way race with the industry leader.

"1984" gave us a lot more visibility than we could have achieved using conventional advertising. It was our statement to the world. If we had just advertised Macintosh and its features, how many people would have remembered the ad after the Super Bowl game?

The ad fit with our marketing strategy, which was to keep public attention focused on our company's very different vision of how technology should be developed. It gave us a high platform from which to tell our story. It also evoked a great deal of curiosity about Apple as an innovative company. That's the difference between a short-term market-share strategy and a longer-term marketing position strategy. One test I used was asking myself whether IBM could have run "1984." The answer was obvious. IBM couldn't have done it with credibility; only Apple was believable with such a commercial.

Although IBM could significantly outspend us in advertising, we achieved double the brand awareness by using bolder and riskier placement strategies. "1984" was just a start. During the year, we exclusively bought all the advertising space in an election issue of *Newsweek* and we became the first advertiser ever to put inserts into major magazines. They weren't small inserts, but twenty-page-long extravaganzas that detailed the advantages of our product.

Lay the groundwork well in advance. Behind any successful

event lay months and months of preparation. One of the most important strategic building blocks to the event was Regis McKenna's belief that you build foundations early. McKenna, an early Apple adviser who dreamed up the friendly-looking and distinctive multi-colored Apple logo, is a master of technology public relations. But he doesn't believe in advertising. He insists that computers are sold best through cleverly crafted word-of-mouth campaigns. To spread the word, Regis adheres to what he terms the "90-10 rule." It means that 90 percent of the world is influenced by the remaining 10 percent. If you can positively reach the influence-makers of the world, you've managed to send ripples throughout the target community. The same holds true for virtually all marketers.

Word-of-mouth marketing has its risks. It's not always easy to influence the influencers who tend to potentially be your most informed audience. The powerful 10 percent, then, can work for or against you. That's why it's so crucial that a marketer focus on substance and credibility. The American public quickly sees through false claims by manufacturers, as it did in the claims of Detroit car-makers who once asserted that their cars were of greater quality than Japanese imports when that was clearly not the case. I wouldn't know how to market a poor-quality car, any more than I would know how to market a poorly made personal computer.

The personal computer industry's infrastructure comprises layers of constituents between the manufacturer and the customer. So Regis and Mike Murray, Macintosh's marketing manager, worked together on a marketing plan to cultivate a relationship with six constituencies well in advance of the launch: (1) third-party developers; (2) dealers; (3) luminaries; (4) financial analysts; (5) trade, business, and general press; and (6) our most critical customers.

Together, they make up the crucial 10 percent that will influence the remaining 90. What's more, all the groups are interrelated. When a journalist, for example, does a story on a topic, he'll call representatives of all the constituent groups. If they are briefed ahead of time and know the product well, they will be more inclined to offer a statement in its support.

To get third-party companies interested in developing products to work with or run on Macintosh, we "seeded" numerous companies with prototypes of the computer and our plans for it months before the debut. Nearly a full year before the actual introduction of the Macintosh, we signed up one hundred third-party software companies to develop software for the Macintosh.

At the introduction, however, we had almost no outside software at all to offer. That's why we bundled MacWrite and MacPaint and used promos of Bill Gates of Microsoft, Mitch Kapor of Lotus Development, and Fred Gibbons of Software Publishing, who promised to support the Mac.

We did, though, gain the enthusiasm of a bright computer scientist, Andrew J. Singer, a co-founder and vice president of Think Technologies, Inc. Working closely with the Mac team, he developed "Instant Pascal," a language the software universities could use to do some programming of their own. This allowed Apple to make tremendous inroads in university computer science departments, gathering more than $50 million of Macintosh orders from the Ivy League that we could announce on day one.

A group of "luminaries" and key decision makers also was chosen to receive free Macintoshes. Our annual report featured eleven of these "great imaginations," experimenting with Macintosh: Entrepreneur Ted Turner; novelist Kurt Vonnegut; Vietnam Veterans Memorial designer Maya Lin; ballet master Peter Martins; designer Milton Glaser; Muppet creator Jim Henson; San Francisco mayor Dianne Feinstein; composer and lyricist Stephen Sondheim; *Life* magazine's art director Bob Ciano; Lee Iacocca, and David Rockefeller. Some fifty people received advance copies of the Macintosh, from avant-garde artist Andy Warhol to Sean Lennon, the son of the late Beatle John Lennon.

The marketing blitz was a calculated strategy. By building the foundations out there, you can eventually reap the rewards when you do have something to say. So one route to 1984 was Regis's concept that you build foundations early. Don't go around and talk to the media when you need them. Lay your groundwork well in advance of that.

Create and structure the mystery. Yet we couldn't tip our hand too soon. So in order to create interest and enthusiasm before the actual event would take place, we had to set the scene for the Macintosh mystery. The "1984" commercial certainly did so. It was the ultimate tease.

Of all the constituent groups, the industry analysts and media representatives were among the most important. For them, we put on a series of "sneaks" around the country: all told, sixty individual seven-hour presentations to pave the way for a successful introduction. There also were sixteen "sneak" days for groups of up to ten people, beginning in late October. Not only would the product be unveiled at these sessions, but people got to meet and interview Steve and me as well as members of the design team.

While "sneaks" were being held at Apple, three teams from our marketing department hit the road in a fleet of trucks for an eight-to-twelve-city tour to roll out the product for our dealers. This was far more than an introduction. In the final three months before the introduction, we trained 4,000 salesmen at dealerships on the Macintosh. Most computer companies announce products before they actually are available. The reason they do this is to preempt the competition. It may then take months before a product hits the market. In Lisa's case, for example, five months passed between the actual launch of the computer and its shipment to computer dealers.

For Macintosh, the plan was to have the product in dealer stores on the day of the introduction. Most of them were purely for demonstration purposes, to whet the appetites of computer fans and convince them to place orders for the computer. That way we could benefit from the massive publicity on the day of the launch.

Seize on external events. Our 1984 event exploited three different and unconnected happenings: our shareholders' meeting, the rapid change and turbulence of the computer business, and George Orwell's thirty-five-year-old vision of the world in the year 1984.

Most shareholders' meetings are staid and legalistic. Ours was like a revival. We had 2,700 people there and another 800 people banging on the doors to get in. I can remember when Kendall used to invite the local Boy Scouts to our annual meetings in Purchase, New York, because so few of our shareholders would attend. More than half of the people in the auditorium, of course, were very enthusiastic Apple employees. Their evident enthusiasm at an event is infectious to all who attend and certainly noticeable by the press. If we could harness the meeting as a platform for connecting the other two occurrences, we could have the makings for a big success.

Establish your own guidelines for success. When Macintosh was introduced, we set our own target for success. If we could sell 50,000 units in the first 100 days, Macintosh would be a successful product. Typically, marketing promises are kept as vague as possible because an unkept promise can severely erode a brand's effectiveness. We seized the initiative to set our own ground rules for establishing Mac as the third milestone product. That preempts others from setting the guidelines by which your success is measured. We established a goal to sell 50,000 Macintoshes in the first 100 days. We sold, in fact, 72,000 units.

It was, of course, no coincidence that we set our deadline so that it would coincide with another Apple event to introduce the Apple IIc. So we knew we could get a double whammy. The press would come back then and we could tell them how we did.

We had no illusion of beating out IBM. Our strategy to succeed in the marketplace hinged not on the defeat of a giant, but on the positioning of Apple and our product.

As we moved through 1984 and into 1985, we had secured a role in a two-horse race with IBM by using event marketing and supportive advertising in non-traditional ways. We redefined the scope of competition, changed its ground rules, secured our position in share of mind, and set the stage for what would become the most important year in Apple's brief history.

8

A Company in Trouble

A misty fog hung low to the ground. In Silicon Valley, it was another morning of waiting for a bright sun to burn off the haze. At 9:00 a.m., a full hour before we planned to begin our annual shareholders' meeting, hundreds of people had already gathered on the steps of Flint Center. By ten, every seat in the large auditorium was taken and a sizable crowd was relegated to a movie theater nearby to watch the meeting by remote video.

Steve and I didn't disappoint the more than 2,000 cheering people who packed the place on January 23. The media facetiously referred to our multi-media presentation as the Steve-and-John Show.

We introduced one another as friends. Then the stage darkened for a theatrical demonstration of AppleTalk, which allows Macintosh computers to communicate and share data with each other.

"Imagine," said Steve, "that we're two middle managers, preparing a joint report to the shareholders. One makes a slightly higher salary than the other."

"Well, Steve," I joked, "that may be true, but the other is worth a lot more."

We both faced Macintosh screens linked by a wire glowing with a mysterious green light suspended overhead. As if by wizardry, a stamped envelope gently glided from my Macintosh onto Steve's.

Just as it did a year earlier when we introduced the Macintosh, the crowd went wild. The notion of a new desk-to-desk battle with IBM struck a chord. It seemed that we had scored yet another triumph. But behind the slick presentations and the hoopla of the event, we were beginning to worry.

We could pull it off because our profit for the quarter ended December 28 leaped nearly eightfold, to a record $46.1 million, while our sales more than doubled to a record $698.3 million. Most people at Apple were ecstatic. But we had forecast far greater revenues and built inventories to exploit them. We had built enough product to allow us to ship close to $1 billion of revenue, some $300 million more than we reported. We stuck our necks out, converting over $100 million in cash into inventory, because we had felt Apple was on a roll when we had to make these decisions during the summer. Now I suspected that our computer dealers were holding huge inventories of unsold product.

The crowd roared its approval when Steve walked on stage blindfolded after we screened the "Lemmings" commercial. But we already knew it had flopped, too. The day after the Super Bowl, our telephone lines were overloaded with calls from irate people claiming they would never buy an Apple product again. They believed the commercial insulted the very people we were trying to court as customers in corporate America. Dealers flooded us with calls saying they were getting complaints from prospective customers.

Independent studies showed the ad laid an egg. *Advertising Age* reported that fewer than 20 percent of the viewers who claimed to have seen it could describe the commercial correctly. Another survey showed it was the most memorable of the ninety-eight ads that aired during the game, but only because it was so unsettingly morbid and absurd. We tried to do "Godfather II," as one wag joked, and wound up with "Friday the Thirteenth, Part 4."

And only a few weeks before this event, I had discovered that two ingredients crucial to the Macintosh Office would not be ready for immediate shipping: the file server, which allows groups of users to share common data and communicate directly with each other in a local network; and an AppleTalk card, which would permit an IBM PC to connect to the Macintosh Office. Steve had shown me the hardware for the file server on several occasions—it looked like the box of a videocassette recorder. But I was too technologically naive at the time to understand that the file server was primarily a software product, and the software was nowhere near ready.

Yet, such a device was crucial to make the Macintosh Office a success. Steve told us the hardware was working in prototype form, but we had no software that worked. We also had a phenomenal product in a laser printer, dubbed the LaserWriter, but we weren't sure we could convince people that a Macintosh and a LaserWriter were enough to constitute a real event.

The Macintosh was starved for business software. We were really getting by with mirrors at that point.

Unfortunately, we weren't doing it well. Unlike 1984, the Mac Office event became mere hype. As the months wore on, our critics knew our announcement was contrived and premature. The media turned against us. We'd created the anti-event. It was like anti-matter; it swung the other way on us. Some of it was a backlash from the previous year. We had told the world the Macintosh was going to change the world. Now it was failing.

In October, Steve and I were the "Dynamic Duo." Four months later, we were a company in trouble. In our efforts to make the Macintosh Office look important, we overlooked the fact that Apple II sales accounted for 70 percent of the company's revenues during the Christmas season. The Apple II division, already at war with Steve's Macintosh group, was furious. Shortly after the annual meeting, an outraged Steve Wozniak called me up, and he could hardly compose himself he was so mad. Woz felt that Apple had lost its direction and that we were walking away from a great product.

He said virtually everyone in the Apple II group was upset. He didn't understand why I had sold out and was only backing Macintosh. It wasn't intentional, I told him. We wanted to give the Macintosh a lot of attention because its success in the corporate environment was so crucial to the company's future. Yet it was true that the Apple II, not the Macintosh, had gotten us through the difficult Christmas period. The conversation culminated in his resignation from Apple.

As the days in the new year wore on, the bad news continued to flow in. Woz was only the most visible of many key executives and middle managers who left the company. Our chief financial officer and our vice president of international operations announced their departures. Dozens of engineers in both the Apple II and Macintosh groups began to leave. The organization chart, as one Apple insider told the media, was filled with TBHs, which stood for "to be hired." The marketing manager in the Apple II group turned over so many times that people put up a sign that read: "If your boss calls, be sure to get his name." Some of our people began to eye the competition with what one of them called "pc envy."

By the end of January, our shipments had slowed to a virtual halt because Apple dealers were loaded with more than a month's worth of inventory. They began to call us up, clamoring to return unsold product to the company. Many dealers still had inventory left over from November.

Indeed, we were overwhelmed with inventory—much of it Apple II product that had been hard hit by IBM's heavy discounting of the failing PCjr. IBM had promised dealers lucrative incentive rebates at the end of the selling season if they pushed the product out over the competition.

IBM's pricing on the PCjr. over the Christmas holidays was surprisingly low. I could not understand how IBM could be selling that product without losing money on it. Dealers who initially tried to sell the PCjr. for $1,698 now were virtually giving it away for under $900. The price undercut the Apple IIc by at least $200, and even worse, IBM was throwing in a full color monitor.

At the time, we had no idea that IBM was getting ready to ditch the product. Every public statement IBM made was, "We're not getting out of the product. We're staying behind the product." This only made their price cutting all the more threatening.

While most of our mounting inventory was in Apple IIs, Macintosh sales were so disappointingly low during the last three months of 1984 that Steve had become increasingly depressed. We thought we would be selling as many as 60,000 to 85,000 Macintosh units a month. They were actually selling in the low 20,000s. Members of his own staff were coming to me and saying they had never seen Steve so discouraged.

He couldn't understand why we weren't selling more Macintoshes. For weeks, Steve simply moped around the office, withdrawn and dejected. He'd shut himself in his office and refuse to talk to anyone.

"I don't understand it," he said, over and over again. "Why isn't it selling? Things just aren't going right, and I can't figure out why."

Steve stubbornly refused to believe that something could be wrong with the product. It had to be something else or someone else—the marketing or sales operations, the dealers, or even the customers. It couldn't possibly be the Macintosh. Mac was a great product.

Steve and I, however, grabbed on to the hope that a deal to sell Macintosh computers to the French might be our possible wild card out of the problem. The potential of landing a single order as large as $500 million now seemed more important than ever. It would significantly build people's confidence that the Macintosh was the computer of the future.

We had assembled a team of people to help advise us how to deal with the French government: Sam Pisar, the well-known French legal adviser; Jean-Jacques Servan-Schreiber, the French visionary; me and Al Eisenstat. Jean-Jacques, who would take long walks with President Mitterrand, had convinced him that computer technology could become his legacy, just as former President Pompidou had been remembered as the French leader who helped to make France a world leader in the use of nuclear energy. We met with leaders from industry, government, and education in France. It consumed a lot of my time, but I saw it as a long shot that could really make a difference for us.

Finally, in February, we received clearance to visit with President Mitterrand at the Elysée Palace. Steve flew in to attend the meeting. I again asked him to be on his best behavior, particularly because on a previous visit to the palace with Jean-Louis Gassée, head of Apple France, he had proved to be his typically irreverent self in meeting with a high government official.

"We went in, and Steve proceeded to lecture the official on how to run France," Gassée said, laughing. "So I'm sitting there thinking, 'Oh my God! We're going to get thrown out or sent to prison.' But the beauty of Steve's incredible power is that this guy defended himself. He should have said, 'Hey, listen. You do computers; we do government! Buzz off.'"

Not wanting to have such a scene with Mitterrand, I asked Steve to keep his non-computer opinions to himself. We drove up in a limousine to the inner courtyard of the palace, passed the uniformed French guards at the gate, and were ushered through a huge marble foyer into a waiting room. After a short time, we were escorted into another reception room where we met the president's interpreter, who briefed us on how to address the president.

Finally, Mitterrand walked into the room. He was not a tall man. Dressed in a blue pin-striped suit, he had a rigid posture and he never cracked a smile. He was accompanied by Charles Saltzman, his science adviser. We shook hands, and he gestured us into his study, a huge room with large chairs upholstered in green silk brocade. Mitterrand, Steve, and I sat in chairs in front of a crackling fireplace. Saltzman, Jean-Jacques, and the interpreter sat along another side.

Through his interpreter, Mitterrand asked how we were enjoying Paris. He said it was nice to see Steve again. It was normal chitchat, no talk of computers. After a few minutes, the president got up and we were ushered into his private dining room for lunch.

"We're very enthusiastic about your vision of computers, Mr. President," I told him. "From everything we know, it goes far beyond what is happening anywhere else in the world, including the United States and Japan. If France is successful in carrying out your vision, it could bring your country to the forefront of computer sciences."

"Yes," the president said, obviously pleased, "this is right for the French people. It is something they would respond to very favorably and would understand because the French have a passion for things that stimulate the intellect."

Steve started to talk about how IBM sold computers as data-processing machines and how Apple viewed computers as tools for the mind that could unleash new creativity in individuals.

"Mr. President," I said, "I'm well aware of France's long ties to the Third World countries. I'm sure you're aware of the tremendous opportunity France would have if it had the leading technology for the next generation of personal computers. It would be a chance to bring the Third World into the twenty-first century by using the computer to rapidly accelerate education in these countries."

Mitterrand's eyebrows arched upward. "That's very interesting," he said. "If we were to do something with Apple, we of course would want to have the rights to sell to the Third World countries. This would be important for our balance of trade."

We told him we were prepared to negotiate with French industry to discuss such matters, but we had to respect other agreements we already had in place.

"Your country does not have the same relationship with the Soviet Union that France has," he then said. "And I think that this would be a very good opportunity to bring your technology to the Soviet Union by way of France."

"That would be a possibility," I said, "but we have to respect the agreements that allow for approval of our government of technology exported into the Eastern bloc nations."

"Yes," Mitterrand said, "I understand. Of course, we would expect that French industry would have to participate in this because we have a very large and a very talented industry in France. This would be important."

I told him we already had met with leaders of the French computer and telecommunications industries and that we were more than prepared to enter into negotiations with them, but were not ready to license our technology. There would have to be a joint venture of some form.

"This sounds worthwhile to pursue," he said.

Meantime, waiters in black cutaways had put before us a fairly exotic meal of some kind of innards. It probably was something of a French delicacy, but I had never eaten anything like it. Each time I swallowed one, I thought, "My God, I hope I can get it down." Steve just pushed them to the side of his plate, but I didn't want to be disrespectful to the president of France.

"What's wrong?" Mitterrand asked me. "Don't you like the food?"

"It's fine," I said.

"No, he doesn't like the food," Mitterrand said.

"No, I like it," I insisted, not wanting to offend him. "It's fine, Mr. President."

"You must get him something else," he said to his waiters. They were scurrying around.

"No, this is fine. I'll eat this."

I took a good swallow of wine to wash it down, and somehow got through the meal. Steve meanwhile never ate anything, but his plate was out of Mitterrand's view, blocked by a vase of fresh flowers on the table. I was at the president's right side, so I couldn't get away with it.

We adjourned to his study for coffee and finally, after a few more minutes, he turned to his science adviser, Saltzman, and said, "Well, should we do this? This is what France needs. Charles, do you believe French industry is willing to work with Apple?"

"Yes, Mr. President," he responded. "There will be many delicate negotiations and things that have to worked out, but I think all parties could work together."

"Well, that's it," the president said, standing up. He shook our hands again and we were ushered out, through the various passageways and halls, down the marble staircase to the marble foyer, past the guards and into our limousine.

Steve and I looked at each other and smiled. We felt like two starry-eyed kids who had just visited a king in his palace. For a fleeting moment, we forgot our troubles back home and believed we had pulled off a marketing coup.

"Wow," Steve said, "that was really interesting. I think he might really do it, you know."

"This is France," warned Jean-Jacques. "You have to be careful. You don't know until it's all done."

We held a few more sessions with cabinet members, wrapping up what we thought were some of the final details. Steve flew back to California, Al remained behind to pursue our proposal, while I flew on to London for another business meeting. As soon as I checked into my hotel in London, I was contacted by a reporter for *The Wall Street Journal.* Our meeting with Mitterrand was supposed to be secret, but the reporter apparently had heard of it from a source in French industry.

Leaders in France's computer industry never thought the proposal would make it this far. They apparently were floored when they learned of our meeting with Mitterrand, and launched a full-force campaign to derail it. Eventually, they were able to convince Mitterrand that there would be huge political risks in a deal with an American company. If it were successful, they believed, it would cost many French jobs because people would want to go and buy Apple computers for themselves, not French computers. Within weeks, the deal was torpedoed. We had invested weeks hoping for a deal that would dazzle the world. Instead, it became an unnecessary distraction at a fragile time.

In California, things continued to unravel. In early March, we decided to shut all four of our manufacturing plants for a week because of the excess inventory problems. Wall Street analysts began cutting their estimates of our earnings for the next quarter. As our stock fell to new lows each day, rumors of a takeover began to creep their way into news stories about Apple.

The media, which had eagerly scrambled to tell the romantic story of Apple's garage–to–Fortune 500 adventure, now were rushing to get the latest gossip about the company's decline. Inside Apple, we were increasingly absorbed with fingerpointing and infighting. The long, meandering chats and intellectual debates about how technology would change the world became far more basic. For the first time since Steve and I had met, we found ourselves entrenched on opposite sides of major issues.

One conflict concerned our distribution system and had been building for months—ever since October when Steve had dinner with Fred Smith, founder of Federal Express. Smith, an entrepreneur as dynamic and riveting as Jobs, ostensibly told Steve that Apple could save on distribution costs by shipping products from the factory direct to the customer by Federal Express.

Conceptually, the idea made good sense because it offered the potential to dramatically reduce the need for a network of warehouses, carrying costs, and extensive inventory. When an Apple dealer reported an order, it would trigger assembly of the product —just like when you put in an order for a new car. As soon as it came off the assembly line, Federal Express could ship it overnight. Steve seized on the idea, thinking we should shut down all six of our distribution sites across the country.

I was in favor of studying it; Steve was convinced it made great sense, and had members of his staff summon the analysis to justify a decision in his favor. It didn't matter that our middle managers were already agitated because they felt that Steve and I had usurped their authority to make decisions. Now Steve wanted to dismantle our entire distribution system without any of the people intimately involved in distribution having a chance to say anything about it. A real morale problem was in the making.

So sales head Bill Campbell and I got Steve to back off to allow the middle managers time to study the problem. But Steve, obsessed with the idea that the distribution system had to change, found it impossible not to get involved. The middle managers directed their anger at me, believing that as chief executive I should have been able to control him.

When I went down to speak with several of them at a leadership seminar, I came up against a hostile group. Many of them were critical of the company, of Steve and me. They were disgusted with what was transpiring.

In an exercise designed to relieve their anger, everyone was asked to draw pictures that reflected their perceptions of Apple. One manager sketched one of Steve and me both trying to steer a single boat; I, however, appeared to be under Steve's control. Someone else drew a caricature of Steve with two hats, one as operating manager and one as chairman, with Steve having to choose between them.

One key manager threatened to resign, prompting a public confrontation between several of the middle managers and me at the seminar.

"Who's really running this company anyway?" someone asked me. "If you're running the company, why is Steve Jobs going around telling us all what to do?"

What made the distribution issue all the more troublesome was that Campbell's team, busy shipping record product during the recent Christmas season, failed to come up with evidence against Steve's Federal Express plan. It was taking months and months for them to get back with answers. The most rigorous analysis at Apple was being done in the Macintosh division by a team headed by Debi Coleman, one of Steve's brightest and most aggressive managers, who now headed up our manufacturing plant in Fremont.

The distribution issue was emerging as a key test of our ability to allow the company's middle management more of a role in decision making, yet it couldn't effectively respond to the Federal Express idea. The paradox was that Steve knew more about what went on in his division—even though he couldn't manage it very well—than the people who were criticizing him.

I felt caught in the middle: drawn in one direction by the middle managers, whom I wanted to have more of a say in company decisions, and dragged in another by Steve, whose people were delivering the needed analysis to support their position.

No matter how often I told him to stay out of it, to allow the middle managers to decide on a task-force solution, he poked his head into it. "If you keep going on and getting involved in everyone's business, we're not going to get anything done," I told him. "You've got to focus on Macintosh and get that solved."

He agreed with me—just as he had agreed to withhold his opinions before our Xerox meeting, just as he had agreed not to verbally abuse people when I told him to go easy. But he simply couldn't stay out of it. Steve had to be involved; and he had to have control.

It seemed that every time I turned around, I discovered yet another problem. And wherever I turned, I got involved with another conflict created by Steve. Some of Steve's closest colleagues from the Macintosh division visited me on several occasions to complain about him. Some maintained that the file server would never ship—that it primarily was a product driven by software, not the hardware as Steve had maintained.

I had always seen technology through Steve's eyes. He was the magician and I was part of his audience. I had taken to heart Arthur C. Clarke's "Third Law" that "any sufficiently advanced technology is indistinguishable from magic." I realized, however, that the development of a file server would be dependent on systems technology, connecting stand-alone computers into systems or networks that could communicate with each other. This was the world of the minicomputer and the mainframe for which Steve showed disdain.

To better understand the technology, I hired a young technical adviser, Mike Homer, from our own management information systems group, and I began to cultivate relationships with other technologists outside Apple for use as a sounding board. I no longer wanted to marvel in amazement at a technological trick, I wanted to understand it myself.

And I started listening to Alan Kay.

"Steve was the sort of perfect visual personality and his main fault was that he couldn't get out of it. The visual mind is quite happy to substitute figure for ground. If you have a black circle on a white background, it's interpreted almost exactly the same as a white circle on a black background. Because your vision takes first derivatives and what it sees is a cartoon outline.

"Take a look at the Mac. If you look at it from the front, it's fantastic. If you look at it from the back, it stinks. Steve doesn't think systems at all. Different kind of mentality. Turn the Mac around and look at the spigots on the back, and you say, 'Holy smoke, what's wrong with these guys? Aren't they thinking about connectivity, about the ability to link up to a larger world?'

"Looking at the original Mac, you can see Steve. It's like Steve's head in a sense because it has the good parts of Steve and the bad parts. It has this super quality control and the parts where his brain didn't function.

"Apple's idea of systems, when I came, was to throw in a floppy disk and say, 'That's all the connection we'll ever have to have.'"

"This is a lot more complicated than we think," I told Steve. "We really need to understand a lot more about systems, about how we connect up to other computers."

"Don't worry," he said. "Stay the course. We know what we're doing. Trust me. This is the right way to go."

Whenever I would mention that other engineers at Apple thought our approach could be wrong, he shrugged their concerns aside.

"They just don't understand," he said.

Other members of his staff privately told me that no one yet knew what the next generation Macintosh would look like—even though more than a year had passed since the introduction of the first Mac.

"John," one said, "you have got to do something about Steve. He's constantly changing his mind about what we should do. The result is we don't know what to do. We all love Steve's ideas, but we can't take his management style much longer."

More and more of my time was consumed with trying to calm people down because Steve intruded into their area. I was getting into the office earlier and earlier—by 6:30 a.m. Yet I couldn't seem to manage my time well enough to have an impact.

As I began to question and challenge Steve, we found ourselves agreeing on less and less. The most devastating part was that we were a new products company in a new products industry, yet we weren't pushing new products out the door.

The friction between us was becoming evident. At one point, my executive assistant, Nanette Buckhout, threatened to resign because of her increasing frustrations with Steve's staff. She had spent eleven years with me at Pepsi, through many difficult times. She could shoulder pressure as well as I, and never before had she gotten to a breaking point. She also had been one to openly defend Steve when members of the executive staff would come to my office to complain about him.

But even Nanette couldn't take much more. She found Steve's staff arrogant on numerous occasions. Sometimes his staff would say that Steve, still depressed over the Mac's lackluster sales, was either "too tired" or "not feeling well enough" to make a meeting.

"I feel sometimes that when I try to arrange meetings for you and Steve, I am trying to get a date with him—it's ridiculous," she wrote. "If Steve is not accessible to you, can you imagine how the other employees at Apple are feeling?"

Bill Campbell brought another major problem to my attention in early April. In January, we renamed the Lisa the Macintosh XL and cut its price to $3,995. We had hoped the new name would strengthen customers' and retailers' focus on Macintosh office products. Campbell had discovered, however, that we might not be able to deliver the product much longer.

"The word's all over Apple and it's getting out to our dealers that we don't have enough parts to build the Macintosh XL for more than about ninety days," Campbell said. "We're going to totally lose our credibility on this thing."

Steve and several members of the Macintosh team believed the original design of the Lisa wasn't good enough and that it never would have the quality of a Macintosh. They felt it wasn't a priority product and wanted it phased out. We obviously couldn't phase a product out that had just been introduced. So someone in the Macintosh division simply neglected, perhaps deliberately, to order parts and components to allow us to continue the manufacture of the Macintosh XL.

We discovered we couldn't get delivery of additional parts for the product until the early fall. Steve felt his division could get a Macintosh out with a hard disk by then and argued that that was a better solution because the product would be more reliable and cost less to build. We found ourselves in the awkward position of having to discontinue a product we introduced only three months earlier. The outside world just crucified us over it. They pointed to it as a sign that Apple was out of control.

I had been losing confidence in Steve's ability to manage the Mac division since the introduction of the Macintosh Office. This latest fiasco only heightened my concern. The Macintosh division was no longer a product development group, it now was a large, complex business with hundreds of employees. I could recall Steve's earlier insistence on never allowing the Macintosh group to go over 100 people. He believed too many people would make the group ineffective, unable to foster the camaraderie needed to get the most from them. He never wanted to become an administrator or a manager. He wanted to be on the front lines, involved in every decision.

Yet that is exactly what happened as Macintosh continued its growth and we folded Lisa into it. A move that had initially seemed logical in consolidating the company's operations was now clearly a mistake.

I had given Steve greater power than he had ever had and I had created a monster.

Initially, I saw Apple in PepsiCo terms. Frito-Lay and Pepsi-Cola could comfortably and successfully exist as separate entities under PepsiCo. The Apple II group could have its own factories and sales organization for the K–12 education and consumer markets. Macintosh, with its own independent operations, targeted the university and business markets. What I didn't realize was that it wasn't working. The two groups became too competitive with each other. People were getting burned out.

It was a mistake for other reasons, too. The organization created two power bases and removed me from day-to-day operating decisions. I became more remote from the business. As chairman, Steve was over me. And as head of a product division, he was under me. He really had more knowledge about what was going on in the business than I did because all the information was coming up through the products divisions. They had all the power. The corporate staff basically became an impotent group, largely a financial organization.

The tensions that developed between the two groups could

have cracked steel. Steve had never made a secret of the fact that he had always thought the Macintosh people represented the best of Apple. Now he and his Macintosh cohorts began to openly call everyone else in the company "bozos." It got to the point where non-Macintosh people began wearing buttons with a line running through the face of a bozo clown.

There was nothing else to do: I had to remove Steve as general manager of the Macintosh division. It was a painful decision because I knew the cost was high. Steve would pay the price of a job that he liked; I would pay the price of our friendship because I knew it could never survive this. For days I wracked my mind for an alternative. But I knew I wasn't doing what I was hired to do. My responsibility was to the shareholders, the board, and the employees. I had to separate my personal interests from the interests of the corporation.

I went to see Steve to tell him what I had decided. He still was in a funk over why people weren't buying the Macintosh. I told him I planned to bring the issues between us out in the open with the board at the next meeting.

"There is no one who admires your brilliance and vision more than I do," I said. "I changed my entire life to come and work with you, Steve. But this is really not going to work. You've either got to get a lot better, or we're going to have to make some changes. Over the past two years, we have developed a great friendship with each other, but I have lost confidence in your ability to run the Macintosh division."

Steve appeared stunned.

"Well, you've got to spend more time with me," he demanded.

True, we weren't spending nearly as much time together. But there wasn't as much time left. I was being pulled in every direction.

"I want you to know I'm going to bring this up with the board and I'm going to recommend that you step down from your operating job of running the Macintosh division. And I want you to know that ahead of time."

"I don't believe you're going to do that," he said.

"Yes, I am. I think you should focus your time as chairman on new technologies and new products that we should look at in the future. We need to reorganize the Macintosh division."

Steve was incensed and outraged. He jumped up from his seat

and began pacing the floor, his eyes focusing in a piercing and defiant stare.

"If you do that, you're going to destroy this company!" he said angrily. "I'm the only one who understands enough around here about manufacturing and operations, and I don't think you understand these things yet.

"You're too far removed from the actual day-in-and-day-out operations, and if I'm not overseeing this, we're not going to get any new products out and we're not going to succeed!"

A violent disagreement erupted. Steve and I had never spoken to each other that way. All of a sudden, we found ourselves battling. Convinced I had lobbied the board ahead of time, he felt I had betrayed him. I hadn't. But it was clear all-out war because this was his company. He had brought me to Apple, and now I was telling him to step down from operating the division of the product he created. I heard rumblings from other people that he had lost confidence in me, too. He was convinced that I was as much a part of the problem as anything. The fact was we both were part of the problem.

I don't think he believed I would go to the board with it. But I felt I had to. At the April 10 meeting, I told our directors they had a choice:

"I'm asking Steve to step down and you can back me on it and then I take responsibility for running the company, or we can do nothing and you're going to have to find yourselves a new CEO," I said. "We've got enough problems and we've got to solve them right now."

I was totally prepared to deliver on my offer to resign. I had come to Apple thinking that I would stay five years, help nurture Steve as a manager, and then quit. I had no idea of exactly what I would do after that, but I thought at that point I wouldn't have many financial worries, given what I hoped Apple's stock options would be worth. Maybe, I thought, I would just go out and start a company of my own. If I walked out on Apple now, the scenario would be quite different. But I could deal with it.

I explained to the board that it had become too difficult to effectively run the company with Steve in dual roles as chairman and Macintosh general manager. Steve had to accept me as the sole chief executive. I wanted him to remain as chairman and be a major contributor as a product innovator who could contribute to our ideas and strategies. My solution was to work out an orderly transition with Steve so Apple could benefit from his product insights, while we would pick the strongest candidate to succeed him as general manager.

I proposed that we strengthen the Macintosh marketing function by appointing Jean-Louis Gassée as marketing director. Steve and I had talked about this earlier because we both believed Murray no longer felt comfortable working in such a large organization. As head of Apple France, Gassée had turned that unit into our fastest-growing and most profitable foreign division. Gassée would have the inside track to succeed Steve, but we wouldn't make a choice until we saw how well he did in the marketing job. Gassée, however, would not accept the job unless he received assurances that he would become the general manager of the division.

Steve, who initially favored bringing Gassée to the United States, argued that he should prove he deserved the general manager's job. But eventually he agreed to Gassée's proposal as long as we kept the time for the change flexible. I was thinking that Steve could move out toward the end of the year. At the same time, we also would launch a new product group that Steve could head up. I felt it was the least traumatic and most dignified way to handle the transition.

The board meeting lasted from 6:00 p.m. until 9:30 p.m. and resumed the following day at 9:00 a.m. It didn't end until after three-thirty. At one point, the board met only with me; at another, it met privately with Steve. The upshot was that the board unanimously decided that we should ask Steve to step down as executive vice president and continue as chairman. It left me with the authority to implement the change.

Steve was stunned and visibly beaten. He couldn't believe it.

The board meeting over, I climbed the stairs to my office and abruptly left—not even saying goodbye to Nanette, who obviously wondered what had transpired during the day. Later she recalled that:

"After the board meeting, John immediately went home. You couldn't even speak to him about it. He just walked into his office, got his briefcase, and walked out. He was completely out of it.

"*Then Mike Markkula called from home. He wanted to see how John was doing and whether he was okay.*

"'*Nan, this has been really tough on him,*' *he said.* '*Is he okay?*'

"*And I said,* '*As well as can be expected. How did it go? I haven't seen Steve.*'

"*And he said,* '*You know, Steve is not really believing any of this. Until he does, he'll never accept it. Somebody really should talk to him. I'm concerned that he's not really willing to accept this, and he's not going to let go. Do you talk to him?*'

"'*Yeah, I talk to him on occasion,*' *I said.* '*Do you think I should try? I don't even know if he'll talk to me, but I'll see how he's doing.*'

"*I called his office, but I didn't know how he would react. I was surprised when I think how that meeting ended and how everybody walked out, that he would even get on the phone.*

"*But he got on and I said,* '*Steve, do you have some time to talk? Do you want to talk?*' *And he said,* '*Yeah. I'll come over there.*' *It was a little after five. So he came over and it was the most unbelievable meeting. It was very emotional. He just broke down and cried. And I cried. My heart really went out to him.*

"*He said,* '*I can't believe this is happening. I can't believe it happened. Why did John do this to me; I can't believe he would do this. He betrayed me.*'

"'*It's a nightmare,*' *I said.* '*What did you do? You and John together have accomplished so much. You blew it. You blew it.*'

"*I couldn't forgive him for what he did to John. Only a week or so earlier, John came into work and said,* '*Nan, I got the strangest call. Steve called late at about eleven and woke me up.*' *And I said,* '*What did he want?*' *He said,* '*He just called to say, "John, you're terrific and I just want you to know that I love working with you and I really appreciate our friendship."*'

"*Now, I had just had a conversation with Al Eisenstat who told me he had gotten a call from Steve that very night saying he's losing confidence in John, that he's real upset about how John's running things and he thinks we should talk to the board about it. I said to Al,* '*Wait a minute. What time did Steve call you?*' *And he said,* '*Nine o'clock.*' *And I said,* '*Al, John got a call at eleven and this is what Steve told him.*' *He said,* '*What the hell is he doing?*' *I couldn't trust him anymore after that but now I just felt so sorry for him.*

"He was just very sad through the whole thing. Very mellow. I said, 'John is the best friend you could ever have, that you ever had . . . He was so loyal to you. Why did you go behind his back?' And he started saying that John wasn't an operations guy or something like that. And I said, 'Why couldn't you work it out with him? He always defended you and he was always the one defending you when people would complain about you. I always defended you, too. I don't understand.'

"And he kind of got quiet, and I said, 'What are you going to do?' And he said, 'I know he was a good friend. I know that.' I think this is what really blows me away. He said, 'And I think what I should do is definitely leave Apple.' And he said, looking straight into my eyes, 'Nan, I don't think I should stay at Apple.'

" 'Steve, you know you and John can work together. Apple needs you. You don't have to leave.' And he said, 'I think I should get away and work on my friendship with John. John's friendship is more important than anything else, and I think maybe that's what I should do, concentrate on our friendship. That should be my priority.'

"I'll never forget those words. It broke my heart. All I know is, he was very emotional and it was real. And he knew that the next day, I was going to sit down with John and say, 'Steve really values your friendship more than anything else and he really wants to work on it.' "

Steve seemed to acquiesce in the decision. He set to work on mending our fragile friendship. But he told me he didn't believe I would use the board's approval to oust him from his operating role. He said he was willing to do anything to stay in the position and prove to me and the board he could be the operating manager we wanted. In return, he said, he would give me all the leeway I required to run the company. He just wanted a chance to prove he could do it.

I refused to relent. As the company's problems mounted, settling problems with Steve became even more critical. Then he suddenly bolted out of his depression and became convinced that only he could turn Apple around. When it became clear I wasn't going to back down, he came to talk to me in early May.

"I think you really lost your stride," he said. "You really were great the first year and everything went wonderful. But something happened. I can't pin it down, but it was sometime during the end of 1984. I think I understand what has to happen at Apple, and I really am disappointed we're not following my plans on more things."

"Steve," I said heatedly, "let's sit down and analyze that. I think it's my fault that I didn't do a better job of managing you because you haven't gotten the Macintosh Office out. And you haven't listened to the marketplace and what people really want. You won't listen to anyone about systems products and the importance of connecting into IBM's products. And maybe you won't believe this, but there really are more IBM personal computers out there than there are Macintoshes."

"Okay, hotshot," he said, rising to his feet. "You were hired to run our company and look where it is. If I'm such a bad manager how come we're shipping so many Macintoshes and getting profit from that? And if you're such a good manager, how come we've got all this inventory of the Apple IIc out there?"

I couldn't give him a good answer. On one hand, he was right, although we had put in place a dealer promotion to stimulate lackluster Macintosh sales and it was working. On the other, he had a short memory. He forgot that we had agreed on how fast we should race together to build the company. When sales of the Apple IIc and the Macintosh were booming during the summer of 1984, we decided to "go for it" together and with the board's blessing. We had bet the company on this race, and it turned out that we lost.

I had been hired for my consumer marketing experience. Steve saw in me the marketer who could help him put a new "appliance" into the home.

It was unclear what the average consumer would do with it. But if you asked people in the nineteenth century why they would need a telephone, few would be able to come up with an answer. If you had asked them what they would do with an automobile, they couldn't tell you, either.

Yet those industries helped shape the modern world.

Mistakenly, Steve and I tried to turn Apple into a consumer marketing giant. I saw in Apple a wonderful company that had come out of nowhere and had been able to develop a love affair with consumers. It boasted a strong trademark and name. Its products were reliable and innovative—all the things you want in a consumer company. I asked myself how we could market technology as it had never been marketed before. I used the techniques that worked so well at Pepsi: going against conventional wisdom, using marketing as theater, making it bigger than life.

Apple would snare the high end of the market by leveraging our strong position in schools to sell into the home. We agreed to steer clear of the low end of the market, which was being sold by mass merchandisers with Mattel's Adam computer, TI's 99/4, Commodore 64, and Atari's 1200.

My theory was to price the product at a premium and then plow some of that back into advertising and build our market share. It has always been cheaper to gain market share when an industry is growing than when it has stabilized. Once we gained position, the economics would be such that no one could afford to come after us. I remember wondering how long it would take us to get to $200 million in advertising expenditures because no one company, with the exception of IBM, could ever afford to spend that. Our economics would all be built around that strategy.

Soon after I arrived, I raised our ad budget—from $15 to $100 million. No one had heard of our advertising the year before. Now Apple had the highest advertising awareness of any computer brand in the United States. We decided that our marketing and advertising would be as innovative as the product—our way of differentiating ourselves and our product from the competition.

What I missed was that the key number in the business is gross margin—the percentage of profits on overall sales. It was critical to have high gross margins to pay for the huge research and development expenses needed to support a proprietary technology. As long as our growth galloped at a 50 percent a year pace, we couldn't spend money fast enough to get ourselves into trouble.

The real problem would come if the growth stopped. But we never had any indications that was going to happen. It just came out of nowhere. One day, it seemed, everything was great. The next day we were in the middle of a storm. The home market, which was really driving our growth, was a figment of everyone's imagination.

People weren't about to buy $2000 computers to play a video game, balance a checkbook, or file gourmet recipes as some suggested. The average consumer simply couldn't do something useful with a computer. Neither could the home market appreciate important differences in computer products. Computers largely looked alike and were a mystery for the average person: they were too expensive and too intimidating. Once we saturated the market for enthusiasts, it wasn't possible for the industry to continue its incredible record of growth.

I had mistakenly thought I could wind expenses down later once Steve and I got the company up to $2 or $3 billion in annual revenues. The first priority was the race. . . . I didn't watch inventories and I didn't watch gross margins closely enough. The inventories kept building and the gross margins kept getting thinner and thinner. Profits remained only because we had reduced research and development. In a consumer product framework, our R and D budget was astronomical. I remember looking at it and saying, "Boy, this company is spending a huge amount on research and development. We spent three million dollars at Pepsi. How can anyone not figure out what they're going to create with forty million?"

Meantime, we didn't worry about increasing R and D because we already were spending $40 million a year. Robbing research to pay for advertising turned out to be a big, big mistake. We lost our new product edge. As it happened, we had become a company that could introduce a new product only every year or two, and burn people out in the process of doing so.

What I hadn't realized was that Apple would never be a consumer products company. It was a computer company in a technology industry. All the other successful computer companies had high gross margins, and the ones that had proprietary technologies were all spending 7 to 10 percent of their revenues on research and development. I should have understood that those were the things you had to watch. Alan Kay once told me that "Point of view is worth eighty IQ points." I realized how right he was. It was, more than anything, a problem of perspective.

When I went back and looked at the $2 billion in total industry losses in 1983 and 1984, I was astounded. I discovered that almost

100 percent of it was inventory-related. Companies either built too much inventory and the industry slowed down, or they had badly forecasted sales. In consumer products, you don't worry about the value of inventories because their value usually remains constant. At Pepsi, you produce soda the night before and ship it the next day.

In the computer industry, that's not true. Because you spend a lot of money on research and development, you amortize those costs into the product price for the first year. You don't know how long the product is going to last. Products didn't become obsolete after two years in consumer packaging. I didn't realize that you priced your research and development up front and that's why the price of computers kept coming down. It wasn't just from competitive products; the whole industry had been pricing computers that way for years. But I didn't understand the computer perspective.

Racing to grow fast was fine—as long as things were growing. But if they ever stopped, the price you were going to pay was astronomical. I was hired to be a consumer marketing person. Yet Apple didn't warrant a consumer marketing perspective. On a superficial level it may have looked like one because the brand was so neat and people loved it so much. But this was a business that demanded a focus on research and development and on inventories which quickly become obsolete.

I had been party to creating a machine that was designed to lose money.

The evening before our May 24 executive staff meeting, I was having dinner at Al Eisenstat's house when Jean-Louis Gassée pulled me aside in the living room. He appeared less playful than usual. Jean-Louis has a flair for flamboyance and for fun but this time he was deadly serious and direct. He suggested I cancel my trip to China the following afternoon. Months earlier, I had made a commitment to meet the vice premier of China to talk about Apple computers in education. With some 980,000 schools and over 200 million students, it is a huge potential market. The trip was important to lay the groundwork for what would certainly be a long-term opportunity.

"John," he warned, "you should be aware that there are real forces going on to try to throw you out of the company."

"What do you mean?" I asked.

"I'd rather not go into all the details of it, but it would be my advice to you not to go to China. You should stay here."

Pressed, he maintained that Steve, obviously unhappy over the likely loss of his operating role, was planning to overthrow me while I was away in China. He had ostensibly been testing his standing in talks with some managers and members of the executive staff.

I was startled. If Steve wanted to mount a serious challenge to my leadership, he could have at least come to me first—as I had first gone to Steve to openly inform him in advance that I was going to seek the board's support for his removal as head of the Macintosh division.

Steve obviously had been bitter ever since the April 11 board meeting, when it was decided that he would be removed as head of the Macintosh division. We still had a cordial, if not close, relationship with each other, but we held different opinions on the direction of the company, and Steve already had made it clear to me that he was the one who could manage Apple out of its troubles.

But I had come from a world where trust was everything. No one would have ever done anything at PepsiCo to undermine Kendall. That wasn't even a remote possibility. At Pepsi, we competed vigorously with each other, but we did so on the basis of trust. We competed openly and honestly.

The board, moreover, was also upset with me because it felt I had been given a clear mandate to remove Steve at the April meeting, and various board members wanted to know why he hadn't yet been removed. One wanted Steve out of operations completely and immediately. He urged that if Steve refused to step down, we have him physically removed from the building. I had believed I could gradually move Steve out of operations and into advanced product development. Now, things were getting out of hand.

"Al," I said, "what do you think?"

"I haven't heard a thing about this," he said.

"Jean-Louis, are you sure of this?" I asked.

"I wouldn't come forward to you if I didn't feel fairly confident," he said.

As much as I respected and admired Jean-Louis, I didn't want to believe he could be right about this. I thought up any excuse for why it couldn't be true—his own rivalry with Steve over control of the Mac division, the tension we'd all lived through lately, the late hour, the wine. Anything.

When Leezy and I returned home, I told her about the conversation. "I'm really uncomfortable getting on this plane and going to China tomorrow," I said.

"My instincts run the same way, John," she said. "You don't belong on the other side of the world where no one can reach you. And what if the board wanted to talk to you immediately or if the executive staff wanted to get in touch with you?"

"That's what I was thinking. How would they reach me? I'd be totally out of touch."

The next morning I canceled the trip. I decided to confront Steve with the allegation in front of the executive staff. I felt it would be impossible for me to lead the company as chief executive if I didn't have the support of both the staff and the board of directors.

Everyone had already assembled in the boardroom for the 9:00 a.m. session. Steve arrived late. When he sat down, I nervously glanced around the table to measure the pulse of the meeting. But I didn't hesitate to bring the issue up.

"Steve," I said, "we're not going to follow the normal agenda this morning because there is a major issue which has to be settled, and I think the whole executive staff ought to be included in it. It's come to my attention that you'd like to throw me out of the company, and I'd like to ask you if that's true."

The executive staff wasn't shocked by the news. Steve had, by now, approached nearly all of them to gain a sign of their support of him. But they seemed stunned that I would spark an open confrontation with him. An uneasy moment of frozen silence passed as Steve looked down and then finally up at me, meeting my eyes with an intense glare.

"I think you're bad for Apple and I think you're the wrong person to run this company," he said slowly, almost quietly, in a tense but controlled voice. "You really should leave this company. I'm more worried about Apple than I have ever been. I'm afraid of you. You don't know how to operate and never have.

"John," Steve went on, getting more wound up, "you manage by monologue! You have no understanding of the product development process. You don't know how manufacturing works. You're not close to the company. The middle managers don't respect you. In the first year, you helped build the company, but in the second, you hurt the company."

I felt sick to my stomach. Steve had originally felt I should be involved in virtually every detail of the operations, but I told him he was wrong. It wasn't necessary or desirable for the chief executive to know every detail of the company. That is the job of individual managers running a good organization.

"It's pretty clear that we have a major point of difference," I snapped. "You can't be involved in all details."

"I wanted you here to help me grow, and you've been ineffective in helping me."

I couldn't believe what I was hearing. Neither could many of the executive staff members around the table. They were a ring of perplexed, sullen faces. I suddenly didn't know if most of them were behind me or Steve, but at this moment it didn't seem to make a difference.

"I made a mistake in treating you with high esteem," I stammered. "I don't trust you, and I won't tolerate a lack of trust." I hadn't stuttered for more than twenty years, yet I could feel myself briefly losing my composure, falling back into my childhood stammer.

"If I left, who would run the company?" I asked in a challenging voice.

"I think I could run the company," Steve said seriously. "I think I understand the things that need to be done."

"Well," I said, "I certainly can't run the company if I don't have the support of the board and the executive staff. I'd like to go around the room and just ask each of the executive staff members how they feel about what you've just said. Because if they agree with you, it would be very hard for me to run the company."

I went around the table as each member of the executive staff gave his opinion. Every one of them said they weren't pleased with how things were going, but indicated they were putting their support behind me. Still, every one had affectionate feelings for Steve and spoke of the tremendous contributions he made to Apple and the industry.

Campbell said Steve was the heart of the company. "Steve needs to have a role and be part of the company," he said.

"I love Steve," said Del Yocam, who ran the Apple II division. "I respect you, John." He made it clear that love wasn't enough anymore, that we had to have leadership that could be respected.

They were not ready to support Steve's proposal that I leave the company.

"Well, I guess I know where things stand," Steve said quietly, his eyes glistening with emotion.

He bolted from the room, and we abruptly ended the meeting. No one followed Steve out to comfort him.

Steve's comments had stung, particularly his remarks that I had failed to teach him anything. During my first year and a half at Apple, all he could do was tell me how much he learned from me.

I felt dazed, but now had to face a group of frustrated middle managers who also had vented their anger at me a few weeks earlier. I outlined the company's problems and a way in which they could contribute solutions. We decided to form a task force of middle managers to increase their participation in the management of the company. The session went well, and the news of a task force was welcomed. It meant that the company's middle managers finally would have more of a say in the company's affairs.

But after the meeting, I felt drained. I wondered if I really belonged at Apple.

I was failing, and the evidence of it surrounded me. The company was in real trouble. For the first time in my life, my power, prestige, and self-assurance were in jeopardy. I had never lost my self-confidence. I had never known failure before. But now I wondered whether I was capable of leading the company through its crisis, or if Steve was right. Maybe I wasn't the best person to run Apple.

Few very successful people think of failure. Throughout my life, I had scarcely thought of the word. My father had instilled in his three sons an ethic to succeed born from his high expectations for all of us. I always tried hard to fulfill those expectations, to ensure that his efforts to underwrite a first-class education for me hadn't been for naught. Now, I privately wondered myself.

I was at a crossroads in my life as surely as if someone had put up a sign. If I panicked, total failure seemed certain. Or maybe I could summon an inner strength to get me through this dream-turned-nightmare. I could scarcely believe I had allowed this to happen to me. The stress was more palpable than anything I had ever experienced.

I wandered into Al Eisenstat's office. Al had been a good, steady friend ever since I arrived at Apple. I trusted him completely and respected him for his reasoned judgment.

"Al," I said, "I need to just drive around with you. Would you mind coming out with me, and we'll just drive around a little bit and talk?"

I looked ashen and shaken, even disoriented from the day's events.

We got into his brown Porsche. Ironically, the license plate had "Pepse" on it. People always thought it was my car, but Al's nickname since childhood was Pepsi because his uncle and father were Pepsi bottlers from Pennsylvania. We began driving onto the freeway. My mind was painfully divided. I had won the support I wanted, yet I knew that few were happy about the ways things transpired. I was unprepared for such a wild swing in fate, from distinction to the near failure of the last turbulent months.

"Al," I said, "I don't know whether I can go through with this."

"What do you mean?" he asked.

"I have to tell you that I don't think I have it inside of me to go through with this. Will you drive me home?"

Al tried to offer some comfort. He told me we had gone through the worst of it, that the board and the executive staff were solidly behind me and that now we could move forward to turn the company around. But his words didn't really register through the pain I was feeling.

We were driving along Interstate 280, toward my home in Woodside, when I said, "Al, I think I'm going to resign."

"You're kidding!" he said. "You can't resign now. Apple will fall apart if you resign now!"

"Al, I just think it's the right thing. I'm going to resign. I'm not up to it right now. I don't think I'm right for the company. Will you call the board to alert them that I feel I should resign?"

"Well, if that's what you really want," he said, "I'll do it. But I think you're copping out. You've got to stand up to him."

Al brought me home. Leezy was surprised to see me so early in the afternoon and so shaken. I told her in detail about Steve's remarks and my uncertainty over being able to lead the company out of its troubles. Leezy had never really liked Steve. She disliked his late-night phone calls to the house, his interminable visits and intrusions, and my endless fascination with him. All the hours I spent with Steve in the evenings and on weekends had worn on her, and rightly so. We had frequently disagreed about Steve, she never quite trusting him, me always defending his actions. Now I could only sadly tell her she was right.

There was the sense that she was losing her husband after following me to a strange place where she had to make new friends and start a new life from scratch. Leezy never cared much for the social hierarchy of the corporate wives at Pepsi. She didn't miss that at all. But Silicon Valley, for all its "new age" trappings, didn't seem hospitable to women who weren't interested in a career in the Valley.

What I told her made her all the more incensed about him.

"Leezy," I said, "I think we've got to go. But I have to tell you that we are bankrupt. I borrowed three million dollars to buy Apple stock, and we can't pay the loan back unless we sell the house."

In my confidence in the company's future, I had borrowed $3 million to buy tens of thousands of shares of Apple stock. Our stock had soared to more than $63 a share in 1983. It now commanded little more than $15 a share. I had purchased my holdings when the price was much higher.

"When we got married," she said, more calmly than anyone could have expected, "we didn't have a very big house. We can do that again. I'm totally with you, whatever you want to do. What should we do about the house?"

"We ought to put it on the market," I said. "But the minute that happens, the newspapers will find out and they will assume that I'm leaving. So I've got to figure out the timing on all of this. And I don't want to leave the board in the lurch because I feel partly responsible for the problems we're in. I guess we'll just have to stick it out for a while, but we ought to start getting ourselves together and figuring out what we're going to do."

"Well, what kind of job will you be able to get?"

"I don't know," I said. "Gerry Roche told me that if it ever blew up, there was nothing he could do, that I'd be on my own. I know what I'm capable of doing, and I have always had a lot of self-confidence, so I'm not worried. I'll come up with something that I can do. But I think this is it. We've lost. I've failed."

I left the house to walk around our yard and think about what had happened. Self-criticism is a seldom-practiced art. Steve wasn't willing to share much of the blame for the company's problems. I had to concede I made mistakes, serious errors of judgment that helped to plunge the company into a crisis. But Steve had made those decisions with me as well, and it was he who failed to bring to market the sorely needed products that would make the Macintosh a success in the business world.

If Steve felt betrayed, so did I. I never plotted behind his back to relieve him of the operating responsibilities I had given him in the first place. Neither did I make the decision lightly to remove him from operations. It was one of the most difficult decisions I ever could make.

When I returned, Leezy turned to me and said sharply, "John, you've never quit anything before in your life. You've never been a quitter.

"You know, I've watched you throughout your whole career. You've had problems before, and you've always had the self-confidence to take them on. You were always the optimist whenever everyone else was pessimistic. I've never, in our entire relationship, ever seen you like this before. I don't know how you lost your self-confidence, but you can't quit. I'm not going to let you quit."

"I put you through too much," I said. "I pulled you out of your home in Connecticut, I brought you out here, and now I've turned your private life into a public scene. Apple is a soap opera. The newspapers write about us constantly. We have no privacy. We have to live in a fenced-in compound with electric gates. We've had bomb scares, kidnapping attempts. And the result is we're bankrupt. All I've given us is a lot of pain, and you never see me. That's not much of a life."

"John," she said, "I have confidence that you can fix this thing, and I don't want you to back out of it."

At the least, I needed some sleep. I felt emotionally and physically spent. According to Leezy:

"I just decided I had to do it. I watched Steve turn from a friend of John's to trying to plant little seeds in John's head about me. I think Steve was jealous I was in the way at all. From the very beginning, I had reservations about Steve. Even before we came, I said, 'I don't trust him. He started this company. What makes you think in a million years that you're going to have a free hand to run it?'

"So I sped over to Steve's office and he was gone. They said he had gone to his favorite restaurant, the Good Earth. I drove over to the Good Earth Restaurant and decided to wait in the car. I didn't think it would be a good idea to go marching into the restaurant to make a scene in front of everyone over lunch. So I waited and waited, and he came out with Debi Coleman and a bunch of people I didn't know.

"I was outraged and livid, but I had it under control. I wasn't sure what I would say; I hadn't planned anything. I hadn't sat there and said, Now I'm going to say this. It just came out. But I knew I had to have a confrontation with him because I was too furious. Whenever I get really outraged about something, I have to let it out. I'm not one of these people who sit back and hide my feelings. I can't do it. That's why John says I'll never have a heart attack or ulcers because I really blow it off when I get upset about something.

"As soon as I saw Steve I got out of the car, very controlled, and said, 'Oh, Steve, could I talk to you for a minute?' His mouth dropped. I don't think he would have talked to me if he hadn't been there with a lot of other people. They were watching his reaction. He paused and then he said, 'Oh, Leezy!'

"He looked sort of surprised, like how am I going to get out of this one? I think Steve honestly knew I was capable of being a tough character to deal with. He turned to his friends and said, 'You guys go ahead. I'll catch up with you in a minute.'

"As soon as I walked over to him, he started hanging his head.

I said, 'Steve, I just have a few little things to say to you. It won't take long.' My normal instincts would have been to slug him. But I was perfectly controlled.

" 'Do you have any idea what a privilege it has been even to know someone as fine as John Sculley? He has been a real friend to you, but you'll never know it, until the day you're on your deathbed.'

"I said, 'Steve, can't you look at me in the eyes when I'm talking to you?' And he kept saying, 'You don't understand, you don't understand.' I said, 'Steve, look at me when you talk to me.' And he looked at me and I said, 'Never mind, don't look at me. When I look into most people's eyes, I see a soul. When I look into your eyes, I see a bottomless pit, an empty hole, a dead zone.' And he turned his head and said, 'You don't understand.'

"I said, 'I think I understand everything there is to understand, Steve. I feel sorry for you.' I left it at that."

The next morning, I woke up and felt surprisingly strong. It was true—I wasn't a quitter. While I had hardly regained the buoyant spirit I brought to Apple only months earlier, I at least believed I could muster the confidence and strength needed to turn the company around.

I immediately called Al at his home and asked him if he had spoken to any of the board members yet about my plans to resign. He had only called Arthur Rock, who expressed shock and surprise at the news.

"Well, call him back," I urged. "I'm staying, if he and the others still want me."

"I'm sure they do," ventured Al.

At this point, I could feel the adrenaline flowing within me. I felt determined that we would get Apple out of its morass. No sooner had I summoned the strength to reverse my day-old decision to quit when Steve called. He wanted to rendezvous on Sunday for a walk in the hills at Stanford University. We had met there often, to walk and talk in confidence.

We used to stroll together there, a bucolic area alongside Interstate 280, past the huge radio telescopes and satellite dishes set into the hills by Stanford University scientists. It seemed to affirm Silicon Valley's role as a technological center. The modernistic telescopes took Venus' temperature, ensured the moon was firm enough to land on, and communicated with satellites and spacecraft.

Yet what I perceived as symbols of the new technological age, Steve saw as low-tech junk, remnants of antiquated technology that polluted the area's beauty. He was right. The giant 60-foot aluminum dish that looks so modern from afar is really a rusty, twenty-five-year-old, outdated piece of equipment. Our differing perspectives, though, demonstrated how different our worlds were. Steve was mentally living twenty-five years in the future. As a newcomer to Silicon Valley, I felt caught between the industrial and new-age times.

It was during these walks that Steve had assumed the role of technology teacher to me, as I had attempted to teach him all I could about my world—marketing and management. Our companionship had blossomed into a close friendship during those walks. Little by little, we talked about life and about the universe; we traded fears and hopes about our futures and we exchanged hundreds of private thoughts.

This meeting, of course, would be different. Shortly after three in the afternoon the following day, we met in the hills and walked for several hours, talking about how we were going to resolve the issue. Steve argued again and again that he should have an operational role at Apple. I insisted it wouldn't work out. But Steve had the ability to totally forget anything that had occurred and to totally rewrite in his mind a new scenario. He lacked the support of both the board of directors and the executive staff, yet he was bold enough to propose that I relinquish control of the company.

"Why don't you become chairman and I'll become president and chief executive officer?" he said, almost matter-of-factly.

"Steve, that doesn't make any sense," I said. "I wasn't hired to come and just be a figurehead, and the company doesn't need that. If I shouldn't be the chief executive officer, then we should find another one. But just creating that for me doesn't make much sense."

"Well, that's how I feel," he said. "I don't want to be a figurehead. I just don't want to be a chairman that's going off and working on long-range projects or thinking of new visions and things like that."

"I know you don't," I said. Steve wanted to prove that he could manage something successfully. He honestly felt he was better equipped to bring Apple out of its doldrums, and he believed a move back into product development would be a sign to everyone inside and outside the company that he had failed as a manager. So Steve was hardly ready to start over again developing products, by starting a think tank within Apple. We'd work through the company's current problems, while he could focus on the company's future.

"Isn't there some way we could divide the things up and you can work on the marketing side of the business and I can work on the product side, and we could find a way to sort of run them like two separate operations?" Steve asked.

"I honestly don't know how that would work. My sense is that Apple's got to pull together as one company. We can't structure it into two companies. Splitting up the company along functional lines without a clear leader wouldn't help anyone.

"We've got a real crisis on our hands, and this is not the time to experiment. One person has got to run the company and I've got the support and you don't."

It was an agonizing meeting. When I told some members of the executive staff about it, they were surprised it even occurred. Why did I let myself in for a pointless, trying scene? Maybe it was a chance to reconcile our crumbling friendship; maybe it was the sheer force of Steve's personality drawing me back to him. We had become such close compatriots partly because there was no sense of competition between us. When I joined Apple, I had come to terms with what I was going to be in life. I believed that the blithe spirit in fading jeans and Velcro sneakers was one of the important figures in our country during this century. I was going to help him succeed. I never imagined that I would run the company by myself someday. Now that was the reality and our friendship was over.

As soon as I arrived at work on Monday morning, I called together the executive staff. They weren't open to giving Steve a major role in the company.

"John," one said, "we've gone through too much of this. The company's being ripped apart. You have our support, but we expect you to show strong leadership, and you cannot let Steve back in operations."

The issue settled, I resigned myself to the more important task of bringing Apple back.

Later in the week, I phoned Steve to tell him, finally and again, that there didn't seem to be any solution that made sense for him in an operating role.

"Well," he said meekly, obviously hurt, "I guess that's it."

"I'm sorry, Steve," I said, "I guess it is."

"Okay."

It was a brief conversation, an abrupt end to our relationship. On May 31, I signed the paperwork removing him as executive vice president.

Managing Through Crisis

It has always amazed me that business magazines give so much praise to people who have turned companies around. They're too quick to say how wonderful a manager is because he got the profits up this quarter. Some of the worst decisions ever made in American business are behind getting the profits up in a quarter or two to please Wall Street. By being mere "fixers" instead of "builders," too many executives either have sold out their company's future or have never been challenged to achieve something especially important.

The turnaround of Apple won me much praise—but often for the wrong reasons. Analysts and observers were quick to point out the increased profitability, the higher stock price, and Apple's success in the corporate marketplace. At best, however, the turnaround is little more than a footnote in our company's history. Far more important is what we preserved and how Apple has reinvented itself for the future.

Turning the company around wasn't the difficult part. Cutting expenses isn't much of a mystery. Closing down an unprofitable plant or operation, while one of the toughest decisions a manager might make, isn't all that difficult, either. The hard part is knowing what to turn the company into—would it be the same company as it was, or had the industry changed so much that it would have to become a vastly different corporation to survive? A tremendous amount of advice poured in from all quarters during the crisis. Most of it, in hindsight, was poor advice. We would have destroyed the

company if we had followed most of it. Instead, we held close to
our dream and vision.

Even in the darkest moments of our crisis, we refused to abandon the things we cared about—our proprietary technology, our
alternative to "the standard," our focus on the individual and the
future of the personal computer. We resisted entreaties to become
just another maker of IBM clones or to license our technology to
others in a last-ditch effort for short-term success. It's important in a
crisis not to become consumed with expense cutting, but to set
aside enough time to work on the company's values, vision, identity, and directional goals. This is the company's future.

Assess the Damage

Since a business out of control is usually hemorrhaging in
many parts of the organization, it's necessary to assess damage and
get control concurrently. There is little time to spare to do these
things in sequential steps. You need your most disciplined and experienced executives in the most important control jobs. This is no
time for amateurs. I knew from my Pepsi experience that a functional organization was the best structure to get fast control and to
quickly eliminate redundant expenses.

The next step is to analyze (usually with imperfect information
since accurate data are difficult to come by in a crisis) what the
swing factors are in the business. Inventory? Excessive manufacturing capability? Distribution problems? Segregate the problems to
understand why the company is failing. What are the assumptions
that have to be in place in order to make money? How do they
differ from the assumptions that had been made? Then, you can set
up your own personal system for scanning for "red flags."

I had made an error in looking at Apple as a consumer business
like Pepsi. That perspective put the business's major focus on revenue growth, using advertising and expanding dealer distribution as
the driving force. We increased the ad budget from about $15 mil-
lion to $100 million and dramatically expanded distribution by tak-
ing on ComputerLand with its over 350 outlets. Meantime, gross
margins were deteriorating (I thought we could fix this later after

we had critical mass), and research and development remained constant in dollars (therefore declining in percentage of revenues).

Enlist Your Experience

Eventually every top executive will face a crisis, particularly in a time when change, even radical change, is normal. So you should constantly be conditioning yourself for it—physically and mentally. Try to determine what you have learned from your experiences as you proceed through life. I have found that I always learn more from my mistakes than from my successes. If you aren't making some mistakes, you aren't taking enough chances.

In the midst of our crisis, I felt prepared to handle most problems because I managed to construct or steer solutions toward what I already knew from experience. For example, I had installed a functional organization at Pepsi and knew what it took to make it work. I understood cost cutting and knew the necessity of cutting deeper than at first seemed necessary. As painful as this would be, I realized then that fast improvement would give the organization a critical boost in self-confidence a few months later when the really hard work would begin—the work of building back the company, not merely stopping the hemorrhaging. I knew how to install a forecasting system which would work because I had done this many times before at Pepsi, too.

Take Big Risks

While it's important to look for some incremental gains during a crisis to gain confidence as you work through a struggle, it's vital that you take big risks overall. Too many managers are hesitant and fearful to assume great risks in a crisis. They play it safe. The goal to which managers in trouble aspire is based upon "small wins." Although logic might argue just the opposite, it's sometimes important to gamble everything in a high-risk situation. It's a counterintuitive notion, but an important one.

When we cut back our workforce by more than 20 percent,

many people were shocked. No one realized that we would cut so deeply. It was a painful and unpopular decision. But once it was done, it helped the company come around far more swiftly than more conservative action would have allowed. Unfortunately, executives often permit peer pressure and company tradition to constrain their options and decisions. That's why so many companies in recent years have announced dramatic reductions in staff, only to follow months later with still more and greater reductions of the workforce. Their so-called professional managers lacked either the insight or the courage to take bolder initiatives in the beginning.

When many people weren't sure we would even be profitable the following year, we also accelerated product development expenses by 70 percent. Not only did we have to gain control of the company, we had to prepare for a successful future. That also led to our $15 million investment in a Cray supercomputer in January of 1986, at a time when the public wasn't yet convinced that we had turned the company around. We bought the Cray to do simulations of future products to speed up the design of software development tools—to eliminate one of the reasons for the initial failure of the Macintosh.

Redesign—Don't Fix

"There is nothing better than a life and death struggle," Lee Iacocca once told us, "to help get your priorities straight."

Yet when most companies are confronted with problems, they try simply to fix them. They fail to use a problem or a crisis as an opportunity to explore a new way to do business. Managers' first instinct is to fix instead of reveal, to solve a problem instead of find an opportunity. Before they ask, how do I make it beautiful or better, they ask, how do I get out of this jam? It's far more important to get interested in taking a problem or crisis apart and understanding it.

Herein lies one of the few positive aspects of a crisis: it creates an environment in which executives have the greatest chance to make significant changes in a company. Who, after all, wants to change something that isn't obviously broken? And how much support can one expect from the company's stakeholders—its employees, shareholders, suppliers, and customers—if an executive radically alters the company when it's not in a state of crisis?

I took a chance that the different array of individuals on the new executive staff would eventually learn to work together as a solid team. I gambled, too, that the crisis was an opportunity to put in place greater discipline, accountability, and process—the management attributes of any successful organization—without sacrificing Apple's soul. The crisis obviously made it apparent to all that we badly needed "process" to run a company as large as Apple.

Throughout a crisis, there's a point where you think you understand it and are tempted to act. But as you further study virtually any dilemma, you begin to realize you fail to understand it at all. This discovery creates only greater curiosity. Rather than plunging further into the problem, I begin to look at things that have absolutely nothing to do with it. Often, the answer is *out there* somewhere.

It's the collision of disparate ideas that alters one's perspective. This is the key to unlocking our tendency toward traditional or superficial thinking that leads to stereotypical solutions. The mystery of life doesn't get less exciting when you learn how DNA and cell physiology work. It gets more intriguing, because you gain an ever greater perspective. In the haste to fix, many executives fail to understand how to build.

Explore External Viewpoints

As a leader you need constantly to be able to shift your perspective to see the business from different points of view. A product view, a finance view, a manufacturing view, a sales view, a people view. You also need to gauge what's going on with some external reference points. Listening to outside constituencies and keeping them informed as to what you are doing is imperative. Your suppliers, customers, and others will give you a different perspective with which to compare your inside information. It's not possible to communicate with the outside world too much—even when you may believe it's a time to cut off all your external contacts.

Never Panic

When you're maneuvering through a crisis, self-confidence is extremely important. At times, there may be no guarantees that you'll make it through. It's critical, then, to maintain your cool, not to panic, and to look for incremental wins that can be built upon and leveraged to further motivate the organization.

Only concern yourself with those things that you can do something about. The things you can't do something about shouldn't keep you awake at night. To keep a clear head, it's important to get some time off alone. You need perspective from the crisis. I gained it by getting up each morning at four-thirty for a long run on the road in the cold darkness.

After the key decisions were made, I felt quite calm—even in the most difficult and tense moments. The reason: I was starting to take control of those things that were controllable. I've often heard top athletes say that the actual event of competition is a calming experience that seems to unravel almost in slow motion. It's the few moments before the action that are the most difficult to deal with. I think this is true in a business crisis as well.

Curiously, I've been widely viewed as the "professional manager" a young, entrepreneurial company badly needed. Yet I only consider myself adequately good as a professional manager. It's nothing I ever aspired to be. If it were true, Apple might look like a completely different company today. If I had come in and just tightened everything down and sanitized it, the very things that make Apple an unusual company would have been lost—the creativity and innovativeness to develop new, exciting products that are changing the way people think, learn, and work.

9

The Brink of Collapse

The world never figured out how two young college dropouts could put together, nurture, and run a large company. In fact, they didn't. Mike Markkula did. Small of stature, intensely private, he has been Apple's unsung hero, the "Fifth Beatle" who works quietly in the background, the company's stabilizing force.

All three founders were a study in opposites. Steve was the brilliant, charismatic folk hero and visionary, never wary of conflict. Woz was a gentle, good-humored genius, who evaded conflict at every turn and was only interested in creating "neat" products. Neither had any business experience at all. For that, the pair turned to Mike. He quietly brought to the partnership greater credibility and maturity from his years as an engineer and product manager at Fairchild Semiconductor and Intel. Mike's breadth of business knowledge was expansive. We thought of him as a rare breed in the Valley —a multilingual talent who could speak comfortably on sales, marketing, financial, or technical concepts.

While encouraging the two Steves to move into the public's eye as Apple's personas, symbols of the youthful, upstart company that Apple was, Mike took to the shadows. He himself had no interest in exercising power, only in making the company successful. His influence was clearly felt, particularly when the company was at a crossroads.

When Steve's original business plan for the company would sell to hardly anyone, it was Mike who went to the Jobs garage to rewrite it, then lined up the venture capitalists to transform the two kids' dream into a reality. He sank his own personal money into the company, recruited all of its outside board members, and enticed many of the company's early professional managers from Hewlett-Packard, Intel, and National Semiconductor, including Apple's first president, Michael Scott. He even played the heavy who delivered the ultimatum to Wozniak, then reluctant to leave his full-time job: quit Hewlett-Packard, he told Woz, or forget Apple.

Mike was one of the Valley's Wise Men. He intimately knew the network of venture capitalists, inventors, pioneers, and corporate dropouts who had made new technology their lifeblood. He believed so strongly in Apple from the start because he realized firsthand how the integrated circuit would make it possible for people, not just institutions, to draw on the power of computers. At Intel, he was product manager for the 8008, one of the first chips. Mike personally designed an electronic slide rule, a precursor to the computer.

Mike worked sixteen hours a day, pulling the strings to make Apple a raging success. He wrote one of the first software programs for the Apple II, and with his handpicked sales vice president, Gene Carter, he began to build a country-wide network of computer dealers that helped Apple to grow quickly. There was no distribution system for personal computers then.

For all these reasons and more, he won the highest respect of the company's board of directors. So when the executive staff and board lost confidence in an increasingly withdrawn and remote President Scott during the failure of the Apple III, it turned to Markkula. Only reluctantly did he agree to succeed Scott, and only for an interim period, because Mike had no interest in running the company. When Apple had to recruit a new chief executive, Mike ultimately was given the authority to hire. At the age of forty-one, he was anxious to retire for the second time in his life, spend more time with his family, and fly around in his own private plane outfitted with an Apple II computer.

Now, with Apple in crisis again, Mike Markkula, as vice chairman and director closest to the company, would play yet another major role behind the scenes. Working secretly without my knowledge, Mike had already launched his own investigation to determine whether I was competent to lead the company out of its crisis. Given the leadership crisis that had unfolded, all sorts of accusations and emotional sparks were flying. It was difficult to know for sure what was the truth. So I had asked Mike for a private meeting to present my own notions about Apple's problems and what I thought should be done about them.

I wasn't going to appease him or plead for his support. I didn't fear my job was in jeopardy. Frankly, I was mad at myself. I felt terrible for letting Mike and the board down. How in the world had I allowed myself to become ensnared in such a mess?

It was a hot California afternoon. As I readied for my session with Mike, my fresh clothes were sticking to my skin. I had assembled a few handwritten notes on some yellow paper and placed them in a file folder along with our latest inventory, sales, and financial figures. The numbers alone showed a company plunged into genuine crisis. Sales of the Macintosh computer continued to fall with no end in sight.

During our most optimistic times, we thought we could sell 80,000 to 100,000 Macs a month; instead, we were selling fewer than 20,000. Our inventories were excessive. Thousands of Macintoshes were stacked up against the walls of our Fremont factory, nearly blocking the hallways and exits. Before the crisis ended, $2.5 billion would be lost cumulatively in the personal computer business, primarily because of inventory losses. It staggered me that no one could forecast accurately in the industry. At Pepsi, we could forecast down to a fraction of a percentage point. A tenth of a point won or lost could make or break careers.

Worse, our manufacturing capacity was equally excessive. At Fremont, we could run three shifts to produce Macintoshes. Now we could barely justify running one. Many of the people on the factory lines were shifted to maintenance work on the equipment.

What the figures failed to show and what severely compounded our problems was a company badly divided into two hostile camps: Apple II and Macintosh. The street that divided the two buildings was known as "the DMZ." You ventured across it only at your peril. The anger was poisonous: hardly a day would pass when I wouldn't hear of another key manager or engineer who had resigned. I feared that when people learned that Steve would lose his operating role, it was likely to worsen. After all, his identity was intimately tied to Apple.

Our problems only began there, inside Apple. Outside it, the mess was stupendous. The network of third-party companies, so critical to Apple's past success in creating software and peripherals to expand the use of our computers, was abandoning us to work with IBM. Many of our dealers, too, seriously considered dumping our product in favor of the competition, which was ready to launch new products for next Christmas when we had none.

Nothing went right. Our hopes for the French deal had collapsed, as had negotiations for alliances with General Motors, General Electric, and AT&T. Instead of chasing miracles, I should have been tightening down the business. Or so it seemed now. All this had been a detour, and that's when most companies get into trouble. But we hadn't realized we were in such a precarious position.

I got into my Apple-bought car, a 380 SEC black Mercedes, and drove north on Route 280 toward San Francisco. Past the polluted prosperity of Silicon Valley, the expensive homes of those who drew their fortunes from technology. In the last six years, houses had sprung up out of nowhere on the Valley's hills, like weeds in a neglected garden. Past the idyllic rolling hills near Stanford University where cows grazed on a rich green lawn.

Everywhere the contrasts seemed to characterize the life I was living. It was erratic, sprawling, and eclectic, as exploding as Silicon Valley. But there often was a serenity and idealism more reflective of the Stanford Hills.

I turned off 280, onto the back roads that led to Mike's house, my mind clicking away, organizing my thoughts for our meeting. I knew from experience that when I came to Kendall or Pearson I was expected not only to define the problems but to come equipped with the answers. I passed through a pair of security gates and drove down a long, unpretentious road to his house in the Portola Valley for the 3:00 p.m. session. Though I'd driven the two miles, I felt like I had run them.

High in the hills, Mike's Mission-style home, in white stucco with a high-arching black-tiled roof, commanded expansive views of the Valley. Mike greeted me warmly and we walked into his study— a large, comfortable room of fine hardwoods, with elegant French doors and a multitude of large windows. Most studies are lined with books; Mike's is lined with electronic gear, an entire wall of rack-mounted equipment from sophisticated video and stereo systems to Macintosh and Apple II computers. I was impressed that he had designed the component layout himself and had written the software to control the equipment from his desk.

Unlike my own cluttered study, with books and equipment piled on a desk, everything here seemed in its rightful place. Even the wiring for his computers was fed through one of the legs of his massive oak desk, unobtrusively connecting one keyboard to control all the electronics mounted in the wall. It was typical of Mike to have the crucial wiring unobvious and neatly camouflaged. I liked how the two-dimensional walls in the house yielded a secret third dimension: over the room's fireplace hung a painting which would disappear into the ceiling to expose a large television projection screen. We settled into a sofa in front of the fireplace and began to talk.

From our very first meeting two and a half years ago, I liked and admired Mike. Like everyone else at Apple, then, he was an unabashed optimist. "Apple will be one of the largest and most successful corporations in the world by the turn of the century," he told me without flinching. He hired me, believing I was capable of helping the company realize his goal. Now, as Apple's second-largest shareholder behind Steve, Mike had seen the value of his holdings tumble by almost $200 million in the past year alone. If I hadn't been so single-mindedly fixed on Apple's problems, I might have wondered whether Mike held me responsible for these staggering losses.

As Mike listened, only occasionally interrupting, I launched into a four-hour monologue about the company's problems and how we got there. I attributed our woes to a series of little compromises and a big strategic error that led to the crisis. The major compromises were of my own doing: before I arrived, Mike was making all the business decisions at Apple. Steve led a small project team without profit-and-loss responsibility. He clearly wasn't Apple's only resident technologist. As an engineer, Mike wielded much influence over technology as well.

Yet I kept handing Steve more power and authority. By the time of the blow-up, he was in a significant operating role, with more than 1,000 people reporting to him; he was the company's public spokesman and Apple's resident technologist. I was supposed to be the chief executive. Yet, hovering above me on an organizational chart was a visionary chairman. Lingering below me was an operating executive running the most critical parts of Apple. They were one and the same person. I was boxed in between a pair of bookends. It created a near-impossible situation for me.

All of this confusion laid the fault lines for our biggest disaster: a misguided vision in whose creation I took part. Apple was supposed to become a wonderful consumer products company. That's why it hired a soft-drinks guy in the first place. By now, however, I knew this was a lunatic plan; our race to realize it had been a death march. Technology companies are only superficially in the same category as consumer product companies. We couldn't bend reality to all our dreams of changing the world. The world would also have to change us.

Our perspective had been hopelessly wrong. High tech could not be designed and sold as a consumer product. And certainly not now. The consumer business had collapsed at the end of 1984. Most people who bought computers stuffed them in the closet because balancing a checkbook wasn't reason enough to flick on the switch. Consumers weren't ready to put computers in their homes as easily as they installed telephones, refrigerators, televisions, and even Cuisinarts. They weren't willing to pay a couple of thousands of dollars for something they didn't know what to do with.

More than we bargained for, the home/education business was frighteningly seasonal. It was like selling toys. In 1984, we racked up almost 40 percent of our sales at Christmas. If you guessed wrong on the amount of product you were going to sell at Christmas, you lived with all that inventory. Much worse, you lived with it in an industry where product development was obsolete in a year and a half. Making forecast scenarios was a high-risk proposition.

We would have to dramatically alter the whole orientation of Apple Computer, I told Mike. Not its values, its groups, its environment—but the kind of business it was in. We would have to shift from being a home/education company to one that served education and business. That's where the money is and that's where the market would grow fastest. That also is where people perceived that technology had some functionality to it and were willing to pay for that functionality.

It was a big shift; but, luckily, we had one beautiful ace in the hole:

What made Apple different and continues to make it different from any of our competitors is that we own the crown jewels, our own systems software technology. Nobody else does. And nobody can clone the Macintosh as they can IBM PCs. That's also Microsoft's advantage: they own the systems software that IBM uses on their computers. That's why Microsoft has grown so rapidly and why Bill Gates, its youthful founder, became the industry's first billionaire.

Without stopping, I went on to describe how I intended to lead us out of these problems.

It wasn't until after my presentation that Mike revealed that he had spent the previous week interviewing some thirty-five people at Apple to gain an independent understanding of our problems. It became clear that if I hadn't been able to convince Mike that I had a grip on Apple and knew exactly what its problems were, I would have been thrown out of the company.

While surprised, I wasn't shocked or offended. An informed and independent board was one of Apple's strengths. A chief executive who becomes paranoid about his board members knowing too much is doing a great disservice to his shareholders. Besides, Mike and I were on common ground. We both wanted what was in the best interests of the company.

He offered his advice and his help. Mike suggested that Steve be given a narrowly defined job in product development to determine future product strategies with some technical people. I told him it wouldn't work.

"Steve has to be out of operations," I said. "We can't afford to have major internal debate over every issue on what we ought to do. What I can't do is add the one more additional risk of trying to figure out how to manage Steve. We don't have the luxury to argue over which new products to produce; we have to get new products out."

Steve hadn't been able to get the products out of the Macintosh group. There was no reason to believe that would change in the near future. And I thought he would make the transition all the more torturous by arguing along each step of the way.

"Yeah," said Mike, "I guess that makes sense."

We discussed my ideas to reorganize the company and whom I would likely select in new roles in a new organization.

"John," he finally said, "I've listened carefully to what you've had to say. I think you know what you're talking about. There are a lot of people, though, who aren't happy about how things are being run. I want you to know you have my backing, and I'm going to tell the board that. We hired you as CEO, and we want you to run the company."

They were comforting words. Mike's support was critical, although it wasn't given unconditionally. He grew stern in reprimanding me for allowing the crisis to reach such a severe stage.

"You've got my total support, but I'm very disappointed that Apple is in this position and that you didn't move forward when you had the authority of the board in April."

If I hadn't agreed with him, I might have flinched at this.

"You're absolutely right," I said. "When I got the board's authority to remove Steve, I shouldn't have waited around. I should have acted immediately. I was trying to make it easier on Steve and what I did was create a big mess. That was my mistake."

I was as disappointed in myself as Mike was. I had made errors, and I deserved the criticism. At Pepsi, I wouldn't have tolerated someone behaving like Steve. But there was no one like him there. He was special. Still, we could hardly sit here and cry over how the company got into trouble. The question now was how do we get out of it.

I left Mike's home at 7:30 p.m. knowing there weren't going to be any more chances. I vowed never to let the board down again. In some respects, this meeting determined my future in much the same way as my quiet evening with Kendall when I told him of Apple's offer. I had left Kendall's home feeling awful about letting my friend down. This time, I felt charged up. True, I was tired, physically tired, and it started to sink in how much work lay ahead of me. Yet I felt a sense of exhilaration. I was moving beyond the tough political issues between Steve and me. I knew what had to be done, even if the task ahead seemed awesome. My adrenaline began flowing. I had to turn this thing around in the next six months, or I couldn't expect anyone to give me a vote of confidence.

The following day, the company's outside directors agreed with Mike to support me. But the board, too, expressed outrage that I had allowed a crisis in leadership to mushroom after entrusting me with the responsibility of getting the company under control at the April meeting. With the board's backing, however, I met with the executive staff for the next two days, in marathon sessions on May 29 and 30, from 7:00 a.m. until well into the night to hammer out our plan for a comeback.

Apple had become two different warring companies. Many of our best people in the Apple II group, angry over the preferential treatment Macintosh people seemed to have, were leaving the company. We sorely needed to rid ourselves of the internal competition; we had to become one Apple.

The real test of any organization is how well it works in the worst of times. Clearly, Apple's decentralized structure wasn't working very well. Each of the two divisions had its own sales, marketing, manufacturing, and product development staffs, which resulted in many overlapping jobs.

It was nearly impossible to get the right information quickly when I needed it most. I was constantly surprised by new and disturbing findings, including the failure to order parts for the Macintosh XL. The management inexperience of many of Apple's key players as well as my own lack of experience in the personal computer industry should have been early-warning signs that a decentralized organization wasn't suited for our volatile marketplace. It set up a system under which people would fight for what was best for their groups, not what was best for the company as a whole.

In a time of crisis, the first priority is to get control. I knew from experience that a functional organization would be the best way for me to get on top of the details of the business. The overriding reason to adopt a fairly traditional functional structure, though, was because it would help us become one Apple.

We had to quickly achieve three goals. In the midst of a computer slump, Apple had to become a more efficient, lower-cost operation. This meant downsizing the company just to reduce our breakeven point. Then, to survive long term, the company had to emerge as more responsive by bringing products to market quicker than it had in the past. Next, the key to all this was a reorganization which would allow us to better coordinate product development, manufacturing, and marketing as a corporate-wide team. We needed to be one Apple all marching in the same direction.

Organizing the company along functional instead of product

lines would mean changing almost every job in the entire company, in addition to closing down facilities and laying off hundreds, perhaps more than a thousand employees. This wasn't just change—it was an apocalypse. I knew this would rip the company apart at the very time when it already was fragile. And if we picked the wrong people in the key functional jobs of operations, marketing, and product development, it could be a disaster.

When I first installed a functional structure in Pepsi's company-owned bottling plants in 1971, it failed to work as planned. I had assumed that such an organization would give us greater skills in each discipline because each person would be a specialist. He would be required to look at marketing or product development overall, not simply through the interests of a single division. Instead of matching people to the new functional jobs, however, we put too many generalists with little management experience in positions for which they lacked the specialized skills. Our appointments had incorrectly been based on rank and position, not pure skills. It didn't help that our new job descriptions weren't tested in the real world, either. So they didn't assist people in fully understanding what their new jobs entailed. We correctly reinstalled a functional organization at Pepsi a year later, with different people.

I hardly mind making a mistake you can learn from. But in a crisis like the one we now were in at Apple, you have only one chance. If you make a mistake, there might not be a company, much less an opportunity to try again! For me, the question was, who would be best for the new organization's top jobs? Every company has its own genes, and you have to live with them. We had to preserve the values that had sprung from Apple's feisty entrepreneurial roots. It was vital, for example, that people could continue to work in an environment in which each person could personally make a difference. I felt we had a better chance of getting ourselves out of the mess by leveraging what we were good at—entrepreneurial skills.

The successful entrepreneur perceives no obstacles and always finds a creative way out of the most difficult and impossible tasks. So while I turned to a traditional organizational concept, I reached for non-traditionalists to fill some of the key jobs. It wasn't the safe choice.

The time to take your biggest risks is when you face your most difficult obstacles. Playing it safe is probably not going to work in the midst of a crisis.

I was, after all, being paid a lot of money to figure out how to make Apple a great company, not just a survivor. The experience might be analogous to a pilot flying a 747. You really don't do an awful lot when the plane's on auto-pilot. But when you have to take it over during those sixty seconds when three of the four engines flame out, you better take any action, risky or not, to control it, and the sense of responsibility is overwhelming.

If we'd played it safe, we might have come out with an Apple-label IBM compatible, which would have been opportune in the short term but would have destroyed our advantage as an alternative technology—the basis of Apple's soul. It would drive away the people who were our most valuable assets because Apple no longer would be unique. We wouldn't do that.

Or, we could have played it safe by following Atari's lead: slash our size and expected income, and preserve our proprietary technology. Atari's focus was to make money, not great products. They wanted to sell the cheapest systems in the greatest numbers.

The riskiest alternative was to stay the course. Do what we did best . . . only do it better. And do it *now*.

To help me, I sorely needed people with tremendous passion for Apple. We couldn't lose the dream in the process of rebuilding the company.

In the key jobs, I wanted people who really represented the best of what Apple had stood for in terms of creativity. Not caretakers, but passionate and brilliant leaders—even if it meant taking huge risks on inexperienced individuals and hoping they would not meet but exceed the test. We had to keep intact the tremendous spirit, innovation, and outrageous creativity of Apple.

I had taken inventory of the management talent, particularly admiring Del Yocam's success in installing order and process into the Apple II division where he was general manager. While the Macintosh division was in a shambles, Del's Apple II group had sustained the company over the Christmas season.

Del was California laid-back. He spoke slowly and deliberately; that's also how he walked and talked. When I first met him, I found him a precise and orderly manager who followed up on the meticulous notes he'd keep in a maroon notebook, which must have looked like the ledger Bob Cratchit carried, always tucked under his arm. Of all the people in that crazy session at Pájaro Dunes in 1983, Del impressed me as a man of precision. He had a swift, well-deserved spiral to the top after joining Apple from Fairchild Camera & Instrument Corp. in 1979 as director of materials. I decided to promote him now to group executive in charge of all operations—product development, manufacturing, distribution, and operations management.

It was the biggest and most important job on the executive staff. Operations would go through the most wrenching changes, so I needed my strongest manager over the area. Del would have the tough work of shuttering and consolidating factories, laying off people, and seizing control over our inventories. Some thought he lacked experience for the job, but I had promoted him a year earlier to head the Apple II group and he had proven he could be tough.

Apple sorely needed more process and control. Giving this job to Del, though, made it more palpable to the organization. If *I* tried to superimpose controls over freewheeling Apple, it would have been as if corporate America had rushed in to clamp down the company. Del, one of the Apple originals, could install process without creating anxiety. If I did it, it would scare people to death.

There was only one drawback. Del was used to managing people who were exactly like himself and who always followed in his steady, precise way. Now, however, I would call upon him to manage people who were vastly different. This is the essence of leadership. The challenge is in balancing their attributes without smothering their differences, or their faults, with too much control.

To balance the discipline Del would provide, I wanted to have a few mavericks who could bring extraordinary talent to their jobs. Under Del, I placed two of Apple's best iconoclastic thinkers: Jean-Louis Gassée and Debi Coleman. Both were exceptionally bright, talented, and quick-witted. Yet neither one was particularly prepared for the job because they had never managed a large organization.

Gassée, the French mathematician who had almost single-handedly built Apple France into our largest international subsidiary, was a charismatic intellectual who cultivated a romantic involvement with the personal computer. A one-time model, a poet, and a

philosopher, he could easily be mistaken for Jean-Paul Belmondo—
right down to his style. Sometimes he would pause in mid-sentence,
raise his eyebrows, and peer up at the ceiling waiting for a response
to the sexual metaphors he'd drop.

"We must always give our user pure sex," he'd say. "It's like a
rendezvous in the back seat of an automobile with a beautiful girl.
One's experience with the personal computer should be better than
the greatest orgasm you could have." He was right. What made an
Apple computer different was that the user did, in fact, have a love
affair with the machine. The intensity was something Jean-Louis appreciated. He wouldn't want to be the father of a computer that
lacked the excitement of a sexual experience.

Gassée represented Apple at its best—slightly irreverent, at
times arrogant, but always incredibly insightful and smart. Gassée
had the gift to articulate the romance of our business as few others
could, or would dare. An IBM executive would risk his career if he
spoke of the sensual nature of computers. "Any source could give
you the facts," political observer Teddy White once teased. "What
you need is the source who can give you the metaphor." Jean-Louis
was never at a loss for metaphor.

"One of the deep mysteries to me is our logo," he once said,
"the symbol of lust and knowledge, bitten into, all crossed with the
colors of the rainbow in the wrong order. You couldn't dream of a
more appropriate logo: lust, knowledge, hope, and anarchy."

Although he is primarily a marketing man, I reached out for him
to become vice president of all product development. Gassée lacked
the technical background to lead an engineering group, but his unrestrained enthusiasm and knowledge of software made him the perfect choice. I had to have Jean-Louis's strengths on the team.

Debi was an English literature major from Brown University
with a Stanford MBA. She traded Nabokov for high technology because she saw in it the means to influence the world far beyond
anyone who walked the streets to protest the Vietnam War. She
exemplified the blend of opposites I felt we would expect of everyone in the brave new world of computers, when the distinction
between "the hard nerds" and "the soft nerds," as Alan Kay put it,
finally disappears. "The hard nerds," he says, "are the ones with the
plastic thing in their pocket; they think Shakespeare is a defunct car

company and Frescobaldi made the trains run on time. The soft nerds are the ones who think differentiation is a social disease." Debi understood science and business and had the perspective of a deeper cultural background.

Recruited on the Macintosh team by Steve from Hewlett-Packard, she had become manufacturing manager of the Macintosh factory a little over a year earlier. I had watched her carefully at the factory and saw firsthand how close she was to her people. She believed in automation, understood just-in-time manufacturing, and knew well the power of using information to control inventory. And she embraced Apple and everything for which it stood, working fourteen to sixteen hours a day and weekends.

"Apple does this to people," she told me when I moved to the campus, agog and slightly overawed by what I saw. "I mean people wear Apple underwear. I have lots of friends that work for big Fortune 200 companies and if they got a better offer someplace tomorrow, they'd jump, they wouldn't think twice about it. That doesn't work here.

"It's almost like faith. Unless you're a Catholic, you may not understand. 'You have to accept this. It's like fate.' That's what the nuns always told us. They'd say you've got to accept it. I was a very bad religion student, which is funny because I never accept anything on faith, except Apple."

Like Gassée, she was wisely irreverent and challenging, forceful and tough, with a voice that no factory could drown out. Many executives would find her and Gassée a handful to manage. But I knew that if there was any chance that Apple would have breakthroughs in manufacturing, Debi was going to be important. She would search for unexpected ways of solving problems, not the textbook manufacturing approaches. That would be critical to our future and our longer-term ability to compete with the Japanese. So instead of putting in a tried-and-true manufacturing executive, I chose her as vice president in charge of worldwide manufacturing.

Next, I merged together U.S. marketing and sales, putting Bill Campbell, the former football coach at Columbia University, in charge of it. Highly admired by his people as head of U.S. sales, Bill had a strong personality and the leadership qualities necessary to hold the dealers and the sales organization together. Bill was the first person I recruited to the company, convincing him to forsake a job in London with Eastman Kodak for a position in Cupertino with Apple. I thought his coaching experience uniquely qualified him to deal with our young marketing workforce. At Apple, he had done an exceptional job, substantially revising the sales staff, creating a 350-person field sales group to call on our 2,600 U.S. dealers.

Now, his task would be harder than ever. We had shifted from a sellers' to a buyers' market, leaving consumer dealers weaker and weaker. Business dealers had begun to mumble about dropping Macintosh because they didn't think it was a business product. With a special promotional program, Bill might be able to prop them up this quarter or next quarter, but I didn't see any out. The distribution system was a faulty design. There were too many undercapitalized retailers; computer prices were too low; and supply far outweighed demand, so few of the dealers could make enough money to survive. By the force of Bill's physical presence, all six feet and booming voice of him, he might be able to knock heads together and pull people together. He had to. We couldn't make it through the end of the year unless he could stop the downfall in sales.

In early winter, I made three other important moves. I put Michael Spindler, a European who was marketing manager for Apple's European operations, in charge of all international sales. He was our bet on growth. He didn't have to carry the baggage of the tremendously bad publicity we were getting in the United States. While we walked away from the most price-sensitive sales and positioned the Apple II line as a premium product, Spindler would have to drive major growth abroad to cover up our declining U.S. revenues.

"You've got to grow," I told Bill and Mike. "We can't be down in revenues because it will scare people to death. Third-party developers will think we're in even greater trouble and won't ever work for us."

We were going to reduce our dependency in the U.S. consumer market, which meant sales growth in the international area would be important because otherwise people could feel Apple was failing.

Then Dave Barram, Apple's chief financial officer, was given the job of putting order and accountability into our financial process. Dave was an experienced financial executive from Hewlett-Packard who had only recently joined Apple. The son of a Baptist minister, he always showed great concern for our people and Apple's role in the local community, like a shepherd with his flock. It was a good balance to the deep-cutting decisions we had ahead of us.

Heading up human resources was Jay Elliot, who had succeeded Ann Bowers when she retired. Jay was a tall, bearded, easygoing former native Californian who had worked in Silicon Valley since its early days, occasionally making trips to Hawaii to surf. He was to play an important role during the lay offs, handling them with fairness and dignity for all involved.

Al Eisenstat, who as secretary of the board was our liaison with the directors, was ultimately named a director. I relied upon Al for his wisdom and his judgment; he was our test of reasonableness. I trusted him without reservation. Al could be tough and insightful, yet he also had a warm, engaging personality. I asked him to perform another crucial task: to keep Steve, who remained as chairman, out of the company's operations. I was fearful that any encouragement would force Steve back into operations and I didn't believe we could risk it. Anything he did could be destructive at such a fragile time.

"I'm asking you to be in charge of Steve over the next few weeks," I told Al. "Go to Europe with him, go anywhere he wants to go. But I've got to buy some time to hold this organization together. I can't risk having another division at this time or it could be the end of Apple. You were planning an exploratory sales trip to the Soviet Union anyway. Why not take him with you?"

Steve always admired Al, and Al always liked Steve, so the two left a few days later and spent a week in Moscow.

What a group to lead Apple out of its quagmire: a soda-pop executive from the East; a solid, though untested, Apple II manager; an Ivy League football coach; a French intellectual; a German conceptual thinker; an English literature major; a seasoned attorney; a Baptist philosopher; and a laid-back surfer!

It was an organization of vastly different nonconformists, an organization in which almost everyone wasn't quite prepared for what they would have to do to turn the company around. Like the Denver Broncos, we became a crew of misfits thrown together to perform under severe pressure. There were obvious gaps in the group. None of us had a strong technical background, yet here we were trying to lead a technical corporation. We were a team of individuals—as paradoxical as that sounds. But as such, we could make dramatic changes while holding the company together at the same time.

A group is more accurately what we were . . . not a team. Trust and respect establish the basis of any good working team. Yet there wasn't much trust in the beginning. We didn't know one another very well; we hadn't worked together as a team before, partly because Steve and I had called all the shots. Suddenly we would be making decisions as a group. Neither was there much reason for mutual respect, including respect for me. I hadn't contributed much to make Apple great at that point. In a sense, all of us were untested for what lay ahead.

This all felt right, these matches of talent, need, and ambition. I thought I had it all figured out. Surely this would have taken us far at Pepsi. But then everyone at Apple started demanding to know the company's new vision.

Sales growth covered a lot of sins, and the vision was always the binding force that kept us together. Growth had now slowed, exposing our errors in judgment as well as an organization that lacked the control necessary to turn it around. The vision was now in doubt, and I wasn't prepared to commit to what our vision would be because I didn't know. People became anxious because I wasn't talking about vision. I was talking about slashing inventories. putting controls in, and cutting the workforce. Before we knew where the ship was going, I wanted to ensure that it wouldn't sink. The new vision would come in time.

Ever since the shootout between Steve and me, rumors had spread through Apple about our confrontation. It was clear to everyone that Steve and I were no longer a twosome. No longer could we be seen together everywhere. He almost never dropped my name, except in a critical remark. I rarely used his. The question that seemed to pervade the company was when the split would become official. And who would win.

I wanted to deliver the answers to our middle managers on May 31, after the two marathon executive staff sessions at which we set the course for a new Apple. I had to demonstrate some success to the company: morale was desperately low. So we had communications meetings every week, every few days. The talk was constant. Nothing is more disconcerting than silence when a company is in trouble. Speculation always leads to negative exaggeration.

It was 90 degrees that afternoon, and the air conditioning barely cooled the room packed with over one hundred people. Some sat on chairs, some on tables, while others lined the walls of the large ground-floor conference room of the DeAnza II Building. It was a room filled with sad, sober faces. They knew I wasn't there to give them good news. Rumors of layoffs already were appearing in the local press with regularity.

Just before I was to begin my presentation, Steve walked in with a handful of his loyalists. They strolled quietly to a corner in the back of the room under the watchful eyes of everyone else. It was as if Steve meant to be the last arrival in the room, just as Kendall had been at so many of the Pepsi Nielsen meetings. Steve had been present at all the major events in Apple's brief history. He had to witness and take part in this next turning point—even if it was to watch his public undoing. He seemed beaten and dejected. But everyone could still feel his presence; it made the room that much hotter.

Once Steve took his seat, his eyes focused on me in a constant, burning stare. I nearly felt like he was publicly daring me to go through with it, to announce before his company—his people—that he had been dethroned. Nobody who's never been stared at can know what Steve's look of contempt feels like. It's unyielding. You "feel" it, just like you feel an X-ray boring inside your bones, down into where you're soft and destructibly mortal.

For a second, I flashed back to happier times, to 1984 when Steve and I made something of a pilgrimage to Cambridge, Massachusetts, to visit one of Steve's heroes—Edwin Land, the brilliant founder/scientist of Polaroid.

Steve lionized Land, saw in him one of America's greatest inventors. It was beyond his belief that Polaroid ousted Land after the only major failure of Land's career—Polavision, an instant movie system that failed to compete against videotape recording and resulted in a near $70 million writeoff in 1979. "All he did was blow a lousy few million and they took his company away from him," Steve told me with great disgust.

I was now about to do the same to Steve, to make public the

fact that I was in charge of the company and that Steve no longer had an operating role. I could feel the tension, and I felt on the spot. Whether people agreed with me or not, I hoped that at least they would understand what I was trying to do and why I had selected a new team to lead Apple.

Trying to evade Steve's glare, I outlined the company's problems, warned that layoffs and major consolidations would result, and then flashed on a screen in the room a slide of the new functional structure. Steve sat atop the organizational chart as chairman. Below him was vice chairman Markkula and myself as chief executive and president. Underneath the three of us were all the functional groups from operations to marketing and sales. It was the first time, though, that Steve hadn't had a dual role in the company. The impression to anyone would be that there had been a showdown and that I had won.

"We are one Apple," I said. "There have been disagreements as to which direction we should go. These are perilous times for us. But Apple has to have one leader and one direction. We have to be one company."

It was a tough, unnaturally quiet meeting. Steve, his eyes still fixed on me, and his cohorts sat there silently. To avoid his stare, I'd look at all the others in the room, at each of them, one by one. Their faces were largely noncommittal. People wondered who among them would soon lose their jobs—and what they'd be left with if they stayed. For all of us, the future seemed less than certain. When the meeting ended, they quietly shuffled out of the room, largely ignoring both Steve and me, not wanting to commit themselves to either of us.

The evening before, Barbara Krause, our public relations officer, had drafted the press release that would announce the reorganization. Now Steve, Barbara, and I met outside the room to review the public announcement. Together, we rode the elevator to my office on the third floor. All that could be heard was the elevator's loud hum—not a single word was spoken.

In my office, Barbara showed Steve the one-page announcement. It was as if someone had gotten the chance to read his own obituary. Steve scoured the document, fixing on a paragraph which stated that he "will take on a more global role in new product innovations and strategies." The statement also quoted me as saying, "As chairman of the board, he [Steve] will continue to be a creator of powerful ideas and the champion of Apple's spirit."

Steve wanted to make the wording ambiguous so that it wouldn't immediately be apparent that he no longer had a day-to-day management role.

"Steve, I'm not going to do that," I said.

He continued to press for a change, but I stood firm. A concession would have been costly; Steve was unwilling to accept that he was out. I had to make it clear that Apple now had one leader. I couldn't risk any further confusion either inside or outside the company.

The tension we felt had dissipated into sadness. Now we were only quibbling over a handful of words in the fine print of a divorce settlement. Barbara's crestfallen face reflected what all of us felt.

He then asked if he could move into an office a few doors from mine that was occupied by Al Eisenstat. But I couldn't risk his interference and I knew he couldn't let go. If I allowed him an office next to the other members of the executive staff, it would only invite trouble. Steve always had to be involved.

"You're not going to have any operational duties, so you don't need to be up here in this building,   I said. "Your role is as chairman, and as this press release says, you are going to take a more global role in the company."

"Well, if that's the way you want it," he replied, tears in his eyes, "I guess that's that."

A few days later, over the weekend, Steve's office was moved out of the Macintosh Building across Bandley Drive to a different building.

What we may have lacked in experience, we made up for in energy and dedication. We gathered in my office at 7:30 a.m. every day—Saturdays and Sundays included. Birthdays, holidays, family outings all got postponed for a time. We were fighting to gain control over the runaway elements of our business. Having revamped the staff, we focused on reducing our inventory, lowering our breakeven point, and boosting our gross margins to a level that would support a handsome research and development effort.

Each morning, Del, Bill, and Jean-Louis would deliver a report on the preceding day's events and outline what further steps would be taken that day. We discussed only tactical moves, what had happened over the last twenty-four hours and what likely would occur over the next twenty-four. There was little talk of the future. For us, long-range planning meant planning the next three or four hours. We were plugging the holes and the gaps as they opened to save Apple. And the company held its collective breath as we met, wondering how our decisions might later affect them.

A near-warlike mentality prevailed. Mention was always made of people who were leaving and casualty lists were created. We had our own war heroes. And war dead. We'd hear reports on virtually every aspect of the business and would vigorously discuss everything, too. No one would leave my office until most of the decisions for that day were made. It was chaotic. Every few days, I would call at least one director to post him or her on events and to get advice. After each session, individually and together, we were absorbed in implementing our way out of the crisis.

I went back to that demanding discipline I had shown at PepsiCo and kept pushing people to the limits of their physical abilities. Not just the exec staff but everyone. Almost daily, someone on the executive staff would warn that we couldn't keep pushing so hard.

Del said, "We can't push people any harder. They are going to break. We're just going to burn people out."

"Del, I know that may happen, but we don't have any choice. We have got to stop the hemorrhaging and get control of the company. We have to take the risk."

We had to race the clock to get things together well before Christmas. There was no way we could sell the tens of millions of dollars in Apple IIc extra inventory then, if we weren't succeeding and doing well in the educational market. If it was going to break, I felt it may as well break early.

Because it was a seven-day-a-week job, Leezy left for our home in Maine for the summer. She realized she would see little of me over the next few months. I was up at 4:30 a.m., thinking through the issues for each day on my run through the Stanford Hills. I'd arrive at Apple at daybreak to ready myself for the seven-thirty staff meeting, after which I'd handle a flurry of phone calls from anyone who had anything to do with Apple. Some wondered if we would go out of business; others wondered when we would go out of business. Throughout the day, people ran in and out of my office for signoffs. I worked until late in the evening, knowing I would go through the same ritual the next day. And then the next and the next.

Our most painful decision would be to significantly scale back the company's workforce. To slash operating costs, I had already reduced advertising, closed our factories for a week, eliminated the Lisa computer and some development efforts, and laid off about 1,500 temporary employees. Now we began to go through in detail virtually every job in the new organization to decide whose jobs would be made redundant by the functional consolidation.

I knew from experience that you seldom do this twice; you do it once and you do it right. If you ever have to make a major change, never be timid, Kendall once told me. Make sure you get it all done the first time because you may never get a second chance. We just went through with a knife and cut very deep.

"We've got to make sure we cut deep enough," I said, "no matter how painful it is."

Apple had six factories but we couldn't afford them all. We decided to close two of the smallest ones immediately—our Mill Street, Ireland, plant, which made computer accessories, could be combined with our facility in Cork, Ireland, while our Garden Grove, California, plant, which produced keyboards and the mouse, could be collapsed into another domestic factory.

The more agonizing decision was whether to close down either our new Macintosh factory in nearby Fremont, or our Carrolltown, Texas, plant which made the Apple IIc computer. It was a Hobson's choice. Our taxes, wage rates, and expenses were higher in California than in Texas, and our California plant was located in an earthquake zone. If we closed Texas, our only domestic plant would be vulnerable in the event of a natural disaster. Our employees in Texas were among the most productive, motivated people I had ever seen. Indeed, only months earlier, we were about to consider a proposal to substantially automate the plant.

The task of studying which of the two plants to abandon went to both Del and Debi. No matter what they decided, the decision would exact a high personal price. It was Del who had opened the

Texas plant five years earlier and personally hired many of the people in it. If Debi were to recommend the shutdown of the Fremont facility, it would mean closing down over a year of her own life because she was instrumental in the plant's creation.

Unlike our Texas plant, which was largely a manual factory, Fremont was a model for what American manufacturing should be. Components coming in were automatically detrashed—as we called the job of unpacking—and put into plastic buckets that rolled on conveyor belts into gigantic three-story elevator storage units. A giant robotic arm on wheels whirled at 60 miles an hour through the storage unit, picking up parts and components, feeding them to robots building Macs on the assembly line. At each build station, a Macintosh would monitor the progress of its newborn. After the assembled Mac gets a brain—its key integrated circuit—its screen lights up and it tells the line's human operator how it's doing: "I'm okay," or "Fix me, I've got a problem with a drive." If it needs repair, it gets vectored off into a hospital area. Next, the good Macs go through a stress test on one of two seven-story, burn-in racks for twenty-four hours before being packed in boxes by robots. A single Mac controlled these stress tests as well.

It was almost a scene out of science fiction: machines replicating themselves, Macintoshes building Macintoshes, little beige boxes thundering along the conveyor belts by the hundreds while other Macs stood by controlling part of the process.

To design the plant, Apple had sent Matt Carter, Debi, and others to view world-class manufacturing facilities in Japan and to study in seminars the best production techniques with such manufacturing gurus as W. Edwards Deming and Philip Crosby. The pair advocated not only state-of-the-art production, but making quality a major part of the process from product design to product delivery.

The result: the Macintosh was a superb product, made in a plant that was one of the most highly automated manufacturing facilities in the world. Moreover, Fremont's close proximity to Apple headquarters was critical because it meant that our design engineers could easily confer with manufacturing engineers to create products that could be produced efficiently. Ultimately, we believed it was worth the extra cost in higher taxes, salary, and expenses to link our design and manufacturing engineering.

We also figured out that even a fairly substantial earthquake wouldn't disrupt production for more than a few days. If this happened, we could always build the product manually in the plant with help from Cupertino until we got the automated systems back up. Another of the advantages of having just-in-time manufacturing is that you don't have a lot of parts inventory lying around that could get damaged.

Our Texas plant wasn't nearly as automated. That was in our plans for the future, but now all those plans were not only on hold, they were being ripped up and discarded daily. We decided to close the Texas plant, which would leave us with facilities in Fremont, Singapore, and Cork, Ireland.

Closing the Texas plant represented our single biggest hit. All told, about 1,200 people out of a 5,800-strong workforce would lose their jobs. About 60 percent of those dismissed would be manufacturing employees.

The remaining cutbacks fell across the board with only one exception—research and development. New product development was our lifeblood, and I wasn't about to slash it.

We would announce the news on June 14: a 20 percent cut in our permanent workforce, in addition to almost complete elimination of our temporary workforce, the closure of three factories, and our forecast of Apple's first quarterly loss as a public company.

Planning for the Future

In the year I was born, 1939, a World's Fair was held in New York. Peering fifty years into the future, the sponsors of the Fair attempted to predict the technologies and advances that would shape the world through 1989.

They envisioned space travel, then only a fantasy in sci-fi movies and books, becoming a reality. They thought television, then a mere curiosity, would be in every home. And they believed that air travel would make the world seem much smaller. Yet they never even mentioned the computer, the laser, the transistor, or the microprocessor.

The future seems even less predictable today. We have never lived in a time of so much volatile change. It makes planning for the future incredibly complex and difficult, and many companies have lost millions of dollars placing bets on the wrong horses.

Consider Videotext—one of the most heavily researched business projects in recent years. Some of the biggest corporations invested millions in it, and yet it has been a total bust. The experience of Videotext and other ideas demonstrates that it takes more than just a rigorous process of research and process to plan for the future—it takes artistry.

That's why planning for the future encompasses more than an analytical approach. Indeed, numerical figures aren't all that helpful. Sometimes a chart filled with numbers appears unshakably credible. It often isn't. In planning Apple's future, I prefer to talk about ideas and beliefs instead. How do my views, my ideas jibe with where people think the industry is going? How do our beliefs differ from the analysis?

Solutions are often obvious once you get the questions right. Many American companies in the 1960s and 1970s, however, were obviously asking the wrong questions. It wasn't the quality of their planning that got many big companies in trouble; it was the quality of their perspective.

At most companies, planning looks forward. The corporate planners, along with the chief executive, decide where the company should go in the next year or two by peering back into the company's past, making judgments and extrapolations on what's to come based on their experiences to date. That's like saying, You have a great future behind you.

Our planning scheme is quite different and simple: We've separated the preparation of our business plan (a moving twenty-four-month planning outlook) from the process of long-term planning about Apple's future direction in the 1990s. For the latter, we project ourselves out into the future and then work backward to the present in small increments of time. We ask ourselves: what will the year 1992 be like? We create in our minds a visual portrait of what the economy, our industry, and our company will look like. Then we move back into the present, envisioning what we have to do in small steps to get to the future. What do we have to do in 1989, for example, to achieve our vision in 1992? We call this "back to the future" planning.

In the midst of our crisis, this process helped us realize that despite our troubles, we could look forward and confidently see a personal computer industry focused on graphics and a better user interface. Luckily, they were our strong points and IBM's greatest vulnerabilities. We figured we had a technology lead of eighteen months to two years over IBM. Our glimpse into the future, however, convinced us we had to make major investments to continue to pioneer advances in both fields.

It's an approach that also has worked for MCI Corp. chairman Bill McGowan. He imagines himself and his company already out there a year or two later. At MCI, then, planning makes 1987 look more like 1989. Once his perspective is adjusted to that more distant date, he looks back to the present. He asks himself, "What would I have done differently back in, say, 1987 knowing what I know now in 1989?"

Stanford University president Donald Kennedy also follows this formula. After mentally projecting himself out to the year 2020 to envision what higher learning will look like, he then looks back over the years. He asks himself what Stanford must do in each of the years from 1987 to 2019 to ensure that his vision of the university in 2020 will occur.

The process extends the timeline of thinking, providing two valuable ingredients for more efficient planning: *different viewpoints* and *insightful questions.* We try to articulate the right questions, rather than get too hung up on the answers. Our sextant to navigate into the future is a statement of identity, as well as sets of directions and values, generated with the help of Professor Steven C. Wheelwright of Stanford's business school.

They provided the framework for what Apple would do to realize its ambitious vision of changing the world and how we would go about it. Some 150 middle managers gathered over several days to vigorously discuss both the meaning and implications of the framework. Then, Apple's executive staff began imagining what Apple wanted to look like in 1992. We did this in considerable detail, function by function, throughout the organization, even before we knew exactly how to get there or whether it was practical that we could.

In each case, we adopted a 1992 viewpoint and then looked back to 1987 to ask ourselves what we should do differently in 1988 to make sure we build the Apple we want by the start of the century's last decade. Not surprisingly, we came up with different priorities than would have been realized under the normal business planning process. That done, we kept extending out further and further into the future. In projecting out at least five to ten years, we realize it's a cultural departure to think beyond a three-year plan; but we're interested in when it will be possible to accomplish some of the dreams we have.

How certain can we be that this process has any accuracy at all? What we do know is that we have a vision of personal computing which only becomes more important as time goes on. We also know that future technologies now being explored in the labs of the best universities are probably ten to fifteen years away from commercialization. We scout them out using the framework of our vision to help us shape the future of our company and our industry.

We ask ourselves what our competitors will possibly be able to do at that time, because we're always looking for meaningful differences that are long-lasting. In high technology, where time is compressed, the sustainable advantages don't last as long. If you try to attach them to a single product or solution, you can make a serious error. Planning, then, becomes a flexible, sometimes intuitive, process of navigation rather than a tight set of procedures based on trends and projections.

Similarly, we take a different approach to product planning as well. It starts out with unconstrained dreaming. We don't limit idea creation to the practical in the beginning—it can only hinder the possibilities. The wild dreams are transformed into pragmatics later on in the process. When Einstein was trying to figure out his theory of relativity, he imagined himself sitting on a photon in outer space moving along at 300,000 kilometers per second.

Larry Tesler, our vice president for advanced development, rides a photon too. He explores new technologies for products at Apple. His team creates technological objects, not products, that help turn the wildest dreams imaginable into realities. Listen to him:

"Like science-fiction writers, we think of the crazy, totally impractical things. We say, 'Wouldn't it be wonderful if I could look up at the ceiling and call someone by their name and have him come down here right now.' Or, 'Wouldn't it be nice if I could reach into that graphic on the wall, grab that silver ball in it, and spin the ball around.' We think the way people who create sci-fi movies or books do. And those are the kinds of people we hire.

"Then we start beating the idea up in many ways. Someone will say, 'That's crazy. This doesn't have any practical application. Why would anyone buy something that would allow him to

*reach into a graphic and spin a ball?' Well, maybe he wouldn't.
But what about a facilities planner in a corporation who might
look at a three-dimensional rendering of a whole building and
he's trying to figure out how to lay out the building? If he could
reach in and pick up the furniture and partitions and move them
around, that might make his job easier. And what if he could
point at the wall, click a mouse, and see where the pipes and
electrical circuits are?*

*"You start to imagine what an idea could really do. Then you
start comparing the available technologies with ways to design
such a thing. We take our fantasies and match them against what
people will need and gradually focus on something a little more
practical. Some of the way-out things might be set aside. Eventually, it becomes a project with a life of its own. Then it's not
vision anymore. It's clever engineering."*

No less crucial, planning has to be a part of the company's
mindset. Our people think about these things all the time. They
don't hold a meeting once a year to dream up ways to plan for the
future. It's part of the company's identity, values, and vision which
can be recited by every Apple employee around the world.

This is the type of long-range thinking that permeates the organization and has nothing to do with the company's annual business
plan process (how do we translate strategic questions and priorities
into the business plan for the next two years; what products do we
have to get out; how will we get them out; and what resources will
we allocate against them?). The difference is matching the norm
against a framework for the long-term future.

In many cases, planning for the long haul in American business
—so preoccupied with quarterly results—amounts to a major break
from tradition. Yet if we are to plan for the future more accurately,
many of our ingrained habits must fall by the wayside.

Let's say we stop judging business and planning its future
strictly by the balance sheet. Every way we currently look at business has been financially focused. Instead, let's look at the creative
value of a corporation: *How much of our revenue comes from*

product we didn't make the year before? At Apple, we now get 30 to 50 percent of our revenue from products we didn't make a year earlier. You couldn't do that if you weren't a creative organization. This measure of creativity becomes essential in planning for our future. We constantly test ourselves on how well we can maintain that percentage.

A few companies are following similar measures. Ford recently changed most of its product line. IBM has made a bold stroke to totally change its entire personal computer line. If they are correct in their choice of product, more than 50 percent of their personal computer revenue will derive from products they didn't make a year ago.

You could also calculate a creative index for countries that would be focused on what you do in the future, not what you did in the past. And right now what you would see is that the United States may be in more trouble than we realize.

Planning for the future, at Apple, means just that. More than anything, we believe that the best way to predict the future is to invent it. We feel the confidence to shape our destiny.

10

A Real-Life *Dynasty*

Arriving for work at daybreak on June 14, I saw a company much different from the one I had joined only two years earlier. Then, Apple radiated energy and fervent hope. The streets that bound the campus were filled with young people who rushed about with unbounded confidence and enthusiasm on their faces. It was a company that boasted the highest morale of any organization I had ever seen. Now it was a company torn asunder.

Young people, their eyes moist with tears, wandered aimlessly along the streets. Many of them, hearing of the coming layoffs yesterday afternoon, hadn't gone to sleep the night before. I recognized an obviously confused and distraught Macintosh engineer roaming the street without direction.

"Have you been up all night?" I asked.

"I don't know," he answered, gazing off into the sky.

"I know this is really hard for you. It's one of the hardest things I've ever had to go through. Can I help?" I asked.

"No," he said, "I just want to be by myself."

He mumbled something incoherent and brushed me away.

It felt like Doomsday. The news coursed through the company campus. Apple people had never known such anguish. These were young idealists, many of whom had never worked for another company. The last time any significant layoff had occurred was on "Black Wednesday," the day in 1980 when president Michael Scott fired forty-one people shortly after the company went public. There was no comparison to the one out of every five people—1,200 in total— who would lose their jobs today.

Groups of twos and threes and fours clustered along the sidewalks and under the small trees of Apple's campus. They spoke in feverish whispers, and when I approached, they grew silent. Some glumly watched friends pack boxes of belongings into their cars and drive away. Many left as soon as they were told of the layoff. It was like sadly watching students going home at the end of a school year, except these people were never going to be coming back.

It was a mess, just an absolute disaster. People openly sobbed in the streets. Television crews cruised up and down Bandley Drive. News reporters circled our buildings attempting to interview people who had just lost their jobs. I felt nearly impotent in my ability to help, yet I couldn't hide or insulate myself from the despair in an office, either. I walked the campus, behind the main buildings to evade the growing number of reporters in search of a story, awkwardly attempting to console people who were either losing their own jobs or whose closest friends were going to be affected.

Our decision to lay off workers shocked and pained the young, dedicated employees who had gravitated to the company seeking a place in a corporate dream, not the nightmare it had become. Was the Valley's Camelot dead?

Frankly, I wondered myself. The news media widely portrayed me as the victor in a boardroom coup. Nothing could have been further from the truth. My so-called victory was the darkest hour of my professional life. My struggle with Steve was also personally devastating. Far from feeling victorious, I now had to battle to win the confidence and support of a company which had lost its entrepreneurial folk hero.

I became the protagonist in a real-life version of *Dynasty*. The plot thickened at every turn. As the media absorbed the real evidence of our plunge, the headlines chronicled all the bad news: a severe drop in earnings, a major reorganization, Steve's removal as head of the Macintosh division, the dismissal of over 20 percent of the workforce, the company's first quarterly loss of $17.2 million, and rumors of a possible takeover of Apple. Every scene seemed to unfold publicly, before an omnipresent and increasingly hostile press.

It was as if people were standing a death watch, waiting for the final collapse. The news reports depicted a sorely troubled Apple whose survival was in doubt. One journalist reported that Apple was like a dead whale washed up on the beach; another wrote that the company had had its heart ripped out. Some newspapers predicted that if the company survived the crisis, it would never be the same; others speculated that Steve might consider selling his stock to a corporate raider under a plan that would return control of the company to him.

When I'd pick up the newspapers in my driveway each morning, I would read how Apple was unlikely to remain in existence. During my drive to work, the local radio stations would hit me with more bad news. When I returned home at night, I would turn the television on and hear an announcer say: "And problems continue to get worse at Apple Computer." I couldn't escape the flood of bad news, so I just turned it off. I wasn't interested in hearing it anymore. I stopped reading the newspapers and magazines as well, if only to protect my own brittle morale and confidence.

Our affairs became as much discussed as the "Who Shot JR?" episode of *Dallas*. It became *the* discussion of Silicon Valley. Some prominent Silicon Valley leaders even wagered on who would win. Shortly after I joined Apple, Ben Rosen, a leading venture capitalist who helped launch Lotus Development Corp., bet a former Apple engineer, Wayne Rosing, that Steve would outlast and eventually oust me. Rosing later sent me a copy of Rosen's $100 check and his letter. I'm sure there was a surfeit of bets that got paid off along the way.

I sought refuge from the avalanche of Doomsday publicity by my early-morning runs through Stanford University's campus and walks through its sculpture gardens. Great art has been my friend for many, many years—my guidance and inspiration. Before I joined Apple, when I was trying to understand the sort of person Steve was, I had taken him on that trip to the Metropolitan Museum in New York. To prove to myself whether or not we could freely exchange ideas, I had talked to Steve about golden age Greek sculpture and architecture. He had explained to me how personal computers would let everyone explore their own ideas, as artists do, in new expressions of creativity and innovation. He had called it "the romance of the possible." I had realized then that we all are on the same journey, only on different schedules. Yes, I had thought that spring, I could work with Steve on ideas that might well change the world.

Now, wandering alone through Stanford University's sculpture garden, I stared up at Rodin's magnificent *Gates of Hell* and felt the agony yet beauty of this medieval epic drama. The bronze relief was almost sensuous; yet it captured the human tragedy of despair. It echoed the painful, almost tragic elements of life at Apple. As far as I wanted to run, there were forces like the Sirens which kept pulling me back.

I had been on something of a marathon journey for twenty years, working at high speeds to sharpen my physical and mental conditioning. Now I tried to squeeze out every ounce of knowledge and understanding I had gained over the past two decades. I had a set of values and skills from which to draw. Kendall and Pearson had taught me the nature of competition and I was, in one sense, a finely honed weapon. I knew how to compete and succeed, how to survive and make tough decisions in a political environment. These were things that gave me an advantage when I faced the tough tasks at Apple.

I drew upon all those experiences, from my years in International Foods when I had to gain control of a company, wind down its costs, and stem its losses. I recalled my experience in working with Pepsi's bottlers, which wasn't much different from the network of Apple's third-party developers and dealers. I drew from my experience in positioning products during Pepsi days to help get our sales back. It was probably the first time I had a chance to demonstrate those skills at Apple. Usually, I had allowed Steve to have his way, coaching from the background.

It was our failure as a management team that forced us to lay off so many Apple people, so it was our responsibility to cushion the blow. It was important for all that the layoffs be handled as compassionately as possible. Jay Elliot mapped out the plans. Affected employees in Cupertino were notified in one-on-one meetings with managers at work and given liberal severance allowances. Psychiatric counselors met privately with people who might suffer great emotional stress. Out-placement consultants were enlisted to help all our employees, not only managers, find new jobs. A placement center was established in one of the buildings, outfitted with Macintosh computers and LaserWriters, for people to write resumes and letters in their search for new jobs. In Garden Grove, we closed our offices at 2:00 p.m. to give employees time to absorb the bad news.

From Texas came word that our employees there displayed an astonishing reaction to the news that they would lose their jobs. Debi, whose study played a key role in the plant's closure, traveled to Carrollton to personally tell them of the decision. Word had apparently leaked out ahead of time because the plant's employees showed up in *"Apple II Forever"* T-shirts and black armbands. Some actually thanked Debi for the privilege of having worked for "the greatest company in the world." There was amazingly little bitterness or rancor. They showed their support of the company and determined that the shutdown be accomplished in a first-class manner. If anything, it reinforced my belief that Apple didn't deserve to be turned into another fine-tuned, expense-controlled company in corporate America.

Indeed, their total cooperation allowed us to transfer production of our IIc line to Fremont over a long weekend. We were doing things that seemed impossible, but that was Apple at its best. Within two short weeks, our employees were building the equivalent of 30,000 IIcs a month on the original Macintosh production line. To keep as many of the employees in Ireland as possible working, we bused them from the closed Mill Street factory to our remaining facility in Cork. By selling our Garden Grove plant to Alps, a Japanese vendor of keyboards and other computer products, we were able to save the jobs of one third of those employees. In Cupertino, we placed 80 percent of the people in other companies within three months of the layoff.

Still, we were hounded by the press, which only heightened the pain, anguish, and drama of our troubles. It had a tremendous impact on our sales. Who, after all, wants to buy a computer from a failing company? The crisis struck at the heart of the company's strength, beyond the financial statement and the loss of control. It badly shook the faith and confidence of the constellation of companies upon which Apple's success is largely dependent. Many of these companies, particularly the third-party developers, had turned their backs on Apple because of our closed boxes—the IIc and the Mac. We had to convince them they could make money developing products that hooked into our world.

Even long-time Apple supporters began to lose faith in our ability to make it on our own. Bill Gates, founder of Microsoft, which

302

accounted for nearly half of all Macintosh software revenue, called to say that he wasn't sure Macintosh would be able to make it unless we licensed the technology to other companies as fast as possible. He thought it was our only salvation. Other outsiders, convinced that IBM had virtually won the personal computer race, advised us to stamp Apple's logo on Asian-made IBM clones. They insisted it was the only way Apple could possibly survive.

Jittery dealers, confronted with IBM's building momentum in the market and reports of more new products by other competitors, were beginning to worry that Macintosh might not make it through next Christmas. Businessland, one of the most important computer dealers, considered dropping Mac because it represented only 2 to 3 percent of their revenues. Other dealers came back with the same message. Some smaller outlets were considering dumping Apple and picking up low-end suppliers, such as Commodore and Atari. Both were launching new products for the upcoming Christmas season that were expected to duplicate some of the features of the Macintosh in color.

Dealers were the company's oxygen; I needed to gain their support. I decided then to use my first public appearance after the reorganization to announce a new business partnership with them. I hadn't made myself available for press interviews because I knew they could lead to an open debate between Steve and me that would only hurt the company. In fact, we had an unwritten understanding to steer clear of the press. So it made my appearance at a Future Computing Forum in San Francisco in mid-June all the more climactic.

Some 700 people were packed into a hotel room where only 400 had been expected. To avoid the press, I snuck in from a side door through the hotel's kitchen. When I reached the podium, you could hear a pin drop because so many people were straining to hear what I would say. I looked out at their faces and told them, "We are one Apple. We have put our individual egos aside and we are putting teamwork in its place."

I told them that Apple would not change either its vision as a company or its commitment to our Apple II and Macintosh product lines.

"But we're also a realistic company that understands we must become more market-driven if we are to achieve our full potential as a leader in the personal computer industry."

I announced two important refinements to dramatically strengthen our relationships with two key groups: our dealer base and third-party developers. To better sustain our dealers I offered, among other things, a program that would make them the seller of virtually all Apple-branded office products to large companies.

"You'll see us take steps to make it easier for other companies to connect their products with ours," I said. "These steps will include a gradual transition to selective industry protocol standards as well as a new priority in the future for work station expandability." This statement was particularly important because it acknowledged the need to return to "open" products for which other companies could make peripherals, plug-in boards, and other devices that enhanced their performance.

"We're solid in our commitments . . . firm in our product foundations . . . and confident that with strong partnerships with dealers and developers, we'll remain a leader in the personal computer industry."

That said, I quickly headed for the kitchen again and into a waiting car.

Back at Apple, the tension was thick. I would get daily sales reports from Bill Campbell. Some days, we wouldn't fill many orders at all.

"We've got to find a way to get it up," I implored Bill at our early-morning executive staff sessions. "Just don't take no for an answer. Figure out which dealers have the inventory and concentrate primarily on them."

"Don't worry, John, I'm not going to let you down," Bill said over and over.

Together, we visited many dealers, virtually pleading for their support until we could demonstrate that we could turn the company around. Bill worked crazy hours—oftentimes scheduling 6:00 a.m. breakfast meetings while still remaining at the office beyond midnight. He spent days on the road, holding the hands of the dealers on the front lines, phoning in to Cupertino to tell us the latest news —good or bad.

There were days he'd call to let me know, "We filled two orders for Macs yesterday, none today, so far." Each unit sold was cause for joy. Like a politician campaigning for votes, Bill had to sniff out who our lukewarm supporters were so we could move them to our side. The slightest bit of daylight would prompt us to send a couple of guys out to get a sale. Bill told his sales people not to leave the dealers' stores unless they got their commitment to buy more product.

We doubled the number of people in educational sales, because I knew we could not go into the Christmas selling season without scoring major sales in key school districts. The only way we could sell parents the Apple II against cheaper, less useful computers by Commodore and Atari was if their children used them at school. We expanded an evangelist group—a staff that encourages outside developers to create new products for Apple computers—and we pledged to change some of the technical features of the Macintosh that hindered other companies in designing accessories for it. We also invested more money into creating developers' tools to make it easier for these outside companies to create software for our products.

By early July, we had gotten through the first shock of the layoffs, but morale sagged miserably. Disillusioned by the downturn, Apple's employees wondered if management had lost its ability to manage the company. I had yet to regain the confidence of our people. There was no greater evidence of this than in some of the questions I received at the first communications meeting before Apple's employees since Steve had lost his operating role. I had asked everyone to submit questions in advance of the July 7 meeting. While two people jokingly asked me my opinion of New Coke, the stack of questions were some of the most difficult and bitter I had ever received. They were brutally frank and they stung emotionally. I felt weak and ill as I read them:

"How can you justify a $1 million salary when you have admitted that you had not been in total control? Don't you think it would be an insanely great gesture to give back part of your salary in light of our current fiscal problems and layoffs?"

"Your salary would pay for a whole department of engineers. Have you ever considered emulating Lee Iacocca and reducing your salary for a period of time to one dollar in order to benefit the company?"

"Steve Jobs is popularly credited with single-handedly picking and recruiting you for the office of president. Now that he is gone, do you feel secure in your job?"

"Why did you, John, let Steve Jobs run rampant for over a year before taking control of the company?"

They were tough questions, maybe even good ones. But how could anyone possibly answer them? I had planned a prepared script on a Teleprompter, but as I looked through a stack of 4-by-5 cards of questions, I realized that Apple people wouldn't want me hiding behind a prepared script.

"I've got to go out and talk to them. Not read to them," I told Barbara Krause, our public relations officer.

I threw my script away, walked out to the centerstage of Flint Center, and stood there with nothing between me and 2,700 employees. I could feel their hostility and their anxiety, their doubts about my leadership with Steve gone. Regardless of what they thought of me when it was done, I wanted to make sure I could explain the decisions we were making, why we did them, and what the outlook for the future was.

I didn't pull any punches. Together we would face a difficult summer, and unless everyone pitched in we wouldn't make it. They recognized that Apple wasn't the only company in trouble. By now, every other Silicon Valley firm was laying off people and closing plants. It was a somber, uninspiring session. No one felt very good about what they were hearing.

It was necessary to work toward four major goals, I explained. To get ourselves together internally; to regain the confidence of our constituents; to heal the divisions between the Macintosh and Apple II groups, and to have a successful Christmas. We could only accomplish these goals if the fourth were met: namely, if people became more disciplined and accountable.

"We don't have to stop doing things in unorthodox ways," I said. "We can still be a company that has soul. I have no intention to structure the company so that it's no more fun. The best is yet to come. We've just begun to see the potential."

It wasn't possible not to say something about Steve. Everyone wanted to hear from me on the subject, so I didn't evade it.

"Neither Steve nor I know exactly what he's going to do," I said. "He loves Apple as much today as he did two months ago, but it's clear that he's going through the process of trying to sort out exactly what he wants to do. This experience has tested our friendship. I don't think there is bitterness between us. I think there's more pain.

"It's also clear that he's not going to have, either now or in the future, an operating role with Apple," I added. "So Steve has got to decide if there's a role that he will enjoy as chairman, doing the kinds of things that he is getting a taste for right now . . ."

As the weeks went on, feelings about Steve changed. The executive staff members who had assumed his responsibilities became bitter toward him because they believed he had misled us about the rate of progress in the Macintosh division. Development projects we assumed to have been active weren't or were nowhere near completion as we had been led to believe by Steve. We were further behind than we ever imagined on our next generation Macintosh, as well as on a host of peripheral products and software.

Every experience stands out when you're in a crisis. When Lucinda Mehran, a friend of ours and the daughter of IBM's Tom Watson, Jr., called to invite Leezy and me for a visit to her family's compound in Maine, I had no idea why. I had never met her father before, and really didn't know what to expect. I arrived at the retired legend's waterfront home, and headed outside to wait for him. All of a sudden, a low-flying plane, coming out of nowhere, zoomed at my head. Then, just as suddenly, it fell into a death roll, pirouetting down toward the ground, until pulling straight up into a series of loops and rollovers that took it well out of sight into the clouds.

Not long after, Watson himself appeared. "Just wanted you young hotshots from Apple to know us old-timers still have guts." In his early seventies, he still flew stunt planes with the same daring he had displayed when taking over IBM from his father and turning it into not just a maker of excellent mainframes, but a world-class institution.

During the weekend I was struck not just by Watson's daring but also by his modesty and by how interested he was in Apple. He seemed so confident that we would get over our problems.

"As long as Apple can continue to innovate and hold together the things it believes in, it will pull through," he said. "It's going to take a lot of work, but what you can't lose is the innovation. You're doing the right things."

It gave me courage to see this great man in action, and to realize that when he took over the company from his father, IBM was much smaller than Apple was now. Watson's generosity was especially touching, coming at a moment when most of my own friends and outside allies stood a safe distance away, mute. And coming from the living symbol of Apple's toughest competitor.

Sometimes comfort appears from the most unexpected places.

Toward the end of the summer, there were fragile signs of hope —light at the end of the tunnel, maybe. But maybe there was another tunnel at the end of the light.

Del and Debi worked out a way to manage the inventory down, partly through a European deal in which we sold thousands of Apple IIcs at steep discounts. More than anything else, the deal bought us time. Our accounting policies required us to write off all inventory beyond six months. This barter agreement siphoned off inventories, lowering the size of our writeoff. By cutting back and curtailing expenses, we pulled our breakeven point down by almost $400 million a year.

Debi zealously attacked the manufacturing job, taking a fresh look at our worldwide operations. Once she got beyond the initial steps of consolidating plants, she began to work up radical new ways of thinking about manufacturing. She quickly forged partnerships with Jean-Louis's product design group and our external vendors. Her goal was not only to "fix" but to make better, to use the crisis to make operations not a service to Apple's creative departments but a strategic weapon in itself.

"I'm rebelling against the establishment, not by protest, but by showing the power of compelling ideas," she told the executive staff when unveiling her plans.

Employing a manufacturing model from Stanford's Steven Wheelwright and Harvard's Robert Hayes, she worked to make Fremont an example of how manufacturing could succeed in the United

States. The Wheelwright-Hayes model, as she described it, included four stages.

"In Stage One, you don't cause any problems inside the company," Debi explained. "You just try to minimize the negatives. Stage Two is externally neutral. So you follow whatever the industry leader does. Stage Three is internally supportive, where you give credible support to the business's strategies, goals, and direction. And Stage Four, when it's externally supportive, is where you have a strategic competitive advantage that is identifiable and sustainable over time. If we do all of this, we're going to get beaucoup profits.

"I think we're in Stage One now. We don't have to worry about operations or manufacturing. It's not performing badly. But we aren't thinking of it as a competitive weapon."

To move us up to the fourth stage, she stressed the need for quality and flexibility throughout manufacturing. Under Del's guidance, Debi helped reduce the number of our vendors from 1,500 to under 250. That provided the remaining vendors with the incentive to locate closer to us and to figure out ways to deliver product without us having to carry the burden of inventory. Instead of ordering piece parts up to fifteen weeks in advance, we could order them six to seven weeks out. While a traditional manufacturing plant turns its inventory over two to four times a year, Debi managed inventories so well we got it to thirty-six or more turns annually at Fremont (that was an important measure of how low we were able to keep our inventories). By the end of 1985, we would have improved our inventory management to the extent that we converted a quarter of a billion dollars in inventory into cash.

She set up parallel assembly lines at Fremont so that vendors would compete against each other on the same factory task. Thus, an IBM automated line would be placed in competition with another one from Hurata, each company wanting to prove it was best. Debi arranged meetings between the heads of our suppliers and Del and me; we exchanged business plans, and shared twenty-six-week sales forecasts with them. They began sharing their costs with us so we could negotiate prices that guaranteed them a fair return but kept us competitive. The upshot: manufacturing was on its way to becoming a key strategic advantage by providing us with the lowest total cost and improved reliability.

On the sales and marketing side, Bill installed an auditing system that alerted us to how much product delivered to dealers had actually sold through to consumers. This was critical to help us forecast sales more accurately and to prevent us from being caught with so much inventory ever again. He put in better dealer programs to boost revenues and put more emphasis on educational sales, the basis of Apple's success. By early August, he finally was getting some evidence that the dealers wouldn't abandon us and that Macintosh sales were slowly increasing.

Public proof that we would survive came at a gathering of Macintosh users and developers called "MacWorld" in Boston on August 21 through August 23. I was expecting a lackluster event, reflecting the downbeat mood that generally pervaded Apple. By the time I arrived, some 15,000 people were swarming the Macintosh exhibition, at which more than eighty new Mac products were introduced by third-party companies. For once, people weren't all consumed in whether Apple was going to survive or what happened to Steve. Instead, they were talking in upbeat tones about how great the Macintosh was. For the first time in months, my spirits soared.

All summer long, Bill and I made the rounds, pleading with the dealers and business customers not to abandon us. Things didn't suddenly improve in the marketplace, but as we walked through the exposition, here was living proof that Macintosh still had a loyal and dedicated following. Many of them were in blue jeans, with beards and long hair in ponytails held together by rubber bands. We hadn't hit the business users yet, but at least there were people out there who loved the product. It was a major morale boost for us.

Our friendship had ended months ago. But Steve and I were destined for a second ending, this one even more bitter and final.

We had little contact over that summer. We spoke briefly about his trip to Europe at the June board meeting, exchanged a few tired words, a quick hello or goodbye. It was like seeing an old friend in a dream where you can't touch him or he'd disappear. I heard rumors —that he was considering a career in politics, that he wanted to apply as a civilian traveler on the space shuttle—and I knew he had sold over $20 million of Apple stock. From friends, I heard he spent days bicycling along the beach, feeling sad and lost, but mostly angry at me.

He told one of his friends that being removed as head of the Macintosh division was like being a small kid on a football team and having the wind kicked out of you as you lay there on your back. I winced in pain when I heard that because I knew I was the person who delivered the blow. Bringing Steve back during those fragile months of recovery would only have run the risk of reliving many of the painful things we had already gotten behind us—all across the company. To many observers, my position seemed cold and hostile, but I refused to budge. The executive staff felt the same way.

I also heard stories that made me feel close to Steve in another way. Al informed me of his adventures with Steve abroad, and Steve's insistence on speaking about Leon Trotsky in the Soviet Union where Trotsky, the revolutionary's revolutionary, was verboten. Trotsky was one of the original leaders of the Soviet Communist Revolution, but his works had been banned because they differed from today's party line. That in itself would have immediately drawn Steve to him. Al says:

"He brooded a lot in Moscow. But with our own personal KGB agent assigned to us, all Steve wanted to talk about was Trotsky. He was making Trotsky out to be one of Russia's national heroes. The natural reaction of the Russians was to rear back.

"The KGB guy said, 'Steve, you don't want to talk about Trotsky. Our historians have studied the situation and we don't believe he's a great man anymore. We think he's no good.' The issue was dropped.

"But then another day we had a guide who brought us to the state university of Moscow, and again Steve starts with Trotsky. One of the last things we did was go to the Academy of Sciences, where both of us were to make addresses before Russia's computer scientists. We climb up to the fifth floor of a building that would have been condemned if it were in the United States, and there was this group of young people with sandals and open shirts. They could have been computer scientists here, except many of them had gold teeth.

"I got up first on the stage and said, 'I hoped we could open up avenues of discussion.' You know, a motherhood kind of talk. Then Steve got up and started talking about education and the future of the computer industry. He talked about how wonderful the world is going to be in the future because of computers. Behind Steve on the stage were huge portraits of Lenin and Marx.

"He points behind him to the pictures of them and says, 'Look, here are the things we can't do today. We know what Mr. Lenin and Mr. Marx believed in. We know what their thoughts were because a lot has been written about them and it is reasonably well documented. But the one thing we can't do is ask them a question and get their current thinking. Ahh, but in the future you're going to have artificial intelligence and you'll be able to ask Mr. Lenin a question or Mr. Trotsky a question.'

"There was a silence I couldn't believe. I was on the stage facing the audience so I could see the expressions on their faces. They were in a state of shock. This was before one of the most august bodies in Moscow. I loved it."

Al's story warmed me. Even though Steve had lost his power, he hadn't lost his nerve. He was still cocky enough to pull a prank in the Soviet Union.

Steve is, like Trotsky, a brilliant revolutionary, overturning whole worlds with his new ideas. He is a zealot, his vision so pure that he couldn't accommodate that vision to the imperfections of the world. Lenin had realized he had to adjust to the world. True revolutionaries like Steve, like Trotsky, are also dogmatists; they ignore the necessity of pragmatism, of working through human failings.

In September, Steve asked, through Al, that I state in writing my position on a couple of issues to come before the directors at that month's board meeting. I wrote suggesting we get together on Friday morning, September 13, immediately after the board meeting.

I felt it was time for us to sit down and see if there was some way we could manage either a business or personal relationship. He had too much talent and energy and life left not to do something great. My priority was to get Apple through an extremely rough summer. Once it became clear the company was getting healthier, I then hoped the two of us could figure out how Steve could again make a real contribution to Apple. But he obviously had no interest in doing that because I never heard from him.

The first I was aware of his plans was when I saw the agenda for the September 12 board meeting. The last item scheduled for the session was a "Chairman's Report" with no explanation attached. I assumed it would be Steve's critique of the company's reorganization, since I had heard through the grapevine that he was quite critical of what we were doing. What came, however, was an even greater surprise.

Late in the afternoon, Steve rose, avoiding my eyes. He said in a flat, unemotional voice, "I've been thinking a lot and it's time for me to get on with my life. It's obvious that I've got to do something. I'm thirty years old."

Steve said education meant a great deal to him. When he looked back on his Apple years, he felt his most important contribution had been to bring the personal computer into the educational world. Offering to resign as chairman, Steve said he intended to leave the company to start a new venture to address the higher education market. But he said his new corporation would not be competitive with Apple, only complementary, and that he would take with him only a handful of non-key personnel. He suggested, too, that maybe Apple would want to buy the distribution rights to his product once he concluded it. Steve also asked if Apple would be interested in giving him a license for Macintosh software.

Markkula seemed visibly irritated by Steve's remarks that other Apple people apparently were going to join Steve. He felt strongly that Steve didn't have the right to hire any Apple employees.

"Why would you take anyone at all?" he asked.

"Don't get upset," Steve retorted. "These are very low-level people that you won't miss, and they will be leaving anyway. Don't look at this as a big issue."

Steve was asked to leave the room so the board could privately discuss whether to accept his offer of resignation. The board expressed surprise over Steve's sudden announcement and wondered if he could really build another company that would be complementary to Apple Computer. One director initially suggested that we should offer to take a position in his company; others agreed. We began to discuss how we could work together with Steve's new company.

When he returned, I said, "All of us have appreciated what you have done for Apple and we recognize you want to get on with your life. On the assumption that your business is complementary and not competitive, and that you're not taking key people from Apple, we want you to reconsider your decision to resign from the board." The board also told him it would be interested in buying up to 10 percent of his new company.

Steve said he would have to think about remaining on the board and allowing Apple to buy a stake in the company. We arranged to meet the following Thursday so I could get a better understanding of what his plans were for his new company. It was a pleasant and seemingly tidy end to the meeting.

However, the next morning, Friday the 13th, ominously, Steve called my office at 7:10 and asked for a 7:25 meeting prior to my scheduled staff meeting at 7:30. He sheepishly entered my office and presented me with an envelope. I opened it and read the typewritten note:

Dear John,

Today these five employees of Apple Computer will be resigning to join me in my new venture. . . .

The brief note said that all five employees would give two weeks' notice to their managers that morning and asked for "as smooth and unharassed" a departure as possible. Steve also attempted to assure me that no more Apple employees would leave with him. The letter was signed in Steve's usual spidery scrawl, all in lowercase.

I was both shocked and alarmed. The people listed on the paper were hardly "low-level." Rich Page, an Apple Fellow and one of the company's most important engineering designers, was in charge of our next-generation Macintosh. Dan'l Lewin was marketing manager for our important higher education business and had developed the plans to sell our advanced work stations to the higher education market. Bud Tribble was manager of software engineering for Macintosh. Susan Barnes was senior controller for U.S. sales and marketing;

and George Crow was an engineering manager with vast Macintosh experience.

Together, they knew our internal schedules, our costs, the focus of Apple's next products, the schedule of when we would introduce them, how they would be used, and which individuals and universities we would work with to ensure their success. Their accumulated knowledge would give Steve a decided advantage to compete directly with Apple in terms of marketing opportunities and technical and product know-how.

"Steve," I said, "these are not low-level people."

"Well," he said, "these people were going to resign anyway. They are going to be handing in their resignations by nine this morning, so I wanted to give you and the executive staff the courtesy of knowing that beforehand because I know you have your meeting this morning."

I knew the executive staff and the board would likely be as surprised and shocked as I was about it. Only hours earlier, I had left the board meeting with the impression that this was still a germ of an idea in Steve's head, certainly not a fait accompli.

I asked Steve how it happened so fast. He said his new team met last night and agreed it was better to do it all at once rather than leave any doubt about what he was doing. I couldn't imagine how five people would suddenly, out of the blue, decide after a meeting the night before that they all wanted to resign and go form a company without some thought going into it ahead of the board meeting.

Our meeting was brief. I went into the executive staff meeting as scheduled, handing the letter to Eisenstat. I told the staff who Steve intended to take with him, and the news provoked an angry uproar. Some suggested that Steve should be exposed for what he was. He had been held in high esteem as a folk hero and now he was going out and trying to destroy the very company he had helped to create.

"We should expose him for the fraud that he is so that people here stop regarding him as a Messiah," Campbell shouted.

All our progress would soon become lost in the glare of this latest episode. The news media jumped all over the story, carrying unattributed remarks from angry executives and directors. "I've never seen such an angry group of people in all the companies I've ever done business with," one director anonymously told *The Wall Street Journal.* "The board of directors and executive staff of Apple are incensed, as I am. I think all of us think he has tried to deceive us."

In Silicon Valley, people resign from companies every day to become entrepreneurs. But a Steve Jobs doesn't rush off every day, and the chairman of the company doesn't often take employees with him when he leaves. Especially after telling the board of directors that he wasn't going to take any important people.

Steve resigned on September 17. So I learned when a *Wall Street Journal* reporter called to ask for Apple's comment. The reporter apparently obtained a copy of Steve's resignation letter addressed to Markkula before Apple did. The day newspapers carried news of his resignation, Apple stock jumped a full point.

When Jean-Louis and Al later met with Steve privately, they learned that the product he planned to build was essentially one we had been working on in the Macintosh division, code-named Big Mac. We commonly referred to it as a 3M machine because it would have a 17-inch, million pixel display, a million megabytes of memory and run a million instructions per second. The computer was to be based on a 68020 processor with Unix software.

Apple already had specific plans to market a computer to the university market. The product we were developing would be remarkably similar to what Steve told Al and Jean-Louis that he was developing. "Jean-Louis and I looked at each other in disbelief. He's doing nothing but a 3M machine, and it sounds like Big Mac," Al said. The people Steve recruited had unique knowledge of our plans to market the product to the universities, as well as of Apple's cost structure and the prices we paid for the machine's components.

I later had a telephone meeting with the board at 3:30 p.m. on Friday, September 20, when we discussed whether to bring litigation against Steve.

No one wanted to prevent Steve from starting another company and continuing to bring innovation and creativity to the industry. But if he did so, the board believed that he shouldn't use Apple's confidential or proprietary information. The board authorized me to begin litigation on the basis that Steve allegedly made plans for the new company while serving as Apple's chairman, and that he falsely represented his company and intentions to the board. We sued one of the fathers of our company on September 23. The newspapers uniformly called it the "end of an era."

A few days later, when a member of the facilities staff went to clean up Steve's office and pack his belongings for shipment to his home, they discovered on the floor a black-and-white photo of the two of us together. It was a warm and inviting picture that perfectly captured our friendship: the two of us deep in thought, conversing about Apple's future as we had done nearly every day. The picture's glass frame was shattered, as if it had been violently thrown across the room. On the back, almost seven months to the day earlier, I had inscribed the words:

"Here's to Great Ideas, Great Experiences and a Great Friendship! John."

It was months before that staffer would tell me about his find, thinking (but perhaps not really thinking at all) that time would make things easier.

Living Out the Genetic Code

How do third-wave corporations perceive their environment and themselves? Second-wave companies see the future as an extension of the past. Third-wave companies invent their own future with only a genetic code reference to their past. Why the difference?

Instead of giving us a vocabulary of action, culture limits us by an emphasis on tradition, on yesterday's heroes, on myths and rituals whose sole value is that they derive from an earlier time. Yet business is in desperate need of a new language for understanding how to use a corporation's strengths in ways that don't also constrain it with weaknesses. A new language would help rescue matters from obviousness. "You draw the near things nearer by making the queer things queerer," as a Danish philosopher once wrote.

Apple has had to smash the icon of culture's central importance to business management. While having a strong culture, Apple has also had to recognize the constraints of culture. The requirement for dynamic process is simply not expressible in cultural terms.

In popular use, "culture" is a closed system; its language is descriptive, and so it misses evidence of action and change. Anthropological categories like "heroes," "myths," and so on are static. No surprise: the job of anthropology is to fix and study closed systems. Businesses that define reality in such terms similarly create closed systems for themselves. They excessively—perhaps unconsciously—venerate tradition and worship habit: "the way we do things around here." Culture is a feel-good tool, a set of behavioral blinders; it makes a corporation comfortable with its habits.

Early in the century, historian Arnold Toynbee urged a cultural strategy of imitating the example of great men. Marshall McLuhan was probably the first to question this advice: "This is to locate cultural safety in the power of the will, rather than in the power of adequate perception of situations," he argued. AT&T may have spent most of this century deifying its service heroes and imitating their examples. But how can AT&T maintain any allegiance to culture and at the same time adapt to the highly competitive environment it is now in? Not by imitating home-grown heroes. It needs a new vocabulary to understand and implement change.

Similarly, Apple's history was rooted in the tradition of making only one product at a time. We'd put our hearts into it, then collapse for two years before we could think about another product. Our history thus kept working against us.

In what new ways can corporations think about the future? I suggest the better concept lies in the idea of genetic change. As cells grow and divide, genetic code is always present, yet the code's message is always expressed differently in different organisms. Genetic coding imprints notions of identity and values as culture does, but in so doing suggests a sense of forward-looking, a sense that everything done today is an investment in the future, not an expression of the past. The code is constant over a lifetime, but cells can change; metaphorically, this becomes a forward-looking model. Moreover, its perspective is not tribal, as culture's is, but biological. Its focus is the individual primarily, the species or group secondarily.

The elements of genetic coding are as follows.

Vision vs. Goals

I like directions better than goals. While the genetic code is predetermined, it's not fixed as habit/culture is. In America, projects have a beginning, a middle, and an end. In Japan, projects have direction, so that what you're pushing for is heading further and further out.

We don't try so much to define Apple's identity; instead, we try to make it recognizable.

Metaphors vs. Myths

Corporate cultures make great use of stories, generally war stories, repeated ad nauseam. At Apple, what's more exciting than myth is metaphor. Metaphor, which literally means movement, focuses on relationships of ideas, images, symbols. Metaphors create tension, collision of ideas, fusion. Metaphor "gives you two ideas for one," as Dr. Johnson said. Apple metaphors like "software artist," or "hardware wizard," or even "desktop publishing," or the computer as "appliance," get you dreaming in two worlds.

The reason we talk in metaphors at Apple is because virtually everything we're doing hasn't been done before. I never had to use a metaphor to describe what Pepsi did.

Directions vs. Rituals

Apple people wanted to form their values very early in the company's existence, on the theory that children do the same. Now that we're no longer children, we had to shed our childish ways during the company reorganization. Most companies don't have to go from infancy to childhood to adulthood as rapidly as we did. Dave Barram, an Apple vice president, said that "Apple is like a six-foot-tall, eight-year-old boy." We always looked a lot more sophisticated than we were.

So there were things we had to shed, particularly the rituals and symbols. In the direction we were headed, some of those rituals and symbols weren't going to help us.

We are measured not by how much we can learn, but by how well we can unlearn, as Alan Kay says.

For example, we had to make it acceptable to talk about accountability with the same reverence as we talk about creativity. Something as creative as architecture requires discipline just to stay

up. We had to separate discipline and control. Controls are insepar-
ably linked to policy, so we rarely talk policy at Apple; we talk in
terms of guidelines and discipline. For a creative-driven organization, control has negative connotations while discipline is an under-
lying process integral to innovation.

Japan and Europe are both steeped in a long history of traditions. Americans, by contrast, have no real tradition of a common
heritage, so the dreams of all that is possible for each individual
become our unifying social force. It's the same at Apple, a company
with no baggage from the past: our people look for a clear vision, a
set of values, and directions for the future as the forces that bind us
together.

Heroes

The heroic style—the lone cowboy on horseback—is not the
figure we worship anymore at Apple. In the new corporation, heroes won't personify any single set of achievements. Instead, they
personify the process. They might be thought of as gatekeepers,
information carriers, and teams. Originally, heroes at Apple were
the hackers and engineers who created the products. Now, more
teams are heroes.

Traditionally, managers could attempt to alter only three things
in an organization: structure, people, and process. In a hierarchical
model, structure is the most important element. In a network
model, though, process is the most critical. Structure is rarely tam-
pered with in a traditional corporation, since it represents stability
and strength. At Apple, there is nothing special about structure except its flexibility to change as needs and opportunities require.
Structure is understood in biological terms (e.g., it grows, adapts,
divides in order to survive), instead of in the rigid hierarchical
terms of the traditional models of corporate America, particularly
the Catholic Church and the military.

In a network model, moreover, people and their values are
linked. Culture links people to the past while genetic code links
them to the future. As an organization grows and changes, its genetic code always remains the same.

Organization Architecture

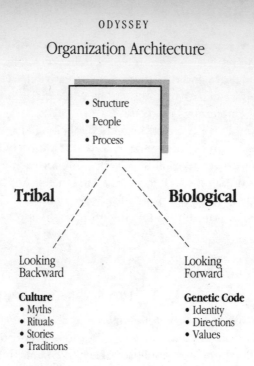

- Structure
- People
- Process

Tribal / **Biological**

Looking
Backward

Culture
- Myths
- Rituals
- Stories
- Traditions

Looking
Forward

Genetic Code
- Identity
- Directions
- Values

By losing some of these traits that tradition exemplifies, we were proving we weren't losing the basics of identity, directions, values. In looking backward, the emphasis is on tribal connections; in looking forward, the emphasis is on the individual, on biological notions.

Genetic coding has displaced the central importance of culture at Apple.

11

The New Spirit

When I arrived in California in 1983, Silicon Valley was the garden of promise. The Valley and its flamboyant, millionaire entrepreneurs lent hope that innovation and creativity were still possible in American business. It was a territory as rich as the country's steel belt became poor, an area which spawned hundreds of new companies with tens of thousands of new employees.

The free spirits who rushed west during the Gold Rush and early days of Hollywood continued their pilgrimage to California in the late 1970s for the promise of a high-tech, high-risk high life in the Valley. The computer lured to Silicon Valley the same kind of people who came westward in the 1800s to pan for gold nuggets in the stream beds of the Sierra Nevada, the jobless dreamers, mavericks from the status quo. For the first time they could become involved in something that not only lent them fortune but also fame.

Newly rich entrepreneurs and venture capitalists cruised the freeways in Mercedeses and BMWs; they glided through the sky in private Cessnas and Lear jets and settled into million-dollar homes in the hills. Venture capitalist Don Valentine appropriately viewed the Valley as "a pocket of entrepreneuring that attracted a breed of buccaneer capitalists and high-risk takers—an area barely big enough to contain the egos."

In what some called the "capital of the future," free-swinging Apple had evolved into its crowning success story. Now, it was no more. Our troubled company symbolized the general gloom and doom that pervaded a once optimistic land of wealth. Was Silicon Valley really dead?

If it was, its death would have bleak ramifications for other industries. The Valley seemed like the country's last best hope. It thrived in a heady swirl of engineering genius and entrepreneurial risk taking when the country's traditional industrial base proved increasingly vulnerable to foreign competition. If the Valley was doomed, so was the country.

It wasn't only Apple and other slumping personal computer companies, it was the entire electronics industry. Fierce competition from Japan was crushing the Valley's semiconductor makers. Layoffs were commonplace. So were bankruptcies. Some 20 million square feet of excess space—the equivalent of the city of Los Angeles—glutted the Valley's real estate market because so many companies either closed down or canceled their plans to grow. The whole Valley was going through a tremendous dynamic change, and it was hard for all of us to follow it.

No less important than the repositioning of Apple was the repositioning of John Sculley. The summer of 1985 thrust me on a pilgrimage into a wilderness of high technology and computers that I had not entered nearly as deeply before. As the company's resident technologist, Steve always maintained the primary contacts with the industry's leaders. It wasn't until after he left that I suddenly found myself in this new role.

Unlike a Jobs, a Wozniak, a Bill Gates, or a Mitch Kapor, I hadn't grown up in the personal computer industry. I hadn't founded my own company. I was brought in and had to adopt someone else's vision and beliefs about where the industry was going. I had now reached a point where I had to develop beliefs of my own, to go back and reach deep inside myself to discover what John Sculley believed in. And I had to do so at a time when the entire industry's future seemed in doubt.

Over the past eight months, I had met with many of the industry's pioneers who helped me define the company's new vision. I devoured books, such as Pamela McCorduck's *The Universal Machine,* which showed that non-technologists like myself could be as passionate and visionary as the Valley's pioneering inventors; and I read *Literary Machines* and *The Mechanical Bride,* whose authors dreamed of the possibilities of what computers could be.

If I were in a crisis at Pepsi, the last thing I would have done was to open a book for answers. But now Apple people wanted to know if there was going to be a new vision. I had to go on a search, to track the dream back to its source. Jean-Louis loved computing but didn't invent it. Woz helped invent it but never realized how the personal computer would change society. So I had to discover the origin of the dream. Alan Kay talked to me about life, science—everything but computers. Jack, my son, gave me Douglas Hofstadter's *The Mind's I*, which helped broaden my perspective.

I was searching for the answer to whether personal computing could really change the world. Or was it one of those great motivating ideas that didn't have staying power?

"You're only going to find the answer," said Kay, "if you go to the people who started the dream. The dream was alive and well long before Apple Computer was invented."

But we still needed to gain the credibility of many of the non-believers, who were less than convinced of Apple's future. I had to navigate through the constellation of companies that evolved around Apple. And this was so new to me. At PepsiCo, it wasn't necessary for Kendall to proselytize to an external network vital to the company's interests. His external sphere of influence was largely the institutions of big business: the Business Roundtable, the Business Council, and the U.S. Chamber of Commerce. Division presidents worked with the independent bottlers.

My new world was a whole galaxy, a world of many circles. Apple, which was always talking about changing the world, was about to be changed by it. In the first circle were the people the Valley engineers called "the suits."

October 1985 wasn't the best time for one of the most powerful "suits" to visit the Valley. But John Akers, the newly named chief executive of IBM Corp., made his first visit to Silicon Valley since he was a Navy fighter pilot stationed at San Jose's Moffett Field some twenty-five years earlier. Ken Oshman, co-founder and chairman of ROLM Corp., hosted a dinner for the new IBM executive to introduce him to the leaders of the Valley's top companies. IBM had recently acquired ROLM, a maker of computerized telephone exchanges, named for the initials of the four Rice University and Stanford graduates who founded the company (Gene Richeson, Ken Oshman, Walter Lowenstern, and Bob Maxfield).

We gathered at Ken's beautiful home in Atherton with modern sculpture in the atrium and the garden, and we sat along a large table in his formal dining room. The group included some of Silicon Valley's true stars, from Robert Noyce, vice chairman of Intel and one of the brilliant inventors of the integrated chip, to Jerry Sanders, the outspoken founder of Advanced Micro Devices, one of the country's largest semiconductor companies to benefit from Noyce's invention.

Akers showed up in a dark three-piece suit and white shirt, what many have jokingly referred to as IBM's standard uniform. ROLM, known for its freewheeling culture, seemed the antithesis of IBM. It allowed employees to work whatever hours they wanted, it gave them three-month sabbaticals at full pay after six years, and it boasted a million-dollar recreation center with a Jacuzzi, steam room, sauna, and two heated swimming pools. When IBM made ROLM a wholly owned subsidiary, Akers teased employees that he wouldn't "fill in the swimming pool [with cement]." For all of ROLM's unusual culture, though, I had never seen Ken without a buttoned suit jacket and a perfect dimple in his tie. He looked like an IBM salesman. It was Corporate America meets Silicon Valley, and I was the hybrid.

Ken set the agenda for the evening's discussion. "Let's have one big conversation so we can all join in and share in it," he said. "What's everyone's feeling about the future of Silicon Valley?"

The general assessment was bleak. Noyce believed Washington needed to take action to protect the Valley's semiconductor makers from intense Japanese competition. But no one's remarks were more depressing than those of Sanders, who had once exuded confidence and bravado.

In Silicon Valley, where people generally looked like professors, businessmen, or aging hippies, Jerry looked like none of them. He liked to shock. With his gold chains, loud clothes, and a shock of white hair, he seemed more like a movie star. He measured his success by the amount of fun he could buy: a gleaming white Rolls-Royce sedan, a Bentley convertible, lavish homes in San Francisco, Bel Air, and Malibu, and outrageously expensive Christmas parties for employees in San Francisco's Civic Auditorium. "I work absolutely as little as possible and that turns out to be more than any human being should work," he was fond of saying. Now he was anything but optimistic.

"I don't know why we're kidding ourselves," he said. "This isn't a recession, it's a depression, and there's no way we'll recover. We have a disaster going on here. The Japs are destroying our industry. They're dumping semiconductors in the market below cost, and we can't make money without some relief. We need help from Washington, we need IBM to take a firm position, or there isn't going to be a semiconductor industry in this country."

His comments, along with the generally known state of affairs in the Valley, threw a chill on the evening. Akers was beginning to feel the effects of the slump in personal computers at IBM; the company found itself losing market share to Asian makers of IBM clones. Digital Equipment Corp., taking advantage of the incompatibility of IBM's computers, was beginning to make inroads on IBM. IBM's profits were to fall for the first time in years. But Akers was caught by surprise at how downbeat an outlook Sanders portrayed. His remarks were somber, but hardly desperate.

"I'm cautiously optimistic, but I don't see a turnaround soon," Akers said carefully. "I think we have quite a few tough quarters ahead of us. I can't see anything favorable happening for at least a year."

Despite all the negative publicity we were receiving, I countered with a more optimistic view of the Valley's future. At least from the personal computer standpoint.

"Look," I said, "I think Jerry is speaking for the semiconductor industry, which is really hurting. But in personal computers, we're starting to see some vibrancy in our sales. And we'll see better results in the late 1980s. As long as we can continue to pursue proprietary technologies that are difficult for Japan and other Asian countries to clone, there's a good future for our industry. But we have to make some radical shifts and move the technology forward. We can't stand still."

It was becoming clear to me the Valley wasn't going to disappear, but it was going through a dramatic change. Leadership in a number of companies was being handed down from the pioneers to a second generation of leaders who were going to have to build a different future. If it would be less swashbuckling, it still didn't have to be less entrepreneurial.

I had reason to be optimistic. We were beginning to work and solve problems together as a team. As we glimpsed some hope, we began to trust and respect each other, and we had regained control of the company. Wall Street analysts had been forecasting that Apple would post a loss or just break even in the fourth quarter ended September 27. We surprised them by bouncing back with $22.4 million in net profits. Supported by price cuts on all our key products, orders from dealers for the critical Christmas selling season were coming in stronger than expected. Indeed, some dealers already were complaining that demand was outstripping supply. We also began to see some progress in international sales as Mike Spindler began building some important success stories in Europe.

In the United Kingdom, for example, Apple's share of the personal computer market fell to 10 percent from 25 percent between 1983 and early 1985. Many of Apple's 450 U.K. dealers were going bust or couldn't provide the kind of service and support to move upmarket. David Hancock, recruited by Spindler from Gillette in mid-1984, began to position the company as a supplier to the corporate market and Britain's professional services industry.

He weeded out 50 percent of the dealers and created Apple Centers that would sell only Apple computers and, therefore, be totally dedicated to the company. When a potential customer walked into a Center, we had a 100 percent share of his mind. And we had a dealer who could provide far greater support and service to the customer. The changes initially stabilized the subsidiary's sales decline and helped form the basis of a major recovery. Apple UK now boasts twenty such centers which helped to boost fiscal 1986 sales by more than 60 percent.

No less crucial, Spindler began to champion a new multi-local approach to international subsidiaries. For far too long, most American multi-nationals simply cloned their U.S. operations overseas, selling exactly the same product around the world that was successful in the United States. "The multi-national format has two drawbacks," Spindler believes. "It means too much jurisdictional influence from corporate headquarters and too much of a nationalist approach. Multi-local means you have a network model that adapts to local markets. You behave and act like a local company, yet you are within the network of the mother company back home. The whole world can thus become one big shopping cart for ideas and capital."

For seven years Apple had tried to sell computers in Japan with little success. It wasn't until we developed a localized product in mid-1986 that sales started to take off. We began offering the Macintosh Plus with KanjiTalk, an operating system that gives users access to three traditional Japanese alphabets. Constructing software to accommodate as many as 3,800 Japanese Kanji characters was no easy task, but we had to make a "Japanese product" to be successful in Japan.

For now, however, the turnaround of our business in the United Kingdom and some other European markets boosted our spirits.

It was one of the first stages of the turnaround. But we still had a long way to go. We had to regain the morale Apple had lost during the hard summer months. We had to rebuild the network of third-party companies so crucial to Apple's success. And we had to demonstrate that while Apple's roots were intact, we would be repositioning ourselves from a consumer- to a business-focused company.

To do this, we had to appeal not only to the "early adopters," the enthusiasts who were willing to take a risk with new technology. We also had to court the "low risk takers," business people who weren't spellbound by the gee-whiz factor of technology as much as they were in search of solutions. Apple, the consumer products company, had to become Apple the high-performance solutions company.

In a major change of Apple's philosophy, I had publicly announced that we would begin to introduce devices that would allow Apple users to plug into IBM and Digital Equipment Corp. communications networks. Our efforts in the past to establish our own standard for office computers left us isolated from the business mainstream of desktop publishing. If we were to succeed in business, we had to coexist in offices with IBM-compatible equipment. These were reassuring comments for companies that were considering buying Macintosh for business use. But they created near havoc inside Apple.

I felt like the religious Crusades were beginning all over again in Cupertino. Even faced with Apple's possible ruin, people still resisted reaching out to business markets, connectivity, and coexistence with IBM—their all-time enemy, the symbol of evil. "How could a soda-pop executive lead us in a direction we can trust?" they all wondered. At a time when morale was low, the repositioning triggered greater anxiety. We had to build products to connect to other computers—"systems" products—something we had never done before.

People rebelled, some refusing to work on products like MS-DOS co-processors cards and IBM mainframe terminal emulators that would allow us to coexist with IBM. They feared the new direction was a sign that Apple was going to abandon the unique technologies —and philosophy—that had made the company an innovative maverick. IBM made institutions stronger; Apple was the productivity tool for individuals: marketing to companies seemed a sellout. It wasn't true, of course. We were simply trying to shift to different markets to protect our technology. Without higher gross margins, it wouldn't be possible to move forward successfully. Many of our largest potential corporate customers already had purchased tens of millions of dollars in IBM computers. We had to find ways for them to connect Mac into these or there was no way we could succeed in business.

The time was ripe. Many corporations had by now installed enough computers to realize that their real cost wasn't the software or the hardware, but the cost of training people to use them. Macs were easier to use by far than IBM personal computers and our research showed they were used more frequently because of it. The average IBM PC in business is used only thirty minutes a day, while a Mac gets more than two hours of use daily. The average IBM uses 2.2 applications; the average Mac, 6 programs.

We couldn't do it without the support of Apple's people. Tilting the company in a different direction meant there would have to be dramatic changes in the way we did business. We had to train marketing and sales people to sell solutions. We had to get our research and development people working on products that allowed us to coexist with IBM.

Now we were ready to reach out into the next public circle— the sellers. We still were cutting expenses and watching every penny in the budget when Bill Campbell and Mike Spindler urged that we hold our usual worldwide sales meeting in late October. I was reluctant.

"How could we justify it?" I asked. "We haven't gotten ourselves out of the woods yet."

"We've got to do it," insisted Bill. "It will get the morale back and be an important event for us."

I gave way, but frankly wasn't sure it would be a good message to put on a major sales meeting only four months after laying off more than 20 percent of our workforce. I was wrong. It turned out to be exactly the right decision. Bill did a phenomenal job of rallying his troops. It bred terrific enthusiasm.

We could speak with confidence about the progress we had made within Apple, and we could show them a crucial revision to the Macintosh that we believed would allow us to sell into the large business environment. We were moving away from hyping technology features to selling solutions, primarily a concept created by our marketing people called "desktop publishing." This was a phrase coined by Paul Brainerd, founder of Aldus Corp., which came up with Pagemaker software that allowed us to package together the Macintosh and LaserWriter as a desktop publishing system. Using Pagemaker, it was now possible to design newsletters, circulars, and even books on the computer and print them with typeset quality on a laser printer. The superior graphics of the Macintosh as well as Apple's LaserWriter combined to give us a pioneering edge.

Instinctively, I felt desktop publishing could be very successful with business. Companies which routinely had to send their printing jobs to outside printers could bring it all in house far more cheaply than ever before. Championed inside Apple by a young Harvard MBA, John Scull, it had the potential to revolutionize the publishing business by virtually eliminating the need for documents to be typeset, pasted onto boards, and printed. It brought centralized electronic publishing down to a personalized scale on the desktop—just as Apple had brought the mainframe to the desktop.

Desktop publishing represented one of the very successful ways of segmenting the market, not to win a small position in a big market as in developing a better spreadsheet program, but in order to dominate a specific segment. Our sales people loved the idea.

The traditional rock concert and dance at the end of the meeting coincided with Halloween, so everyone dressed up in costume. I showed up in long woolen underwear with a silver-painted face and multicolored stars for eyes as the Spirit of Apple. I didn't look the part of a traditional corporate CEO. It was the first sign that the spirit hadn't died.

My own transition was not moving without difficulty. Only a few months earlier I had addressed one hundred of Bill's managers at a sales strategy meeting in San Diego. I had flown there late in the afternoon, and after a cocktail reception had begun talking to the group about how these were very tough times for Apple.

"Before we have a chance to get new products out, we're going to have to sell the products we already have to the outside world. Otherwise, no one will buy them," I told them. I should have stopped there. "That can only be done by you people, and you've got to do it. We have to face up to the fact that we don't have the best sales organization. Dealers have more respect for IBM and Compaq sales people than they do for Apple."

I went on, sounding more critical than I had in months because of my frustration and impatience at not having made even more progress.

"That is unacceptable to me. We have to raise our standards of excellence and I'm raising my expectations of what I want each of you to do. I'm proud of what you've done in the last month in turning the Macintosh around, but it's not time to relax. We can't pause to catch our breath. We're not going to get well unless we get a lot better soon."

Bill couldn't believe it. We spent the entire night talking to each other about it. He expected me to come in and thank his sales organization for holding us together over the summer months. While I didn't explicitly warn that we would replace them if things didn't get better, my remarks had that impact because they were made at a moment when the company was fragile. Bill threatened to quit.

I fell back on my PepsiCo roots just when I shouldn't have. I was too hard on them. When we were up against Coca-Cola, no words were minced. At Pepsi, toughness counted; Pepsi people counted on those types of remarks. No one apologized for any critical comments. If you had a problem, you fixed it. If you couldn't, you would be replaced. But it was a horrible mistake to speak to Apple people like that. It created tremendous anxiety at a time when the company was barely holding itself together.

There are times when you can lean hard and people get mad at you yet perform beyond their own expectations; and there are other times when, leaning too hard, you can cause damage. This was a time when leaders are supposed to inspire. If anything, it reinforced in me the belief that tomorrow's management leaders are going to have to be very different from those of the past.

The image of the chief executive as a tough, aloof, nearly macho hero is an anachronism in today's world. The new-age leaders will lead not with toughness but with powerful ideas. My natural instincts were to be authoritative, cool, and distant. I was too consumed with solving a problem instead of building for the future.

Yet, the new-age leader almost has to show his fallibility. Making mistakes is a very real and important part of succeeding. In a traditional corporation, too often a mistake is a sign of weakness. At Apple, making mistakes is the only way to learn. If you fail to convey the idea at the top that you can make mistakes, you can send the wrong message, isolate yourself from the people.

If I needed another lesson in sensitivity, I'd soon have an important reminder when Woz came back. Along with Apple Fellow Alan Kay, he assumed the role of goodwill ambassador, circling the world to speak before user groups to sustain the support of our core enthusiasts. Over one six-month period, Woz and Kay delivered more than eighty speeches to corporate groups. This was an unusually vital element in our success because Apple, unlike IBM, had an almost fanatical following among people who could identify with it as a company of the counterculture. Some owners felt emotional attachments to their Apple computers, and it was important not to lose their enthusiasm.

Woz's homecoming was momentous. I had reestablished ties with him at an Apple picnic in south San Jose during the toughest part of the crisis in July. I hadn't seen Woz since the previous winter when he stormed out of the company in disgust over the widening divisions between the Apple II and Macintosh groups. Our last conversation was an angry telephone call, when he accused me of giving Macintosh too much public credit to the neglect of the Apple II group at our shareholders' meeting.

"As the third-largest shareholder, I want you to know I'm upset and so are a lot of people in the Apple II group," he told me. "These people work on Apple IIs and all they hear is Mac, Mac, Mac. It hurts me to see people so demoralized. When I came to work this morning, the engineers, managers, and secretaries were just ready to send in their resignations, they were so angry about it. The shareholders were given the impression that the company's total revenues were coming from Macintosh."

"Steve," I said, "we really did mention the Apple II and the education markets."

"Yeah," he countered, "I heard the word two times in the entire thing, once in a question from the audience and once in a film clip at the start. It was the wrong impression to give."

Woz left, and since then, he had founded CL-9 (Cloud 9) to market a programmable remote-control video device he designed and to spend more time with his two children, Jessie and Sarah.

Contrary to popular belief, Steve had never officially resigned from Apple. He still drew a token salary so he could get his ten-year pin. It was typical Woz—never interested in the prestige of a title or fame, but simply caught up in the Apple culture. More than anything else, he wanted to become a teacher, a goal he wouldn't be able to achieve unless he earned his college degree. So he had returned to Berkeley to complete his electrical engineering degree. Wanting to go incognito and being the practical joker that he is, he enrolled as Rocky Raccoon Clark. Clark was his wife's maiden name, while Rocky Raccoon was his dog.

When he graduated in June 1986, Woz gave the valedictory address before hundreds of people at Berkeley's open amphitheater. The dean of the engineering school introduced him by saying, "This is a first because usually we select the person who's the most likely to succeed. This year we've done things a little backwards. Our speaker is someone who's already succeeded and made his fortune." Woz ambled to the podium and spoke about his theorem of life! He translated it into a formula: $H = F^3$.

"Happiness is the only thing life's about," he said. "You don't buy a computer unless you think it's a road to greater happiness. You don't do anything in life unless it's for happiness. That's the only way you can measure life, by the number of smiles per day. It's food, fun, and friends."

There was nothing more important to him. Woz was not only a computer pioneer, he was a greatly admired folk hero, and Apple sorely needed him at such a delicate and fragile time. Apple people loved him.

I approached him at the Apple picnic, not knowing whether he was still angry at me for focusing so much attention on the Macintosh the previous January when his Apple II group kept the company alive. He wasn't. We sat for hours with the other engineers talking about computer hacking and technical tricks he played on the Apple II microprocessor, Woz growing animated over "software interrupts" and "instruction sets."

For a moment, as others went to fetch hot dogs and cans of soda, Woz and I were alone. I decided to take advantage of our privacy.

"Woz, how do you feel about Apple now?" I asked.

"Actually," he said, "I feel pretty good. I really feel we're back on track. The engineers are doing wonderfully exciting things on the Apple II. I talk to them regularly now and it's fun for me to hang out at Apple again."

"Steve," I said, "I know you have your own company now and you're working on your own products, but we sure would like to see more of you around Apple. A lot of people have a lot of respect for you and look at you as the soul of the company. Would you consider coming back?"

"Sure, that's great. Look, I still love Apple. I care about what it does and I want Apple to be a success. My problem was I thought you and Steve lost perspective on how important the Apple II was."

Woz's return was greeted by both thunderous applause and a standing ovation, particularly when he announced that he had recently purchased $7 million worth of Apple stock. It was an important vote of confidence.

"It's not an investment," he told reporters. "It's just because it's right. I'm very excited about Apple. The morale is up, and the company's products are moving in the right direction."

Meantime, the attitude of the outside world was assuming great symbolic importance. We were switching to a more powerful Macintosh. While Woz and Kay worked the grass roots, Jean-Louis and

Debi struggled hard to get a revision of the Macintosh out by January and to initiate greater improvements over the long term. It was difficult because many engineers had left the company. Some were simply burnt out, exhausted in the whirlwind of activity that allowed them to put out the original Macintosh. A number of others quit with Steve. Wayne Rosing, former general manager for Lisa and one of Apple's senior engineers, resigned with many of his staff to go to Sun Microsystems.

A lot of the work started by Wayne's team would later show up in the open Macintosh II—an expandable computer with vast memory and built-in hard disk storage—that wouldn't debut until 1987. I had backed Wayne's project in late 1984 thinking we needed to develop other versions of the Macintosh that Steve wasn't prepared to build at the time.

Inside Apple there were raging debates over whether future versions of the Macintosh should be open, like the Apple II. Open, the Mac could accept additional circuit boards that adapt it to a variety of uses. Steve had preferred a closed configuration, which is less flexible but more reliable and cheaper to build. It was Henry Ford's 1908 theory for the automobile market transplanted into the 1980s for computers.

Indeed, the parallels between Steve and Henry Ford were striking. Neither man was educated as an engineer nor invented the technology behind the product that would bring him massive wealth and attention. They were, instead, leaders of a social revolution to empower the common man. Ford envisioned the automobile as a mass-produced tool that would give the average person incredible new freedom to explore the world. Steve saw the same in the personal computer.

And both men seemed to be born in the right place and time in history with the right idea: Ford in Detroit, and Steve in Silicon Valley. Detroit was an ideal spot for the birth of the mass-produced automobile because it was already home for a large number of skilled northern Europeans. It was an easy transition for the city's cast iron stove workers to turn their talents to casting engine blocks. The area's carriage producers would become the craftsmen for the auto's bodies and seats, while Detroit's bicycle makers would produce the bicycle-like wheels of the Model T. The Valley, home for the burgeoning semiconductor industry, provided an ideal infrastructure of engineers and technicians to launch the personal computer business. It already was the base for myriad vendors of electronic parts, components, and accessories.

Ford had a vision of creating a total industrial community in River Rouge, Michigan. Not only was he fascinated by his product, but also by the manufacturing process. He got the idea for putting the automobile on a conveyor belt assembly line from Detroit's slaughterhouses. Steve was equally obsessed with the Macintosh factory. To learn as much as possible about the latest manufacturing advances, he visited numerous Japanese plants. Steve insisted from the very beginning that the Macintosh factory be the most automated factory ever built for computers in the United States. Eventually he wanted Apple to have a technology park he dubbed "Supersite."

Without the discovery of vast oil resources in Texas in 1901, a development that provided a cheap energy source for the car, the Model T might not have been possible. Without low-cost microprocessors and integrated circuits, it would not have been possible for Steve to bring the computer to the common man.

Both men took tremendous pride in their creations, personally dictating many of the products' most minute details. Ford often would reject out of hand suggestions from colleagues to change his beloved Model T. Steve, too, held fast against those who would dare tamper with *his* child.

An open system, though, allowed users to personalize their computer by customizing it to their specific needs with add-on products. An open system also expands the technical life of the product because upgrades can be accomplished with add-ons as technology advances. Keeping early adopters' loyalty intact is paramount and this was one way of doing it. Closed products are frozen in time.

Ford, for all his greatness as a pioneering entrepreneur, became too firmly wedded to his breakthrough product, the Model T. He failed to comprehend that a single-product strategy could eventually lead to a steady erosion in sales. The Model T conferred on Ford not only fortune and fame but leadership in a new, exciting industry, not unlike the Macintosh, which bestowed the same attributes on Steve. But as history has proven, it simply wasn't enough. The Model T succumbed to Alfred P. Sloan's strategy of "a car for every purse and purpose," a strategy that would one day permit GM's worldwide supremacy in the automobile market.

Jean-Louis Gassée saw things differently. "The computer is a mind expander," he said, "an enhancer for the mind just as a turbo-charger is for an automobile engine. It will let people do things far beyond what they are capable of doing." His car sported license plates that read OPEN MAC.

He loved great products. Jean-Louis had built an enviable soft-ware industry in France around the Apple II and the Mac. Now, as head of product development, he had to create a product strategy to lead us into the next decade when the second generation of com-puters were going to be systems software products as hardware became less important. It was the software that would unleash the computer's power and potential. His presentation to the executive staff was a tour de force, with Jean-Louis, often dropping into an exaggerated French accent, intentionally butchering words in put-ting a French twist on them to emphasize a point. Sometimes he would pause, raise his eyebrows, and look up at the ceiling, waiting for a response to his sexual metaphors. He used them to shock, yet they skillfully captured the intellectual value of what our products really stood for.

The first result of Jean-Louis's work was the Macintosh Plus, an upgrade that came with both cursor keys and a numeric keypad for spreadsheet users and nearly ten times the internal memory of the first Macintosh.

Only months earlier, in September, Microsoft hit the market with a superb spreadsheet program for business users on the Macin-tosh called Excel. The combination of Excel with Macintosh Plus meant that we no longer had to force the power user to compromise on functionality for the advantages of ease of use and superior graph-ics. These were crucial revisions, changes that would transform the Macintosh into an excellent business product for power users.

Instead of using our annual meeting as a platform to launch the Mac Plus, however, we decided to announce it at an event we staged in San Francisco called "AppleWorld" immediately preceding our annual meeting. That we should sponsor an "event" at all was very controversial because we had been so badly burned in early 1985 by hyping the virtually nonexistent Macintosh Office at our share-holders' meeting.

There was tremendous resistance to it.

"This is wrong," Bill Campbell maintained. "Haven't we learned our lesson with the Macintosh Office and 'Lemmings'?"

"We have to do this because it's clear that we can't be successful unless we can build the self-confidence of our major constituent groups," I countered. "We'll never do it on our own resources."

We no longer could afford to spend $100 million on advertising. But by bringing together all of our constituent groups, the very people our competitors were chasing, the K–12 educators, the university people, enthusiasts, third-party developers, and dealers, we could gain critical mass. I felt sure the enthusiasm of our core constituents would rub off on other people, just as it did at MacWorld in August.

We had pockets of support, loyalists in each of our constituent groups who really wanted Apple to succeed. But it was a lonely, brutal winter because their support wasn't all that publicly evident. AppleWorld was designed to build their confidence that they weren't alone in their support for Apple, to inspire them that Apple still had a vision and a passion for the romance of the personal computer, to get them informed and talking about the Mac Plus and desktop publishing, and to simply say "thanks" for their efforts.

I finally overruled anybody who opposed it. Ironically, the only facility we could find to hold the event was a microcomputer center mart whose construction was halted because of the slump in the computer industry. To add interest and build credibility, we enlisted business and industry gurus like John Naisbitt, Alvin Toffler, Sherry Turkle, author of *The Second Self,* and maverick economist Lester Thurow to give speeches. We sponsored a variety of seminars centered on the use of Apple computers in education, business, and the home, and in one day I delivered eleven different speeches to enlist support. I had to.

In repositioning Apple as a business-focused company, I became the symbol because I was "the guy from corporate America." I used the label; it was a way to leverage the negative press. The media kept saying that Apple wasn't going to be a fun company anymore, that it was becoming sanitized and too professional. I asked myself, how can we turn that around and make it a positive? It's like trying to turn a boat. It's much easier to turn away from the wind instead of into it.

The event itself was a "spectacle of Apple II and Mac fans united in a kind of religious ecstasy, a useful reminder that the IBM option is simply irrelevant to some people," as Jeffrey Tarter, editor of *Soft-letter* put it. But when the product was announced, the consensus was "Too little, too late." "Those are the things they should have done in the first place," the critics said in unison. It was a disheartening response, but we knew the new Macintosh would have an impact. For once, Apple had been listening to its customers and had come up with a product that answered many of their complaints.

By January 1986, we had good news to report: our first quarter, which encompasses the Christmas selling season, had shaped up as a phenomenally big success. Even the most optimistic people thought we would be miracle workers if we could report 50 cents per share in earnings for the quarter. Instead, we turned in a record 91 cents a share, and people were blown away. Atari and Commodore, our tough low-end competitors, failed to hurt us. Their new computers lacked the software and the distribution to become a significant threat. A couple of days later we reached an interim out-of-court settlement with Steve, attempting to put the past behind us.

The most important, intricate circle was the personal computer industry's infrastructure, three layers deep. The biggest layer was the quirky network of influencers, 2,000 of them, mostly small, unconventional companies founded by independent entrepreneurs, corporate dropouts, and computer buffs. Apple provides a technology platform upon which hundreds of other companies can innovate. They are the real champions of the business, companies like AST Research, Broderbund, THINK, Borland.

For every dollar of Apple's sales, they sell three dollars in hardware and software products. And who knows how many computers their popular new products help us sell? Desktop publishing, for example, was only possible because third-party developers, such as Aldus Corp. and Radius, Inc., provided the ingredients like software and full-page screens to make it a reality.

Inside that network was the second layer—value-added resellers, companies which package computers and software into systems for specific uses for engineers, doctors, lawyers, small businessmen. Some of our dealers simply sold the computer as a box; other more sophisticated retailers sold "solutions" to their customers. Each one had different interests, concerns, and problems.

Hovering over it all was a surfeit of industry consultants, analysts, academic technologists, trade and general press. They are the Apple "watchers," but they do more: they also sit in judgment. We are their "opening-night" material. In my three years at Apple, I had met many of them. As the leader of Apple, however, I needed to get to know them as I had never done before. And earn their confidence.

Many in the network were suspicious and questioned our sincerity over a new partnership. We had a reputation for not being an easy company to work with. They'd develop add-on products for the Apple III and then we'd introduce Lisa. And when they made products for Lisa, we were ready to release Macintosh.

"The words sound right," they said, "but we want to see hard evidence." We couldn't afford to have them on the fence. We needed a few big wins. Both the general and the trade press suggested that developers were abandoning the Macintosh. "Venture capitalists are running, not walking, away from the Mac," claimed one software publisher. The *San Francisco Examiner* reported that even Gates of Microsoft was saying privately that his company wouldn't develop new Mac programs. "Development of innovative new Macintosh software by major software publishers is dead," stated one analyst.

I would have to politic hard for their support. I started out with the doyenne of the industry, Esther Dyson. Her Personal Computer Forum in mid-February would be something of a trilateral commission of personal computing. The industry heavies show up because they know that anyone who counts will be there. New faces come to listen and learn. And the industry's pioneers give their talks, then disappear into the backrooms and bars to make deals. Dyson presides expertly over all this.

"People are always coming up to me and saying, 'You know this deal you've just read about. The way it really happened was I spent an hour with the other guy at your Forum.' I love to hear that.

"You'd like to think this is a business like any other, driven by

*ROIs and spreadsheets. But it's really much more than that. The
industry is small and cohesive enough so that personality plays a
tremendous part. Individuals make things happen. You negotiate
with facts and capabilities and troops. But you also negotiate with
the power of your personality.*

*"Perhaps I have a natural instinct toward order or fertility. I
always wince at the word matchmaker but it's true. It's like some
lady a hundred years ago would say, 'Such a pretty young girl and
such a nice young man. It would be nice to see them join productively.' Someday I'd like to fall in love myself and have my very
own company, but I'm too fickle and I have too short an attention
span. I like to see new things. I like to help other people create
babies, but not raise them myself. So I can make a lot of things
happen without doing a lot of work."*

Dyson is our point of contact, the industry's Gertrude Stein. She
sees in the computer a product which brings together all of the
exciting intellectual possibilities that can shape the thinking of the
world. A pixieish woman in her early thirties with short hair, invari-
ably seen with a wringing wet bathing suit tied to the outside of her
backpack, Esther is highly intelligent, well read, fluent in many languages, including Russian, German, and French. She is a self-taught
technologist, daughter of award-winning physicist Freeman Dyson,
and she chronicles the industry's passages and probes its frontiers as
a journalist and spokesperson.

Her vehicle, published out of a pack-rat office on the twenty-
fifth floor of a Park Avenue office building in New York, is Release
1.0, a reference to the first release of a less-than-perfect software
product. When the bugs are worked out, release 2.0 may likely replace it. For now, though, it's the best you can get.

Esther supported my efforts to reorganize Apple, though she
had her doubts about our strategy. "Does Apple really belong in the
corporate marketplace?" she asked only a few months earlier. "Or is
it like Dorothy, searching for happiness far away in Oz when the true
riches lie at home, in the small business and education markets so
familiar and friendly to Apple?"

Everybody seemed to share her skepticism at the conference.
While cheered by the positive receptions we had received at

MacWorld in August and AppleWorld a few weeks earlier, I was essentially preaching to the converted then. Here the praise was for IBM. Every time someone mentioned the word "standard," the audience of 400 would applaud. And no one was applauded more than Rod Canion, chief executive of Compaq Computer Corp., the most successful maker of IBM-compatible computers.

In an impassioned speech, Canion strongly argued in defense of a standard. "Far from being a limitation," he said, "we view the standard as an accelerant. Now, users are able to stick their toes in the water of innovation and be safe within the industry standard. If [end users] are hooked into your proprietary system, they're trapped."

Few of my colleagues took me seriously when I maintained that we, not IBM, would redefine the direction of the industry with a new generation of computers that were graphics-based and boasted a better user interface. We believed the standard wouldn't be a fixed operating system, but that it would be standards of connectivity to link up and communicate with DEC and IBM products.

"We are committed to being the alternative technology company," I said. "The world doesn't need another MS-DOS or IBM-compatible company. We want to be the leader in setting off the second revolution in the personal computer industry."

In a series of private meetings in my hotel suite with the industry's major software pioneers, the most important work was done. Third-party companies are small firms, with limited resources, that can only focus on a few projects. If word were to travel that one of the software giants isn't working on Macintosh projects, no one else would venture to stick their neck out, either. I had to reassure the biggest developers—Microsoft, Lotus, and Ashton-Tate—that Apple still had the target machines they should develop for. If I could convince them to put their efforts behind Macintosh, then we would have a real chance. All of them, however, were sitting on the fence.

The most critical was Bill Gates, founder and chairman of Microsoft Corp., who runs the largest computer software company. Bill is quiet and thoughtful, with mussed blond hair and a slight build that makes him look like Woody Allen. He's often allied with us as the supplier of our most important software, yet he's often at odds with us as our biggest competitor because he wrote and controls the operating system software for "the DOS world," and therefore would be motivated to further enhance his position by producing additional DOS application software.

Back in July, Gates wasn't sure Mac would make it through the end of the year. Then, in November, a conflict between Apple and Microsoft threatened to mushroom into a major crisis. Gates had flown down from Washington State with his attorney for a 10:30 p.m. meeting with me and Al Eisenstat in Apple's boardroom. Gates was developing a program called "Windows" which would allow forthcoming versions of IBM personal computers to boast Macintosh-like features in graphics. In the recent past, we had negotiated with another company, Digital Research, regarding their release of a product called GEM that gave the IBM many of the Macintosh's look-and-feel features. It was a highly unpopular move, prompting many critics to argue that Apple was stifling industry innovation. But we had to take action to protect the proprietary technology that was the future of our company.

Before Gates came down, he phoned.

"I'm really upset with how things are going between Microsoft and Apple," he said. "I hear through the grapevine that you are getting ready to sue us. If that's true, I want to hear it from you."

"There are problems between our companies," I said. "We're not about to let our proprietary technology fall into the public domain. We're going to protect our property."

"I respect that and what Apple is trying to accomplish," Bill replied. "But if we're on a collision course, I want to know it because we'll stop all development on Mac products. I hope we can find a way to settle this thing. The Mac is important to us and to our sales."

Before Bill showed for the meeting, the executive staff met and the sentiment was: we shouldn't cave in. Some believed Microsoft would take our technology and move it to the MS-DOS world. We had worked too hard to turn Apple around. We couldn't let our emotions get in the way of what was right for the company. Open warfare with Microsoft would destroy everything we had accomplished with our reorganization. If we sued our most important software supplier, our business customers would think we'd lost our minds.

"Al and I will represent Apple's best interests, but I'm not ready to bloody the company," I said.

Unlike Digital Research, Microsoft had obtained a license from Xerox on certain technology and had past agreements with Apple that lent Gates greater flexibility. While who was right was legally debatable, we couldn't afford to sue the only company developing successful software for Macintosh at a still turbulent time. Gates and I hammered out a compromise license agreement, which was satisfactory to Microsoft yet protected the integrity of our Macintosh technology for Apple.

That was an important event. This was the crucial time we needed in order to establish that Apple could be a real player with the Macintosh in business. I was betting that desktop publishing would be the stalking horse to get us into corporations and that Microsoft's Excel would expand the use of the Macintosh to more general purpose productivity uses.

We made our peace back in November, and we had since reported our highest profitable quarter. Nevertheless, when Gates and I met privately in my hotel suite, he wasn't sure how much effort he could justify to support Macintosh software. Our Mac sales were still fairly low compared to IBM's, and most outsiders had great doubts that we could be successful in the key business market with the Macintosh.

"I'm not sure I know where Mac is going in the future," he told me.

"Bill," I said, "we're headed into the business market."

"That may be right, but it's going to be really hard. You're really going to have to demonstrate that Mac can be a success in business this year. You don't have much time."

"We've got a plan inside Apple I call 50-50-50," I said.

"What does that mean?" he asked, with a quizzical look.

"It means we expect to sell 50,000 Macintoshes per month a year from now. We expect to have gross margins at least 50 percent or greater, and we expect to have a stock price of $50 a share."

I knew sales of 50,000 Macintosh units a month were required to keep third-party developers over the long term. Gross margins of about 50 percent were vital to support the significant investment a proprietary technology required in research and development. And there was no way the stock price would go up, of course, unless the company was healthy again. Gates smiled.

"Those are pretty ambitious goals," he said. "I don't know whether you can do it or not, but I've been impressed with what you've done with desktop publishing. We're seeing an increase in the Mac run [sales] rate. I think that may work."

Gates promised to honor the agreement we reached at the end of 1985 and to put marketing and technical resources behind Macintosh applications. We also agreed to do co-marketing together to support Microsoft's Excel program, which began to garner rave reviews from the critics. It was showing the signs of success that we had originally hoped for Jazz, the first major software product for the Macintosh, published by Lotus, the second-largest software company. As an integrated spreadsheet, Jazz combined an electronic spreadsheet, word processing, graphics, communications, and a database—the five major software products in personal computing. The program, however, was a big disappointment for both Lotus and Apple.

It was a setback of sorts for Mitch Kapor, Lotus's charismatic and gregarious founder and chairman. A former disc jockey, Mitch was a jocular, heavyset man with flowing black hair. He studied transcendental meditation, wrote code for VisiCalc while an MIT student, and was behind the best-selling spreadsheet program for IBM, Lotus 1-2-3.

Mitch told me he was retiring from the management of his company, but that he remained a strong believer in the Macintosh despite the failure of Jazz to live up to expectations.

"I want to see Lotus continue to develop for Macintosh," he said, "but I still have to persuade some of my colleagues. There's a lot of controversy inside Lotus about whether we should do any more Macintosh products. I'm going to do everything I can to get Lotus to continue to put resources behind it. John, I'm sorry for Steve, but I think you've made the right decisions."

Even if Kapor's support failed to translate into actual products, it was an important boost to our morale. Mitch had a strong following in the industry, and our conversation would allow me to say that he was among the people who strongly supported the efforts of a reorganized Apple.

Soon other players pledged their support. But of all the leaders I privately met with at the conference, none had been more publicly critical of the Macintosh than Philippe Kahn. Kahn, a large, extroverted, flamboyant Frenchman given to quotable metaphors, founded Borland International. He was a superb marketer of low-cost applications, making Borland one of the fastest-growing software houses by selling programs for lower prices.

In the past, Kahn had criticized the Macintosh as an improperly conceived toy without enough memory or speed, with too small a keyboard, and no hard disk support. Yet in the confines of my hotel room, he admitted to being impressed with the changes we had made with the Macintosh Plus.

Like the others, he was skeptical. But Kahn, too, left agreeing to put resources behind a programming language for Macintosh developers and said he was even interested in acquiring at least one other Macintosh software product to market.

With four big developers behind us, I was convinced we had passed one more critical milestone on the way to success in the business market.

I always believed that timing in life is everything. Now was the time for me to hit the speaking trail personally. At every opportunity, I attended business forums, dealer group meetings, industry conferences, and other public forums, giving two or three major speeches every week to help reposition the company. Word of mouth, as Regis McKenna had often pointed out, was still our most important marketing effort. I knew it would take about nine months to convince all constituent groups that we had a workable plan to succeed in business. Nine months would take us up to the end of 1986, just a short period before our new business products were to be announced.

Corporate critics continued to ridicule the Macintosh's unique look by claiming it was little more than a cute toy for grownups. I believed our advertising had to convince people that Apple doesn't produce toys. The Macintosh Plus was the latest evidence of that. Beyond this message, though, it was important to sell the computer not as a box but as a solution to a market need in desktop publishing. I wanted our advertising to focus on two goals: to sell power and to sell solutions.

Advertising always assumed great importance at Apple. From the beginning, advertising and design were integral parts of the Apple II concept. They broadened the market for computers by demystifying the computer for consumers. Until Apple came along, most computer ads were loaded with technical specifications, virtually unreadable to the average consumer. Some people facetiously quipped that Apple was nothing more than "a vertically integrated advertising agency." We viewed our advertising agency as something of a strategic marketing department, making it privy to Apple's most confidential and sensitive projects. We had always used advertising to differentiate ourselves from other computer companies, and this strategy had worked.

Now it was absolutely necessary for advertising to play a crucial role in repositioning the company in the marketplace. Our instructions to Chiat/Day were to develop less expensive newspaper advertising with the impact of expensive television commercials. The concept was to run about four to six pages in a single issue, almost like a TV commercial storyboard. Bruce Mowery and I worked closely together, overseeing every detail of the advertising for the Mac Plus and desktop publishing, and the agency came up with multi-page ads that successfully told both stories. There was no "1984," no "Lemmings." Indeed, no television commercials for Apple at all, mainly to conserve spending. We introduced the new products with a print advertising campaign in only two newspapers, *USA Today* and *The Wall Street Journal.* Chiat/Day came up with stunning four-page ads that visually told the story of desktop publishing.

Chiat/Day's advertising campaign for desktop publishing helped us begin to secure that important market, but I was becoming concerned that Apple's advertising needs were changing faster than the agency's ability to meet them. Chiat/Day was a superb creative shop, but Apple's needs were now vastly different. We were trying to reposition a company, not stun the world with a home-run commercial to win awards. With less money, our advertising had to become more strategic. It had to sell specific solutions to business, home, and school users, not simply irreverent lifestyle messages.

Bill Campbell and I first began to speak about it before the Christmas holidays. I wasn't convinced that Chiat/Day had gotten the message of the need to change. Their initial advertising to sell our desktop publishing concept and the Macintosh Plus continually came in with cute headlines that I believed wouldn't win over business users.

During our October sales meeting, the agency introduced a series of black-and-white testimonial commercials which were greeted with silence by our sales and marketing people. The advertising looked as if it came from two different companies; it had nothing to do with where we were trying to take the company. An earlier attempt in March to produce a commercial to appeal to women also resulted in a $600,000 dud that never aired.

I felt women were an untapped market. Apples give women an advantage: they can learn how to use personal computers that aren't degrading products, reducing women to secretaries. IBM, as the very symbol of male-dominated corporate America, would have trouble positioning itself for the female market.

Set to pop singer Cyndi Lauper's "Girls Just Wanna Have Fun," the commercial was going to depict the power of professional women. They weren't going to be bunnies or Diet Pepsi girls. Feminist Gloria Steinem had a bit part, along with 1984 Olympic Gold Medal winner Joan Benoit, and Margaret Thatcher and Sandra Day O'Connor look-alikes.

By the time we were getting ready to run it in May of 1985, we were already in trouble. The timing was all wrong. Our goal then was to convince the low risk takers that Apple could be trusted in the business world. A commercial that appealed only to a female audience had little to do with that. I learned, too, that women didn't want to be talked to because they were women but because they were smart. Women didn't want pink computers any more than they wanted pink cars.

Bill and Bruce Mowery agreed to hold a competition. Our two leading agencies, Chiat/Day in the United States and B.B.D.O. outside the United States, would compete in a winner-take-all shootout for Apple's $50 million advertising account. We assembled a four-person selection committee, with myself, Del, Bill, and Bruce agreeing to hold the contest.

I called Jay Chiat and Allen Rosenshine, chairman of Omnicom Group Inc., parent of B.B.D.O., who had worked with me on the Pepsi business ever since he was a copywriter on the Diet Pepsi campaign. Understandably upset, Jay wasn't sure he wanted Chiat/ Day to compete. He felt the decision was a fait accompli and that his agency would only be going through a meaningless exercise. Rosenshine, meantime, wanted assurances that we weren't on a fishing expedition, trying to put pressure on Chiat/Day to do better work.

So frantic and pressured was the competition that both agencies began to woo Steve Hayden, the one-time Chiat/Day copywriter behind the masterful "1984" commercial. Hayden, now working for B.B.D.O.'s Tracey/Locke group in Los Angeles, became a hot property because both Chiat and Rosenshine knew how highly I respected him for his previous work. Chiat characteristically joked that he had just two things to offer Steve: "fame and fortune." Ultimately, it was out of a sense of loyalty for his old agency that Steve returned to Chiat/Day. B.B.D.O. suddenly feared its opposition had seized the inside track. To shore up its team, B.B.D.O. recruited a key person from Lord, Geller, Federico & Einstein, which had devised IBM's popular Charlie Chaplin campaign for the PC.

The two agencies were as different as New York and California. Jay Chiat, a witty eccentric with silver hair and a perpetual tan, ruled over one of the most undisciplined yet most creative advertising agencies that ever existed. His people took big risks, did outrageous things, like "1984," and set new directions in both print and television advertising. Their work was an extension of themselves. "It's not your work that's being rejected, it's you," Chiat would tell his people. They joked that they routinely worked eight days a week, the final day being "Chiat day." The usual result: spectacular, award-capturing work that stood out from the clutter for Apple, Nike, Pizza Hut, Porsche, and a slew of other clients.

Next to Chiat, Rosenshine was a no-nonsense, buttoned-down businessman, and B.B.D.O. was a serious, buttoned-down agency. It proved it, too, could do outstanding work as it did with Pepsi, but some thought the agency lacked Chiat/Day's beyond-the-fringe creativity.

For the competition, we gave each agency $75,000, sixty days, and the instructions to devise creative solutions to penetrate the business market and to maintain our advantage in Apple's important education market. We needed ads that would *support* our efforts to reposition the company. The ads had to work with all the products we wanted to advertise—to unify the company as "One Apple" externally and internally. We needed a theme we could live with for several years, and it had to be something Apple people could be proud of. The advertising had to reflect the importance of the individual, yet appeal to the low risk takers we were shooting for.

Usually shootouts are done with five agencies. We knew we'd get better work out of them if they each had a 50 percent chance of succeeding. I did the briefings because advertising was crucial to our repositioning of the company. I spent hours and hours in individual and group interviews and meetings with agency executives, articulating our strategy to reposition the company. Each agency was given half a day for their presentation, with Chiat/Day scheduled to compete on Friday, May 9, and B.B.D.O. on Monday, May 12.

The competition already was generating tremendous attention in the advertising world, the subject of widespread conversation and front-page stories in the trade magazines. Apple was a showcase account that could attract the best creative people to the agency. The best creatives want to put together ads that millions of people will see; to work on soft drinks, beer, cars, or computers—anything that spends a lot of money on ads becomes a glamour product.

The review sent shock waves throughout the advertising community because it failed to appreciate what had gone sour in a relationship that generally yielded superb creative work. "It was like the 'perfect couple' getting divorced," as Hayden put it. "She's beautiful. He's charming. They're both rich and famous and desirable. But no one knows what goes on behind closed doors."

Chiat's team arrived the night before from Los Angeles with a rented van loaded with materials for the presentation. They had made up black T-shirts sporting a Hell's Angel–style skull on the front with a banner that read: "God. Guts. Creativity," and a white Apple logo on the back captioned: "The Final Assault." They rearranged the tables in the room and set up a large screen television, rigging a Macintosh to project slides for their visual and graphic section. The show began at 9:00 a.m. in a nondescript conference room in the Mariani Building on the Apple campus.

To make its pitch for the business, Chiat showed up with an entourage of seven people including Jay and president Lee Clow, all in conservative suits. I couldn't believe it. Jay, who often dressed in bulky Italian knit sweaters, was suited. Clow, a tall, lanky man with a long beard and dark blond shoulder-length hair, generally would come to Apple in sandals and shorts. Today, he donned a dark blue suit.

"I've never seen you in a suit before," I said, somewhat amused.

"We want to prove we can be grown-up, too," Clow retorted.

They seemed weary and exhausted, as if they had been living on coffee for a long time. I was later to learn that most of them had been working sixteen- to eighteen-hour days in a near-hysteric state for the past seven weeks to prepare the presentation.

The group launched into its "assault" with a short video alternating images of Apple computers with cowboys, steelworkers, children, and others cut against emotive music. It was the kind of warm, touching film that brought tears to one's eyes. "If you think Apple's first ten years was something," an announcer intoned, "imagine what we're ready to accomplish in our second. Decade Two: Delivering the Promise."

A jittery Hayden stood before us for the opening remarks.

"Obviously when this began, Chiat/Day had something of a disadvantage," he said. "You don't call an agency review if everything is happy and wonderful. But from that negative position we first created an even playing field and now think we have pulled ahead. We've built a new team for Apple that combines the best of what we had before with some new blood."

The tension was evident. Everyone in the room had a sense that this could be the last time Chiat/Day would ever present a campaign to a client which helped to establish the agency in the advertising world. Chiat spent close to a quarter of a million dollars to mount this last-ditch effort to retain its most important account. We sat scattered around the room's table, with Jay and me sitting next to each other. They felt it was unfair that they had to go through a shootout because they had done some of the best ads in history. And they were scared.

As each of the Chiat people moved to the front of the room to play their roles, it seemed as if the presentation had never been rehearsed. People were blowing their lines, losing their places, and apparently speaking over their allotted times. For the first three hours, Chiat devoted its presentation to its overall strategy, an analysis of the market, and a $75 million media plan, before ever getting to the creative point, the actual advertising.

At one point, as Hayden set the "Delivering the Promise" theme for the presentation, he gulped hard when his boss, sensing perhaps that things weren't proceeding as well as he had hoped, joked, "I guess that means we can't sell the idea to Pizza Hut."

When Hayden got his turn again to show off nearly 150 pieces of creative work, he began with a well-conceived series of print ads to build the momentum for Macintosh credibility in the business world. The opening shot consisted of case histories of how large corporations, from General Electric to John Deere & Co., were using the Macintosh.

One huge, three-page color newspaper ad featured a gold King Tut image on the screen of a computer called the Apple IIgs we intended to launch later in the year. The headline read: "It's the future. Do you know where your kids are?" Yet another mockup, paraphrasing Apple's initial "One person, one computer" vision, touted the tagline: "We're Changing the World, One Desk at a Time."

The four of us from Apple watched intently, occasionally generating a comment. "That's hot," Bruce said, after Hayden suggested the use of a dummy credit-card newspaper insert that consumers could take to their dealer for $2,500 of instant credit. But Hayden began rushing through much of the creative because the agency was clearly running out of time. Indeed, I noticed that he began skipping over several pieces of creative instead of presenting it all. Near the end, Clow elbowed him out of the way for a harder sell of the creative work.

Although the team conjured up some terrifically innovative ideas, I felt the agency failed to devise a single theme that could embrace the entire campaign. "Delivering the Promise" didn't seem to fit.

Jay Chiat completed the presentation with something of a heritage statement. "The quality of the people we have assembled for Apple is simply not something you'll find at any other agency of any size," he said. "The overall quality of our work was some of the best we've ever done. The only safe decision to take Apple through the next ten years is Chiat/Day."

Clow, handing out "Delivering the Promise" canvas bags with

T-shirts and three-ring-binder notebooks of the presentation to all of us, said, "We're all ready for the Apple sales meeting next fall, and this is how it could look."

While disappointed, I remained noncommittal. "Thanks very much," I said. "You've done a lot of good work here."

Del was the most enthusiastic of us, but even he had mixed feelings. "It had its high points and its low points," he told Hayden. When we returned to our offices, each of us had a personal letter on our chair from Jay Chiat, a last appeal explaining why we should retain the agency:

Chiat/Day has always worked very hard for Apple. Maybe we haven't always listened too carefully, but we've always been dedicated and passionate about the work. These past weeks we've never worked harder. We've had our hearts, our souls and our guts in it. . . .

Apple helped build Chiat/Day. Apple is our heritage, our value system, our creative focus, our standard. Apple represents for us the ideal client in many ways. And, now more than ever, knowing the rules, the expectations and the commitment you expect, we can only be more effective than in the past. . . .

The B.B.D.O. team flew in from New York in a rented jet over the weekend in time for Phil Dusenberry, the architect of the Pepsi campaigns, to begin his presentation on Monday morning. In contrast to Chiat/Day, he breezed through the marketing part of the campaign in less than an hour and then focused very quickly on the themes and the creative. A short, soft-spoken man, Phil is a master of understatement and good taste. Rising creative stars would almost kill for the opportunity to work on an account with him. But he also can be tough as nails and uncompromising on creative work.

Phil, extolling the merits of "magic words" just as he had spoken of "magic moments" at Pepsi, presented the theme line: "The Power to Be Your Best." We tried not to smile when we heard the theme, but I realized it was exactly what we were searching for.

Dusenberry said he believed the theme told the story about Apple building powerful, usable products for serious users, yet it emphasized personal achievement, too. It was a line, he felt, that could be built into a wide range of creative executions. Some of them were good, and others weren't usable. But the agency demonstrated that it was a theme line that could be developed equally well for the home, education, and business markets.

The best advertising reaches deep inside the product and finds its soul. That was the inherent beauty of "The Power to Be Your Best." As a theme line, it said everything about what we were trying to become. It had emotive appeal to our new target group, the power users in business, while it worked in our educational market with as much force as it spoke to our enthusiasts. I thought it would let us speak with one voice as a company at a time when unity was imperative and ad dollars were scarce.

"Delivering the Promise," on the other hand, suggested a smug self-confidence, a nonexistent continuity, and the expectation that our target market knew what the promise was in the first place. While Apple's true enthusiasts might interpret the line as our pledge to create wonderful personal tools for the individual, the power users in business we now sought as customers might not have cared about it. They viewed Apple as an arrogant company, which had failed to listen to customer needs and which produced underpowered home computers also used in schools. We suffered a real credibility gap after our failure to deliver the promise of a Macintosh Office. Chiat/Day's theme line would have the sting of a Ford Motor Company running such a line after introducing the Edsel.

We delayed a decision for a full week to allow both presentations to sink in, and then unanimously chose in favor of B.B.D.O. I called Jay first to give him the news late on Monday night, May 19. Although obviously disappointed, he took the news like a gentleman. Then, I called Rosenshine at home at about midnight in New York.

"Allen," I said, "we've reached a decision. We thought about dividing the account between you and Chiat/Day as one possibility, but we've decided not to do that."

There was a pause and then I finally said, "Allen, congratulations. You won the whole enchilada."

He was ecstatic, of course. A few days later Jay published a public response, running full-page ads thanking Apple for having employed Chiat/Day for seven years. "You've done for us what VW did for Doyle Dane Bernbach, what Hathaway did for Ogilvy & Mather, what McDonald's did for Needham, Harper & Steers."

It was another break from the Apple of old.

As we repositioned the company, I realized I had repositioned myself. "The guy from corporate America," the calculating-at-any-cost competitor from Pepsi, no longer lived in the body and mind of John Sculley. I became more mellow, more thoughtful, more settled, too. I found more time for my family and for the things unrelated to work that I enjoyed: sailing, hiking, and horseback riding with Leezy, reading, traveling with my children, Meg, Jack, and Laura.

Leezy is one of the few people who can shake me out of my obsession with work and bring me back to everyday reality. She created a private world behind the walls of my public life. My home is a low-tech world: we have chickens on the property, two dogs, Rudder and Tinker, and two beautiful Morgan horses. At one point, we even had a 1,000-pound bull named Lucky. Leezy spotted a sick-looking calf in a field adjacent to an outdoor Apple party and brought it home. She nursed it back to health until it was consuming 42 gallons of milk a week and weighing in at one ton—when we finally had to send it off to a nearby ranch.

I would see Meg and Jack, who lived on the West Coast after my divorce, once every three weeks for sixteen years. My deal with Pepsi was that I could travel to visit them as often as I chose, and I did. Now, I got to see them more often. Meg, a Los Angeles teacher, would sometimes come to Apple events. Jack, an undergraduate student in applied physics and honors English at Stanford University, and I would now discuss technology, which brought us together.

I was speaking with very different kinds of people, people I never would have met at Pepsi: Alan Kay, Marvin Minsky, Seymour Papert, Nicholas Negroponti. These weren't young kids, they were as old as I was. But they were the founders of computer science and personal computing, and they had seen the potential of computers when Steve Jobs was still just a small child.

I realized, too, how possible it was to overcome your limitations, to achieve well beyond what you believe yourself capable of. David Hancock, managing director of Apple's British company, laid down this challenge to his new management team to build their confidence: "If we can climb the highest mountain in Africa, we will have the confidence to climb any mountain in business." A group of fourteen people—all but one non-athletes, along with one who was a severe asthmatic—climbed 19,000 feet to the top of Mount Kilimanjaro in Tanzania in a six-day trek through bad weather. Some literally clawed their way to the top; others moved just 10 feet at a time before collapsing to reach the summit. It was an extraordinary example of achievement. As Hancock recalls:

"For months as a business team, we weren't quite working. We were losing our hold on the U.K. market daily. And inside the company, we weren't getting synergy. All the operating people, for example, didn't believe they had a role to play outside their functional disciplines and outside Apple. But I knew the controller could use his knowledge to help our marketing staff find new ways to finance dealers.

"It all came to a head at a business planning meeting when the marketing guy was presenting his business plan. Some people didn't contribute to it or even show up. One said, 'Oh God, I'm fed up hearing marketing people going on.' I exploded. We were all in this together, but we didn't give each other support.

"I asked myself and everyone in that room, 'Why don't we do something that is impossible and if we can do it then maybe we can do impossible things.

"We came up with crazy ideas: raiding countries, smuggling ourselves across the border to Jordan and taking a camel ride to the Red Sea, climbing the highest mountain in Africa—all teamoriented adventures. The mountain was physically and mentally demanding. It wasn't short-term because you had to walk many miles and you had to train for it. We decided to go for it.

"But at the last minute, I threw them a curve ball by saying, 'We're going to bring spouses.' The reason I wanted them involved is because Apple challenges the other side of a person's life. You get so involved in it. One way around it is to make sure the rest of your life is totally exposed to this thing called Apple. So we decided we would have an evening dinner to talk about it—we invited the person who walked to the South Pole by foot, retracing Scott's footsteps. He told us how close to death he came and how his supply ship got crushed. And a journalist we had invited told us what she went through at Kilimanjaro. One wife said, 'I'm not sure we're going to go on with this.' Only one of us was an athlete.

"We started off on a Saturday from Heathrow Airport, flew to

Amsterdam, and then took a seventeen-hour flight to Kilimanjaro Airport in Tanzania. We piled into a van for an hour and a half to get to our hotel, the Marango Hotel in Moshi. It was 1930s and could do with a little paint. There were lizards on the floor. Someone found a tarantula in one of the toilets. We went from the luxury of Western Europe to this and it was a real culture shock.

"On Monday, we had to walk with backpacks six miles through a rain forest from 4,500 feet to 9,000 feet. The first night all twenty of us slept on boards with slim mattresses in a hut with no lighting, no heating, and appalling sanitary conditions. We had a single tap for water outside. The next day we walked 12 miles through very thin air to 12,500 feet. Some of us suffered severe headaches and diarrhea from altitude sickness. One person who suffered from sun sickness had to return on her own, walking 18 miles back to the hotel so her husband could continue on. That night we slept in little 12-by-6-foot huts and washed in a stream.

"On Wednesday we went for a four-hour practice walk to 14,000 feet and came back. One of our guides told me, 'These people will not make it to the top.' We already were tired and exhausted and sick. But we were getting to know each other extremely well. You couldn't avoid it. The next day was the most memorable twenty-four hours of my life. We walked from 12,500 to 15,000 feet across an alpine desert to the foot of the final climb. We walked 11 miles and were lashed by rain. The air was incredibly thin. We were all sick, with severe headaches. It was terrible. But we found out so much about each other.

"At 7:30 p.m., we dressed in our final clothing, with two layers of thermal underwear, and then we tried to sleep—ten to a room —for five hours on these thin boards in intense cold. At 12:30 a.m., all thirteen of us left the hut and went out in the pitch-black into a horrible snowstorm to climb to over 19,000 feet. Our guides told us the final assault had to be made during the night because you're going up scree and it's frozen at minus 20 degrees then. During the day it's difficult because you're sliding. It would have frightened us. It was almost a vertical climb in the snow. One woman, a chronic asthmatic, dropped out at 17,000 feet because she had diarrhea. Since you can't see what you have to climb, my wife had to count steps for me to make it. I fell asleep twice standing up

*and had severe leg and stomach cramps. Another couple talked
each other to the top after reaching total exhaustion at 18,000 feet.
They moved just 10 feet at a time before collapsing. We reached the
top at 9 a.m. and it was just a fantastic view. We were up there for
twenty minutes.*

*"Anybody who climbs Kilimanjaro who hasn't climbed more
than two floors of steps in his life before gets great confidence.
There's a much greater sense of understanding and a willingness
to talk with each other today. The wives have become great friends.
They fell into each other's arms at a get-together I had at my home.
Our business planning meeting was like telepathy. It was like
brothers and sisters coming together.*

*"It changed me and reinforced something that I always felt.
Management suppresses talent, and leadership gives you an opportunity to succeed. If you say to someone tomorrow that you're
going to manage 100 people they start putting controls on it. They
look down and inward, and you end up suppressing this great deal
of talent they have. The other way is to set a destiny and get your
people to buy into it. Vision is an incredibly misused word... a
Hollywood word in business. But if you give people the freedom
and the means to reach their destiny they almost always will."*

Like me, David Hancock came to the business with a consumer
marketing background. He left Gillette as international marketing
director and joined Apple in 1984 as head of our troubled British
subsidiary. Between 1983 and early 1985, Apple's share of the U.K.
personal computer market fell from 25 percent to 10 percent. After
their climb, our British subsidiary began to turn in record results.

Amazed at such effort and confidence, I became more
outward-looking, searching into the future, wandering through new
possibilities.

The Geography of Learning

Sometime in the late 1990s, the newspapers are likely to run headlines of two events that may well change the course of our nation. By then, the Soviets will have landed the world's first manned mission on Mars, creating a second "Sputnik effect" of fear that our kids aren't learning to the degree they must. And at that moment, we'll discover that up to 35 percent of our teachers have retired—and nobody will be on hand to teach our kids.

In 1957, the Soviets launched Sputnik 1 into outer space, startling the world and shocking the United States. It took just such an amazing surprise to galvanize the nation to action, creating NASA and committing hundreds of millions of dollars to technical research.

Now the average age of our teacher is the late forties, and fewer people are entering the teaching profession than in any period in recent history. Women, for years the richest resource for the teaching profession, are pursuing different careers. And unfortunately, our society has turned teaching jobs into low-esteem, badly paying work. Many of our teachers, their morale incredibly impoverished, have been reduced to becoming babysitters in large urban schools.

These two unrelated events may spark a general reawakening not only that America has lost its presumed technical edge in the world, but that our only solution out of the crisis lies with the youth of the country, a generation likely to be denied the needed numbers of teachers to bring it along. But maybe this won't be so bad.

As a nation, we seem able only to respond to a crisis. The problem is we have one now in learning that we have yet to acknowledge fully. Some 23 million American adults are functionally illiterate. About 13 percent of our teenagers can't read. From 1963 to 1980, a virtually unbroken decline took place in average scholastic test scores. When compared with students from nineteen other industrialized nations, U.S. students ranked in last place seven times, and never have we achieved first or second.

The personal computer isn't the panacea for this problem, but it is a tool around which solutions can be sought. This is really how computers will change the world, by changing the children who in turn will alter our perspectives of the world. Computers certainly will have a deeper impact on children than they ever will have on the linear, book-fed people of my generation. The personal computer provides us with a better "book," one which is active (like the child) rather than passive. Future generations of the personal computer will offer the attention-grabbing powers of TV, but be controllable by the child rather than the networks.

"It can be like a piano," Alan Kay notes. "A product of technology, yes, but one which can be a tool, a toy, a medium of expression, a source of unending pleasure and delight . . . and, as with most gadgets in unenlightened hands, a terrible drudge!"

The personal computer's promise has been far from fulfilled. Most of the computers on school desks today are used for simple drills and rote learning. We're still preparing our children for the same old repetitive jobs in the industrial age—the very jobs that are disappearing daily. Instead, we should be preparing them for the jobs of the future, jobs that will require thinking skills, not rote memorization and repetition.

Computers, with their library of knowledge at students' fingertips, will make it possible for children to enjoy learning by making them explorers, active participants in educational adventures. But we can't just parachute computers into the schools to do simple drill and practice routines, as Sherry Turkle has pointed out. We have to build computers into the core curriculum.

The Carnegie Foundation has been quick to notice part of the potential:

The [new] technologies should make it possible to relieve teachers of much of the burden of imparting information to students, thereby freeing them for coaching, diagnosing learning difficulties, developing students' creative and problem-solving capacities and participating in school management. The substantial productivity advances that can be expected from computer use will result not from replacing teachers with machines, but through greatly improved achievement by students when good teachers are augmented by properly used technology.

For years the Apple II has been the workhorse in schools across America. Enthusiasts have had a long love affair with this wonderful machine. When we decided to add the Apple IIGS to our Apple II product line, we did it with the belief that we have only begun to tap the potential of personal computers in education.

Wouldn't it be fantastic if we could build an Apple II compatible that had the ease of use of the Macintosh and could also share its data files? When the engineers began this task, it seemed almost impossibly difficult, but once again they surpassed themselves. What makes the IIGS so great is its superb color graphics and stereo sound, two important features for the new age of CD-ROM optical media. Bill Gates has said that optical media will be the technology behind the next big revolution in personal computing. I agree with him. Nowhere will this be more important than in public education. It's one of the reasons why National Geographic, Lucas Films, and Apple have joined forces to work together on educational products for the schools.

Some of the most interesting work in learning today is occurring at MIT's Center for Arts and Media. The Center's experiments with mixed media, combining text windows, full-motion TV-quality video windows, and speech as part of interactive learning tools, have astounded researchers. Children, contrary to what their parents believe, can listen to U–2 on the radio and watch *Miami Vice* on television with an opened book on the floor, doing their mathematics homework. Rather than being distracted by the bombardment of media, they find that the "mixed messages" have the potential to help them learn.

If individuals can simultaneously get relevant information in a choice of media, they will become far more effective learners. That's the capability MIT is trying to discover a technological way to harness. We've come a long way from the days when Henry James criticized Balzac for presenting "too many facts . . . ideas and images." Balzac, he groused, "becomes obscure from his very habit of striking too many matches," distracting readers by quantity and intensity. To the computer generation, both of these are pluses.

Why, after all, should we all learn exactly the same way? Every individual learns differently—by reading, by looking at pictures, or by listening. Personal computers of the 1990s will be able to customize the learning process to best fit the specific needs of the individual. Some are intimidated by the math on a basic proficiency test, yet they can mentally add and subtract numbers in a supermarket looking for the best deal. When we can put even apparently difficult information into an interesting, unintimidating context, it's not so threatening. This is exactly where personal computing is headed in the 1990s. The MIT experiments will help us design personal computers that will work better with children who can do several things at one time than with us.

On the West Coast, meanwhile, Apple is sponsoring some of the most interesting research on how to integrate computers into the curriculum. It's all going on in an old, run-down building in Los Angeles with an asphalt jungle–like playground in the back—yet this is one of the most innovative schools in the world, a very special version of L.A.'s Open Magnet Schools. The computer project, called Vivarium, is headed up by Alan Kay, who is looking for ways in which artificial intelligence, computer graphics, user interface, and curriculum design can be altered to allow people to learn better.

The children, first- through sixth-graders, will interactively design animal and plant ecologies to test, sharpen, and enrich their understanding of what they have learned. The big question is what would it be like for novice users to be able to create their own computer agents, semi-intelligent processes that could carry out tasks, find resources, advise, and coach their users.

Alan is beginning a process whereby children will be able to create their own computer agents in artificial intelligence—processes that can perform functions normally associated with human intelligence such as learning, adapting, reasoning, and automatic self-correction. The children are now learning to design their own dinosaur-like creatures. Currently they are using Macintoshes and even low-technology tools like paper, crayons, and scissors. But eventually they will have the help of an extremely powerful computer. Kay has thus taken a difficult technical issue and turned it into a major project around which some of the world's most intelligent artists, engineers, and computer scientists have gravitated: Muppet designer Jim Henson; Paul MacCready, inventor of the novel flying machine, the "Gossamer Condor"; and Marvin Minsky, one of the true pioneers in artificial intelligence, are just three of the people already involved.

Why set kids loose on the project? The breakthroughs in personal computing Alan originally achieved were through fifth- and sixth-graders at Xerox PARC, experiments which led to many of the Macintosh's user-interface features. Kids' minds are fresh. They are more adaptable to the new technology and more likely to come up with new ways to use the system unencumbered by biases of experience, of doing things in old ways.

The experiments will help us in our lifelong learning—another education issue that will grow in importance, as skill renewal becomes essential in training people for the four or five careers they will have. In the future, the people who fail to learn may find themselves excluded from the country's affluent middle class. The notion of a middle class based largely on economics might change to one that is rooted in information and knowledge.

Unfortunately, it may take a crisis to stir us to action. But if it does, education can emerge as the new frontier, just as in the first half of this century science was the arena for discovery and enlightenment. Innovation will require not only education reform but a reformation of our concepts of learning, working, and management. Making the experience of learning self-engaging, creating an environment for learning that is fun, and providing personal tools to make technology as transparent as possible are all necessary steps.

The real computer revolution will take place years from now, with our children's generation, not our own. Around fifty years after the millionth Model T rolled off the assembly line in 1919, Jack Kerouac published his beat novel, *On the Road*. Though cars had been around for fifty years, Kerouac's was the first generation to internalize the car's power, and he wrote vividly about the need for spontaneity and rush, according to scholar Frederick Karl. The car changed from being a "thing" to being part of the Beat Generation's soul. It meant life and escape to Kerouac; so probably will the personal computer to this new generation of kids.

12

A New Apple

A half-mile procession of well-polished limousines and Mercedeses inched toward PepsiCo's brilliantly lit corporate headquarters in the darkness of a beautiful June evening. Bathed in white light, the Erdmans, Moores, and Mirós strewn about the corporate campus seemed to blend easily with the guests. You could smell the freshly mowed, immaculately tended grass. The trees in the courtyard glittered with miniature lights.

One of the guards beckoning us on with flashlights poked his head into our car.

"John Sculley," he said, surprised. "How great to see you!"

The friendly face greeted Leezy and me with a quick salute and ushered us through the broad iron gates.

My last memory of Pepsi was my farewell party of three years ago. By company standards, it was modest, held in a single room, and most of the PepsiCo executives stayed away. PepsiCo president Andrall Pearson didn't show; Kendall couldn't be there; and I had initially refused to go unless the security guards, the fitness center workers, and the maintenance staff were invited.

All the indications were that tonight, June 25, 1986, would be a different occasion—a formal dinner party honoring Don Kendall, who was retiring as PepsiCo chairman. It was the first time I had been back at PepsiCo, in Purchase since I left for Apple. When we reached the main corporate headquarters building, a company chauffeur approached our car and insisted on driving us over the cobblestone pedestrian pathways right up to the front door. The offer was highly unusual; no one except Kendall or a visiting dignitary ever had that privilege. But the carefully hand-chipped stones that had been imported from Europe were difficult for women in heels to walk on. Leezy took advantage of the ride while I strolled up the path with the other guests.

Walking up the jagged path on this soft, hypnotic evening, I felt for an instant as if I had never left Pepsi. Everyone—indeed everything—beyond the two sets of sliding glass doors looked exactly the same. I wondered if Apple had been a dream. And then just as suddenly it looked small, like a return visit to an old hometown or high school when everything somehow seems a miniature version of what you remembered.

A butler announced our names as we entered a spacious reception room. A long receiving line greeted newcomers as waiters in formal dress served Dom Pérignon. I shook hands warmly with Wayne Calloway, the new PepsiCo chairman, Kendall's successor—the job I had, in another life, spent years competing for. Don was next in the receiving line, and he was beaming. This was his gala evening, his farewell, an event to surpass all the other extravagant celebrations ever held at PepsiCo. It was the culmination of a brilliant career.

The party signaled the end of one of the most daunting achievements in corporate history. As chief executive of PepsiCo for twenty-one consecutive years, from 1965 to 1986, Kendall had led the transformation of a lackluster soft-drink maker to a $9.3 billion consumer services giant. PepsiCo's overall revenues, which placed it among the fifty largest corporations in the United States, even exceeded its arch rival, Coca-Cola Co., which once dominated Pepsi on virtually all measures.

"Big John," Kendall boomed, as he lifted me off the ground with a bear hug. "I am so delighted that you could come tonight. You don't know how much this means to me!"

"I wouldn't have missed this for the world, Don. You know how much you mean to me and this is a very special evening. I wanted to celebrate it with you."

I went down the line, shaking hands with each of the company's directors, then moved on into a room crowded with the country's corporate elite. They were the leaders or former chairmen of some of the most powerful corporations in the world, an in-person *Who's Who* of modern capitalism representing General Motors, IBM, Exxon, General Electric, RCA, Johnson & Johnson, Union Carbide, Pan Am, Union Pacific, General Foods, Goldman Sachs, and Citicorp.

The 400 guests later gathered under an expansive white marquee, erected near the man-made lake and the spotlit PepsiCo fountain, which spewed water more than forty feet into the air. Stunning flower arrangements decorated the huge tent under which the guests sat according to prestige and rank. The company's junior vice presidents and their spouses were seated in the far reaches of the marquee, while the corporate Right Stuff sat in front. There was music—Mozart and Copland and Prokofiev—by the forty-piece Philharmonia Virtuosi orchestra. Pop singer John Denver, a friend of Kendall's, played an engaging series of songs dedicated to Don, too. It was Lincoln Center transposed to Westchester County.

The contrast between this and an Apple event was striking. We would sometimes erect a large tent on the asphalt parking lot behind the building for an employee party at which people would show up in blue jeans and dance into a sweat to blasting rock music by Jack Mack and the Heart Attacks. On the few formal occasions, Apple people would don rented pastel-colored tuxedos and ruffled shirts. Alan Kay would arrive in a black silk top hat and cane, others in black tie and Velcro-strapped Nike sneakers. Dressing up at Apple was a game. It was as if people dressed for a Halloween parade. Here, it was a sign of arrival, of success.

But the contrast went much, much deeper. It reflected vast differences between second- and third-wave companies, whose leaders ran institutions as formal in their way as the Catholic Church or the U.S. Army. I realized just then that many second-wave CEOs were former fighter pilots and military men, like John Akers of IBM, James E. Burke of Johnson & Johnson, or Don Kendall himself. Theirs was a religion of *strategy,* of *beating* the competition—of war games raised to the level of business. War was an ill-fitting metaphor for what I did, because strategy had little to do with success in the third wave. In the world I had adopted as my own, Apple, the *romance* of business was what we lived—and lived for—every day.

As the waiters poured Stolichnaya vodka into the guests' glasses for a toast, Calloway strode to the front platform to make an announcement.

"I've been asked several times if I'm the person who's replacing Don Kendall," he said. "No one can replace Don Kendall. I'm merely taking over his old job. I want to report that you are all helping us rewrite our corporate history books. That's because this is the last time anybody will visit the PepsiCo Sculpture Gardens."

Knowing in advance of Calloway's announcement, I watched Don carefully. After a pause, Calloway continued, his voice growing more excited. "We're officially changing the name of this beautiful setting to the Donald M. Kendall Sculpture Gardens, starting right now."

I saw Don's eyes well up in what was an emotional moment for him. The gardens were the symbol of all the might and power of PepsiCo., of all that Kendall had achieved in a magnificent corporate career. It was Kendall who insisted that PepsiCo embrace the fine arts as corporate patron, public benefactor, critic, and connoisseur. From the outset, he concentrated the company's energies on collecting major twentieth-century sculpture, and at his retirement Kendall could rightly claim, as PepsiCo did, a veritable museum-without-walls in its thirty-nine works of modern sculpture—each personally chosen or commissioned by him.

Later, I bumped into Pearson in the men's room. The last time I saw him was behind a PepsiCo desk, when I told him I was leaving the company. Stonefaced and terse, he had refused to even stand or greet me; it was a frosty farewell to someone who had betrayed the corporate loyalty. This was a very different Pearson. Retired from PepsiCo to a Harvard Business School professorship, he was now friendly and outgoing, fascinated by that West Coast company he had barely heard of a few years earlier. As a tough and demanding boss, he had provided the training that helped me through the worst of the crisis at Apple. Pearson had been instructor to a corporate samurai, and he seemed to take pride in my apparent success in the outside world. I knew I owed him a lot. Only now, after what I had been through, could I really appreciate what I had learned from Andy Pearson. It felt good to be friends again.

But I quickly realized how far removed I was from a business that once obsessed me. My friendship with Kendall was greater than ever and so was my respect for his achievements. But PepsiCo held little interest for me. I had never had second thoughts about my decision to leave the company and this trip only confirmed it. Somehow, I felt as if I didn't belong anymore.

I had seen too much, changed too much. My three and a half years at Apple curiously left a greater imprint on my life than some sixteen years here. Sometimes, someone will show me a picture from Pepsi days and I'll honestly wonder if that was really me or someone else. Pepsi was part of a big industry. Apple is a way of life.

I was now part of something important happening in the world. I was living an experience that few chief executives would ever get the opportunity to know. The suburban corporate campuses of New York City and its buttoned-down executives were as incongruously different from Silicon Valley and its inhabitants as soda pop was from the gargantuan potential of computers. No wonder it seemed so small upon my return.

Few people better illustrated the vast dissimilarity with my past world than Apple Fellow Bill Atkinson, one of our most astute technologists. Every day, he plans what life will be like when neither he nor I will be here to sample it. If at Pepsi the horizon for most people was the next Nielsen period, at Apple we glimpsed into the decades ahead. As Bill says, "I bought the dream."

"I bought the dream of making a dent. Not only did I buy it, I tasted it and knew it was right. I looked at the creation around me, starting with the stars in the galaxy and thinking about our planet and our little team and what can we do as part of creation. I thought, How could I contribute? I have been so incredibly lucky and blessed with so many opportunities that I can sit back and loll the rest of my life as far as money goes. But I have some talents I can contribute.

"After I did MacPaint, I worked on this idea I had for a laptop computer called Magic Slate. I had two guys work with me at the house on it. But the technology wasn't there and wasn't going to

be there within five years. I like to get stuff out, I don't just like to dream. I'm a product man. I got real depressed at the realization that we couldn't build this thing. I was doing this for Apple. I went through a dry period where I couldn't write code and couldn't do much, and I went to Bud Tribble, my manager, and said, 'Look, I'm not interested in these computers anymore. I can't do anything with them. I feel like I shouldn't be drawing a salary until I'm producing again.'

"He sat down with me and said, 'The work that you do, going around and kibitzing with people and teaching them about our user interface, is worth more than your salary. So don't worry about your salary and quit feeling guilty.

" 'Go and do what tickles you.'

"So I started reading about cosmology and stuff. I wasn't doing much work—I'd make the rounds and talk to people, but that was it. That dry spell was formative for me. I started to realize I was missing a great opportunity to contribute. At one point, I turned things around. Instead of what can I get out of the world, it was, my God, I was so blessed, what can I put back in? That was when I realized that given who I was, what I knew, who I knew, who would listen to me, the smartest thing I could do was to continue working at Apple and create an application for sharing information.

"I have a certain ability to reach people because Apple will publish me to a lot of people. Without that, it's really hard for an individual to affect a lot of other people. My work will get out to a million people. That's a golden opportunity to shape the world. I feel it's not only a responsibility, it's a joyous opportunity. Wow.

"So, after I got my fill of credit and I asked what really matters and how could I change things, I asked myself what's really important to me."

I had never met anyone like Bill at PepsiCo. A six-foot-tall, wiry man, with curly light brown hair, Bill Atkinson is Apple's cosmic thinker. When solemn, he speaks almost in a whisper. His eyes gaze off into galaxies light-years ahead of our own. Bill believes, as do many other technologists, that he is contributing to the intelligence of a future species that might someday inherit the planet, if not the universe. In his office hangs the motto: "Now is the time for all good men and women to come to the aid of their fellow men."

At one point, he wanted to be a writer. Now, at Apple, he feels he is communicating.

"A thousand years from now," he believes, "the dominant form of intelligence on the planet earth will be more of a descendant of our current generation of computers than it is our DNA. It might not even be two hundred years before there is a computer considerably more intelligent than a person. We are at a fork in evolution where a species dies and gives birth to another. It isn't going to happen while we are alive, but we are contributing to something that is much bigger than us. We're not the apex of intelligence. We're a beautiful example of how far it's gone on this planet, but there will be other intelligence."

Never at Pepsi had I heard such thoughts. Yet his ideas were not uncommon in Silicon Valley, where few boundaries existed for creativity or thought. Of the thousands of computer programmers in the Valley, however, Atkinson stood out as one of the few technologists who could dream, conceive, develop, and deliver a product.

At the age of thirty-five in 1987, Bill was already a legend. Recruited to Apple from his own small company in 1978, he was issued badge number 51 and immediately became the "applications software department." His first job was a thirty-page program in BASIC, a computer programming language, that allowed Apple II users to monitor stock quotes. It was Atkinson who was responsible for the Lisa computer's user interface, the unique way in which a computer user interacts with the computer. He became an honorary member of the Macintosh team because he had designed many of the computer's features ported from the Lisa, including pull-down windows, the one-button mouse, and the graphics program Quickdraw. He wrote some of the tightest, most elegant code ever written for computers.

Steve enticed Bill to write MacPaint by promising to bundle it in the box for free to everyone who purchased the Macintosh. Like a poet who's chiefly interested that his words touch as many people as possible, Bill urgently wanted his work disseminated to the widest possible audience.

"If you're an artist," he explains, "you want people to like your work and you want it to have an impact on people's lives. You want it on public display instead of locked away in some closet. I use computer code as my artistic medium to express myself, to leave my mark on the world, to steer the world in ways that I will be able to tell my grandchildren I made a small contribution."

In October of 1985, though, a badly disillusioned Atkinson came to see me. He wasn't the typically buoyant Atkinson I had known from Macintosh days, when he was living on fruit juice and Big Macs, laboring twenty hours a day and thriving on it. Now, he seemed crushed and nearly defeated. Apple, unbeknown to me, had decided to "unbundle" MacPaint without consulting Bill. He feared that his current work on a new program called HyperCard wasn't being appreciated, either.

"I need a relationship of support and trust," Bill said. "What I'm doing is going to require immense amounts of energy on my part, and I'm only willing to do it if it's not going to get squashed. If that's going to happen, I want to know now and I'll do something else."

I was both shocked and surprised. Atkinson had already spent nearly two years developing HyperCard. And as he explained what it could do, I began to realize that it was one of the most exciting products I had seen in my more than three years at Apple. In its most basic form, HyperCard is a database program which uses the Rolodex card as a metaphor for storing information in a computer.

But HyperCard isn't really an application, like word processing or a spreadsheet, as much as it is a software engine. Until now, users could only type their own information into applications that used both text and graphics. With HyperCard, users will be able to better use information in the form of text, graphics, video, music, and animation provided by other people. It's a personal tool kit for using, customizing, or creating information.

HyperCard allows users to quickly browse through large stacks of information and find what's most important to them fast. That's incredibly important because it will help people more easily access information from CD-ROMs, which look like stereo compact discs but can store virtual encyclopedias of knowledge. A single CD-ROM, a development likely to revolutionize personal computing in the next few years, will store the equivalent of 1,500 floppy disks.

HyperCard makes all this information manageable, and it helps them organize information the way they think—by association and context—in addition to hierarchy. Users, for example, can simply click on the wheels of an automobile in a graphic to find other wheels in a graphics library. Or they can click on a map of Africa for a picture of what the country looks like. By pointing to a lion in the photo, a user can access information on carnivorous cats.

Because HyperCard is so easy to use, it will turn many subject-matter experts who aren't computer programmers into information providers. Professionals, business executives, and educators—people who work with information daily—will be able to realize more of the power of the personal computer and share it with others. In his description of its potential, Atkinson is animated and his enthusiasm infectious. "This will allow even your grandmother to write computer programs," he laughs.

This was more than just another program from one of the true computer wizards of the Valley. It was a personal creative effort born of emotion and trauma—After the Macintosh was launched, Bill tried to develop for us a small laptop computer he called Magic Slate. As the Mac team scattered and as Bill's early hopes for his new product failed to materialize, he became increasingly depressed and fell into a slump.

"I went through a dry period where I couldn't write code and couldn't do much of anything," he told me.

"That lasted about six months," Bill continued. "Then I spent one night on a park bench down the street from my home, staring at the stars the entire night. It was the first time I really got it—that the odds are we really aren't alone. I felt very small, but I also felt very proud. That was the motivation that got me going. This is coming from inside me. It's not coming for fame and glory. It's not coming from money. I've got enough of that. At that point, I turned around and asked what could I do and how could I contribute. I knew I was a really good programmer, and it suddenly dawned on me that I could teach a little of what I know."

Bill's searching night under the stars in January of 1985 jolted him out of a six-month slump and propelled him into a flurry of activity on HyperCard. His work habits are productively compulsive. In a typical day, he puts in as many as sixteen to twenty hours in an overheated, cluttered room in his home in the hills of Los Altos. The place is a junkshop array of old and new technology. Computers are stripped to their innards, outside their cases. The wooden counters along the walls are covered with fragments of electronic gear, a spare keyboard, tangles of wire, and pieces of circuit boards. Computer magazines, computer paper, and thick binders of written code are heaped in high piles on the floor. The laboratory sports the locker-room smells of young programmers sweating through hot nights over gutted computers, inputting thousands of pages of code line by line.

Now, because of Apple's decision to sell MacPaint and because of lackluster interest in HyperCard, he was concerned that his work would be for nothing. I decided to call together the executive staff and allow Bill a chance to tell his story in person. I urged support of the project, and we eventually struck a deal with Bill under which Apple would either agree to "bundle" HyperCard with every computer or we would give Bill the complete rights to the program to distribute as he pleased on his own.

I took a great interest in championing his project, watching its progress over the months and helping to guide it as well. Adopting the role of end user, I asked what people would want to use it for. Initially, Bill conceived of HyperCard as a program that could help him organize his own life; it lacked use as a tool for programmers and as an interface to optical media. I urged Bill to add these because they would bring new dimensions to the program. With Joe Hutsko, my technical adviser, I sat around my house at night, playing with the program to see what improvements we could make in it. I told Bill not what his project should look like, but what it could be.

The spirit was coming back. Our lifeblood is our products—and there were plenty rolling out. We proved there was great vigor in the Apple II line by launching in October of 1986 the Apple IIgs, a computer with astounding graphics and sound capabilities. Esther Dyson was among its many fans. And we would soon deliver on the promise of the Macintosh computer. By now, the press was reporting a comeback. One local rock music station, KMEL, began to refer to me as "Skullman." Oftentimes when KMEL's "zoo crew" read the day's problem news, one of its disc jockeys would suggest that maybe "Skullman" would have the solution to it—from the trade deficit to vagrants in San Francisco to high taxes and a nuclear-arms agreement. Ten years ago, who would have guessed that corporate chief executives would be thought of as celebrities? No one in the world could have been more gray and boring than a businessman. Now even a rock music station was making complimentary remarks about me.

The mail and phone calls changed, too. Investors and Apple fans sent letters and made personal calls to congratulate me on the company's better performance. Letters from Eastern Europe asked if I could send people brochures of Apple products so they could look at them, because they knew they'd never have computers in their lifetimes. It was a far cry from when the stock was crashing. Then, between fifty and a hundred people would call every day screaming about what I was going to do to pay them back for the money they lost.

The third-party companies which were sitting on the fence only a year earlier all came through. Bill Gates delivered a new, more powerful version of Microsoft Word. Philippe Kahn, who once called the Macintosh "a total failure," bought a Macintosh software company in San Jose which created a sophisticated database program. And he told people he had several products for the Macintosh under development in the past year. Ashton-Tate was the last of the "big three" personal computer software publishers to offer software for the Macintosh when its chairman, Edward Esber, promised to come out with a database management program for Macintosh.

Desktop publishing, meanwhile, had become a huge success. Far from the tiny niche critics initially contended, it emerged as a crucial entry point for Apple into the corporate world. For under $12,000, it provided many of the benefits of centralized electronic publishing systems, which cost $250,000 in 1984. The market for desktop publishing systems was expected to increase to some $750 million in 1987, double its size of the year before, and to explode to $4.8 billion by the end of the decade.

While it was obvious that design firms, advertising agencies, and newsletter publishers would want desktop publishing, we knew it had to reach well beyond this market to become more than a niche product. Large corporations had long used high-end graphics tools for their engineers. These technical managers often had the authority to buy computers independent of the corporation's management information systems (MIS) department. We used our small direct sales force to aggressively go after the large aerospace corporations, and I became a salesman, willing to pay personal visits to let our potential customers know they could trust us as a vendor. In each instance, we were careful to cultivate relationships with the heads of MIS, because while we may have first gotten through the back door with desktop publishing, we knew we would eventually have to march through the front door for reorders.

We leveraged early success stories at companies such as Boeing, Hughes Aircraft, General Dynamics, McDonnell Douglas, and TRW into greater selling opportunities. Once these systems were put into place to serve the in-house publishing needs of major companies, the Macintosh began to be used for other computing purposes as well. Other large companies like Arthur Young & Co., Peat Marwick Mitchell, SeaFirst Bank, and Du Pont were among many who already had bought several thousand Macintoshes. The Plessey Co., one of Britain's largest corporations, agreed to buy multiple thousands of Macintoshes throughout Europe.

Such support demonstrated how we had become a value-added marketing company instead of a commodity marketing company. We weren't aiming for the lowest price, we were going for the most value. It would also form the basis for such things as interpersonal computing, the ability for people to work within groups via a connected network of personal computers.

Desktop publishing is really only the beginning of a new generation of knowledge tools that will help us rethink the way we perform work. The more important revolution it will spur hasn't yet come. As we move into the information economy, the desktop, not the factory floor, is becoming the workplace of the future. Increasingly, workers are at desks utilizing their minds, instead of at factory machines using their hands.

This is merely the beginning of how Apple will play a small but important role in redefining the way work is done. We have an opportunity to extend document processing further by connecting our personal computers into work groups which can communicate with each other via desktop. We're going to discover huge opportunities to improve productivity by changing the way people work.

For more than thirty years, since the introduction of the first computer, people have focused on using the machine to speed up work. The computer made it easier for companies to process their payrolls, manage airline-ticket transactions or traffic control. Yet the most significant and important gains in productivity really will come as people work differently, not faster.

The work-group concept will connect people around the world, creating pockets of creativity in teams that could not have existed before. Regardless of distance, they will be able to share common resources—pass messages to each other, access huge databases of information and analysis, and benefit from the collision of ideas that occurs in a team atmosphere. The result of their work will emerge in an "intelligent document," intelligent because it will contain up-to-the-minute. data that will influence decision making. Documents will become persuasive, insightful, customized, and highly relevant because of the timeliness of the information in them. Documents intelligent enough to automatically update themselves as well as routinely distribute themselves to appropriate individuals on the network will dramatically change the way companies are organized and their decision-making process in the years ahead.

Apple's changes didn't come without an occasional uproar. When I began to speak of our expanded role as a small computer systems company, many of our middle managers rebelled. I knew that data communications among computers was becoming increasingly important and that it was vital for Apple to connect into the large installed base of computers from IBM and Digital Equipment Corp. Apple had to peacefully coexist within those worlds because business already had made huge investments in them. No one could expect a company to throw out thousands of dollars worth of IBM equipment to install Macintosh.

Yet it struck Apple people as incredibly unpopular. It turned me and anyone else I asked to work on it into a lightning rod of controversy. We attracted a large number of computer scientists with systems backgrounds who demonstrated that we could connect users to foreign environments as elegantly as we connected users to their stand-alone machines.

But it was a major philosophical hurdle for a company that had always done everything by itself. The very nature of the word "systems" suggested that we had to recognize others' standards to allow various products to link up to each other. Apple people had long considered so-called systems products to be dull and boring. To them, systems represented a sellout of the things they were trying to change about computers.

Toward the end of 1986, in fact, a group of middle managers demanded a showdown meeting with me. They didn't want to work for a systems company and they marched in revolt. Yet business and education were demanding connectivity. I had to convince them that our primary goals hadn't changed.

I explained that I saw Apple as a company that constantly reinvented itself and we were now going to reinvent ourselves into a "small computer systems company." That didn't mean giving up being a great personal computer company that focused on individuals. What it did mean was that we were going to build very powerful systems—desktop computers and work stations—that could connect to other work stations that were either our own or in foreign environments. I had chosen my words incorrectly, and it frightened people at Apple. When I explained that we were really trying to build a foundation for interpersonal computing by moving from stand-alone to connectivity using a range of systems products, the crisis was averted.

Apple would still change the world, I believed. But we had to admit the world had also changed us.

The good news continued for us.

B.B.D.O.'s first advertising efforts were previewed at our sales meeting in October of 1986 at the Boca Raton Hotel and Club in Florida. As we rolled the tape in a nearby university auditorium, the crowd of hundreds cheered, taking Phil Dusenberry aback. These weren't ordinary commercials; they were tight little dramas with well-constructed dialogue and cinéma vérité effects. There was tension in the scenes, long pauses in the dialogue, actors who didn't look like actors, and even dialogue that grabbed the viewer before the picture appeared. To sell the Macintosh to business power users, they emphasized the edge an executive would have in communicating his ideas to management with flashy graphics through Macintosh's desktop publishing capabilities.

One of the commercials, called "Red Eye," showed two businessmen in the first-class section of a night flight. In the dialogue, the older man catches a glimpse of a report the younger man is studying. He shows terrific surprise when the younger executive explains that he wrote it himself—graphics and all—not on an expensive computer system or by using a freelance graphics system.

"If I had to send this out, I couldn't afford to ride up here," he says. B.B.D.O. took such great care in creating this commercial that the details enlarge the drama, down to the younger executive's overbite, which was a touch that made the character wonderfully winning.

United under the theme, "The Power to Be Your Best," B.B.D.O. did eleven spots in all, including a power-image commercial. It captured the split seconds of a rush of power—the surge of a jet at takeoff, an Olympic swimmer plunging into a pool, a train barreling forward at full speed—all with subtle images of Apple woven into the scene, and culminating in the simplest, most powerful movement of all: the approach of a human hand to the Mac keyboard.

We would spend about $45 million on advertising in 1987, less than half the amount we spent in 1984. Without having nearly as much money to spend on advertising, I still wanted B.B.D.O.'s work to at least become advertising that was talked about. So I came up with the idea to publicly debut the new ads at a press conference in New York, to launch the ads as if they were a new product.

To add an element of suspense to the event, we asked film critics Gene Siskel and Roger Ebert to critique the advertising. It was a risky bet, because the critics had to be able to give their honest impressions before a group of some of the toughest reporters in the country. But I believe in marketing as theater, and this was another chance to make an event out of a typical marketing occurrence.

Siskel and Ebert were the independent arbiters—like the people who tested the taste of Pepsi against Coke—who would give our advertising greater credibility and attention. That, too, was a controversial move. Bill Campbell was totally against it. He feared that

Apple could be accused of hyping things into an event once again, just when the company was getting its credibility back. He also thought the risks far outweighed the advantages. What if the film critics tore the commercials apart in front of the media?

Other members of the executive staff were worried about it as well. I disagreed. "Look," I said, "we have some great new advertising. There's a lot of excitement about the change of agency. Apple has been off television for a year. And I don't want the advertising to get lost in the product introduction. At the same time, we don't have as much media as we like to be able to advertise. There's a risk, and if it fails, you can all point your finger at me. I'll take the blame, but I think it's worth the risk.

"If we don't think our advertising is good enough to withstand their criticism, then why are we even running the advertising?" I asked. "Why did we spend so much work trying to get it? We're trying to seat a new theme, and it would be a lot easier if the people in the advertising business have a chance to hear it from us."

Few companies, of course, hold press conferences to show their new advertising. We sent out invites in large, Hollywood-style tin film cans, filled with popcorn, a film strip from one of the commercials, and a formal invitation. And we planned to show every one of the B.B.D.O. commercials except one.

The only commercial that failed to get an enthusiastic response at our sales meeting was a sixty-second montage of power images interspersed by subtle references to Apple. In some ways it was too strong, too many of the images were almost violent, and it didn't leave the right message. The style overpowered the advertising message, becoming virtually a cliché of vignettes; it could have been a promo for ABC Sports. It seemed like an attempt to come up with another single blockbuster to set the stage for the rest of the commercials in the series.

I asked the agency to do another edit of the commercial, to excise some of the more violent images, and install more Apple references, withholding my decision to show the commercial before our New York media critics. When B.B.D.O. came in with the revision a few days before the New York event, we screened it a few times.

Everyone seemed to love the new version. I liked it, too, but thought to withhold my enthusiasm. The commercial hadn't been shown to any focus groups nor to Apple employees on an informal basis. I believed it would be a good idea for B.B.D.O. to work a little harder to show it, to gain the support of others before I would give the final go-ahead.

"It's better," I said. "But I don't know that it's good enough to show."

They edited the commercial again and we indeed showed it in New York. It was a skeptical crowd, however. Was this, in fact, another example of the brash company on the West Coast coming to New York to stage an "event" where none existed? The truth was that my reputation was on the line. Everyone wanted to see what B.B.D.O. could produce after Apple fired one of the hottest creative agencies in the country. Had I made a mistake?

"We're a company that does things differently," I explained. "We've been known to take whole divisions of our company off to the movies when there is a new film in town, like *Raiders of the Lost Ark* or *Return of the Jedi.* So it felt very natural to us, because we like good movies, to have good movie critics come and give their opinion about our advertising. But there's one catch. We had to pay Siskel and Ebert to come here and do this, and we don't have the slightest idea of what they are going to say."

Until now, few in the room even cracked a smile. Finally their eyes sparkled with the thought that two tough movie critics would be allowed unrestrained to assail our $6 million advertising production. I introduced the two of them and Roger Ebert explained how they would score the commercials. A 4 was the absolute best, while anything over 3 was outstanding. Anything under a 3, however, would be a pretty good excuse to walk off to the refrigerator for a snack. If it were less than a 2, Ebert advised people to make arrangements to be out of town when the commercials screened.

We started off with what I thought would be the most popular commercial—the power commercial. Ebert said some nice things and then rated it a 2.5. I thought "Oh my God! If that's our best commercial and he rated it two and a half, then what's to come?" Then Siskel rated the same commercial 3.5. Later on, the reviews were very good. The pair, who had reviewed advertising in the past for the publication *Advertising Age,* said it was the best campaign they had ever critiqued.

When the stories were written, journalists didn't write what we said. They matched it up with what Siskel and Ebert said. We received a huge amount of publicity and hardly a word of it was negative. After the commercials aired, an independent study showed they really clicked with viewers. We scored the highest advertising awareness of any company in November, a month after we launched the ads on the World Series. Although outspent by our competitors, we posted an awareness score that was twice as high as IBM and nearly ten times as high as Radio Shack.

The advertising set the stage for our tenth year in business in 1987—a year in which we planned to celebrate by launching more new products than ever before in the company's history.

The day, February 2, 1987, began in darkness: up at 3:30 a.m. to catch a 4:45 limousine that would bring me and a small group of Apple supporters to a Los Angeles television studio to spread the good news.

Already in the sleek black limousine was evidence of our efforts to tell the world that Apple was back. The morning's papers, *The Wall Street Journal,* the *Los Angeles Times, The New York Times,* and *USA Today,* all carried stories about the new products Apple was launching to up the stakes in the personal computer market. Even Stan, our driver, told us he had heard a pre-dawn report on Apple's new products on National Public Radio.

The new products represented the second generation of the Macintosh family—the Macintosh II, the open Macintosh designed for advanced applications with a color display, network connections, and compatibility into the IBM world, and the Macintosh SE (system expansion), which with added internal-storage capacity and a slot for additional functions was expected to become Apple's mainstream system for business users.

The band of technology pirates who created the original Macintosh had proclaimed that they made the computer for themselves. The team that pushed that technology further ahead with the newest additions created them, as one of the engineers said, "for the rest of us." This wasn't an ordinary product introduction; it was really the story of the comeback. Jean-Louis said it best, in launching the two new computers: "It's the people at and in Apple who found in their gut and in their brains the will and the skills to turn the company around."

Macintosh was a product several years ahead of its time. Only now were we getting to the point where we could build them powerful enough and at a low enough cost so people could really gain truly useful machines. And the people behind these new computers were the new heroes and leaders of Apple Computer. As one of the youngest engineers put it, "We are all leaders because we all want something to be good. It's not direction from above. It's not the word of John Sculley coming down, saying, 'Thou shalt make good products.' It's because we want to make good products."

Now, throughout the early-morning hours, I sat wired before two TV cameras in a small studio beaming a series of live interviews by satellite to a spate of TV broadcasters: Canada AM, Financial News Network, Cable News Network, Hearst stations in Boston and Baltimore, CBS affiliates in Detroit and Denver, and local stations in Philadelphia, Dallas, Knoxville, New Orleans, and Indianapolis.

I could tell them all the story of a comeback. Now we were no longer dependent on a single market as we once were, we had a pipeline filled with new products into the early 1990s, the company had never been stronger financially, and today we would unveil the products to win greater success in the business marketplace.

The scene for this meeting was the Universal Studios Amphitheater in Los Angeles, where we launched the second AppleWorld conference on March 2. Some 3,000 educators, business people, government officials, dealers, users, developers, financial analysts, and press converged in L.A. for the two-day event. About 200 reporters and financial analysts congregated in the orchestra pit in front of the amphitheater stage for the opening session and introduction of our new computers.

This event was not nearly like the first one. A year earlier, we were under the gun. We were fighting for the very support that would ensure our survival. We brought together our constituent groups in an effort to show them that Apple was still alive. Now we brought them together to show them how far we had progressed and how much potential the future held for us both.

Throughout the development of these products, we had been involved in a race against time to beat IBM. If this event had occurred only a month later, we might have been forced on the defensive. IBM would have announced its new Personal System/2 line of computers and Apple would have been perceived as playing catch-up. Worse still, the introduction of our products would have been overwhelmed by the millions IBM spent to launch its new personal computers. Once again, the events proved how valuable timing is in life and marketing.

The difference in our products, however, is greater than four weeks. Because the new Microsoft operating system that is to take advantage of IBM's computers won't be available for at least another year, we boasted an eighteen-month to two-year advantage over IBM. It would take at least that long before IBM had the software for these new computers to do what we already could ship to customers. By then, however, we will move to the second and third evolutions of system software for Macintosh and further performance advances on the hardware side.

In many ways, IBM's new products are a confirmation of Apple's direction. Besides increased speed and power, the new line eventually will give users an improved user interface and better graphics —the things that already differentiate the Macintosh from all other personal computers. Some analysts may wonder about Apple's ability to compete with IBM several years from now when its PS/2-computer system is fully implemented.

It's much preferable for Macintosh to be recognized as a significant competitor in the industry's mainstream as it is today rather than where we were only two years earlier. Then, we were sitting on the sidelines trying to explain to the marketplace why graphics and ease of use are important. Before the 1974 oil crisis, Japanese automotive companies were virtually alone in selling small cars in the U.S. market. When the American automakers finally shifted to the production of smaller cars, some analysts predicted that Japan would dramatically lose market share. After all, the reasoning went, Detroit wouldn't permit foreign competitors a dominant share of the small car market once it became part of the industry's mainstream. History, however, has shown that the best technology and quality ultimately results in the highest consumer satisfaction and a correspondingly high share of market.

The second generation of personal computers—both Macintosh

and IBM's PS/2—are really software machines, not hardware products. Apple is the only computer company which has complete ownership and control of its system software technology. Consequently Apple has been able to optimize the system software and hardware in order to maintain meaningful differences in our solutions for the end user. The strict rules the Macintosh's operating system imposed on software developers forced them to create programs that offer users greater consistency. That's why they can more easily move from one application to another and why users require far less training time on Macintosh computers.

In systems software, we have the important building blocks in place to do the basic things better. And we're investing hundreds of millions of dollars to ensure that is the case. In applications software, we have another often overlooked advantage. The elegance of the Macintosh as a technology platform is best appreciated by the most creative and talented third-party developers. That's a major reason why Macintosh has become over the last two years the target machine for the most exciting and innovative new software programs.

Apple will continue to stress the meaningful differences while taking advantage of IBM's own work to allow our products to coexist in the same environments. Ironically, IBM's move to PS/2 greatly simplifies the technical issues for Macintosh connectivity into IBM computer systems. IBM's adoption of 3.5-inch diskettes, of graphic-based application programs and system standards for connectivity across their own product line means that Macintosh can nicely coexist even in IBM-dominated worlds.

The press turned amazingly positive, from the general media to our industry pundits. "This has been a good year for John Sculley," agreed Esther Dyson. "What sounded like outrageously confident statements last year have turned out to be true. The Mac has gained a solid if limited following in corporate America, and its prospects look brighter each month. . . ."

Measured against the 50-50-50 goals set in the heat of the crisis in 1985, we have achieved or surpassed each milestone. We hit the 50 percent gross margin target at the end of 1985 and quickly exceeded it to about 53 percent in early 1987; the 50,000 a month Macintosh target in early 1987; and the stock price zoomed upward, reaching about $50 a share in early 1987. Just before the introduction of our newest products at AppleWorld, our stock hit its highest level ever at more than $70 a share. By spring of 1987, the company market value rose to $5.5 billion, compared to under $900 million in June of 1985.

A black-tie tenth anniversary party at the Santa Clara Convention Center brought 5,500 Apple people together for a dinner and concert with the rock group Huey Lewis and the News. Under the theme "Over the Rainbow," the convention arena was transformed into the Emerald City. Actors dressed as characters from *The Wizard of Oz* strolled through the crowd of party-goers on a fabricated Yellow Brick Road. It truly was a fantasy come true for so many of us at Apple.

Ten years ago, a revolution began that changed the world. It was a revolution that put incredibly powerful tools into the hands and minds of individuals—not computer experts, but ordinary people who were to discover that they could do extraordinary things. I've been lucky to be a part of that revolution, which has vastly improved the way people learn, think, work, organize, and communicate.

Indeed, as I look back at Mike Markkula's original business plan for Apple Computer, dated November 18, 1976, I can't help but feel great pride that in virtually all areas the company has exceeded the initial dreams of its three founders.

Under major objectives, Markkula had hoped the company would:

1. Obtain a market share greater than or equal to two (2) times that of the nearest competitor.
2. Realize equal or greater than 20% pretax profit.
3. Grow to $500 million annual sales in 10 years.
4. Establish and maintain an operating environment conducive to human growth and development.
5. Continue to make significant technological contributions to the home computer industry.
6. (Possible) Structure company for easy exit of founders within 5 years.

Under key strategies, Markkula listed:

1. It is extremely important for Apple to be the first recognized leader in the home computer marketplace.

2. Continually market peripheral products for the basic computer, thereby generating sales equal to or greater than the initial computer purchase.

3. Allocate sufficient funds to R&D to guarantee technological leadership consistent with market demands.

4. Attract and retain *absolutely* outstanding personnel.

5. Rifle-shot the hobby market as the first stepping stone to the major market.

6. Maintain significant effort in manufacturing to continually reduce cost of production.

7. Grow at the same rate that the market grows.

8. Design and market the computer to be more economical than a dedicated system in specific applications, even though all features of the Apple are not used.

In many ways, we've met and exceeded almost all of the goals and strategies set onto paper when Apple was little more than a dream with a home in a two-car garage. When Apple was founded, there were probably fewer than 50,000 computers that had ever been built in the entire world. Today, more than 50,000 computers are built and sold every day. The decade saw a hobbyists' dream materialize into a $46 billion industry.

Apple helped to change the world, and the world helped to change Apple.

For the first time in its history, the company also has products in the pipeline not only for next year and the year after that but into the early 1990s. In 1987, Apple was pouring about $185 million into research and development of new products, more than four times as much as the $40 million spent on R and D in 1983. About 20 percent of the money is supporting ideas that have nothing to do with products for the next two or three years. By 1990, we expect to spend well in excess of $300 million a year on R and D to support what should be a $4 billion corporation. By the year 2000, we expect Apple to be approaching $20 billion in annual revenue, with several campuses around the world—all united by the vision to change the world. In Debi Coleman's words, we went through "a total transformation."

"We've gone through a metamorphosis. It's like the caterpillar became the butterfly, but we were really ugly, slimy caterpillars

*before we became a beautiful butterfly sort of thing. On al-
most every level, every function, every approach, we've changed. I
think people have really matured. The middle management part of
Apple today feels revitalized. I think they really feel like they participate. There was no middle management participation in anything before. We really kind of argue passionately about just
about everything from the color of the products to the shape of
the package.*

*"There are no fewer battles. There is no less excitement and
intensity of feeling about anything, but I think that there's much
more willingness to listen to the other side, to not win the battle
for the sake of winning a battle, of really waiting and measuring
and making tradeoffs. Not compromises because people still don't
stand for compromises. That's one thing that hasn't changed.*

*"In the early years under the guise of no compromise and
integrity, we really were intellectual bullies lots of the time. And
in some cases, intellectual terrorism, as Jean-Louis will say. People
really believe it now. It isn't rammed down anybody's throat. It
isn't like sacrificing the vestal virgins because you're supposed to,
you know? It's like you have the Olympic Games because it's a
wonderful contest of spirit and strength and flexibility and we'll
get swifter, higher, stronger by working at it."*

We are, as Thoreau so eloquently said, not noblemen, but a
noble village of men and women. We're trying to build a model
corporation for the future. Not a company for the rational world I
left—a world too consumed with power and competition, a world
that rewarded people for building corporate empires, not beauty.

The new corporate models aren't to be found in the military,
the Catholic Church, any more than they are to be discovered in
Japan, a country which has shaken us into this new reality. The clues
and inspiration for business systems in the future are to come from
new disciplines and new paradigms. From biological cell theory,
from Tao, from architecture, and from art.

Through this journey, I have made another important discovery.
Only through a radical shift in our thinking can we succeed in reaching and achieving in this new age. It calls for nothing but a complete
break from the tradition-bound ways of the business leaders and

managers of the industrial age. It demands major educational reform so that learning becomes less an exercise in memorization than it does a way to think and discover.

If we fall into the trap of adopting some cleverly put clichés about how to manage better, we will end up a second-rate country in the next century. If we are unable to tap the creativity of our people, we will fail. If we lack the ability to envision bright ideas as the truest source of power, we may watch from the sidelines as other nations lead the way.

The story that Apple has to tell is the gospel of innovation. It's a time to stop using technology simply to systematize the old ways of doing things. Apple offered a new view on productivity and innovation. It started with the people, not the institutions of government or business. Give people exciting new tools to work with—tools which are both easy to use and interesting—and they will devise better ways of working and learning.

We want technology to be the source of new tools for creating a new world. The new world we already have created inside Apple, where creativity permeates every facet of our work environment, is but one small example of what an exciting new company can be in the information age.

The computer industry won't exist as we now know it. The driving force will be an information technology industry, with personalized knowledge-based systems at its epicenter. Apple will remain a company based upon a community of bright, talented people who enjoy doing innovative things. People like Bill Atkinson, Alan Kay, and others whose passion for the personal computer is limitless. We will remain a creative, driven people, with egalitarian values that will focus on building enabling tools for individuals.

When you think how much the personal computer has changed our world in the past decade, just imagine how far it can take us in the next. When I look back on the four years I've spent at Apple, I feel lucky I've been a part of it all.

The dream continues.

Spinouts

The movie *Logan's Run* is set in the twenty-third century, when no one is allowed to live past their thirtieth birthday. Those who try to escape this fate are hunted down in their elaborate, dome-enclosed city by a special police force.

At Apple today, the average employee age is only twenty-nine, not because we have police tracking down the over-thirty crowd, but because we've come up with a new management model to keep the workforce young, their entrepreneurial spirit high, the groups small and intensely motivated: we've started creating what we call the spinout.

It may be one of the most exciting alternatives for a company like Apple. Because we believe that interdependencies—networks of smaller companies—are a major source of strength, we are spinning out from the Apple mothership new ideas, new business directions in the form of new companies. While many former Apple employees have gone off to create companies that evolve around us, Apple has for the first time created one of its own, and more are likely to follow. Our aim is to nurture the strengths of our people, strengths that have been typical of Apple for ten years.

Our first offspring announced this year is Apple Software. This spinout fills a gap in the market for us, because now, the three major personal computer software companies garner most of their revenues by selling products for the IBM world. We wanted to make it possible for much more Apple software to be created: that's the new spinout's charter. However, this wasn't a mission Apple itself could directly undertake. If we were to sell a great deal of software under the Apple label, our third-party developers would have been at a disadvantage; and that would have discouraged them from creating new products for us. We didn't want to jeopardize their support, so we are simply going to spin the business out to run on its own, and produce software under a new non-Apple trademark.

For the first year, we plan to incubate this new child until finally granting it independence as a separate company without the Apple name. But spinouts are effective in many more ways than simple marketing.

For bright, ambitious people, the spinout is a dream opportunity. It combines the allure of a small, intense start-up with the romance of Apple. Like the denizens of the under-thirty world in *Logan's Run,* we'll spin out one of our most senior managers to head each new cell—whether it is 100 percent owned by us or an entity in which Apple will hold a minority position. For Apple Software, we placed in charge Bill Campbell, executive vice president for sales and marketing and one of our "over-thirty" executives. Bill will recruit a team from some 200 Apple employees who immediately applied for a chance to work for a start-up—so they will transfer to this new cell Apple's genetic code as well.

Financially, any company wants to attract investors to something new. Spinouts thus may well offer a way to enrich the market capitalization of the mother company and also allow the company to become larger and enhance its position without having to become big and fat in the habit of traditional conglomerates.

The ultimate aim is to expand the network further than it has gone. In the future we envision a federation of companies spun out of the mothership in such fields as systems products and in markets like engineering or industrial training.

We are networking out of opportunity. We think we can become stronger, faster, more flexible, and hold on to more creative people by creating a federation. Its ties to the mothership should be similar to our ties with our third-party companies, offering clear direction to where we are going so the spinouts have a place in our future, not just in our present. The difference with independent companies is that we can more directly influence the spinout's course. The mothership manages the federation through the bonds of interdependency.

Why are spinouts so right for the times?

A number of major corporations have shed subsidiaries and divisions in recent years, only to find that these thrive when they are spun off. Part of the reason is that large corporations are only capable of doing a few things at any one time. All the resources and focus of the corporation are directed toward those few things. If you want to do something else, you don't have the corporation working for you—you have the bureaucracy and expenses of the company working against you.

Looked at another way, the difference is not cell division but cell association. The federation emerges like the slug worm, a unique living organism formed in the collision of many single-cell amoebas—not the traditional cell division—to achieve a higher order of living. While small isn't necessarily better, smaller is better. One of the reasons behind the tremendous success of Japan is its people's tendency to reduce things to their smallest and simplest forms. It's an integral part of Japanese culture. The essential Japanese outlook toward the world is to reduce it in order to understand it, express it, and manipulate it. From the miniature trees of bonsai to the tiny transistor which allowed Japan to break into the international market after the war, the Japanese have an innate propensity to shrink things. In design and philosophy, Apple has been guided by the Japanese. It was no accident that when launched, the Macintosh was the smallest desktop computer ever produced.

Even Japanese poetry or Kabuki theater are the constant refinement and simplification of ideas. These forms are reduced to the point where they become almost symbolic, rather than truly representational. It is an American characteristic to look at things in a real way—we want to touch and feel. We like art that is realistic, The Japanese like art that is stylistic.

The Japanese mind, says O-Young Lee, a South Korean professor and one of the most insightful observers of Japan, "idealizes the dwarf over the giant . . . as a company grows bigger, it gets more and more abstract, and direct contact becomes more difficult to maintain. As a result, a marked tendency has arisen among large Japanese companies to spawn 'child companies.' Sometimes these child companies outdo their parents, as when Victor Japan, an off shoot of Matsushita Electric, developed the VHS video cassette."

The mothership, then, not only attempts to preserve creativity and innovation in "smaller" environments, it seeks to simplify the structure and process. The fact is that new or small enterprises have been more successful at this than large ones. We want to postpone the natural tendency for an Apple to become institutionalized. By creating the federation, it can become the mother of invention without having to give up the small company values we pride.

The lucky paradox here is that smaller actually gives Apple a wider scope. Our ideal working arrangements derive from the Gaia hypothesis, in which the planet itself is believed to be the core of a single, unified, living system. James E. Lovelock, the British biologist and inventor who conceived this hypothesis, views the earth as a self-controlling, whole system, not a conglomeration of discon-nected parts and discontinuous functions. We see the same in the networked entity of the future. We are creating not just a company here or a company there, but a greater cell around which all its parts are interconnected.

This is the distinguishing feature between the more common occurrence in corporate America for "spinoffs" versus a "spinout." A spinoff means "goodbye and good luck." It's the stripping off of assets that the corporate parent no longer has an interest in. Our spinouts will remain a vital part of the network of interdependen-cies around which the third-wave corporation garners its strength and flexibility. Rather than "goodbye and good luck," we're seeking a long-term relationship with our spinouts because we believe they are essential to the success of the mothership.

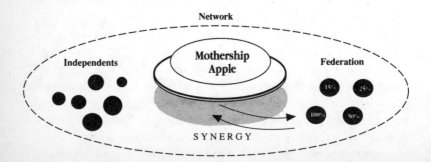

The Gaia model is, as one scientist put it, "a brilliant organizing principle for bringing together people." The lifeblood of the network is the free flow of information and mutual support. Any single entity is only as strong as the other parts make it. Within the living organism lie not only entities partially owned by Apple but totally independent ones whose survival is dependent on the mothership.

Unlike *Logan's Run,* this scenario is set in the current century.

Epilogue:
A Twenty-first Century
Renaissance

"Silicon Valley is different from anything else I've ever experienced. It's like Florence must have been in the Renaissance. It's where all the bright minds are coming together and it's a place in time where wonderful things are going to happen."

That promise the headhunter made to me more than four years ago turned out to be true. A romantic at heart, I allowed that extravagant hope to start me on an odyssey that is far from over. It's a journey which now heads toward the twenty-first century with the dream that Apple can help change the next generation more than we have changed our own. I'm optimistic enough to think that we can do it. Perhaps it's because Apple is a new company in a new industry founded by a generation that will spend a large part of their working lives in the next century.

I'm setting out now on a new odyssey with new goals. It's a journey of imagination that takes me into the future. For Americans, ten years is a long time. I have been trying to project myself—and Apple—into the twenty-first century, a mere fifteen years away. Navigators "shoot the sun" to chart their direction; using a distant point on the technology horizon, I've been trying to fix Apple's course by looking far ahead. Even on this virtually uncharted frontier, there are already footsteps to follow. Japanese industrial leader Konosuke Matsushita, now in his nineties, was recently preparing not his company's five or ten-year plan, but its 150-year plan.

What I see and hear gives me great hope for the future of our country and our world. I now believe more than ever that another renaissance may happen in the United States in the twenty-first century. I have become a technological optimist in every sense.

But such a glorious future is hardly assured us.

It is far from clear that the next 100 years will belong to the United States as the last so thoroughly have. Like most of my contemporaries, I grew up in a vastly different world—an economic hierarchy with the United States at the top. That is no longer the case.

Corporate managements must share some of the greatest blame for the global economic descendancy of the United States. From 1952 to 1980, American companies licensed over 32,000 technology agreements to Japanese firms, at an estimated cost to develop this technology of well over $500 billion. These were important technologies, like transistors and semiconductors and robotics. We sold all this technology to Japan at a scandalous fire sale price of slightly over $9 billion. Japan not only seized on these technologies, but skillfully turned them into high-quality products. And we still haven't learned the lesson from it: Not only do we continue to rent out our technical and business inventions to foreigners, but now they are significantly increasing their share of technological innovation and ideas. Some twenty years ago, 16 percent of all U.S. patents were issued to foreigners. Today, 45 percent go to inventors and scientists outside the United States.

Our educational system is also at fault. It continues to prepare students for rote, mechanical jobs that won't exist anymore—because corporate America is automating its factories here at home, shifting more manufacturing offshore while continuing to lose market share to global competitors. Only 9 percent of American employees work in factories today. Thinking skills are replacing manual skills in the new age. Yet, inside the classrooms, the schools still emphasize memorization and repetition over true learning.

Most at risk is America's affluent middle class, the source of our strength and power in the world economy.

Inherently, the strength of the American economy in the industrial age was the consuming power of our affluent middle class. It paid for and supported the massive buildup of American industrial might, from the carmakers of Detroit to the steel mills of Pittsburgh. U.S. companies acquired natural resources at advantageous prices from less developed nations and then added value to them through technological and manufacturing know-how. We not only sold these mass-produced goods in our own market; we also sold them back to many of the less developed countries where we had acquired the primary materials to make them. We even financed their purchasing habits, much as Japan now finances ours.

Today, that once exclusive know-how to produce products is available in many countries around the world, including the newly industrialized ones, such as Japan, Korea, Taiwan and Singapore. We no longer have something unique to offer the world or ourselves, something upon which our affluent middle class has been based. And as a society we aren't productive enough to afford the standard of living many of us have come to expect. The short-term panacea has been to go deeper and deeper into debt as a nation and a people.

The middle class must be preserved; it is as important to life everywhere as the rain forest in Brazil—the source of power and the beneficiary of power. Up to 80 percent of the world's oxygen is being created in these rain forests—they are the perfect ecosystem. The collapse of our affluent middle class society has global implications that equal the threat of unbalance to these rain forests. For decades we have supplied nourishment to industry around the globe; our standard of living has become the model for the world's population. We now must redefine our middle-class expectations and learn how to reduce over time our habits of voracious consumption. The adjustment might not mean a less satisfying lifestyle, just a different one. Would we be willing, for example, to give up the extra car, the multiple TV sets, and other unnecessary purchases, if the tradeoff becomes a four-day work week and the chance to live to one hundred years of age?

Long term, however, we will not be able to sustain an affluent middle class unless we are able to create the corresponding added value which will pay for our expensive consumption habits. But how do we maintain a middle class when we have to do more than consume value, when we have to create value? How does American industry create value as it moves from the hierarchical model we dominated to a networked paradigm in which our country is but one of many participants?

Our hope is innovation. We will need to become more innovative—particularly in the workplace and the classroom. Balancing the budget or easing the trade imbalance become short-term tactical goals. To "add value" in the information age requires major reforms in the ways we learn and work.

What is required, as physicist Fritjof Capra and others have pointed out, is nothing less than "a cultural and political shift from a mechanistic and patriarchal world view to one informed by holistic, ecological, and post-patriarchal concepts and values." The mechanistic world view that evolved from Cartesian-Newtonian science in which everything worked with clocklike precision has given way to acceptance of a more volatile, chaotic world in which such order does not exist.

Yet we have been living in a world which was largely defined by the seventeenth century. Galileo, Sir Francis Bacon, Descartes and Sir Isaac Newton all envisioned a universe in which everything was explainable. It was only a question of unraveling the puzzle and explaining the order rather than questioning whether a rational ordered universe actually existed.

Gradually, however, a new paradigm in science emerged. Exploring the outer fringes of quantum mechanics, German physicist Werner Heisenberg proved that we can never know everything with complete accuracy. In studying atomic particles, he found that the more we know about a particle's position, the less we know about its velocity. The more we know of its velocity, the less we know of its position. Later, Einstein introduced the notion of time as a dimension, which challenged Newton's thinking and changed the entire discipline of physics. Such a simple but powerful idea changed our world. Only recently have discoveries like Heisenberg's Uncertainty Principle begun to interest those who still live in the seventeenth-century world of mechanistic business.

We are at the crest of a wave of similar discoveries and innovations—both philosophical and technical—in economics and business that will change our perceptions and notions of how to manage and compete in the information age. These fundamental changes require new ways of thinking, learning, and working if we are to fulfill the promise of the new age.

If innovation is our only chance, then only a respect for individual creativity will lead to innovation. Our future will be found in the value Americans can add to products and services through ingenuity, resourcefulness and flexibility—all qualities of the individual's perspective. To reshape our institutions, we must nurture the natural intuitiveness buried within ourselves. We desperately need new tools to help us become far more creative, to give us access to broader fields of knowledge, to unlock new points of view, and to encourage experimentation.

Once we have thousands and thousands of ideas to harvest, we may have the chance once again to create a renaissance, perhaps every bit as important as the first, in the early part of the next century. It would represent a rebirth and revival of learning and culture unleashed by new technologies and the rediscovery of both arts and sciences as one and the same discipline. Technology could lead the way not to a twenty-first-century artificial/bionic man, whose life is led in the shadow of institutions and bureaucracies, as George Orwell predicted, but to a renaissance person whose existence is celebrated in a new age of the individual.

How do we convince people that innovation is the key? By taking as our inspiration the first great Renaissance, which redefined the importance of the individual to society. In medieval Europe, people were subservient to the institutions of church and government. It was largely Gutenberg's invention of printing with movable type which stirred a revolution in thinking, habit, and behavior, and so triggered the end of the medieval world.

In the year movable type was invented, only one out of every one hundred people could read. And the few who had that advantage read in Latin, the universal language of the elite. By 1500, 80 out of every 100 could tap the knowledge in books which were then published in the vernacular of the common man. More than eight million books were printed within fifty years after the invention of the printing press.

The press not only democratized knowledge in the fifteenth century. It opened people's minds to the Golden Age back in fifth and sixth centuries B.C., a time when there was no artificial separation between the disciplines of arts and sciences. Ethics, culture, science, and mathematics were one subject. Thus was born the notion of the Renaissance Man, whose culture was characterized by multiple points of view and a focus on the individual. Suddenly art made a dramatic change. It shifted from an absorption in the spiritual, in which most great painters depicted great religious events with the most important figures always appearing the largest. Suddenly, everything took on a logical order of scale and the element of perspective—that is, looking at the world from the point of view of the individual observer—was introduced.

The printing press was a tool for the mind which gave power to a few to change the world for the many. The result was a new self-esteem for the individual. An explosion of invention. An excitement of the power of wonderful ideas. A few exceptional people were able to use these new tools and ideas to dramatically change the paradigms of their day. They changed art. They changed science. They changed literature and commerce and medicine. They introduced new ideas in philosophy and religion.

In our time too, our society has become overly institutionalized. In the industrial age, institutions obscured the individual's importance. They blocked worker after worker from making a meaningful and noticeable difference. Though large institutions helped the country grow phenomenally, they meant the loss of human perspective. So today the individual is overwhelmed by forces well beyond his influence, no less control.

In many companies, people have become mere shufflers of papers and nonthinking bodies in meetings. They often lack the authority to approve ideas and projects, yet unfairly have the burden of responsibility for them. At one point, the big three auto companies had an astounding ten layers of staff between the factory worker and the chief executive. (One of them still has eight!) In many school systems, we have significantly increased the number of people in education but the size of the classes hasn't changed proportionately. Most of the additions have gone not into the classroom to create more intimate settings between teacher and student, but into the infrastructure.

Many of us have been curious why we have not seen more productivity gains in the 1980s from information technology when the cost of that technology has continued to dramatically fall while the power and performance of that same technology has risen significantly. Unconventional wisdom suggests that we have been trying to solve the wrong problem. If we want our institutions to be more productive, then we must learn how to focus the power of information technology not on the institutions themselves but on the individuals inside the institutions. We should be trying not to make institutions work faster, but to help people discover imaginative new ways to work better. It's not such an outrageous idea in a third-wave corporation for people to find their work experience exciting, interesting, and actually have fun!

Second, we can feel the effects of institutional dominance in the rise of overspecialization, in our universities and in our businesses. Years ago, most medical students strived to become doctors of medicine. Now they become specialists. While we have successfully enhanced the depth of knowledge in specific fields, we also have lost the opportunity to draw contrasts and comparisons between knowledge from field to field. Specialization has worked to narrow our perspectives and options. It encourages mechanistic and linear thinking.

If you believe, as I do, that point of view is one of the sources of new ideas and creativity, then specialization only narrows the vision of the individual. It doesn't broaden it, allowing the mind to explore new and vastly different horizons.

Third, time compression has nearly crippled our ability to cope with change. Technology has made the world a smaller, faster place that penalizes the slow-moving and stable institution. Companies that can quickly get ideas and information through their organizations for discussion and action will have distinct competitive advantages over others. In the next century, the world will become even more compact as computers permit real-time language translations. The lifting of the language barrier is likely to have as revolutionary a change on making the world a smaller, faster place to live as the airplane or the satellite.

Unfortunately it is unlikely we will be able to preserve our affluent middle class through gradual evolutionary steps of improvement in our businesses. Yet revolutions only occur in a democracy when there is sufficient discomfort or crisis so that enough people demand a change. And peaceful revolutions are only successful in a democracy when the proposed alternatives are obviously better than what it had previously. By the twenty-first century, we may well suffer a crisis in business and in education that will be intolerable enough to support vast changes in our society.

If these problems—institutional stranglehold, dominance of overspecialization, and rapid change—are to become the trigger points for a new renaissance, then what's missing today is the positive catalytic force. Society needs a breakthrough tool equivalent in our age to what the printing press was for the first Renaissance. A tool which will help stimulate individual creativity by awakening our minds to new points of view and giving us access to more knowledge than any human could possibly discover by any other means.

The odyssey ahead is to assure that we create the ancestor of a tool that might well be crucial to us in the next century. This is the context in which our dream to change the world with personal computers like the Apple II and the Macintosh is so compelling. It's why we view our role as artists and impresarios. It's why we wear with pride T-shirts emblazoned with slogans championing the passion and the romance of our journey.

A future-generation Macintosh, which we should have early in the twenty-first century, might well be a wonderful fantasy machine called the Knowledge Navigator, a discoverer of worlds, a tool as galvanizing as the printing press. Individuals could use it to drive through libraries, museums, databases, or institutional archives. This tool wouldn't just take you to the doorstep of these great resources as sophisticated computers do now; it would invite you deep inside its secrets, interpreting and explaining—converting vast quantities of information into personalized and understandable knowledge.

Imagine the Knowledge Navigator having two navigational joysticks on each side, like a pilot's controls, allowing you to steer through various windows and menus opening galleries, stacks, and more. You might even be set free from the keyboard, entering commands by speaking to the Navigator. What you see on the large, flat display screen will likely be in full color, high-definition, television-quality images, full pages of text, graphics, computer-generated animation. What you hear will incorporate high-fidelity sound, speech synthesis, and speech recognition. You will be able to work in several of these windows at any time, giving you the possibility to simultaneously compare, for example, the animated structural system of living cells with the animated network of a global economy.

Or you might want to explore the depths of Zen philosophy in which beauty is in the details, comparing it with examples of the architectural details of the Parthenon from ancient Greece and then contrasting these ideas with the design details of a Japanese camera. Various windows on the display will give you a choice of text, audio, animated graphics, or television-quality images, letting you simultaneously grasp ideas through a mix of media alternatives. Most important, the Knowledge Navigator will customize knowledge for you—it learns as you use it—to make navigating through information and ideas as interesting and understandable as possible. If you are visually oriented, you could work with the animated windows; if you are textual, you could work primarily in a text mode.

What the Navigator looks like is not as important as what it does. Just as radios and phones today come in all sizes and shapes, from a Pepsi bottle to a plastic apple, the Navigator's "form function" isn't critical. Indeed, within the next decade, the most powerful personal computer available today will be "invisible," like a motor; it will fit into a machine the size of a pocket calculator. Or it will be encased like a car engine in some highly powerful and useful new device. By then, computers may be sewn into the fabric of your shirt or embedded into the walls of your home. The Apple II chip is already small enough to wear on an earring.

Of far greater importance is how this new tool may change the way we learn, think, work, communicate and live, how it will dramatically change the computer industry from a producer of hardware or software to a producer of mass-personalized knowledge systems.

New communication and information technologies not only give us new things to think about, but new facilities to think with. The form of the printed book created a new way of organizing content and, in so doing, it promoted a new way of organizing thought. The current generation of personal computers has only hinted at the possibilities in "idea processors"—such as outlining software—for people whose product is their thinking. Bill Atkinson's Hypercard is another important step toward giving us new ways to access and organize information. Bill's dream was to create an erector set of software tools that will let us follow our natural instincts to browse through stacks of cards on our personal computer screen and then have the capability to link to other cards by merely pointing at a word or picture on the card. The ability to interact with ideas and information in a random intuitive manner has not been possible with the relatively inflexible structure of traditional database software found on large mainframe computers. Even today we are shaping some of the root technologies which will show up in far more advanced form in our personal computers of the twenty-first century. It would give the user:

The power of a point of view. The perspective to compare and contrast and so free ourselves of the limits imposed by specialization. As Marvin Minsky says, "You don't really understand something until you understand it more than one way."

In the twenty-first century, the walls between the various areas of specialization will come down—in business, education and life. Already, a number of world-class universities, from the University of Michigan to Carnegie-Mellon, have installed computer networks on their campuses that now give them the ability to connect students with their professors and the arts with the sciences.

At Brown University, technologists have "wired" Shakespeare; they have attached little active buttons to certain words in his plays so that a curious reader can click them on to explore the deeper meaning of the tragedy of King Lear or Macbeth. Brown technologies employ an idea that computer visionary Ted Nelson had in the 1960s called Hypertext. In fact, Atkinson's Hypercard also has its roots in hypermedia. Hypertext is a branching concept, which means a user can explore in depth the links of a reference in one document with other related references or documents, going deeper and deeper into the meaning of a text. What might take hours in a library, manually flipping through a card catalog, writing down numbers and searching through the stacks, can be done casually, at any time, on any subject, at a desk at home or under a tree in the park.

If, for example, a passage suggests the cold nights King Richard's men had to battle, you can click on this passage to learn something of the weather patterns in Shakespeare's time. That discovery may trigger another question, maybe dealing with the feuds among monarchs, or the state of the British economy during the harsh winters of the sixteenth century. You can thus keep clicking onto subjects, some of a political/social/economic nature, some totally unrelated to Shakespeare, and keep broadening *and* deepening your intellectual bandwidth.

Approaches like "marketing as theater" or the management style of the impresario might have value for business school students. The students would need easy access to information from the fields of the performing arts in order to draw connections and benefit from comparisons. The Navigator will make this possible—on and off the nation's campuses.

Analogy is a wonderful source for seeing new points of view and explaining them in ways that add depth and clarity. We can find new metaphors because we will have the ability to navigate in real time across vast frontiers of knowledge. When I first came to Silicon Valley I was startled by the constant use of metaphors. Soon it became obvious that this was the perfect way to inspire people about things that hadn't yet been created by showing analogies to things we already understood. Indeed, it will provide users access to almost all the knowledge in the world, whether it's in Texas or Timbuktu. By the early twenty-first century, all scholarly knowledge will be fully digitized, electronically sitting in computers around the world. The process has already begun. Access to this information may at first be possible only in the universities; but over a period of years its availability is likely to expand into the commercial markets where everyone will be able to enjoy its use.

Just imagine the implications. As communications theorist Neil Postman has written in *The Disappearance of Childhood,* "A group is largely defined by the exclusivity of the information its members share. If everyone knew what lawyers know, there would be no lawyers. If students knew what their teachers know, there would be no need to differentiate between them. . . . G. B. Shaw once remarked that all professions are conspiracies against the laity. We might broaden this idea to say that any group is a 'conspiracy' against those who are not in it by virtue of the fact that, for one reason or another, the 'outs' do not have access to the information possessed by the 'ins.' "

For the first time in our history, the world will have a tool that will provide not mere information, but true knowledge, cheaply and efficiently for all the "outs" and the "ins" willing to use it. People will have the power to wander through centuries of knowledge as true explorers. We can skim the surface, occasionally diving in to incredible depths when we choose.

Our ability to exercise our point of view won't be limited to substance; it will extend to style. We will be able to stimulate our imagination by choosing the most interesting ways of navigating through knowledge which personally turns each of us on. For example, we will be able to look at the same subject in different ways at the same time—selecting from alternative media windows on the screen.

The power of simulation. Simulation may be the ultimate destiny of personal computing. It lets us say, "What if we were to try this . . ." based on some set of assumptions we can define. Personal computers do this today but we will be able to do such things in even more remarkable ways in the future.

In the future, sophisticated 3-D modeling will, for example, be possible with animated graphics and special effects as strikingly impressive as today's fantasy films—all within the control of the individual. Imagine a clothes designer who wants to see how a new fashion design might look in action. The computer would transform his simple sketch into a 3-D drawing draped on a human figure. The designer's sketch will now have been enhanced to show color, fabric texture and the smallest of details. Then the mannequin will saunter around the screen as if on a catwalk. All of this would be accomplished in real time on a twenty-first-century personal computer.

Simulation gives us the power to take risks, to experiment, to fail and try again. It will let us do extraordinary things in time compression. These are tremendous stimuli to creativity and innovation.

The power of ideas. To access source material from anywhere, with the internal artificial intelligence to draw links between ideas from totally different fields, a machine like the Navigator will require a network of informational highways just as the automobile needed roads and highways to become very useful as a transportation tool. The construction of a superhighway of knowledge will have as profound an impact on the American economy as the development of the national railroad system in the mid-1800s and the interstate highway system in the late 1950s.

Eventually, you will find yourself able to hook into a telephone "highway" (an intelligent network) to get streams of information—voice, text, and images—over the same wire simultaneously. Today, we're limited by slow modems, long log-on times, and hard-to-memorize commands to get costly information from only a few sources. By the early part of the next century, few limitations will prevail and the process will become transparent. Users won't even have to give a moment's thought to where the information resides—the tool will navigate its own way through these highways to capture it.

The Navigator will not only travel such highways. It will also perform content analysis of the information, meaning that it will tailor information to your precise needs. That's an important feature because the quantity of information in the world is doubling every three to four years. We will either cope with it or it will overwhelm us. By the early twenty-first century, the world will be suffering from information overload unless we can achieve significant changes in the way we deal with the increasing number of facts, figures, and opinions.

This tailoring of information would represent a quantum leap in the way we think and use computers—particularly because so many companies, industries, and institutions still fail to use the full benefits of existing technology. Each of our most sophisticated naval ships, for example, requires more than 20,000 pounds of paper and filing cabinets simply to hold the documentation for training, support, and maintenance. Yet all of this can be stored on a few small optical disks, weighing in at a pound or less.

Artificial intelligence will play an important role in the Knowledge Navigator. Inside the soul of the computer will be intelligent software "agents." Over time, they will become smart enough to learn that you like certain types of information presented in certain ways. The agent will learn along with you and work invisibly, turning information into useful knowledge for you.

The agent is your opinion surrogate, the ultimate objective observer. It will wander around throughout dozens of databases, pulling together whatever it thinks you, the user, are interested in. You won't have to search through the stacks of libraries—the world's largest library will exist on your desktop or your lap.

The power of enjoyment. Throughout history the telling of stories has been a fundamental way of transferring knowledge from generation to generation. Stories can illustrate, illuminate, and personalize information into scripts. Eventually, "agents" may be able to tailor information to stimulate our imagination and help make both learning and work interesting and fun.

If we can't get people excited about these tasks, then we'll never get them to be innovative and creative. Versions of the Navigator will give students the opportunity to learn at their own pace and to learn in a personalized way that is best for them. The computer can become a personal tutor that will track a student's progress, ask questions, and assign homework to correct specific weaknesses.

By customizing knowledge so each of us—individually—can learn or work at our own pace, this new personal computing device will be a tool that is fun and comfortable to use. Just as a car takes you wherever you want to go without your worrying over how the ignition key works the engine, so the Knowledge Navigator will drive you anywhere through the available store of knowledge.

Innovation will never take root in our society unless a revolution in learning begins at the start of one's education. If we had the Navigator tomorrow it would, therefore, change nothing. Widespread changes, particularly in education, must first occur if there is to be a new renaissance.

I have grown disheartened about educators' discovery that high school students show little interest in learning. Some teachers are so fatigued that they just want to shuffle students from one class to the next. There are 2,000 community colleges in the United States today, compared with only 500 back in the sixties, but they are mostly engaged in filling in the gaps of a poor high school education.

Making learning fun will also improve the self-esteem of our teachers. Educators want to feel that they are doing something important to shape the lives of their students. Too much of the discussion about education centers around budget deficits, when inadequately prepared students are being advanced through grades and when discipline in the schools has broken down. The experience of learning needs to become important and respected by society again. The process of teaching must gain recognition as the process of human resource enhancement. These are the roots of our society, and nothing short of a revolution in American public education will be required to restore our position as innovation leader in a twenty-first-century world. If we are to turn the schools into a resource that builds the talents of our people, it is essential to make the experience of learning interesting again.

The power of creativity. The supporting premise behind the Knowledge Navigator is that innovation is the best option we have to add value in a global dynamic economy where our goal is to preserve the economic importance of America's affluent middle class. Innovation requires extraordinary personal creativity. The Navigator is a tool designed to enhance our creativity. That's where we're headed with information technology—toward mass personalized knowledge systems with transparent technology.

If we do it right and create and mass-produce such tools, we can leverage the strengths in individuality again. We can bridge the specializations to restore a balance between knowledge in depth and generalization and abstract thinking; we can generate enthusiasm for different points of view. By making the exploration of knowledge fun and interesting, the Navigator will qualify greater numbers of people for the "deeper mysteries" that will help lead us toward a new renaissance.

Ultimately we may become a society of information sharers. A tool like the Navigator could expose one of the great limitations of the printing press, too, opening the doors of knowledge to millions of people who have not been able to take advantage of one of the world's greatest inventions. As Postman notes, "The great paradox of literacy was that as it made secrets accessible, it simultaneously created an obstacle to their availability. One must qualify for the deeper mysteries of the printed page by submitting oneself to the rigors of a scholastic education. One must progress slowly, sequentially, even painfully, as the capacity for self-restraint and conceptual thinking is both enriched and expanded."

My dream is to see the Knowledge Navigator become the legitimate descendant of the Macintosh. We have come so far in the computer industry in just the past fifteen or twenty years! It proves how far we will be able to advance the technology by at least as much in the next two decades.

Seymour Cray, supercomputer pioneer and founder of Cray Research, Inc., said it best:

"I'm exaggerating just a little bit when I tell you this story, but I think it's real. I want to compare what's happening in the personal computer business with what's happening in the supercomputer business.... Today when you buy a $10,000 personal computer, which is pretty much the high end of the line, you can get a central memory of 4 million bytes. That's the same size memory as we delivered with the CRAY-1 [in 1976]. Now that kind of astonishes me.

"There's a revolution in the personal computer industry that is as impressive as ours or more so... Apple just announced a Macintosh II. Some of you may have seen it. Do you know what they said their memory size was going to be when they expand it in the early 1990s? They said it was going to be two gigabytes. That's exactly the size of the CRAY-2 memory today! So in a few years, Apple is planning to deliver a system with a memory the size of our current supercomputers. Now the processor probably won't be as fast, and it won't cost nearly as much either. But they're putting multi-processors in their box as part of their plan. So what does this mean?

"Well, in my mind, it's going to be a real revolution because people with minimal financial resources, individuals with out-of-pocket money, will in a few years be able to do physical simulations on personal computers, simulations that used to require a supercomputer. What a revolution that might be! Instead of a few hundred customers for this kind of work, we're talking about hundreds of thousands...."

Astonishingly, few major technological breakthroughs are necessary to achieve this—it's largely a question of building the critical mass of technologies that are already in motion to make the computer *a mass personalized knowledge-based system. Mass* means it has got to be affordable. *Personalized* means it will be easily adaptable to the individual's needs and tasks. *Knowledge-based* suggests a major leap from solely providing information. Wisdom, reflection, points of view, and opinion will be offered by the new technology.

System means we need an infrastructure of intelligent information networks analogous to the infrastructure of highways that was needed to transform the automobile industry into a mass personalized transportation system.

For those interested in technology, the details of what we can do and what we will soon be able to do are fascinating. We will require a "distributed database" under which all information we could possibly desire is accessible to the Navigator regardless of where those data reside in the world. Today, the necessary distributed processing technology is fast becoming a commercial reality, and new database technology offers one of the most exciting opportunities for growth and new uses of personal computing in the 1990s.

To better handle all this information, we also will need a dramatic reduction in the cost of active memory and mass storage memory technology. These are both reasonable expectations over the next thirteen years. Memory expansion is crucial for three-dimensional simulations and animation on the computer screen.

A revolution is about to occur in mass storage as optical media becomes a full commercial reality. Optical media in the form of CD-ROMs, which look like stereo compact disks, is one of the most exciting developments ahead. A single CD-ROM can hold more than 500 megabytes of data, which is equivalent to putting the entire twenty-six volumes of an encyclopedia on a single disk! Large libraries of text, sound and television-quality pictures can now be etched on the small round pieces of plastic by precision laser beams.

Next, we will want all the important information in the world to be digitized and electronically scored (meaning scanned or typed into computers) so it can be retrieved by personal computers. As awesome as that may sound, it's a likely probability sometime early in the twenty-first century. Already, savvy investors are buying up the rights to many databases in the belief that they will be very valuable in the next century, just as investors previously bought up the rights to old film libraries.

We also should expect to see a wide choice of digitized media, from speech and text to animated computer-generated images and full-color, high-resolution TV-quality video, on a computer screen. Imagine watching Dan Rather deliver the news in one window of the Knowledge Navigator screen, while simultaneously your computer brings up relevant facts and links to other aspects of the same story he is reporting. The computer would generate only what it knows you might enjoy from its experience of working with you.

Then, the use of such mixed media will require multiple processors working at the same time. The microprocessor is the computer's brain. In the early twenty-first century, that brain will be one hundred times faster yet cost no more. Yet if we add more of them to each computer, we can obviously boost performance to even greater levels, since several processors can share the load of handling data in a single program. That could significantly speed up the process of doing long, complex tasks and becomes particularly important in 3-D imaging, speech recognition, and high-resolution animation.

Parallel processing is no easy task, however. Learning to write programs for parallel processor computers looms as one of the biggest challenges because all our computer science knowledge has been directed toward the single linear processor architecture first envisioned by Turing and von Neuman nearly fifty years ago. Coprocessing, on the other hand, is a closer reality. This technology requires several processors to be programmed separately to support several different dedicated tasks that can run on the personal computer at the same time.

In addition, trends already are underway that will lead to the eventual convergence of telecommunications and personal computing. The essential worldwide network and communications standards are already being defined. These necessary efforts are supported by all the major telecommunications and computer companies around the world.

Finally, we don't want information, only access to better information that interests us individually. What we really want is to be able to understand better. Ideally, we want the computer to do the hard work of figuring out what is important, drawing relationships between data from different sources and performing analysis on it. What we need, then, is a very sophisticated level of a knowledge-based system better known as artificial intelligence.

This is where significant breakthroughs are still necessary for the Navigator to be a reality. But much work is underway and incubating at the best universities, research laboratories, and start-up companies to make this more than a possibility in the early twenty-first century. Typically, it takes ten to fifteen years before such work slips out of the university lab and into commercial use.

Computer pioneers throughout the country are pushing the edge of the envelope, exploring concepts and ideas that once were mere dreams. Douglas Hofstadter, author of *The Mind's I,* has been working at the University of Michigan with the theory of analogy as the basis for artificial intelligence. Doug Lenat, a brilliant computer scientist at the Micro Computer Consortium in Austin, Texas, has undertaken one of the most ambitious AI projects. He is creating a total encyclopedic knowledge base to be linked and accessed by the computer using principles of common sense.

Meantime, however, we will see a continued explosion in expert systems. An expert system takes the wisdom of individual experts and interprets their experience into a long list of rules to follow under various conditions. Expert systems have unique software which uses predefined rules based on expert experience combined with the ability of the computer to infer probable answers. An expert system allows the user to ask questions in plain English and get answers back in English. But whatever intelligence it may appear to have is limited to the imputed experience or rules built into its inference engine.

While expert systems are an important step, the Navigator must have innate intelligence of its own. The real distinction between expert systems and artificial intelligence is the ability of the computer to be able to learn from its own experience. Only true artificial intelligence will allow computers to become smarter over time. Computer scientists have been dreaming of the possibilities of artificial intelligence for over three decades. Yet the more they learn, the more they realize how little we know.

Still, this exploration is unfolding some fascinating developments. Some of the best researchers in this field at MIT have just learned to create digitized cockroaches that incredibly set their own willful, deliberate tracks over a programmed terrain. Of course, these roaches look primitive, almost silly, like images straight from the light show at the old Fillmore East. Their slow lumbering movements can't compare with the fabulous antics of the simplest Disney creatures. But then Mickey and Minnie Mouse are really puppets following completely their animators' will—not their own! These roaches are the "prehistorical" incarnation of our agents.

Marvin Minsky and Seymour Pappert, long-time collaborators at MIT in artificial intelligence, are trying to understand how the human mind works. They are particularly focusing on the mind of the child because it is less complicated by experience than the mind of the adult. In Minsky's book *The Society of Minds* he envisions the mind as a vast society of very small and very simple modules, each having the capability to carry out specific tasks. Consider the beehive: Each worker bee has relatively low intelligence, but when you put thousands of them together, they take on a high level of brilliance. AI may work on this very premise: that clusters of "agents" will assume higher levels of intelligence. In trying to unravel how these agents cross-connect and associate with each other, he hopes to discover how intelligent computers of the future may be designed to do the same. But to scale this theory up to the level of the human mind is an awesome task. The human brain is estimated to have over 10 billion neurons—equivalent to individual processors—with over 10 trillion interconnections (synapse junctions).

As Yale psychologist Roger Schank points out, "at the root of our ability to understand is our ability to find the most relevant memory at just the right time." He defines a memory organization as one based on an indexing scheme of failure-driven events. Put simply, we learn best by remembering our mistakes. His work is directed toward writing little scripts based on trial and error experience as a way of understanding the dynamic nature of human memory.

Myriad steps are required to get there, and they are being taken all over the country by hundreds of pioneers. Consider the development of Danny Hillis's Connection Machine. As he says only partly in jest: "We want to build a computer that will be proud of us." He's well on his way. A software program called the Indexor* is now capable of indexing every word in a full-length novel in less than a second. This is an essential technology for content analysis of vast databases, since we must have the potential to link every word with every other word to draw logical patterns of content understanding. The computer could therefore search for patterns of recurring ideas and connected themes between different documents, which would otherwise be physically difficult, if not impossible. The Connection Machine uses what is called massive parallelism, or literally hundreds of thousands of microprocessors in one computer. Today's personal computer uses all of one processor. The personal computer of tomorrow will likely use several.

Another alternative to artificial intelligence is the neural network. It takes a very different approach. It is founded on the observation that the human brain is composed of billions of neurons connected through synaptic junctions, with each neuron acting as a potential neural chemical transmitter. In a neural network computer, many small individual processors called perceptrons are linked to each other. Statistical weighing is used as the basis to determine clusters and patterns of individual processors which either promote or inhibit activity. Conventional computer logic forces answers into discrete true or false categories. Neural networks can make judgments of approximation.

Already, there have been successful experiments of neural networks learning from their own trial and experience. They start out rather dumb, but in a matter of hours are able to become quite accomplished at such tasks as handwriting and speech recognition.

Twenty years ago, Alan Kay envisioned the Dynabook, which became the progenitor of the personal computer. The Dynabook was a small, compact computer, something that could be tucked under the arm and carried like a notebook. It could recognize handwriting and tap into large computers via radio frequency. Kay never built the product, but he and others became so excited by his vision of what it could be that it spurred a revolution in computing.

Vivarium may never get completed, either, just like Dynabook. But along the way, Kay and others who have rallied around the project will make the discoveries necessary to give us the pieces to complete the Navigator. Bill Atkinson's Hypercard, too, the next logical step to making computers truly accessible to people, is another of the building blocks for the next revolution.

The most exciting part of the odyssey lies ahead. It's everyone's odyssey. But we must do something now because there will be no quick fixes in the twenty-first century. We must revolutionize our institutions, using our technologies and our people as vast resources. If America is to regain its competitive edge, it will have to regain the initiative in innovation and creativity. It may well take a full generation, at least twenty years, for this to occur—a perspective few Americans seem capable of taking.

Consider the twelfth-century cathedral. Each one took more than a hundred years to complete, and workers could spend a lifetime without seeing either the beginning or the end of the building. Yet the cathedral was a mirror of its age—an age measured not in years but in centuries. It was a project of experimentation. Structural design was achieved not through scientific formulas of load factors and stress equations but through a process of trial and error, guided, of course, by master masons who had a wealth of practical experience. The master builders behind these projects didn't have clearly defined goals in mind, only clear directions of where they were headed. During their journey of construction and experimentation, they never regarded their work as finished; they kept pushing their goals beyond all limits. It was management by direction, not management by objectives.

We, too, must be ready to reach for a new direction through risky trial and error, through a workforce that has pride in the things it does, often prepared to undertake a journey which will exceed its own lifetime.

Such tools, such aims, may help us realize the potential of the very best elements in our society.

The United States has a chance of creating a twenty-first-century renaissance . . . if we can learn to make the heterogeneous character of our country an asset again. Despite the weaknesses of our public elementary and secondary school systems, we have as a nation an extremely good higher education system. It's a fact recognized by the large and growing number of foreigners who attend our best universities. It's also no surprise that the single largest contributor to a region's economic health is the strength of its educational community. Silicon Valley sprouted from open apricot and prune fields in part because of its proximity to Stanford University; Harvard and MIT have had the same effect on the emergence of Boston's Route 128 as a haven for entrepreneurial activity.

As the artificial walls of our great universities come tumbling down through technology, and as electronic networks expand the reach of university campuses, the range of influence of higher education will increase. Libraries, as noted, will no longer be bound by bricks and mortar but will be electronically connected to students far from the physical campus. The teaching skills of the best professors at the best universities will be available by "template" to anyone who wants to learn. The universities in networks of interdependencies can indeed become the models of the new institutions in this new renaissance.

If the next renaissance will be based on a new age of individualism, the United States has many of the right attributes to enhance the individual's stature in the world. In Japan, it is not inherent in the rigid social order to champion the individual. While Japanese team accomplishments, pride, and morale are extraordinary, the Japanese are less likely to achieve the cosmic breakthrough of a Bill Atkinson or an Alan Kay. The rigidity of Japanese society and the aging of its population leave some doubt about the country's ability to quickly adjust to new paradigms for learning, working, and communicating. Yet we must not disregard the high respect Japanese have for education and family and their ability to assimilate new outside philosophies without abandonment of their traditions.

Europe also seems less likely as the place for another renaissance. Though blessed with bright, educated people and a rich culture, Europe remains overly institutionalized and bound by near unshakable traditions that look backward rather than ahead. Europe is constantly expending its energies in opposing directions between the fragmentation of nationalistic interests and the oversimplification of pan–European alliances which often fail to live up to their lofty objectives.

It's interesting to note that the Soviet Union is the only sophisticated country in which the Renaissance never occurred—largely because it is a country which has no respect for the individual. Up until ten years ago, even the copying machines in that country were kept under lock and key.

The genetic code of America has been defined as one of heterogeneous revolutionaries and immigrants. They can be the source of strength for us in the future as they have been in the past. We still have the best chance of launching the twenty-first-century renaissance if a consensus of Americans grasps the seriousness of the crisis ahead—losing our affluent middle class—and seizes on the equally imposing opportunities we have to use technology and education to build on our strengths.

The Japanese may seem to have many advantages over us—their understanding of the global economy, their use of technology, and even their creativity. It is naive to call them mere copiers as many critics have suggested. Their creativity is channeled into product miniaturization and quality maximization. They see that the beauty of Buddha is in the details while we in America are more conscious of creativity at a larger, more obvious level.

But Japan, now being severely tested by its less developed neighbors, draws upon the intellect and strength of only half its workforce. Although many women in Japan are employed in clerical or assembly-line jobs, they have not been tapped as a significant resource for management jobs.

As we shift toward a work world which learns to leverage intuitive and creative skills, women will emerge as the country's most important hidden resource. Some 30 percent of the students in the nation's top business schools today are women. A disproportionate share of them also are getting the high honors and distinctions in our universities. At Apple, where 50 percent of our managers are female, some 70 percent of our performance awards for management last year went to women.

If creativity and innovation are important in regaining our world competitiveness, women leaders may prove ideally suited for our own country's renewal. Many of the characteristics of the new-age leader are the typical personality traits that women possess.

Steve Jobs will be especially significant to all of us on the voyage out of this century. His beliefs and actions helped us dream of how to restore the individual's power in a society thick with institutions. His motivating idea—that we can change the world one person, one computer at a time—was fundamentally right. So Apple and many others have proven and are continuing to prove.

In some way, I want Apple to be the living laboratory for the model corporation of this new century. As new discoveries appear, new ideas will occur inside the company. Ideas will constantly be refreshed over time. Other corporations, such as AT&T, now find themselves consumed trying to disassemble all the things which prevent them from turning into true twenty-first-century companies. Whether we succeed or not isn't as important as the fact that we will aim for that direction and ask the insightful questions.

At Apple, we think in terms of "paradigms" to help us adapt to change, to remind us of the plastic nature of categories; it helps us realize we all wear blinders created by our culture, our language, and our attitudes. As Thomas Kuhn wrote in *The Structure of Scientific Revolutions,* when Sir William Herschel discovered in the late 1700s that Uranus was not a comet but a planet, he opened the eyes of other astronomers to the existence of new planets everywhere.

His discovery had far-reaching consequences: it triggered a paradigm shift. Before that discovery, every scientist saw a galaxy populated by fleeting comets; suddenly they were thinking in terms of the greater permanence of planets. In the first fifty years of the nineteenth century, twenty "new" planets were discovered. It was almost as if astronomers lived in a different world. We are now on the verge of a massive shift in the paradigm.

Our transition toward this "new vision of reality" has been a wrenching roller coaster ride—yet one that is part and parcel of the new reality of constant change. Ilya Prigogine, the Russian-born Nobel laureate, perhaps described it best by drawing from the world of physics in noting that order often follows chaos. Instability imposes revolutionary change when managements may only be ready to instigate change in increments. The disorder leads to what Prigogine terms a bifurcation point at which the organization can either crumble into chaos, as many businesses have, or jump to a new, higher level of order. Crisis can often have value because it generates transformation. In a sense, Apple had reached the bifurcation stage during its severe downturn. Our chaos, however, led to the creation of a new, different, and stronger entity whose roots still remain intact.

Apple is in the business of making tools for the individual. These tools are only going to get better and better and may well be the key to education reform, reintroducing creativity and individual resourcefulness as our most important natural resource in the information age. Innovation, I believe, is the only way that America will regain the initiative in a global dynamic economy. The way to increase our productivity is to make people more creative, resourceful, and innovative in the things they do.

It means a right-brain, intuitive tilt for the country which will take at least a generation to implement. But the rewards could possibly lead to another renaissance and a tremendous increase in productivity which will be hard for other nations to match. The roots of our American society are perhaps better suited to this change in the ground rules for world competitiveness than any other country in the world. Americans are by nature an individualistic and resourceful people once we see the way.

I sometimes think of where the world was before Apple began ten short years ago, and of how far we've come. . . . It's as if we already are a twenty-first-century company that has miraculously been able to come back to the late twentieth century to make sure we don't fail or compromise our mission along the way.

But I'm also aware of how far all of us must go to discard the industrial-age models of economics, business, and education and replace them with the new ideas and paradigms of the information age. I feel sure that the next thirteen years will transform the world. We are still at the very beginning of the information age.

When Napoleon Bonaparte wanted to extend the reach of his armies, he believed he should allow them to march in the heat of the summer. So strong were the sun's rays that he proposed lining the major roads in France with shaded trees.

One of his ministers responded in shocked amazement:

"But Emperor Napoleon, they will take thirty years to grow!"

Replied the adventurer who created a French empire: "Then we don't have a moment to waste!"

About the Book

Novelist John Gardner once said there were only two themes in all of literature: someone goes on a journey, and the stranger comes to town. Perhaps publishers sensed both themes in my experience. That may be why since late 1984 they have been asking me to write a book. When I arrived at Apple, they wanted a modern-day version of *A Connecticut Yankee in King Arthur's Court*. By early 1986, they were looking for a book about Apple's ability to survive the turmoil: What lessons were learned along the way that could be helpful to other business people?

The problem was that some of the experiences of that time had been so personally painful that I wasn't sure I could face the effort of recollecting them. Still, I began to feel there was a book starting to develop inside of me. The story was far from over, and the best part of the adventure was still to come.

Finally, in the summer of 1986, I agreed to work on a book project with Harriet Rubin of Harper & Row in New York. I found in her the enthusiasm, talent and youth so characteristic of our people at Apple. And she showed as much excitement about my management and marketing ideas and perspectives as about the narrative of my journey. We decided from the start that we wanted to write a book unlike any other business story. Not another self-conscious CEO tract, but a book which would expose my mistakes and vulnerabilities and what I had learned from them. Too many of these books had celebrated the leader's successes, making their stories almost unapproachable for many readers. But to accomplish this would mean opening myself to unknown others in a way that I had never done before. When I had arrived at Apple I came as a samurai warrior in all appropriate suited armor. Now I was still healing from my wounds. Was I ready to expose my own failings and vulnerabilities? Could I open up enough to tell what I was learning along the way?

Harriet and I then persuaded John A. Byrne, management editor of *Business Week,* to devote the next eleven months of his life as the coauthor of this story. From the start, it was a true team project. We mapped out the outline and scope of the book and plunged into the job of interviewing, reporting, organizing, writing and polishing. John and I met in Florida, New York, Boston, Los Angeles, San Francisco and Cupertino; we even retraced the footsteps of my walk with Steve Jobs through Central Park. Harriet significantly enriched my ideas, often challenging me to come up with newer and fresher perspectives on my experiences.

Over several hundred hours, we developed more than two thousand pages of transcripts and assembled additional material from the hundreds of pages of speeches and essays I had written while at Apple. We conducted interviews with Apple's executive staff, former associates at PepsiCo and others to gain as much perspective as possible on the events in the book. Many ideas came from my notebooks and meetings with Apple people. The project served as a useful forcing mechanism for me to articulate where Apple and the industry was headed. Frequently, I found myself using newly developed material for the book as the source of new ideas in my work at Apple, and I began to borrow new ideas from Apple for the book.

Harriet and John have been such wonderful teammates that the hardest part has been to realize the project is finished. The greatest rewards of a significant creative undertaking are in the doing, not in having done it. The standards that we set for ourselves stretched our intellectual curiosity.

We have attempted to employ the principles of new learning in this book by trying to make my experience as interesting and fun to read as possible, while embedding in the text what I hope will be valuable lessons and insights on business. The narrative serves as the roadmap for my journey. In it, the reader will find billboards that highlight various stops along the way in the form of miniature essays on management, marketing and technology. The intent here is to add depth and perspective to the experience of the adventure.

Readers are likely to find fewer answers at these important way stations than insightful questions. Above all, we have tried to engage the reader on another journey—an odyssey of opinion in which ideas will hopefully find challengers. If we can convince only a handful of people to break with convention and explore on their own different ideas and perspectives, then this book will have served its purpose.

After my break up with Steve Jobs in the summer of 1986, I found a new teacher: Apple Fellow Alan Kay. He led me on an extraordinary journey by sharing with me many of his unique and inventive ideas. It was Alan, perhaps more than anyone else, who expanded my range of viewpoints. We have regularly held weekly discussions which are usually accompanied by his suggestion of a new book or two for me to read. When I trace the origins of the most exciting and outrageous ideas behind the personal computer revolution, most paths lead directly to Alan. He had been both my friend and mentor on this journey.

Without the tremendous efforts of my executive staff team and all the people of Apple, there would have been no story to tell. Their efforts were truly remarkable.

This book became, like so many things in my life, an obsession which deprived my family of much of the little free time that I have had over the past year. Leezy and my three children, Meg, Jack, and Laura, were all tremendously supportive.

My good friend Albert Eisenstat served as a constant adviser and spent many hours reading drafts and suggesting improvements.

My loyal assistant, Nanette Buckhout, who followed me across the country, provided the sanity and balance that helped me through some of the most difficult moments. A true friend is the one who is there when most needed.

Jane Anderson and Barbara Krause devoted many hours of their personal time to help recall details and track down published sources and references. Their enthusiasm for the book was a big motivator.

Joe Hutsko, my twenty-three-year-old technical assistant, helped me discover the wonderful things we can do with our Macintoshes.

Amy Bonetti and Nancy Kelly, my area associates, were superb at managing the logistics of coordinating transcripts, files, speeches and articles as well as helping with many other details along the way. John Michel graciously provided additional support at Harper & Row, as did the Harper production team, Dorothy Gannon, Antonia Rachiele, and Jean Tourott.

Apple's New York office became a working home-away-from-home during my travels east. Everyone there was enormously helpful, Ken Landau, Susan DiClemente, and Francina Roe in particular.

Vincent Virga came to Silicon Valley from New York to assemble the material for the wonderful photo essay he created. His ideas were an inspiration.

This book could never have been possible without the Macintosh technology. Most mornings I rose early to write a few pages before going to Apple. With the click of the Macintosh mouse, I sent my files to John and

Harriet on the East Coast via AppleLink, an electronic communications network. They retrieved my files with their Macintosh systems at home. John, who lives in New Jersey, then would send his work to Harriet, who resides in Virginia, for editing on the same network. The Macintosh, they say, became a "presence" in their lives—its lit screen from early mornings to late evenings a constant reminder of both the book and the benefits of technology.

Indeed, even the jacket of this book was partly created by the Macintosh. Clement Mok, of Apple's Creative Services group, digitized my design sketch of the cover with an Abaton flatbed scanner onto a MacPaint document. Then he used an artist's stylus and Adobe's Illustrator software to enhance the title "Odyssey," giving the word its smooth, natural curves. It took him twelve hours to do this—versus the fifty-two or eighty hours it would take an experienced lettering artist to accomplish the same task without a personal computer.

Clement handpainted the letters' colors using a system called Chromatec. Finally, he employed the Macintosh's desktop publishing capabilities to set type and work out the final mock layout of the cover before outputting the finished art on a Linotronic 300 typesetting machine. The running figure that appears throughout the book is Clement's design, and the book's typeface, Garamond, is part of the design language for Apple's graphics.

Finally, no acknowledgment could be complete without Rudder and Tinker, our dogs, who were faithfully by my side whether I was working on my Macintosh or walking the Stanford hills with Leezy.

To be on this journey with so many friends has been the real reward.

Where They Are Now . . .

BILL ATKINSON, still traveling on a cosmic star somewhere far in the future, is looking over the shoulders of the young programmers who are enhancing Hypertalk, the new software language he invented for Hypercard.

DAVE BARRAM, our new vice president for corporate affairs, is often in Washington, building a presence for Apple in government agencies.

BILL CAMPBELL became president of Apple's first spinout company, Claris, which will create and market new software products. Along with Bill went a team of Apple managers who understand and believe in our genetic code.

DEBI COLEMAN was promoted to chief financial officer, making her the youngest CFO in the Fortune 200 and the only woman in that ranking to hold such a post.

AL EISENSTAT has taken on a much expanded role as Apple's senior vice president. He is overseeing the federation of spinout companies and is in charge of corporate strategy. He has also become chairman of Claris.

JEAN-LOUIS GASSÉE, now on sabbatical in France, has begun to write his second book and learn how to program on Hypercard. He has been promoted to senior vice president of research and development.

ALAN KAY is pursuing his love for chamber music while continuing, in his laboratories in Los Angeles and MIT, to invent ideas which will change the future for all of us.

MIKE SPINDLER was promoted to senior vice president for our international division. He is moving back to Europe, where he will personally lead a major expansion effort for Apple.

LARRY TESLER recently married his long-time astrophysicist companion and is continuing to push the outer limits of graphic technology in personal computing with the help of our CRAY supercomputer.

DEL YOCAM was elected Apple's chief operating officer. Del and his family have recently moved to one of the most beautiful homes in northern California.

Since repositioning Apple from a home/education company to a business/education company, we have added a number of new members to our executive staff team:

CHUCK BOESENBERG, a sales leader on the fast track, came to us from Data General to replace Bill Campbell as head of U.S. sales and marketing.

ALLAN LOREN, from CIGNA, is our new vice president of information system technologies, with the charter to make us a model company for personal productivity with computers.

RALPH RUSSO, a rising star in Apple manufacturing, was selected to succeed Debi Coleman as vice president of operations.

KEVIN SULLIVAN left Digital to join Apple as head of human resources and to help nurture our genetic code.

Finally, the founders:

STEVE JOBS has started a new firm, Next, to build a computer for the higher education market. Chances are he will once again be wondrously ahead of his time.

MIKE MARKKULA began his own aviation company, called ACM (his initials), and has also become involved in cattle ranching.

STEVE WOZNIAK is pursuing his dream of becoming an elementary school teacher, working as an assistant teacher in the California school system.

Bibliography

When Steve Jobs first visited my Connecticut home his eyes were drawn almost immediately to the bookshelves, where he spent some time taking in all that was there. The same thing happens to me when I visit someone's home. Books have always been important to me and to the people around me.

Some of the most interesting and valuable books I have read over the past few years are well out of the mainstream of business trade publications. So I want to open up my library to readers who are curious about the books that have helped shape my thinking during my Apple odyssey.

I've had two strong guides in creating this library. At Oxford and Cambridge universities in England, the don's role is to help stimulate one's intellectual curiosity, not by endless lecturing as is done in schools here, but by "leading you to all the good stuff,' as Alan Kay tells me. That is exactly what Alan has done for me, and I am deeply indebted to him for the many books to which he constantly introduces me.

My interest in books about technology has also been stimulated by my conversations with my son, Jack, who is currently in his final year at Stanford majoring in honors English and applied physics. He works in Silicon Valley as a part-time laboratory technician for NASA Ames Man to Mars Mission. He once took a year off from college at Steve Jobs' encouragement to start his own company; but his real desire in life is to be an astronaut on some future manned mission to Mars to be launched, he hopes, around the latter part of the 1990s.

I hope readers will find the sources listed below as enlightening as I have found them to be.

ABEGGLEN, JAMES C., and GEORGE STALK, JR.: *Kaisha: The Japanese Corporation* (Basic Books).

BIBLIOGRAPHY

BERGER, JOHN: *Ways of Seeing* (The Viking Press).

BLOFELD, JOHN: *Gateway to Wisdom* (Shambala Publishers).

BUZAN, TONY: *Use Both Sides of Your Brain* (E. P. Dutton).

CAPRA, FRITJOF: *The Tao of Physics* (Bantam).

————: *The Turning Point* (Bantam).

CHRISTOPHER, ROBERT C.: *The Japanese Mind* (Linden Press).

CLARKE, ARTHUR C.: *Profiles of the Future* (Warner Books).

COHEN, J. BERNARD: *Revolution in Science* (Belknap—Harvard Press).

DAVIES, PAUL: *God and the New Physics* (Simon & Schuster).

DAWKINS, RICHARD: *The Blind Watchmaker* (Longman).

DRUCKER, PETER F.: *Adventures of a Bystander* (Harper & Row).

FEIGENBAUM, EDWARD A., and PAMELA MCCORDUCK: *The Fifth Generation* (Addison Wesley).

FEYNMAN, RICHARD P.: *Surely You're Joking, Mr. Feynman* (Norton).

GALLWEY, W. TIMOTHY: *The Inner Game of Tennis* (Bantam).

GASSÉE, JEAN-LOUIS: *The Third Apple* (Harcourt Brace Jovanovich).

GAZZANIGA, MICHAEL S.: *The Social Brain* (Basic Books).

GREGORY, R. L.: *Eye and Brain* (World University Library).

GUILE, BRUCE R., editor: *Information Technologies and Social Transformation* (National Academy of Engineering).

HAYES, ROBERT H., and STEVEN C. WHEELWRIGHT: *Restoring Our Competitive Edge* (Wiley).

HOFSTADTER, DOUGLAS R.: *Gödel Escher Bach: An Eternal Golden Braid* (Basic Books).

————: *Metamagical Themas* (Basic Books).

HOFSTADTER, DOUGLAS R., and DANIEL C. DENNETT: *The Mind's I* (Bantam).

HUMPHREY, NICHOLAS: *Consciousness Regained* (Oxford University Press).

JAYNES, JULIAN: *The Origin of Consciousness in the Breakdown of the Bicameral Mind* (Houghton Mifflin).

KOZMETSKY, GEORGE: *Transformation Management* (Ballinger).

KRIEGEL, ROBERT, and MARILYN HARRIS KRIEGEL: *The C Zone* (Doubleday Anchor).

KUHN, THOMAS C.: *The Structure of Scientific Revolutions* (University of Chicago Press).

LABIER, DOUGLAS: *Modern Madness* (Addison Wesley).

LOYE, DAVID: *The Sphinx and the Rainbow* (Bantam).

MCLUHAN, MARSHALL: *The Mechanical Bride* (Vanguard Press).

MINSKY, MARVIN: *The Society of Mind* (Simon & Schuster).

NAISBITT, JOHN: *Megatrends* (Warner Books).

NAISBITT, JOHN, and PATRICIA ABURDENE: *Reinventing the Corporation* (Warner Books).

NEGROPONTE, NICHOLAS: *The Architecture Machine* (MIT Press).

NELSON, TED: *Literary Machines* (Theodor Holm Nelson).

PETERS, THOMAS J., and ROBERT H. WATERMAN, JR.: *In Search of Excellence* (Harper & Row).

PINCHOT, GIFFORD III: *Intrapreneuring* (Harper & Row).

PORTER, MICHAEL E.: *Competitive Advantage* (Free Press).

POSTMAN, NEIL: *Amusing Ourselves to Death* (Elisabeth Sifton/Viking).

————: *The Disappearance of Childhood* (Dell).

PROGOGINE, ILYA: *Order Out of Chaos* (Bantam).

SANDERS, SOL: *Honda: The Man and His Machines* (Charles E. Tuttle Co.).

SCHANK, ROGER C.: *Explanation Patterns* (Lawrence Erlbaum Associates).

————: *Dynamic Memory* (Cambridge University Press).

SCHEIN, EDGAR H.: *Organizational Culture and Leadership* (Jossey Bass Press).

STEVENS, ANTHONY: *Archetypes* (Morrow).

SUZUKI, SHINICHI: *Nurtured by Love* (Exposition Press).

TOFFLER, ALVIN: *The Adaptive Corporation* (Bantam).

WRISTON, WALTER: *Risk and Other Four-Letter Words* (Harper & Row).

Index

INDEX

438

BUSINESS

Odyssey is the chronicle of one of the decade's
most dramatic corporate turnarounds—
written by the CEO who transformed
a foundering Apple Computer into the country's
top marketing powerhouse.

John Sculley, at age 38, had been Pepsi-Cola's youngest president when he rewrote the
rules of marketing, masterminding the "Pepsi Generation" campaign that toppled Coke
from its position as the number-one brand for the first time in history. Compelled by
Apple's fabulous success and cofounder Steve Jobs's promise of "a chance to change
the world," Sculley turned his back on East Coast corporate orthodoxy and joined the
high-risk, gold-rush atmosphere of Silicon Valley. *Odyssey* re-creates the painful
struggles between Sculley and the brilliant Jobs and explains how Sculley managed
Apple out of a severe crisis. It reveals the story behind those dramatic events and
provides a blueprint of business strategy, with tutorials on managing creativity, the new
loyalty, and spin-out management techniques.

"If there is one man whose career exemplifies the experience of American management
over the past 25 years it is Mr. John Sculley. . . . This book is Mr. Sculley's own telling of
his transition from sugar-water salesman to technopreneur. The story is engaging,
intelligently and honestly told. [His] account of Apple's crisis and recovery belongs on
the required reading list of every business school student." —*Economist*

"*Odyssey* is entertaining, detailed and visionary—it shows not only what the dream of
the Information Age is, but how it can be bought by all of us." —*Houston Post*

LIBRARY

PUBLISHERS

ISBN 0-06-091527-7

90000

9 780060 915278

1088N   >$10.95